GHOST EMPIRE

How the French Almost Conquered North America

PHILIP MARCHAND

PRAEGER

Westport, Connecticut
London

Library of Congress Cataloging-in-Publication Data

Marchand, Philip, 1946–
  Ghost empire : how the French almost conquered North America / Philip Marchand.
    p. cm.
  Includes bibliographical references and index.
  ISBN 0–275–99417–1 (alk. paper)
  1. French–North America–History–17th century. 2. French–North America–
  History–18th century. 3. Canada–History–To 1763 (New France) 4. France–
  Colonies–America–History–17th century. 5. France–Colonies–America–
  History–18th century. 6. North America–Discovery and exploration–French.
  I. Title.
  E29.F8M29 2007
  971.01–dc22   2006037767

British Library Cataloguing in Publication Data is available.

Library of Congress Catalog Card Number: 2006037767
ISBN-13: 978–0–275–99417–4
ISBN-10: 0–275–99417–1

Published by arrangement with McClelland & Stewart Ltd.,
Toronto, Canada

First published in 2007

Praeger Publishers, 88 Post Road West, Westport, CT 06881
An imprint of Greenwood Publishing Group, Inc.
www.praeger.com

Printed in the United States of America

The paper used in this book complies with the
Permanent Paper Standard issued by the National
Information Standards Organization (Z39.48–1984).

10 9 8 7 6 5 4 3 2 1

"History, history! We fools, what do we know or care?"
 – William Carlos Williams, *In the American Grain*

"Pauvres sots! comme si la religion catholique n'était pas la
plus avantageuse et la plus agréable des religions!"
 – Alexandre Dumas, *Les trois mousquetaires*

To James D. Howe

Contents

Acknowledgements

This book would never have appeared had it not been for my agent, Anne McDermid, who helped to shape the idea of the book and who stayed with me through many a discouragement. She never lost faith in the project. My thanks to her and to her staff — it was always a pleasure to drop in to their office on Willcocks. Thanks are owed, as well, to the publisher, McClelland & Stewart, and to two old friends in the publishing business, Doug Gibson and Doug Pepper. Alex Schultz, my editor, rose to the challenge of taking an overly long manuscript and performing editorial wizardry on it.

At the very inception of the project, and assisting at its birth, were my fellow participants in the 2001 workshop at the Banff Centre's Creative Non-Fiction and Cultural Journalism program. My special thanks to the chair of that program, Alberto Ruy-Sanchez, and to two superb editors, Ian Pearson and Moira Farr.

All of the following I remember with particular warmth and gratitude for their help and their presence in the course of research-ing the book: Henry Wolff, Jr., and his wife, Linda, of Victoria, Texas, who did more to make my visit to Texas rewarding and pleasurable than is indicated in the book; poet and novelist Paulette Jiles and her husband, Jim Johnson, of San Antonio; Jillian Cook, who provided me with a secure base of operations during the siege of Fort Niagara; all the members and family relations of the Compagnie LeBoeuf, for putting up with me; my old friend Tom Dilworth, of Windsor; Katherine Ashenburg, who gave me a helpful hint from her forthcoming book on the history of personal cleanliness — the reader of Chapter Seven will know what I'm talking about; Ken Fleurant, professor of French at the University of Wisconsin at Green Bay and co-director of Wisconsin's French Connection Project, and his wife, Paula, who were extremely helpful and hospitable; Donald Claude Noel, extraordinary sculptor and authority on French Wisconsin; Paul Karton and Karen Moeller and the beautiful Rebecca; Joseph Coté, another old friend; Jim Baker, site administrator at the Felix Valle House, and Lorraine Stange, director of the Bolduc House Museum, both in Ste. Genevieve, who pointed me in the right directions; R.H. Dick, co-author of the recently published *An American Art Colony: The Art & Artists of Ste. Genevieve, Missouri 1930–1940*, Barbara Hankins and Bernard Schramm, who provided particular insight into the artists' colony and the town itself; Judith Edwards and her mother, Kathleen Edwards; Barbara Dever Gutierrez, author of *Charlene: The Little Cajun Saint* (see Mrs. Gutierrez's website, www.charlenerichard.com, for details on how to obtain that very interesting book); Dean and Sylvia McGee, who not only served a wonderful crawfish etouffée but opened a window on their part of Louisiana, with additional thanks to their son Joseph and their daughter Donna Onebane, whose dissertation entitled *The Stories We Tell: An Oral History of a Prairie Cajun Community* was an invaluable resource (the Pierre Daigle quotation in Chapter Fifteen is from that work); Jane and Jed Horne, for their French Quarter hospitality; and Greg Osborn, historian and archivist with the New Orleans Public Library, for helping me wrestle with the question of just who is a Creole.

I am especially grateful to the historian Jacques Monet, S.J., whose insights into the formative years of New France steered me in the right direction during early work on this book, and who very kindly read the manuscript and corrected a number of errors. Those that remain, now more or less permanently embedded in print, are entirely my responsibility of course. May they not haunt my sleep. A special note of thanks to the always perceptive and knowledgeable Jeet Heer, who pointed out relevant sources and originated the metaphor of French Canadians as hobbits, and to my brother Peter, environmental scientist and the reincarnation of a *coureur de bois*, who advised me on certain woodland issues. Many thanks to John Bentley Mays, Gerald Owens, and Katherine Anderson, who share a table with me at Ari's after 11:30 mass at St. Vincent de Paul's and, among other items of discussion, hash over what the hell modernity means.

You old stalwarts, William and Veronica Ellis, thank you, too. And Patricia, a light shining over the book.

Chronology

1669   La Salle sells his land in Montreal and begins a career of exploration.

1672   The Comte de Frontenac becomes governor of New France.

1673   La Salle enters a business and political alliance with Frontenac.

1674   La Salle takes possession of Cataraqui (Kingston, Ontario).

1678   La Salle, with the permission of Louis XIV, begins exploration of the west.

1682   La Salle reaches the mouth of the Mississippi and claims the land he has traveled for France.

1685   La Salle lands in Texas to found a settlement at the mouth of the Mississippi.

1687   La Salle is murdered by members of his expedition in Texas.

1688   Jean Gery is discovered by soldiers of De León.

1689   Renewing hostilities, the Iroquois raid the settlement at Lachine.

1699   The French found a permanent settlement near the present-day city of Biloxi, Mississippi.

1701   The Iroquois promise neutrality in wars between the English and French. The French empire in North America, often described as a "colossus with feet of clay," reaches its greatest extent, from Hudson Bay in the north to the mouth of the Mississippi.

1713   The Treaty of Utrecht ends the War of Spanish Succession and begins the long process of eradicating French rule in North America. From their North American possessions, the French lose Newfoundland, Hudson Bay, and the Acadian peninsula (Nova Scotia).

1748   The War of Austrian Succession ends inconclusively. The British, however, attain clear maritime supremacy over France, spelling the end of France's overseas empire.

1754   Fighting breaks out in the Ohio Valley between French and American colonial forces led by George Washington.

1759   The British under General James Wolfe seize Quebec City.

1760   Montreal, the last French stronghold in North America, surrenders to the British.

1763   Conclusion of Seven Years' War leaves France stripped of North American possessions, except for Martinique, St. Lucia, and Guadaloupe in the West Indies and the fishing islands of Saint Pierre and Miquelon off Newfoundland.

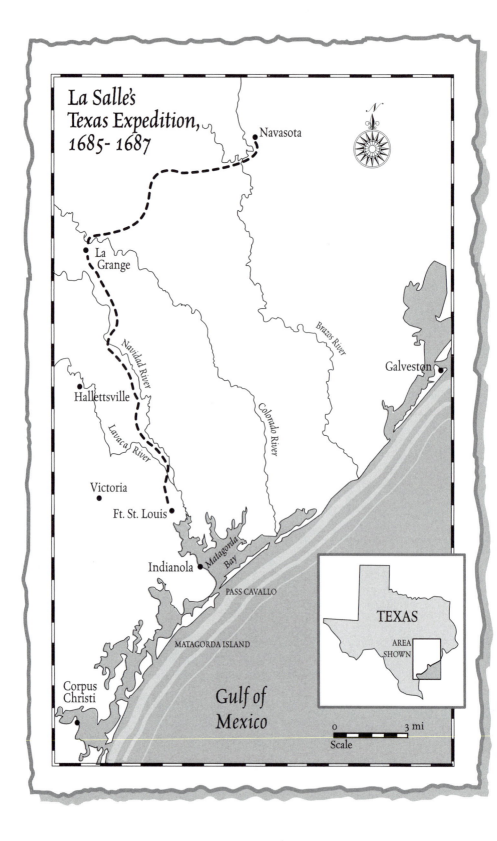

La Salle's Texas Expedition, 1685-1687

La Salle's Explorations, 1678- 1687

Montreal

Ft. Frontenac/Cataraqui (Kingston)

Mackinac Island

St. Ignace

1680   1678

Toronto

Niagara

Green Bay

Detroit

Chicago

Ohio River

Starved Rock

Kankakee

Ft. Crevecoeur (Peoria)

Ste. Genevieve

Ft. Prudhomme (Memphis)

Mississippi River

Arkansas Post

Country of the Quapaws

La Salle's death

1687

Lafayette

1682

New Orleans

1685

Ft. St. Louis

Gulf of Mexico

0   300   600   900 mi

Scale

ONE

The Persistence of Blood

*What the Spanish found in Garcitas Creek • The persistence of the
alligator and the roseate spoonbill • The most hated man in the history
of Texas • A momentous lesson in Grade 4 • The amazing and
dangerous consequences of a passion for history, viz. two historians feud,
and a widow does the devil's work*

For two or three years the court of the Viceroy in Mexico City
had been troubled by rumors of a French settlement on the northern Gulf Coast of New Spain. Shipwrecks had been spotted. Then
in 1688, soldiers under Captain Alonso De León found a strange
Frenchman ruling over a tribe of Coahuiltecans in the high
country north of the Rio Grande. Interrogated in Mexico City, the
Frenchman, who said his name was Jean Gery, told a story of
landing on the swampy, storm-wracked Gulf Coast far to the east,
three years previously, with two hundred Frenchmen equipped
with cannons and small arms, and awaiting a rendezvous with four
thousand Indians from Illinois to march against New Spain.
Smelling disaster, he had deserted at the first opportunity.

The Spanish did not know quite what to make of this testimony. His account was garbled and contradictory; he had a crazed

look in his eye of an old man – he gave his age as forty – who had seen too much. Of the few Europeans who ventured into the wilderness north of the Rio Grande, a high proportion seemed to be liars and madmen – born that way or turned so by their experience. And his story made no sense. Nevertheless, the Viceroy sent Captain De León with one hundred soldiers to find the settlement, if it existed. Guided by Gery, De León set out with his men on March 24, 1689. On April 22, marching along Garcitas Creek, a few miles from where it emptied into Matagorda Bay, they found the place – a few huts built of stakes, with buffalo hide roofs, and a rudimentary house or fort constructed of ship's timbers. Everything had been ransacked.

What most struck De León was not the broken pieces of chests and furniture, or even the eight pieces of artillery lying on the ground. It was the books. More than two hundred of them were scattered on the ground, their pages torn out, their bindings ripped apart. Many of the local Indians, the Karankawas, it turned out, now had pages of print in their possession. From time to time they would look at them, finger them, ponder the strange power of these marks that could speak silently to the white men. They could not know that these marks – more than gunpowder, more even than the smallpox virus – heralded their inevitable destruction. The new spirit of print – uniformity, rationalization, mass production – was the demon that drove their enemies. Those scattered and torn books were deadly.

But where were the inhabitants? De León found no traces except for three skeletons. From the bits of fabric still stuck to the bones of one of these skeletons, De León deduced that it was a woman.

❧

The sign had a distinctly unfriendly tone:

POSTED
NO HUNTING
NO FISHING
ALL VEHICLES SUBJECT TO INSPECTION
ENFORCED

We had business on this property, however, and Shirley Shirley had the key to the padlock on the chain across the fence. And so, on a hot June afternoon with a hint of a coming rainstorm, we entered the dirt road winding through the K-8 Ranch. "This dig has been going on for almost three years come October," she said. "They thought it was going to be six months."

"Why so long?"

"Digging conditions. 'Intractable clay' they called it. That scared me – I knew what that meant. Really hard, dense clay. You had to use a pickax. No way could you use a hand trowel." We drove through the flat range where cattle grazed between mesquite trees, the domain of the ranch where a foreman discovered a buried cannon in 1996. I had flown in from Canada a few days earlier to see this site; in my suitcase was a copy of the *Journal of Henri Joutel*, a lieutenant of René-Robert Cavelier, Sieur de La Salle, and one of the few survivors of La Salle's attempt to plant a settlement here.

As we headed south to the site, the pasture gradually turned to a wooded area thick with scrub oaks, ash, cottonwood trees, the thorny shrub known as cat's claw, mesquite. The cattle disappeared, and deer emerged from the brush. A great blue heron and a roseate spoonbill wading in a pond took flight. Joutel was much struck by the latter bird, with its grotesque spatula of a bill, and its pretty plumage – *un rouge pale . . . fort beau*, according to Joutel. We turned into a clearing about fifty or sixty feet above the brown waters of Garcitas Creek. This was the site of what historians called "Fort Saint Louis," although it was more a collection of huts than a fort. Eastward, the creek was bordered by grassy, yellow-green bottom land, ending in a row of trees about a mile away. Southward, the water flowed into a bayou before it emptied into Matagorda Bay, too far off to be visible.

Not a bad view for La Salle's settlers. North and west was less scenic. In those years, grass grew as high as a man's head. The climate was cooler and wetter then – it was the tail end of what climatologists called the Little Ice Age, lasting from the fourteenth to the nineteenth centuries. Climate change, and the cattle brought by the Spanish, spelled the end of the grassland – no longer would vast fires, some natural, some set by the Indians, sweep through these lands, rejuvenating the grass and preventing the growth of trees and shrubs. Instead, the cattle ate the grass and spread the seeds of oak and mesquite in their manure. The site itself was free of brush only because the archeologists had cleared the area – at first with axes and chainsaws, and then, when it became clear that this would take forever, with a hydro ax, a tractor with a nine-foot-wide mulcher in front that mowed down shrubs and trees.

Now the dig was nearly finished. The only way you could tell it was an archeological site was from the row of empty wheelbarrows and the holes in the ground that still needed to be filled in. If you ignored the busy fire ants and scorpions and looked hard, you could see ceramic chips still lying around. That was it for visible evidence of the French or the Spanish, who took over from the French after Captain De León's visit. "I don't know how the French did it," Shirley said of La Salle's followers, trying to make a home in this strange country. "We had fans going while we dug, but it was still miserable – and we could go home at the end of the day." Our attention was briefly diverted by an armadillo snuffling behind a tree. He went about his work diligently, his snout in the dirt, then scurried off into the brush. "I was used to working in the heat out west, but the humidity here took its toll." Shirley, who had been on aboriginal sites with the National Park Service, worked as crew chief in her shorts and T-shirt with a half-dozen or so volunteers under her, retired engineers and other dedicated, educated people –

volunteers are the lifeblood of North American archeology; practically nothing of importance could be excavated without them. Everything, it seemed, was taken in stride – not just the heat and hard work but the swarm of scorpions in the ladies' portable toilet and the fire ants that crawled up your legs and burrowed under the elastic of your underwear.

This landscape was probably more beautiful when the French were here three centuries ago. They were also spared the fire ants, a later arrival. But the mosquitos that plagued Shirley's crew were in force in Henri Joutel's time. Joutel says they were the worst thing they had to put up with. Scorpions were also present, although Joutel didn't think the Texas variety was any nastier than some he'd seen in Europe. As for the evil-looking spiders on the site – the crew fed grasshoppers to one eight-legged favorite – it's hard to know. Joutel doesn't say anything about spiders.

In any case, there were a lot worse things crawling around. Joutel mentions one poor fellow named Dumesnil who tried to cross a stream and was dragged under the water and *devoré par un crocodile*. That was doubtless not the way Monsieur Dumesnil expected to depart this world when he was hanging out on the streets of La Rochelle, before naval officers came around recruiting for a new expedition. Joutel's friend Sieur Le Gros was bitten by a rattlesnake while hunting in a marsh. His leg swelled up and had to be amputated, and then he died of fever, on the Day of the Beheading of St. John the Baptist, Joutel notes. (Two good men who did not survive their encounter with a sharp-edged instrument.) The reptiles have not gone away. According to Shirley, an alligator hung around Garcitas Creek near the dig for weeks on end, as if fascinated by the activity. The crew named him Wally. Rattlesnakes, on the other hand, remained anonymous. "We killed four of them," Shirley said. "Not me, but the boys. The guy crew would just go kill 'em."

Now their work was done. The artifacts – the rings and the glass beads the French brought with them as trade goods, the bits of copper kettles – had been cleaned up, put in Ziploc bags, and stashed away at the laboratory of the Texas Historical Commission in nearby Victoria. Only one major archeological mystery remained, a mystery with macabre overtones we will consider later on. There was also the enigma of La Salle himself, the man responsible for all this activity, someone historians have tried to fathom with psychiatric precision for years. His personality, too, was a mystery that might never be solved.

❧

"Dear old La Salle," said Gary Dunnam. "The most hated man ever to walk the soil of Texas." Dunnam, the Victoria County heritage director, was leading a tour of the restored 1892 Victoria County courthouse, one of those "cathedrals of the plains" that Texans are so proud of. I was there a few days after my visit to the site. On a wall of the courthouse hung a banner with a portrait of La Salle. As with most busts and portraits of La Salle, it didn't remotely resemble the man. No clues there as to his personality, or to his talent for making enemies. Why was he so hated? Dunnam didn't elaborate, other than to cite "ego problems." Clearly, in the view of Dunnam and many historians, La Salle was asking for trouble the day he set foot in Texas. One might almost say he got what was coming to him, on the banks of the Navasota River, where he made the last of his misjudgments. If it weren't for his being the first European to found a settlement in Texas, you'd never see his likeness in a Texas courthouse, accurate or otherwise. And that settlement, that historic encounter of early modern France and Stone Age hunter-gatherers, was as fleeting as a shadow on the grasslands. La Salle and his men might as well have vanished from the surface of the earth the moment they landed, for all they accomplished. The standard view in Texas is that La Salle is important only because he put a bee in the Spanish bonnet. Once they heard the French were moving in – De León was the first in a stream of soldiers and friars who crossed the

Rio Grande, building missions – the Spanish became serious about their own colonization of Texas.

Not much of a legacy for "dear old La Salle." Yet he was important to me, if only as an echo of an old nostalgia. One day in my fourth-grade class at Egremont Elementary School, in Pittsfield, Massachusetts, in the year 1956, our teacher, Mrs. Drennan, who in memory seems to be eighty years old, asked the class a tricky question. She had been talking about the French and Indian Wars, and then she asked who we supported, the French or the English. I raised my hand. "The French," I said. "Oh? Why the French?" For a moment I was flummoxed. The honest answer would have been: I support the French because the blood of Québécois ancestors runs in my veins, still trilling to my inner ear its old resentment of you New England *Bostonnais*. Or something like that. But of course I couldn't give an honest answer. "Because they won so many wars," I said desperately. "Oh, and what wars did the French win?" I thought for another agonized second. "The Hundred Years War!" (We had also been talking about Joan of Arc.) Then she pounced, the merciless old bat. "The Hundred Years War was a *civil* war," she said. "It was between the French and the Burgundians."

In 1956 it was still possible for a fourth-grade teacher to discuss history in this idiosyncratic manner. Not today. (The Burgundians? Were they aliens on *Star Trek*, Mrs. Drennan?) But of course she was right. The French, despite their flashes of military genius, have never been all that fortunate in the field of battle since the days of Clovis, king of the Franks. I "supported" the French in the French and Indian Wars because they were my people. My paternal and maternal bloodlines go back to the Marchands and the Touchettes who came to French Canada in the middle of the seventeenth century. My ethnic background, my tribal DNA, is about as unmixed as it's possible to be in this day and age, pure Norman French with a dash of Breton French thrown in.

Which means, I admit, very little. La Salle was Norman French, and I'm Norman French in blood, but I can barely speak the language. La Salle has never haunted my dreams or altered my thinking in the slightest. But history held a charm for me when I was a boy, and nothing was more alluring than the wilderness epic of the French and the English and the Indians. At the age of twelve and thirteen, when my contemporary Susan Sontag was reading Proust and Kafka, I was thrilling to the historical novels of Kenneth Roberts, in which the author celebrated the heroic virtues of his forebears, the English settlers of colonial Maine and New Hampshire. In a novel such as *Northwest Passage*, my forebears, on the other hand, were described as "swarthy, stunted Frenchmen." (At least they weren't Indians. You should read Roberts's description of Indians.)

This may be why I'm still intrigued by the career of La Salle, the greatest of the French explorers. He ended up claiming virtually the whole of the North American continent for France, and by the lights of the seventeenth century, his claim was a good one. There was a real chance, near the end of the seventeenth century, that France might back up the claim. A few different turnings of history and you, reader, would be reading this book in French and speaking to your children in French. The United States would not exist. Some sort of French, Catholic state would dominate the continent, and the Ojibway, the Sioux, the Shawnee, the Chickasaw nations would have the same political and cultural presence as African-Americans now do. The English-speaking portion of the continent would still be largely hemmed in between the Alleghenies and the Atlantic.

I don't pine for this counter-historical world, the way some neo-Confederates pine for Lee's victory at Gettysburg. Counter-history exists to help us appreciate real history more profoundly, not to daydream about a Chicago run by the French and the Kickapoo instead of the Irish and the Poles. But there is something else that La Salle and I have in common that is much more intimate and crucial and permanent, and this is why I'm writing this book and following the footsteps of La Salle across North America. Before I explain this bond, however, it may be well to say more about La Salle himself.

❖

La Salle was born in November 1643 to the rich bourgeois family Cavelier, merchants in the old city of Rouen, on the banks of the Seine. The family owned a country manor called La Salle and awarded the title of this estate to their second oldest son – hence the honorific Sieur de la Salle. Just before he turned fifteen, La Salle, who had studied at a local Jesuit school and was uncommonly bright, with an aptitude for mathematics, joined the Jesuit novitiate in Paris. Perhaps he was lured by the promise of adventure as a missionary – the Jesuit *Relations*, the extraordinary collection of narratives of the Jesuit priests in the North American wilderness, was a bestseller at the time. The only certain thing is that La Salle was receiving the best education in the world, superior to anything offered to adolescents today. Ancient and modern languages, the exact sciences, with an emphasis on physics and geography – the Jesuits were mad about cartography and the use of navigational devices such as the astrolabe – mathematics, logic, rhetoric, theology, it was an education calculated to turn a boy into a man at ease with both the rigors of science and the arts of persuasion. The Jesuits wanted their members to be capable of taking care of themselves without help in any situation.

Just before his seventeenth birthday La Salle took his religious vows and entered the Jesuit school in La Flèche, the same school Descartes attended forty years earlier. After two years at La Flèche, he alternated between his own studies and teaching in various Jesuit grammar schools. The latter was torture for La Salle, a restless soul stuck in a classroom all day supervising a bunch of boys. He was full of energy, tall (just under six feet), with an athlete's arms and legs. While capable, it seems, of controlling his sexual drives, he had less success controlling his temper and urge to dominate others. My own suspicion is that La Salle was favored by his parents over his older brother (he got the title of the family-owned farm). Perhaps they knew that the younger was more gifted than the elder. That brother, Jean Cavelier, who was seven years older than La Salle and became a priest in the Sulpician Order, and was indeed a man of mediocre talents, later displayed both resentment of and sub-servience to his younger sibling. So it must have been from the start. It is easy to imagine the drama in the Cavelier home – the eleven-year-old trying to thwart the four-year-old, the beloved of the mother, but always yielding in the end. (The beloved of the mother, Freud reminds us, feels like a conqueror.)

La Salle's superiors noted that he lacked prudence and judg-ment. He was also "scrupulous"; that is, morbidly anxious about the state of his soul and easily convinced that he had sinned mortally. It is not a state, pastoral theologians emphasize, that is invariably con-nected to mental illness, but when it does indicate neurosis, it seems to be symptomatic of obsessive-compulsive disorders or of depres-sion and anxiety. The latter would explain certain aspects of La Salle's later behavior. He was often castigated by observers for with-drawing into himself at various moments in his explorations, of being secretive and refusing to take counsel or reveal his plans. But if he was depressed and anxious, then he was too busy listening to the voices in his own head, the gloomy interior conclave that would not be stilled, to pay attention to his flesh-and-blood companions.

In 1666 the twenty-two-year-old La Salle did a most un-Jesuit thing – he wrote to the general of the society in Rome begging to be sent to China as a missionary. Jesuits don't plead for assignments. They wait to be given orders. The inner pressure on La Salle must have been intense for him to resort to this appeal, which, pre-dictably, was turned down. "A restless urge drove La Salle from one place to another, a peculiar impulse made him think that wherever he was his presence was necessary elsewhere," wrote the Jesuit scholar Jean Delanglez in a summary verdict on La Salle's career. Nothing more acute has ever been said about the man. He always wanted to be in a different place.

The following year he asked his superiors to release him from his vows and his membership in the Society of Jesus. By this time his superiors had ample evidence that La Salle was not cut out to be a Jesuit – their pet name for him was Inquietus. One of them had described the young man as possessing *ingenium bonum, judicium tenue, prudentia parva* – good parts, questionable judgment, very little prudence. A looser translation of the Latin would be "The lad's smart enough, but he doesn't have the sense God gave a flea." La Salle's request was granted. The Father General wrote to him, "Try to live ever in union of heart with us and with Jesus." Some part of La Salle, however, could never forgive the Jesuits.

La Salle now found himself without money or prospects. His father was dead, and his initial religious vows of poverty had legally deprived him of any share of the family inheritance. Nevertheless his family staked him to a voyage across the sea to Canada and sent him off with a few coins in his pocket. A lot of people in Rouen, including some of his relatives, had made money out of Canada, dealing in its fish and furs. Not that you'd want to live there. Founded by Samuel Champlain in 1608, a year after the first permanent English settlement in North America at Jamestown, French Canada was for the first half-century of its existence a string of tiny settlements along the St. Lawrence River, hemmed in by rock and forest, under constant siege by the dreaded Iroquois, gripped half the year by a bone-chilling winter. Jack Kerouac, who never escaped the spell of his own Québécois ancestors, called it "the utterly hopeless place to which the French came when they came to the New World." Walt Whitman, visiting the province in 1880, called its landscape "an extreme of grimness" and one of the scariest places he had ever seen. This is a point always to be remembered about French Canadians.

Things had begun to improve, actually, in the years just prior to La Salle's arrival. Louis XIV, then commencing his long, splendid, tragic reign, took an interest in this outpost of France. It would become, he decided, a province of France, and therefore he took control of its affairs away from the trading monopoly that had hitherto ruled and exploited the colony. Jean Colbert, the king's great minister, would henceforth be responsible for its fortunes, while

Canada would be directly administered by a royal governor, an intendant, and a bishop. An army regiment was sent to teach the Iroquois a lesson. The soldiers burned a few abandoned Mohawk villages – not a great military *coup* – but it was enough to persuade the Five Nations to make peace. More immigrants were sent in an attempt to create a genuine, self-sustaining agricultural community, like the English settlements along the seaboard. The fur trade would continue, for its revenues were indispensable, but now at least not every Frenchman in Canada would be roaming the wilderness like a *sauvage*. By the time La Salle took ship for Montreal, the colony was beginning to flourish, with real farms, real industries, real towns taking root.

This was the base from which La Salle, for the next two decades, conducted his journeys into the unknown heart of the continent. It was as an emissary from the court of Versailles and stone and wood farmhouses of Quebec that he followed the course of the Mississippi to its terminus in the Gulf of Mexico and made a name for himself in history.

⚜

After he accomplished this feat, nothing went right for La Salle. But a century and a half following his death, La Salle did enjoy a tremendous stroke of luck – he attracted the attention of a Boston intellectual named Francis Parkman. Parkman was the son of a Unitarian minister and descendant of a long line of parsons. He had no love for the court of Versailles or the stone and wood houses of Quebec but he was a devoted reader of Sir Walter Scott and James Fenimore Cooper. Something about La Salle inspired him. Anybody who now tries to do justice to La Salle feels Francis Parkman's prose beating a sublime tattoo in the background, which can be a terrible distraction. There are times, probably, when any historian of the period wishes that Parkman, greatest of American historians, had never existed, he is such a beautiful writer and so misleading.

When young Francis Parkman was seven, he was sent to live at his grandfather's farm in Medford, Massachusetts, bordering on a tract of woods known as the Middlesex Fells. For six years the boy roamed these woods. He shared them with the Indians and the pioneers of his brain, as they hunted or conducted their fierce ambushes behind trees, refreshed themselves from running streams, made shelters of pine boughs. At eighteen, he conceived the idea of writing the history of the French in America in the shape of a drama staged within a slightly larger version of Middlesex Fells, which is to say the North American wilderness. I know how that works. Our house on East New Lenox Road, on the outskirts of Pittsfield, was a few minutes away from a woodlot of about thirty-five acres on the other side of the road, which I explored with my brother Peter and another boy named Peter Rice, whose family owned the lot. No patch of earth on this planet will ever mean as much to me.

An ecologist would describe these thirty-five acres of woodland off East New Lenox Road as hemlock and mixed hardwood forest, typical of southern and central New England and characterized by the growth of white pine, hemlock, red maple, sugar maple, yellow birch, chestnut, ash, elm, and red oak. This is what it was. But what mattered to me then and now was the impact of its shaded corridors and its hollows covered with moss or pine needles or ferns on my eight- or nine-year-old imagination, the feelings evoked by the slowly moving stream in one corner of the woods where the muskrats lived. Nature is a haunted house, Emily Dickinson remarked. The very young feel this. When Francis Parkman, as a historian, rhapsodized about "stern depths of immemorial forests, dim and silent as a cavern" or painted a woodland scene in which a "wild shy rivulet steals with timid music through breathless caves of verdure" – and you could see the *coureur de bois* lighting his campfire by the rivulet or Rogers's Rangers filing through the green cathedral on one of their murderous expeditions – he was summoning this romantic prose in an attempt not to describe a particular landscape but to make the reader feel what he felt remembering Middlesex Fells, and what I feel remembering Rice's woods.

With countless thousands of readers, he succeeded. He succeeded so well that we forget how disheartened visitors can be at the sight of Parkman's "immemorial forests" in their actual state. The vista of the northeastern forests of the United States struck the English painter and critic Wyndham Lewis, for one, as a barren desert. "The tundra, or the dune, dotted with the eternal fir tree, comes right up to the back door of the last house in almost any Pennsylvanian or New England townlet," he complained in 1934. Far from being the paradisal wilderness of Parkman and James Fenimore Cooper, our forested landscape, in Lewis's eyes, was hard, crude, and uninspiring. It was a great monotony. "There are no nuances on the North American continent," he wrote, which also explained, Lewis believed, why you never ran across an urbane American.

In fact, the wilderness has expanded since Lewis's complaint. By the time Parkman died in 1893, so many trees had been harvested to produce furnace charcoal that New England was almost de-forested. Since then, with charcoal no longer in demand, and dairy farms ever shrinking, the New England forests have been growing and spreading. When I was a boy in Pittsfield, bears in the neighborhood were unheard of. Now they are a common sight in backyards. That's fine with me, but I don't confuse this growing wilderness with my remembered woods or Parkman's breathless caves of verdure. These exist only in our reconstructed childhoods, in a parallel universe of memory.

All of this helps me to understand Parkman, but in no way can I identify with him as fiercely as he identified with La Salle. Parkman was a headstrong little boy, adored by his mother and sisters. The figure who traditionally fills the nursery door with his ominous shadow and curbs the headstrong little boy – dear papa! – was in Parkman's case an affable, mild-mannered gentleman whose blood had been permanently thinned by generations of high-minded Unitarianism. Dr. Parkman would sit at the head of the table in his coat and tie and make dry, witty puns as he passed the turnips. His son grew up to despise men of the cloth of whatever denomination; he had to make an effort even to acknowledge the incredible heroism of the early Jesuit missionaries. There was nothing wrong with his corpuscles. As a boy he showed himself determined to have his own way and command the will of others. Like La Salle, he possessed the forcefulness to be a leader. Also like La Salle, he lacked the charm or charisma to make his authority palatable. Men generally didn't obey Parkman or La Salle unless they had to.

Parkman, to his credit, did everything he could to live up to the hero's role. He hired professionals to teach him how to box and ride a horse. He practiced marksmanship. He slept in the woods without a blanket. He risked his life. An account of a youthful New Hampshire mountain-climbing expedition depicts Parkman literally hanging from a rock face by his fingertips. He managed to get a jackknife out of his pocket, open it with his teeth, and use it to carve handholds in the crumbling rock.

Why shouldn't he be a hero? He was tall, brave, handsome, strong, athletic, and brilliant. What other gifts could the gods bestow on him? But any visitor to the Parkman house could see signs of trouble for the boy. "The Parkmans had so many illnesses that they were a microcosm of a vast, Victorian sickroom," one biographer writes. "At one time or another, the Parkmans suffered from a host of ailments: temperatures, coughs, aches, painful headaches, despondency, and defective eyesight. The family was often disturbed by Dr. Parkman's severe depressions. . . ." Francis Parkman's blood might have been red, but it was not untainted. Even as a boy, Parkman recalled in later years, he felt "sensitive and restless, rarely ill, but never robust." The reason he was sent to his grandfather's farm, in fact, was to build some of that robustness. There's a Teddy Roosevelt-like obsessiveness in Parkman's attempt to be a rugged, thoroughly masculine specimen. Parkman's body, unfortunately, was not as compliant as Roosevelt's. By his early twenties, he was complaining about insomnia, indigestion, and eye strain. After his return in 1846 from a trip out west – the trip that would form the basis of his first great work, *The Oregon Trail* – the twenty-three-year-old Parkman suffered a nervous collapse. In addition to his earlier symptoms, he experienced what he called a "wild whirl" in his brain, a kind of mental overstimulation that left him prostrate.

At various periods of life he would face this condition, which he called "the enemy." At its worst, Parkman wrote,

> I could neither listen to reading nor engage in conversation even of the lightest. Sleep was difficult, and was often banished entirely for one or two nights during which the brain was apt to be in a state of abnormal activity which had to be repressed at any cost, since thought produced the intensest torture. The effort required to keep the irritated organ quiet was so fatiguing that I occasionally rose and spent hours in the open air, where I found distraction and relief watching the policemen and the tramps on the Malls of Boston Common, at the risk of passing for a tramp myself.

But this affliction, too, solidified his feeling of sympathy for "the masculine form of Cavelier de la Salle," who was not free of his own internal enemy. Addressing the charges of some of La Salle's contemporaries that the man was frankly insane, Parkman defended his champion but admitted that there were times when La Salle clearly lost touch with reality. "It is difficult not to see in all this the chimera of an overwrought brain, no longer able to distinguish between the possible and the impossible," Parkman wrote, in regard to La Salle's plans for his last expedition. (We will come to that.) By 1878, when this was published, the historian was an expert on the subject of overwrought brains.

Parkman's spiritual bond with La Salle – of all the extraordinary figures that populate Parkman's multi-volume epic of the French in America, La Salle comes closest to being the principal hero – gives his book on the subject, *The Discovery of the Great West*, its imaginative drive. That bond also explains what readers find most objectionable about Parkman today, which is his devotion to a combative, male, aristocratic ideal. La Salle failed to embody completely that ideal only in the respect that he happened to be a French Roman Catholic instead of an Anglo-Saxon Protestant. Influenced by Social Darwinism, Parkman viewed his New England ancestors as the vanguard of a manly, independent, resourceful race ordained to triumph over the French Canadians. Although the French had heroes, from the Jesuit martyrs to Champlain and La Salle, eclipsing anything the English colonists produced, the society they left behind, in Parkman's view, was priest-ridden and backward. To do anything in that society of early Quebec, you had to get the permission of some authority. How could the peasants who toiled on the banks of the St. Lawrence under the thumb of their feudal overlords – the fur trader and the *coureur de bois* were conspicuous exceptions to this picture, of course, but they were on the fringes of society, and often downright outlaws – defeat sturdy, tough-minded New England farmers?

The answer was they couldn't. What's more, they should have been grateful the English destroyed their feudal regime. "A happier calamity never befell a people than the conquest of Canada by British arms," wrote Parkman. Like Kenneth Roberts, he had very little patience, in the end, with "swarthy, stunted Frenchmen."

Worse, in twenty-first-century eyes, is Parkman's attitude toward Blacks – he denounced Reconstruction for bringing the "monstrosities of Negro rule" to the South – and toward women – he was a notable opponent of female suffrage – and toward Indians. Talk about a race ordained to defeat. Parkman did admire the pride, heroic virtues, and intelligence of the historic Five Nations Confederacy, but generally he viewed Indians as fatally maladapted to the progress of civilization. His opinions in this regard were solidified by three weeks spent with the Oglala Sioux on the Oregon Trail. These Sioux were dashing hunters and warriors, as robust as they come, but when they weren't hunting or fighting, they reminded Parkman of children, stuffing themselves with food, lying around in the sun, bragging of their exploits, begging for anything that caught their eye. In later life, Parkman adhered to the most wretched aspects of nineteenth-century anthropology – measuring the skulls of racial inferiors with calipers and so on.

Yet we cannot get rid of Parkman. That's the problem with people who write well. They penetrate your brain with their images. No amount of subsequent history will efface Parkman's great dramatic portraits, in the same way that no amount of scholarly research into Richard III will take away the hunchback Shakespeare gave him. I will be quoting Parkman throughout this account, when I need some red corpuscles.

⚜

Everything that happened to La Salle after he reached the mouth of the Mississippi in April of 1682 was anticlimactic. Even so, in my journey in the footsteps of La Salle across the continent, this is where I chose to begin, with this last voyage to Texas, this sad denouement of his career. The voyage was a reckless and futile venture on La Salle's part – it often seems as if the entire French experience in North America was a reckless and futile venture. But out of the darkness of this episode something human survived. Later, when I encountered striking evidence of that survival, at a point when my own journey following the footsteps of La Salle was almost over, I took it as a sign. If one read the sign, I thought, one could glimpse the meaning of the French in North America. One could make some sense of these faraway events, when La Salle came to the shores of Texas and the end of his wandering.

What happened after the discovery of the mouth of the Great River was La Salle's return to France to persuade the king to build a fort and a colony near that spot. This was not an easy sell. Despite, or because of, Louis XIV's decision to solidify his settlements in

Canada, he was never enthusiastic about spending a lot of money to penetrate the heart of the continent and build a vast inland empire. Moreover, there were powerful interests who also stood to lose if the French expanded into the continent – notably the merchants of Montreal and Quebec, who wanted to retain their position as exclusive middlemen between the fur traders in the interior and the consumers in France.

La Salle might have been ignored by the king were it not that war had just been renewed between France and Spain. Louis XIV had always been annoyed by Spain's declaration that the Gulf of Mexico was a Spanish lake, closed to shipping of other nations. Here was a chance to settle the issue. La Salle, meanwhile, had friends at Versailles – lobbyists, we would call them today – who helped him frame his proposal to the monarch. La Salle in that proposal urged that France enforce its claim on the Mississippi, lest foreigners seize it first. From this base, the French could spread the gospel to several Indian nations and also launch an attack on the silver mines of New Biscay, in northern Mexico. To this latter end, all La Salle needed from the king was a ship, a few cannon, and two hundred men. He could easily raise fifteen thousand Indian troops in the neighborhood, since they already hated the Spanish, and call upon another four thousand of his Indian allies in Illinois.

This was bizarre. La Salle apparently believed that the mouth of the river he had just explored was right next door to Mexico. It was as if the state of Texas did not stand between the Mississippi and the Rio Grande. La Salle had only the foggiest idea of where he had been. The inability of Europeans to measure longitude at that time partly accounted for his confusion; the wildly inaccurate maps of the area he consulted compounded it. He just didn't know any better. But he certainly did know that the business of fifteen thousand Indians from the lower Mississippi region was pure moonshine, as was the promise of four thousand Indians from Illinois. It was true that he had built alliances with Indian nations in the Great Lakes. But you were lucky if you could persuade two dozen of these allies to follow you beyond their familiar hunting grounds and trading routes.

He was in a tight spot, burdened with crushing debts to people who had lent him money in the supposition that he would bring back furs. La Salle had no furs to bring back. If the post on the Mississippi proved lucrative in this regard – and there was no reason it shouldn't – that problem would be solved. When the king said yes to his proposal, La Salle no doubt felt some relief. The relief was immediately replaced by a flood of anxiety. He now had the task of organizing the expedition, finding men and supplies, and working with the naval captain, the Sieur de Beaujeu, commander of the warship that would lead the expedition. La Salle had never undertaken anything of this scale, and he certainly was no administrator. But even this he might have coped with had he not been burdened with the knowledge that he had just promised the impossible. Perhaps there were days when he convinced himself he could do it. Perhaps there were days, as Parkman suggests, he convinced himself that peace with Spain would come before he had to make the attempt. In the early hours of the morning, however, when he woke from a troubled sleep, he knew better. Some men can carry on with their plans even when they know they have compromised themselves and that ultimately they will have to face the consequences. The Bill Clintons of the world apparently can function quite cheerfully under these circumstances. But La Salle, the boy who had been weighed under by scruples as a Jesuit novice, was not of that kind. A nagging sense of his own duplicity, as well as impending failure and disgrace, brought out the worst aspects of his personality, his paranoia, his secretiveness.

He quarreled with outfitters in the port of La Rochelle, accusing them of taking pay from his enemies to sabotage his voyage. He quarreled with Beaujeu virtually from the moment they met. The captain's main complaint, entirely justified, was that La Salle would not tell him his plans. Were they sailing to Canada or to the Caribbean? It would make a considerable difference in the amount of supplies they had to carry. Also, there was the small matter of the pilot. Should they choose someone familiar with the waters off the St. Lawrence or someone familiar with the Gulf of Mexico? Get somebody familiar with both, La Salle replied. Further quarrels ensued over the number of men and the amount of material La Salle wanted to pack on board Beaujeu's ship – Beaujeu complained that there was hardly room on deck to maneuver the cannons and the capstan – over who would command the soldiers when on board, and over the all-important matter of who would dine at the captain's table and who would not.

La Salle no doubt put himself in the wrong on a number of these issues. The pressure on the man was great. I suspect, for example, that he didn't tell Beaujeu where they were going not just because of his secretiveness but because he himself was torn. He probably preferred to go to Canada, which was familiar to him, rather than the unpleasant swamps and bayous of the Mississippi delta, where he would be expected not only to build a fort and settlement on grounds barely dry enough to light a fire, but to launch an attack on an enemy of unknown size and location. He may have hoped that something would occur to settle the matter for him. But nothing like that happened. Meanwhile, Beaujeu seethed.

Historians sympathize with the captain. Basically he was a decent sort who, off the shore of Texas, finally parted on good terms with La Salle. But he could sense right off that La Salle's heart was not in this expedition, and he knew, with an infallible instinct, that La Salle was looking for other people to blame. What better candidate than Beaujeu? Beaujeu had already felt the sting of government displeasure when he was held responsible, some years earlier, for a disastrous episode in a war against Spain. Captured by the Spanish, he was then imprisoned by his own government upon his repatriation. Ultimately he had been freed and reinstated in the service, but he was now fighting for compensation and was in no mood to become a scapegoat twice in his career. Thus he wasted no time in complaining to the government about La Salle and making sure there was no mistake in their eyes as to who in this expedition was the problem.

Beaujeu had other stresses, as well – a sick wife, a difficult son. Many allowances may be made for him. But what a difference to subsequent history if he had proven a more generous and large-minded individual. Admittedly, that's a rare commodity in military and government establishments, and La Salle could have been saddled with worse. But still, such a pity. Beaujeu relieved his feelings in a series of confidential letters to a friend – La Salle, by the way, found out about this correspondence, which did nothing to ease his paranoia. Very few people don't believe that this man La Salle is cracked (*frappé*), Beaujeu commented in one letter. Those who have known him for a long time, he continued, say that he has always been *un peu visionnaire*. That word is usually translated "visionary," but in French it means more like someone given to sheer fantasy. La Salle could not distinguish between his dreams and reality. Beaujeu, in addition to listening to tittle-tattle, may also have noticed a certain look in La Salle's eyes, a staring into the distance. More evidence he was not quite right in the head.

Beaujeu, of course, was a tough guy who had seen the inside of a Spanish prison and had commanded in the heat of battle, whereas La Salle, he sneered, had "never commanded anybody but schoolboys." But that stare should have told him. La Salle had experienced something neither he nor Beaujeu had any vocabulary for. No one who had not been in the wilderness of North America could understand that experience, the way it made a man feel he could be reborn, but only with terrible hazards, the way it made him distrust language and the life of the streets or the court or the army encampment. Once it had you, the wilderness would not let go, it was magnificent beyond telling, it was worse than your worst nightmare. It may well have made La Salle seem a little *frappé*.

Beaujeu offered his correspondent a further tidbit. A certain inhabitant of Canada named Saint-Michel, he wrote, had crossed swords with La Salle and spoke none too well of his bravery. This Saint-Michel has never been identified. It was just a nasty story Beaujeu happened to pick up, a delicious calumny. Whatever La Salle's faults, he was no coward. In his vantage point from beyond the grave, Beaujeu must keenly regret having written that sentence. Seeing him toss it off is like seeing a baboon bare his canine teeth. If we pause over it and ponder it, as a kind of specimen of malignancy, we can feel the ugliness of gossip, its spitefulness, and the perfect ease with which it can be used to destroy an extraordinary and vulnerable man. Beaujeu did not want to destroy La Salle. But what irresistible pleasure to pass on a rumor that suggested this fine fellow the king thought so much of, this Hercules of the wilderness, was not such a hero after all, that in fact he was not one bit better than Beaujeu himself, or you, or me.

Somehow by late summer they managed to load the ships, get everybody on board, and set off across the Atlantic. The expedition consisted of four ships: Beaujeu's warship *Joly*; the *Aimable*, a cargo ship of three hundred tons; a bark called the *Belle*; and a ketch, the *Saint-François*. The *Joly*, under Beaujeu, would return to France after reaching its destination; the other ships would remain with La Salle. On board were some three hundred soldiers, tradesmen, and "volunteers." Among the latter were six priests (Sulpicians and Recollets, the two orders in competition with the Jesuits for religious supremacy in New France), including La Salle's brother, Father Jean Cavelier; two of La Salle's nephews; a family consisting of a Monsieur Talon, his wife, Isabelle, and five children; and six other women "lured by the prospect of almost certain matrimony," according to Parkman. The volunteers also included an ex-soldier, Henri Joutel, thirty-four, and an engineer named Jean-Baptiste Minet, twenty-three. Both wrote accounts of the expedition, one sympathetic to La Salle (Joutel), one hostile (Minet). With these passengers went provisions meant to sustain the colonists for nine months: trade goods, cannon and cannonballs, small arms, tools, ironware, and a blacksmith's forge.

Beaujeu now knew he was sailing for the Caribbean. The trip took nearly two months – August and September – during which relations between Beaujeu and La Salle continued to deteriorate. At the Tropic of Cancer, the crew of the *Joly* wanted to follow custom and threaten passengers who had never crossed the line with a dunking in a tub of salt water – it was a way of extracting money or liquor from these passengers in exchange for not carrying through on the threat. After La Salle told the crew they could forget this tradition, Joutel wrote, "The sailors would have gladly killed us all." It didn't help that these sailors had to sleep in the open deck, in the sun and rain, because of La Salle's extra baggage. Heat prostration, dysentery and other ills soon swept through the crowded *Joly*. More serious was the wave of heat prostration, dysentery, and other ills that spread in the crowded *Joly*. At one point, fifty people on board were ill. Shortly before they arrived at the port of Petit Goave, Haiti, La Salle joined their number. For more than a month he fought a persistent fever. The sailors expressed their sentiments by carousing all night in front of the house in Petit Goave where he lay at the point of death. "The more one begged them to be quiet, the more they made a noise," his brother reported. The port itself was a hellhole, populated with the dregs of the Caribbean. "The air was bad, the fruit the same, and there were a great many women worse than either," Joutel wrote. As soon as he was able, La Salle ordered the sailors and soldiers back on the ships, before too many were lost from disease or desertion.

As it was, by the time the ships sailed again on November 25, the number of La Salle's party had been reduced to two hundred. Missing also was the ketch *Saint-François*, which had been captured by the Spanish. The loss of its cargo – provisions, tools, ammunition – was the first of the truly serious blows to the prospects of the settlement. Regardless, the three other ships, their company augmented by freebooters recruited in Haiti, sailed to Cape St. Antoine, the westernmost point of Cuba, and then, after a lengthy delay, set course north-by-west for the mouth of the Mississippi. If the angle of their course had been a few degrees more easterly, they would have hit their mark. As it was, when they sighted land on December 28, 1684, they were already west of the Mississippi, near the current border of Texas and Louisiana. On New Year's Day, they attempted to land but found only mud flats as far as they could see. La Salle, who had been warned about strong easterly currents in the Gulf and the need to compensate for them, continued to sail westward. He passed Galveston Bay and then Matagorda Bay and approached Corpus Christi Bay. More mud flats. The coast, he noticed, was curving southward, and finally he realized he had passed his river. In fact, he was about four hundred miles west of it.

The best course would have been to sail back along the coast until the river was found. Neither La Salle nor Beaujeu had much stomach for that, however – Beaujeu because he didn't want to expose his ship to the treacherous winds and coastal waters of this region, La Salle, Parkman suggests, because of "impatience to rid himself of his colleague." His conflicting objectives made it impossible for him to exercise good judgment. In a sense, this region was as good as any place to launch an attack on Mexico. Why not just stop all this poking around the coast, sailing a bit and then halting with fogs and winds, and constantly worrying about wrecking one of the ships? Or just backtrack a bit, to that bay a few miles to the east that looked so promising? Maybe that was the Mississippi, or a western branch of the Mississippi, obscured by marshes and mud flats.

If relations between La Salle and Beaujeu had been better, sanity might have prevailed and the ships and the men remained together until they found the Mississippi. Instead, La Salle ordered the soldiers to land on Matagorda Island, a narrow thirty-five-mile-long strip of land, and march eastward while he and the ships followed. On February 14, they rendezvoused at the eastern tip of the island, off Matagorda Bay, which La Salle declared was indeed the western branch of the Mississippi. Here he would build his settlement.

On March 12, 1685, the *Joly*, relieved of the two hundred soldiers and settlers who landed on Matagorda Bay, finally sailed back to France. Before then, however, two incidents occurred that doomed the settlement. The first was the shipwreck of the *Aimable*. On February 20, as it attempted to enter Matagorda Bay, it foundered on a sand reef. Much of its precious cargo was salvaged, but much was lost: sixteen hundred cannonballs, fittings for the forge, tools, arms, trade goods such as axes, knives, tobacco, and a great many provisions, including sixty casks of wine and brandy. This incident, too, should give pause to those who sigh over La Salle's "paranoia." In this case, that paranoia seems fully justified – the wreck was almost certainly an act of deliberate sabotage on the part of the ship's captain, a Monsieur Aigron. No other explanation accounts for his deliberate ignoring of the orders and advice he had been given for entering the bay. In fact, he was thrown into prison for destroying the ship when he returned to France. The reason for his betrayal appears to have been sheer spite. He despised La Salle.

The second incident occurred early in March, when La Salle discovered that the local Indians, the Karankawas, who up until that time had seemed wary but tractable, were pilfering his goods. He sent some men to recover the stolen goods and predictably they got carried away, helping themselves to a few canoes. A fight ensued, two Frenchmen were killed, and the Karankawas were permanently alienated from their visitors.

With these disasters hanging over their heads, the followers of La Salle remained, already much reduced in numbers from disease, and with only the little frigate the *Belle* as their link with the outside world. Once again, it is hard not to quote Parkman on the pathos of their situation:

> Here, among tents and hovels, bales, boxes, casks, spars, dismounted cannon, and pens for fowl and swine, were gathered the dejected men and homesick women who were to seize New Biscay, and hold for France a region large as half Europe. The Spaniards, whom they were to conquer, were they knew not where. They knew not where they were themselves; and,

for the fifteen thousand Indian allies who were to have joined them, they found two hundred squalid savages, more like enemies than friends.

❧

I picked up a hint of what was coming in my first telephone conversation with William C. Foster, though all we said was that we would meet Sunday morning at ten in the parking lot of the McDonald's in Cuero. It was a sensible place to rendezvous because the golden arches were on a pole that towered above the restaurant and could be seen for miles around. I spotted the yellow landmark easily, near the center of the town, which advertises itself as "The Way Life Ought To Be" and, on somewhat more solid grounds, the "Wildflower Capital of Texas." I pulled in to the parking lot and waited only a few minutes before Foster arrived in his black Mercedes SUV. A lean man with glasses and a full head of wavy gray hair, wearing a white shirt and a tan pair of shorts, got out of the Mercedes. He hadn't shaved yet. We introduced ourselves and he suggested we drive back to his house.

This, it turned out, was a grand two-story edifice from the mid-nineteenth century, surrounded by live oaks – a species of tree complete with trumpet vines and long, twisty branches growing close to the ground that always looks transplanted from Oz. Foster, a trim, energetic, retired lawyer in his mid-seventies – he works out at a gym religiously – showed me around the house. The parlor and the living room, with high ceilings and wallpaper in somber tones of bronze and brown, looked like they hadn't been touched for decades, except for the presence of a Sony television. The two rooms, Foster told me, were covered in the oldest wallpaper in the state still hanging on a wall. I could believe it. In the spacious, almost vacant room where his mother and his banker stepfather, a man of German descent like many of the townspeople in Cuero, might have entertained in the old days, he pointed to the floor. "See this parquet," he said. "The light-colored parts in each square are pecan. The other parts are oak." It was a beautifully intricate pattern, repeated too many times to think about. Bill Gates couldn't buy a floor like that today. "Germans put those in. That's the kind of thing Germans would do." We walked down a corridor with portrait photographs on the wall. One was of a woman, past the first blush of youth, but still charming. Foster's mother. "Isn't she cute?" Foster said. "A doll." Actually, she had a slightly forlorn look. Next to her was a portrait of a bulky, middle-aged man wearing very small eyeglasses and a tux with white tie. He looked every inch the banker and prominent citizen. "My mother was cute as a bug," Foster said. "And Daddy Reiffert was sixty and he always wanted to marry somebody cute like that. Here she was, divorced with two kids in the Depression, and he married her. You just didn't *do* that. But he did it. I love him."

We sat down in Foster's study, a bright, airy room with lots of windows and a long table covered with stacks of paper. There was no hint of the decayed Southern manse in this part of the house. Here was where Foster did his work. He had been a partner in a Washington, D.C., law firm for twenty-five years, a lobbyist for the oil patch, working on behalf of the Alaska oil pipeline. Now he was an amateur historian – or "independent scholar," to use a less prejudicial term – and the author of a number of books on early Texas published by the Texas State Historical Association. Along with another independent scholar, Robert S. Weddle, he was probably the best authority on La Salle's Texas adventures. His work as editor and annotator of Henri Joutel's journal, in particular – his edition of that journal had recently been published under the title *The La Salle Expedition to Texas* – was invaluable.

It didn't take me long to realize that the connection between Weddle and Foster was a sore point. Foster leaned back in his chair with his arms folded and talked about La Salle's journey to the Gulf Coast and how a minor nautical error made at the departure point in Cuba resulted in the landing four hundred miles from his intended destination. He straightened his right arm and pointed at the ceiling, at an angle to his head, to indicate the path that could have led to the mouth of the Mississippi had it not been for that slight mistake of about three degrees. "After going all that distance, he barely missed it. People say, 'Poor La Salle, he was completely lost.' Screw that 'poor La Salle.' This was in foreign territory, foreign seas. Spanish seas. No one had ever been there before, and he comes in and missed the thing by three degrees. Rather than saying the guy was lost, the truth is the guy was remarkably accurate."

Foster dropped his arm and sat up. A light was in his blue eyes. "Weddle and I have fought and tussled on this thing from the get-go. We've never met. I don't know him. But all my books and articles have been reviewed by Weddle, and he's been a reader of my manuscripts prior to publication as well, because he's been – he is highly regarded by the association. And although his remarks have been caustic and, uh . . ." Foster paused. "Well, I'll just leave it at that. They have been extremely critical, but they haven't been devastating." Foster flashed a wicked smile. "Then I reviewed his recent book, which was a joy to me." He meant, of course, the reviewing, not the book. "I was critical, but complimentary where that was appropriate, and uh, yes, he and I are just quite different human beings. He's Catholic, I'm not. He's authoritarian, and I'm not. He loves to be able to say he knows it all. If the explorers say something like they woke up and the moon rose soon after, Weddle is ready to say that the moon doesn't come up in the morning. And I'm ready to say, 'I'm not sure what they mean, and I'm not prepared to say they're wrong.' I will stick to the last goddamn minute to what the explorers actually say, unless it was a priest who said that 'we had mass this morning and five million Indians attended.' Then I'll say the good father was probably exaggerating. But by and large I really go with the explorers, and I don't take any pride in being able to one-up on them."

In *The La Salle Expedition to Texas*, Foster traced the route of La Salle's attempt to reach the Mississippi overland by assuming that whatever data Joutel provided – chiefly estimates of distance traveled and compass direction – were accurate. "They knew where they were," Foster insisted. "They could count. When they said six leagues, it was six goddamn leagues. It was 2.4 miles if it was a French league, and 2.6 miles if it was a Spanish league. And you use that information. You get out a United States Geographical Survey map and you use it and you plot it out. You can rely on their distances. They're very consistently accurate to within a 10- or 15-per cent margin of error, 95 per cent of the time. And the rest are just anomalies or something. Ninety-five per cent, probably more, but at least 95 per cent of their distances are accurate. They're not precise to the foot, but if they say six leagues, it could be seven leagues long, but it's not going to be eight or nine leagues. It's not going to be four leagues. These were professional frontiersmen. They relied on the accuracy of their distance and direction to get back home. For someone to come along three hundred years later and say they weren't accurate really bothers me."

To understand Foster's annoyance you have to take a look at a footnote in Robert Weddle's book, *The Wreck of the* Belle, *the Ruin of La Salle.* (Footnotes in scholarly works are often like torpedos that travel with lethal intent, under the surface of the text as it were, toward enemy shipping.) In this particular footnote, Weddle quoted Foster's claim, in *The La Salle Expedition to Texas*, that one could repose "a high degree of confidence" in Joutel's accuracy. "Not quite so," Weddle replied, citing disagreement among scholars as to the conversion of the French league to English miles, and the difficulty, in any case, of giving more than a rough estimate of the distance traveled on a given day. This was a controversy I had no opinion on, although I admired Foster's doggedness in trying to chart La Salle's route. Parkman didn't even bother to attempt the feat. "It is impossible, as it would be needless, to follow the detail of their daily march," Parkman wrote in his book, and the casual reader sails right past that statement. By all means, get on with the story. But when Foster drew my attention to that sentence, it gave me pause. I admired the slyness of it. You could call it the Parkman

Maneuver, a handy rhetorical device for any journalist or historian who didn't want to be bothered doing a bit of hard or boring research. I must remember it.

This business about leagues was beyond me. Weddle might be right. Foster might be right. I did notice, apart from this controversy, that Weddle's book took, in general, a rather harsh attitude toward its subject. The author clearly did not have much patience with La Salle in Texas, where, I have to admit, he did everything wrong. I wasn't sure what Weddle's Catholicism had to do with all this, however, unless Catholicism encouraged a judgmental attitude in combination with a cavalier disregard for the empirical, as Foster implied. It wasn't as if La Salle was an enemy of the Church. He seems to have been a believing, practicing Catholic to the end of his days, who wouldn't dream of going anywhere in the continent without a priest in tow. He got very annoyed with some of these priests it is also true, but that's another time-honored Catholic tradition. When Joutel discovered that a few of the priests were recording their own accounts of the expedition – "These gentlemen are extremely fond of writing," Joutel observed acidly – he put a stop to it. Weddle, in his book, attributed this act of censorship to Joutel's "guarding jealously his own role as expedition historian." La Salle no doubt wholeheartedly approved the measure. If anyone was going to put a spin on events, it would be him and his friends. Foster, however, thought La Salle and Joutel – he pronounced it Joe Tell – had a point. "La Salle had enough with these priests writing these notes," he said. "He didn't want the priests sending their special messages back to France. It had nothing to do with La Salle or Joe Tell wanting to be the only one to write about the expedition." La Salle had suffered already from bad publicity spread by his clerical enemies, notably the Jesuits up north.

Then there's the case of Jean Gery (sometimes spelled Jean Jarry), the deserter who lived among the Indians and eventually led the Spanish to Garcitas Creek. "I think the guy was absolutely brilliant," Foster said. "I think he's one of the jewels of the French exploration. He endears himself to everybody, he learns the languages of the Indians, he marries one of them, like a Frenchman would. Like anybody who had any goddamn sense would. Weddle, who's still a Catholic, sees this as an abandonment of the faith. You know, treachery. I'm thinking, man, if I could do what he did, that's what I would have done. Weddle would belittle him, just like he did La Salle, just like he did Joe Tell. He takes great pride in being able to tell the readers, these guys I'm talking about, I know a lot more than they do. But I – I just look at them and marvel. There's no question, on the trip to Texas La Salle got himself into some trouble. Joe Tell himself was critical of La Salle; he said La Salle was overbearing, and he didn't handle the local Indian situation correctly, which he didn't."

Most readers of Joutel's journal come away with high regard for the man's good sense, diligent observations of nature, and loyalty to his commander. Weddle's own attitude toward him is not as censorious as Foster implies, but he does caution about placing entire trust in the man. "Serious efforts to assess his character and motivation have generally been lacking," Weddle writes. "Certain facts, however, stand out: he seldom credits the work of others and rarely mentions anyone by name except his superiors, the clerics, or those with whom he had a personal relationship. . . . Although Joutel's accuracy and objectivity have seldom been questioned – any more than his omissions or his inconsistencies – it should be remembered that he never strayed far from his allegiance to La Salle and the Cavelier family; what he said or failed to say is known in some instances to have been influenced thereby." In another footnote aimed at the good ship Foster, Weddle writes, "Notably missing from Foster, ed., *La Salle Expedition*, is an assessment of Joutel the man."

Easier said than done. If Joutel hadn't made those priests burn their diaries, we might have a better grip on what the expedition was like and therefore who Joutel was. Like Foster, I tend to believe what he writes, but the affair in Texas from beginning to end was full of unpleasant mysteries, and Joutel, too, undoubtedly had his secrets. He certainly was not about to tell everything in that journal. But Joutel is transparent compared to somebody like Gery, a figure who could have been happily dancing with wolves out there in the wilderness, or as compliant with the spirits of evil as Kurtz in the jungle. Weddle passes no judgment on the man in his book, which refers to him only briefly. In January 1689, writes Weddle, while Gery was in Spanish custody, just before he set out with Captain De León to find the French, he "petitioned through the Holy Office of the Inquisition to marry Antonia de Lara, a thirty-five-year-old Spanish woman from San Luis Potosi who was employed as a servant at the military post." Gery "satisfied his interrogators that he was a devout Catholic," Weddle continues. "Apparently, the ecclesiastic authorities raised no questions as to his mental soundness. His admitted liaison with an Indian woman who had borne him a daughter was disavowed, as she was considered a pagan." After the return from Garcitas Creek, Gery disappeared once again into the wilderness. I gathered he never did marry the servant woman, who was also, by the standard of the age, well advanced in years. Weddle quoted the lament of De León, on another expedition to east Texas. "On this journey I sorely missed the old Frenchman, because of his knowledge of all the Indian languages of the region. He was always found faithful."

At this point in my conversation with Foster I was beginning to feel that I was harboring my own secret, namely that I was a communicant in the same church that La Salle belonged to, and apparently Robert S. Weddle. I was a practicing Catholic. This was the link between the explorer and me. We believed the same doctrines and observed the same religious practices. Our mutual bond in this respect outweighed, in my view, the differences in language, time, circumstance, and personality. That we happened to share this bond was also in large part because of his travails in North America, and those of the other men and women who made the unthinkable journey from France to the New World. This was La Salle's legacy to me. This was why I was interested in him. Part of my intention in following his path was to explain along the way something about this bond and why it hasn't come unstuck, why it persists.

I didn't reveal this sneaky agenda to Foster. I limited myself to declaring simply an interest in the French in America. In response, Foster was more candid than I was. "I might as well go on and say it. I'm not interested in Spanish or French or American Texas, their expeditions and what went on in them and what they did per se. All right? I'm not interested in that. That just never did grip me. What I'm interested in is what these good men, the explorers and diarists, saw with respect to the North American environment, particularly the natives, but also the wild animals and the plants. That interests me. The natural and the ethnographic history. I don't care that much about La Salle. I end up extremely close to and fond of people like Joe Tell because they're the ones who tell you what you want to know. He knows that there are people like me, crazy Foster, who really wants to know about the Indians. So Joe Tell asks them all sorts of esoteric questions like, what do Indians know about this and that, the questions I'd like to ask. So I have great respect for these people who led these expeditions and wrote journals about these expeditions, because they convey to me information about the land and the people. To hell with the French. To hell with all that. I'm off on the American Indians and the Mississippi culture and how the Mississippi culture related to the Southwestern and Meso-American cultures in Mexico. That interests me."

This hardly struck me as crazy. If anybody should have put his cards on the table and justified himself it was me, with my interest in these dead, white, European imperialists. Nowadays, Indians and flora and fauna seem innocent and appealing by comparison. Together, they belong to Mother Earth. They have nothing to do with some patriarchal sky god who doesn't exist.

"I'm an agnostic," Foster volunteered, although I hadn't broached the question. "I really ran out of the religion thing long ago." He folded his arms and leaned back. "That's unusual, certainly for Cuero. I believe, by the way, that when Weddle dies and goes to heaven, he's going to give his papers and books to the Catholic Church in San Antonio." I asked Foster if his agnosticism troubled his God-fearing neighbors. "They got to put up with me," he said. "My family moved here in the 1850s. I played football in high school – not very well, but I played football here. I grew up here. I have family all over the place. They can't do anything with me. They have to put up with me – I put up with them. I'm here and they know it." We rose from the table, the interview over, and Foster walked me to my car, parked in back of his black Mercedes SUV. "Nobody else in Cuero would drive something like this," Foster said. "They'd be afraid people would talk about it."

❧

A few days later I drove north to the prairie country just below the Oklahoma border, to see Foster's nemesis, Robert Weddle, at his cattle farm outside the town of Bonham. To get there I drove past a state prison, where highway signs warned you against picking up hitchhikers, and then down a dirt road to a sign with a picture of a cow that read Ash Grove Angus. Weddle, taller than Foster but just as lean, and dressed in a polo shirt and a pair of slacks, was waiting for me inside his ranch house.

We began by talking about his past career. "I left the news business in 1967 and went to work at the University of Texas Press in Austin, as a production manager," Weddle told me. "Life at the University of Texas in the sixties was pretty wild for a country boy." His tone was not nostalgic. That was one clear difference between Weddle and Foster, in fact. The latter I could imagine taking delight in any scene where devilry was afoot. Not Weddle. Foster was excitable, but Weddle was deliberate in his speech and movements. When Foster sat down and crossed his arms, it was a temporary defensive position before he uncoiled those arms to point to something or emphasize his words. When Weddle sat down and crossed his arms, he sat still and rubbed his upper arms slowly, in a contemplative fashion. Weddle, older than Foster by nearly a decade, did not strike me as authoritarian or a know-it-all, but he was a sober fellow, no doubt about it.

I gathered he hadn't stayed long at the campus. "A bunch of us started a little publishing venture that never really got off the ground," Weddle continued. "Then we came back here in 1981, my then wife and I – she died about two years ago." This was the "Nan Avis Williamson Weddle" to whom Weddle dedicated *The Wreck of the* Belle, *the Ruin of La Salle*. In the dedication Weddle had written, "Until her energies failed, she read these pages as they were written. At last I held her dying hand and told her the book was finished." Weddle gave a shy smile. "I've just recently remarried. Today marks our first month." This was said almost by way of apology for not being more hospitable – his home was still unsettled from the effects of the wedding and joining of two households. "We bought our first herd just before we moved here twenty-two years ago," he continued. "Twenty-one years, actually. Really, my most productive years have been the last two decades since I moved here. I was born about a mile back there, so this is home country to me. I came back here when I got to the point I could do what I wanted to do." What he wanted to do was raise cattle and write history. "It takes some work and commitment and time, but I never was happy being tied to a desk full time – and yet I have intellectual interests that demand I not be just a farmer. So they worked pretty well together for me. I've always said it was the best of two worlds. Sometimes they were worlds in collision." He gave that faint, shy smile again. "But it was really satisfying."

He is now giving up the business of raising registered Angus. "I've always tried to manage it myself," he explained. "You can't get good help. But I just got to the point where I'm not physically able to deal with all the problems that come up." I raised the subject of his last book. Had he been too judgmental about La Salle? "That's virtually the only criticism I've had of the book, that maybe I was hard on La Salle," Weddle replied. "But I don't think so. The man was a paranoid personality to begin with. Very strange. And his brother was about as strange as he was – maybe even a little more so. His brother was as greedy as he could be, and the two of them had no intention of going back to that settlement. They took all the goods with them and followed that march across Texas. They made their men carry their own loads, and they loaded the horses with buffalo hides that they expected to take back to France and sell at a great profit. There's no evidence of any concern in their minds for the people they left behind. That's severe condemnation for a military commander. But that's what happened."

Weddle's verdict was not formed hastily, either. "It took me years to form the judgments that I gave in that book. The thing that bothered me all along was how many accounts were told that were false. The Abbé Cavelier was one of the worst, but all the men that were captured and sent back to Mexico told different stories." (Weddle was referring to a handful of survivors of the expedition captured by the Spanish following La Salle's death.) "And La Salle himself wrote stories that were patently false. It's just amazing how much false information was written by the participants." No historian denies this web of deceit, woven in particular by two priests who survived the expedition – Jean Cavelier, La Salle's brother, and Father Anastase Douay – and by the testimony of the French who ended up as prisoners of the Spanish. Of course, the latter had good reason to be economical with the truth. Other survivors could not afford to be too candid, either – with La Salle's creditors, the French government, perhaps even the families of the dead. The divided motives of the expedition and its leaders cast its permanent shadow on the affair – a shadow that fell on Joutel also. "The thing you have to remember about Joutel is that he was closely allied to the Cavelier family," Weddle said, echoing his book. "You read his account and see that he doesn't tell the whole story. He concealed a lot – as much as he revealed. He's the self-appointed historian of the episode, but he didn't tell the whole story."

I mentioned Foster's accusation that Weddle's Catholicism affected his judgment, soured him on the explorers. Weddle looked as if he hadn't heard right. "I'm not Catholic," he said. Not Catholic? There went that thesis. He shook his head over Foster, whose antipathy he appeared fully to reciprocate. "As to how Foster might have gotten the idea I'm a Catholic, my papers are being given to the Catholic Archives of Texas. I'm not Catholic, but the Catholic Archives is really a valuable resource for the early history of Texas, particularly the Spanish colonial period." I was disappointed. It would have been interesting to talk to a Catholic historian about La Salle, especially a historian whose view of the man might have been influenced by his faith, as mine was. Instead, the conversation wound down. The last thing we talked about was Weddle's great-grandfather, a Methodist preacher and bootmaker, who brought his family to the area around 1846. Like Foster, Robert Weddle grew up in a country full of kinfolk. "My mother's first cousins were everywhere," he said. "I couldn't get away with any mischief because it would get home real fast."

⚜

What the archeologists still did not know about the settlement on Garcitas Creek was simple. Where was the cemetery? They located the three skeletons De León said he had found and reburied with the rites of the Church. But where were the dozens of other men and women who had died in the settlement before its final catastrophe? The archeologists were eager to find them. With today's technology, bones can reveal a great deal about the dead. (We know, for example, that the Karankawa were generally taller and more robust than their French visitors. They had tapped into a great ecosystem with year-round sources of protein in the Texas coastal waters, an ecosystem they defended fiercely against other Indians and were fully prepared to defend against the hairy-faced strangers.) Aside from the scientific value of the settlers' mortal remains, however, it was plain frustrating not to find their resting place. It was unsettling. The French must have buried their dead somewhere very close to their settlement. And yet the archeologists had gone over the whole area, uncovering plenty of animal bones in the process. If the burial ground was there, they would have found it.

What happened to the dead? Suspicion pointed to the Karankawa, who might have dug up the remains and desecrated them or even eaten parts of the bodies. That's what you did to enemies you hated and feared. It was the consummate insult. (On his earlier trip down the Mississippi, La Salle had witnessed his Indian allies opening the bodies of two slain enemies. A Frenchmen with La Salle reported that their allies found the bodies "fat and appetizing.") Jeff Durst, the project director, told me of another possibility. "One of my theories is that they were buried right along the edge of the bluff and that because they were disturbing the soil to bury them, the soil washed out and their bones just got washed into the creek." Durst's superior, Jim Bruseth, director of the Texas Historical Commission's archeology division, thought the French might have buried them in the creek to begin with, hoping they would drift out to sea and remain forever beyond the reach of the Karankawa. At one point in his journal, Joutel, after noting the death of a friend, wrote, "I had him buried as honorably as the conditions of the place would admit." That suggested something other than an ordinary burial – perhaps even the equivalent of a burial at sea.

Speculation is hardly as satisfying as evidence, however. At one point the archeologists became so desperate they engaged the services of two "witchers," a local man and woman who claimed they could find dead bodies using coat hangers, the way dowsers can find water through their wood switches. I thought it would be interesting to talk to them. One of them was a woman named Dorothy Albrecht, who lived in La Grange, about a two-hour drive north of Victoria. Her address was a brick ranch house not far from downtown La Grange. When I rang the bell, it took so long for somebody to appear at the door I thought I might have gotten the appointment wrong. But Albrecht, who was seventy-two, just took a long time coming – she was rotund and suffered from a bad knee, and had to walk with the support of a cane. She greeted me cheerfully enough, however, and showed me into a very commodious den. On bookshelves, tabletops, on every available level surface in this room, stood an army of ceramic chickens and roosters. She collected them. "My husband was in the chicken business," she explained. "I used to say we had the only legitimate chicken ranch in town." This was a reference to the Chicken Ranch, a local brothel made famous by the Broadway hit and movie *The Best Little Whorehouse in Texas*. It's long gone – the building removed to Dallas, I was told, and converted into a restaurant. How the La Grange Chamber of Commerce allowed this historic monument to slip away from them I'll never know.

Albrecht told me that she had been taught the art of witching by Judge Norman C. Krischke of neighboring Schulenberg. The tools of the art were simple: a pair of coat hangers, bent so that a handle of five inches stood at a right angle to a straight rod of fifteen inches. (Lengths can vary somewhat.) She took out her pair and held them so that the rods were pointed straight at me. "What happens is when you get over a grave, these will just automatically start doing this with no reason at all," she said. The rods swung toward each other. "If you want to find the gender of the person, you can hold a rod in one hand. It goes to the left, it indicates that it's a male. It goes to the right, it indicates a woman, because you know women are always right." I smiled at the pleasantry. "Just hold them loosely, so they can move without you moving them."

She and Krischke had gone down to the site of the Garcitas Creek settlement three months previously, in March. "I didn't have any trouble convincing him to go," Albrecht said of Krischke, who was seventy-seven and recently had a leg amputated because of diabetes. "But I had trouble convincing his wife to let him go. We probably spent three hours there – something like that, not really too long. I was getting all kinds of signals there. The rods were going like this" – the coat hangers in her hand started swinging like the saloon doors in a western after the bad guy walks in. "I don't know if that's where the massacre took place. They were really flipping back and forth like they couldn't make up their minds." Had she ever discovered graves before? I asked. The coat hangers had located graves before, she replied, but nobody had done any digging to confirm their presence. "I never dug anybody up and I'm not going to," she laughed. I felt badly, because I realized she did not know that the archeologists had already dug in the locations indicated by her and Krischke and found nothing. The feeling worsened as she added, "I don't know whether it really works. I'm real anxious for them to dig down there so I can see how close the judge and I were." The dig at the settlement, I realized, was as close as Albrecht and Krischke would ever come to a scientific test of their witching. And the results, unbeknownst to them, were negative.

Following our interview I drove down to Schulenberg to meet Judge Krischke. In his living room, sitting in his wheelchair, the judge – actually the title "judge" is an honorific, derived from Krischke's years as a county justice of the peace – demonstrated the rods the same way Albrecht had, holding them away from him and showing how they crossed in the presence of a human burial. Then he held up one. "Instead of two wires, you can use one in either hand, left or right," he explained. "If it goes to the right, it's a female because the woman is always right. If it turns to the left, it's always the male." This business about the woman always being right was, I perceived, not so much a little joke as a mnemonic device. Krischke, a man of middle height and build, with thinning white hair and a red face, spoke with a relaxed, authoritative voice, wasting few words, straight to the point, as if communicating information in a forthright, military style. In fact, he had spent twenty-six years in the Air Force. He wasn't much prone to irony, but there was a vein of it there, somewhere.

Krischke discovered the power of the coat hangers in 1996, when he was surveying a graveyard near Ledbetter, Texas. "I was copying all the names on the tombstones, the names and dates for historical records, and I noticed that there were more tombstones at the front of the cemetery than there were at the back, and I wondered if there were some way of discovering whether there were graves there, too," he recalled. "So I went home and made these rods. I tried them on some known graves and it worked. I was surprised, very surprised. But anyway I've found all kinds of graves since then." His use of the coat hangers, which he calls "a tool for me to find history," does not proceed from some love of the occult or the paranormal. He does not believe in ghosts. A good Episcopalian, he does not even believe in the devil. He simply has a passion for local history and genealogy, which finds its keenest expression in a love of cemeteries. That's all his witching comes to – a way of making sure we know, literally, where all the bodies are buried. A way of charting old cemeteries so that all the unmarked graves are accounted for. Albrecht and Krischke's fascination with old cemeteries was not that different from my following the footsteps of La Salle, although no one knows where his bones lie either. I was trying to find sites where the dead and the living connect. They were doing this in a more immediate, concrete fashion.

Krischke's wife, Jan, who looked a decade or so younger than her husband, joined us. She shook her head over the judge's coat hangers. "Every time he goes out there with them, I'm afraid he's going to get in trouble." She wasn't scolding him, she was cautioning him. Go ahead with this stuff but the first sign of "trouble" and you're done hunting up graves. Jan wasn't as censorious as one of Dorothy Albrecht's daughters, who viewed witching as "the devil's work," and wanted her mother to stop it, but she clearly distrusted her husband's witching. In her defense, witching for bones, while not in the same category as using crystal balls, has a mystical, uncanny side. "It's my opinion these are not dowsing rods," Krischke said to me. "These I call – hell, what do I call it?" He laughed. "Divining rods. I think the power that makes these rods move is from a divine source manifesting itself through the blood." Through the blood? "Even though it's dried, you can still find out where a person died because of the blood he left behind, in many instances. For example, three women were killed at a railway crossing, and I applied the rods there and things went crazy." This might account for the activity of the rods at the Garcitas Creek site. The bones were gone, but the blood was still there.

If the idea has no scientific warrant, it certainly has biblical warrant, beginning with the Book of Genesis, in which the Lord asks Cain, "What have you done? Listen: Your brother's blood cries out to me from the soil!" In his version of the Apocalypse, the prophet Isaiah foretells: "The earth will reveal the blood upon her, and no longer conceal her slain." You can scatter a body to the four winds, you can burn it, you can eat it – but you can never entirely remove the traces of blood from the earth, and that blood will cry out. No matter how long it has soaked into the earth, blood is persistent – it will cry out. Australian novelist Peter Carey has a different metaphor to suggest the same phenomenon. "History is like a bloodstain that keeps on showing on the wall no matter how many new owners take possession, no matter how many times we paint over it."

TWO

La Salle on the Prairies

*A dubious real estate opportunity • An unclean animal roams
Matagorda Bay • The man in the cocksucker hat • La Salle in a bad
mood • On cruelty • The pathetic end of the Sieur de la Salle*

In the middle of nowhere they were placed on a pedestal, somebody's feet. Somebody's feet and calves and shins, standing in a pair
of boots. If you drove on a dirt road about a mile inland from a
place called Indianola, on the shores of Matagorda Bay, you would
come across the sight: a lonely stretch of grassland, a sky with the
tremendous billowing clouds of the Gulf, an old cemetery nearby,
and this pair of lower legs. There was not a single clue as to whom
they belonged, except the boots, which might have been worn by a
Confederate general.

I walked off the road into the thick wet grass to take a closer
look. "Look out you don't step on a snake," my companion advised.
I decided I was close enough and returned to the road. Henry
Wolff, Jr., who drove me here and who wrote a column of local
history entitled "Henry's Journal" for the *Victoria Advocate*, told me
the story of the statue. Like many of the stories of this area it spoke
of impossible plans and faded dreams and bad faith. The statue was
made by a woman named Nora Sweetland in 1928. Sweetland had

her own interesting history. She was a red-hot suffragist who threw a rock through a store window that displayed a sign that read "Decent Women Do Not Want To Vote" when she was fifteen years old. She was also known as the Madonna Sculptress for her many statues of the Blessed Virgin Mary. Whether she managed to combine strong feminism with equally strong devotion to the mother of Our Lord, or whether she simply happened to get a lot of church commissions, I do not know. In any case, her statue of the Sieur de la Salle was unveiled on Labor Day, 1928, as an ornament for what people were calling La Salle Memorial Park. It was part of a scheme to promote this spot into a land development known as Bayside Beach. Several people actually paid for lots.

The Great Depression put an end to the enterprise, but it would have failed anyway, for a simple reason. Every few decades a hurricane comes by and flattens the place. In the middle of the nineteenth century, for example, Indianola was actually a thriving port on Matagorda Bay, at that time considered the finest harbor on the Gulf of Mexico. It was a rival to Galveston. Then in 1875 a hurricane killed nine hundred citizens of Indianola. Undaunted, the survivors rebuilt. In 1886 an even worse hurricane removed every trace of the town. The lesson was learned, although by 1928 enough people had forgotten it to give rise to Bayside Beach and a cheap concrete statue of La Salle. A hurricane in the 1930s toppled it. Vandals removed the various parts lying around, leaving only the pedestal and boots. Sweetland particularly lamented the loss of La Salle's head, which she thought was the best part of the statue. Perhaps the head is still perched on a shelf somewhere, in some basement or garage or den, puzzling anyone who sees it with its look of (I'm sure) undaunted courage. Perhaps no one remembers who the head on the shelf represents or where it came from. I hope it has not brought misfortune to its possessor.

Near this area, La Salle and his men set up a staging area, a third of the way between the initial landing on Matagorda Island and the eventual settlement of Garcitas Creek. It was not a lucky spot. No spot on this coastline is. When Joutel and his men landed on Matagorda Island, for example, they found a windswept terrain, flat except for the dunes, with salt pools instead of fresh water and an enticing little reddish-yellow fruit that Joutel tried to prevent his men from eating. Of course they didn't listen and became so sick they vomited blood. (Foster suggests it was the yaupon, a toxic plant used as an ingredient in a tea brewed by local Indians and drunk as a purgative in their purification rituals.) Joutel generally had a good deal of trouble keeping his men, who were not used to self-restraint, from devouring their rations – a sign of much trouble to come. As for the five different species of poisonous snakes on the island, Joutel apparently knew nothing about them yet.

I paid a visit to Matagorda Island one day shortly after my pilgrimage to La Salle's boots. It was a dismal day. Clouds blowing in from the Gulf loured over the waters as the ferry began its passage to Matagorda Bay by navigating a narrow channel beside a sandbar. Cattle grazed on the bar. "Some of those cows only got half a tail," the ferry pilot told me. "Coyotes bit 'em off." I thought he was funning me, but apparently he wasn't. Coyotes swim this channel and, in their characteristic never-say-die spirit, also swim the seven miles to Matagorda Island. About a thousand deer, who have also swum to the island, await them. No wonder the coyote features prominently in American Indian mythology. As a species, we are far more closely related in every way to these shrewd and resourceful, tough and unstoppable animals than we are to apes and monkeys, no matter what the anthropologists say.

We got off the ferry at Matagorda Island State Park, which occupies the northeast end of the island, to face a driving rain – a taste of the misery that Joutel's men endured when the winter weather turned wet. Displaying my own never-say-die spirit, I walked a few miles to the tip of the island and Pass Cavallo, the entrance to Matagorda Bay, where Joutel and his men finished their march across the island. In this weather you could see why, when the ships arrived, it took so long for them to unload supplies. Joutel often noted how the crashing waves made it impossible to manage any vessel, large or small, when the wind blew in from the sea. As for the island itself, its landscape was no more enchanting then, I suspect, than it is today. Then and now it is a fragile interlude between sea and sky, a level ground covered by coarse grasses and a few trees. The French left only one lasting legacy of their brief presence here – the hogs they brought with them from France. (The Karankawa thought these strange animals were the Frenchmen's dogs.) Wild hogs now roam the island, at least some of whom – other strains have since been introduced – carry the DNA of their ancestors from France, forming one of our few direct links with La Salle. Once a year the park holds a hunt to thin their number, open to the public, and from time to time a parks employee does a little thinning on his own. On the ferry ride home I noticed some teenaged boys looking inside a Styrofoam cooler. I peeked inside, too, and saw a splotch of red, and a pair of black, cloven hoofs under a layer of chipped ice.

Here on the island, Joutel and La Salle made their first contact with the Indians. Joutel noted their "guttural" language – they made "a sound with the tongue like a hen" – and their peaceful gesture of embracing the French and blowing in their ears. These gestures came to an end with the fight over the canoes. Afterwards, the French tried to fortify their camp with some loose boards that floated ashore from the wreck of the *Aimable*. At night the Indians prowled around, howling like wolves, until somebody fired a musket in their direction. In the meantime, La Salle decided they had to leave their camp on Matagorda Island. It was vulnerable to Indian attack and also far too exposed to the view of any passing Spanish ship. Near the end of March 1685, after the *Aimable* had sunk and the *Joly* returned to France, he and some of his men explored the western shore of Matagorda Bay. After a week, La Salle decided on the site of Garcitas Creek – well watered, with good soil, an abundance of game, and the defensive advantage of the bluffs – as the site for his settlement. The nearest anchorage for La Salle's remaining ship, the *Belle*, however, was the port later known as Indianola.

In 1939 they put up a monument to La Salle on the beach of Indianola. This granite statue was so massive – La Salle stood about eight feet high – no hurricane could possibly damage it. In fact, it has already survived a few. La Salle was sculpted with flowing locks, thigh-length boots, and a two-handed sword fit for Conan the Barbarian. Oddly enough, he didn't stare at the horizon with chin uplifted, as if glimpsing a vision of the future, but turned his head sideways and looked down, as if a little saddened by his failures. On one side of the base of the statue, however, a quotation from Francis Parkman's history was incised: "America owes him an enduring memory for in this masculine figure she sees the pioneer who guided her to the possession of her richest heritage." This was one way of looking at La Salle, as a nineteenth-century man of action and proto-American.

Now La Salle looked over what Henry Wolff called "the ugliest damn beach in Texas." To halt erosion, local authorities had dumped rip-rap – hunks of concrete and other rubble from demolition sites – on the shoreline. It certainly did not improve the scenery. "On beaches like this, you get two kinds of people," Wolff told me. "You get the people who want to build a nice, smart, vacation home for fishing, and you get drifters who come down here and throw up some kind of a shack." That was evident. In addition to some houses that looked like they cost a lot of money were mobile homes that were falling apart.

I wondered if some of these residents of Indianola woke up in the night from a dream of a wall of water, in the midst of screaming winds, breaking over their rooftops. It was possible. In the meantime, life went on. I stopped by a beachfront bar called Taylor's for a beer one afternoon, though I hesitated for a moment before entering. You could hear loud rock music and raucous laughter emanating quite a distance from this bar, which was not an inviting sound. On the other hand, there were no signs of life anywhere else on the beach, except for a few fishermen out in the water. Saturday night, I was told, teenagers came to the beach to drink, and things livened up then, but this was Thursday afternoon. In I went. The place was dark and empty except for three men sitting in a corner, who were producing all the laughter. The ceiling was made of particle board and the flooring was wood that had turned gray with age – nobody was going to lose a big investment of capital when this building was blown all the way to San Antonio.

The three patrons nodded when I sat down. *This is a family place!! Please control your language!!* read a printed sign. Other hand-lettered signs above the bar were jocular. *Throw a punch and win a trip to the Calhoun County Jail. Tommorrow Free Beer.* The bartender, a pleasant middle-aged woman in a T-shirt and cut-offs, fished a can of Budweiser out of a cooler full of ice for me. "One dollar," she said. I must have looked startled – in Toronto, you can lose the better part of a Canadian ten-dollar bill buying a beer. "Happy hour," she explained. "How you doing?" said the man next to me. He wore a dark, thin mustache and a black straw panama hat, a little the worse for wear.

"Good. How are you?"

"I'm okay. I'm getting divorced."

A younger man sitting on a stool the other side of me, wearing a baseball cap and a work shirt, guffawed. "You better hold it right there. He don't want to hear the rest of it." The man with the hat muttered something I couldn't hear. The third man kept quiet. He didn't say much generally, but he was nice enough to buy me another can of Bud after I'd finished the first. "You say you're a welder," the man about to be divorced said in an accusing tone to the man with the baseball cap. That tone said, If you don't want to hear about my divorce, then we'll talk about you. "You told us you're a pipe fitter."

"I said I was a carpenter too."

"Well, get your story straight."

"I don't have to tell the truth to nobody wearing a cocksucker hat."

The man in the panama hat grinned. The exchange was actually pretty genial. "Cocksucker hat?"

"They say you do it once, you're still okay. Once is okay," the younger man said, with an air of imparting a rule of thumb no reasonable person would dispute.

"Is that right."

"What's a cocksucker hat?" I asked.

"It's just something different is all. Anything unusual like that. When I was a kid I had a straw hat with this brim that was built up around here." He cupped his hands on both sides of his head. "This man saw me wearing it and he said, 'Look at that guy in the cocksucker hat.' You know that hat of yours has holes in it," he said to the man on my other side. "Your head'll get tanned in spots. Look like you have the measles."

"Not if I ain't bald. You be careful what you say."

"I am careful. One time I was talking about cocksuckers, I was talking too loud, and this fellow heard me, he hit me right in the eye. I said, 'Why'd you hit me in the eye? It was my mouth that caused it.'" The man in the hat yelped, stood up, and pounded the bar with the flat of his hand, as if he had never heard anything funnier in his life. *It was my mouth that caused it.* This was turning out to be a pleasant conversation, until the man in the hat suddenly asked me what I did. Stupidly, I had not thought of an answer to this question before I walked into the bar. The ideal answer, of course, would have been something that totally deflected curiosity, like saying I checked inventory in a warehouse. Instead I answered truthfully, that I was a newspaperman. I might as well have said I was a cop or a social worker. The man in the hat narrowed his eyes and then pondered the can of Budweiser he held in his two hands. "I'm a rotten son of a bitch," he finally said. "But these are my friends. You with me on that? People think we're stupid." I wanted to reassure him that I wasn't going to write an exposé about the stupid drunks who hang out on Indianola beach. I didn't think they were stupid, although they did really guffaw and say "git" for "get." The man in the baseball cap at least was a good-natured drinker, and that to me is high recommendation. I myself come from a family where our disposition is actually improved by a few drinks. The man with the cocksucker hat, however, was not so easygoing. In fact, it was clear he was nursing a grievance of some kind, no doubt connected to his divorce. But he was at the stage of drunkenness where he could not stick to a train of thought very long. "When I was a kid my daddy bought me some land here," he said after another pause. "Said honess . . . honessly . . . you'll always have a place to live." He looked up from his can of Budweiser to see if I comprehended the importance of what he was saying. "My mamma said you don't understand it now but you will." Land in Indianola – it sounded like a bad joke, like Bayside Beach revisited. He fell into another brooding silence and then launched into a story about his wife, which became very confused in the telling.

⚜

In July 1685, Henri Joutel, who had been in charge of the temporary camp on Matagorda Island, arrived at Garcitas Creek, where the building of the settlement was in progress. "Everything was in a sad state [*une triste situation*]," Joutel noted. Very little had been accomplished. The major problem was housing, compounded by a lack of trees; the nearest stand of timber was nearly three miles away. In the absence of draft animals, La Salle sent his men to cut and drag the timber to the settlement, a back-breaking task in the hot July sun. "Even the strongest were overcome," wrote Joutel. "The work was excessive, and the rations for the workers were limited and too often cut back for having failed in their task. La Salle's disappointment at not succeeding as he had imagined led him to mistreat his people at the wrong time. All this brought a cheerlessness upon many workers who declined visibly." Joutel tried to tell La Salle it might be easier to bring the wood they had salvaged from the shipwreck, which was still on Matagorda Island and could be transported by water. La Salle told him to keep his opinions to himself. According to Joutel, thirty men died trying to haul logs over the prairie.

In fact, by the end of July, half of the two hundred-odd souls who remained with La Salle in Texas after the departure of the *Joly* were dead. A few had been killed by the Karankawa and in other mishaps, the rest had fallen victim to the sun, bad food, and bad water. (The fruit of a local prickly pear was edible but had to be wiped clean of numerous small quills on its surface. A famished soldier devoured one without bothering to do so, Joutel wrote, and subsequently died a slow, agonizing death. The quills inflamed his throat and suffocated him. A few other members of the expedition perished in the same way.)

Under the circumstances, it was not surprising that they made little progress toward building proper shelter and a fort. La Salle managed to construct a house with four rooms, to accommodate himself and some of the other gentlemen and priests; the crew had to fend for themselves in the open air. Morale, never high to begin with, sank lower. "Our people were not too vigorous [*pas trop alertes*]," Joutel wrote. It was highly desirable to build a stockade, but the project languished and the only stronghold of the settlement remained La Salle's house. Of course, the lack of ready timber accounted in large part for this failure, but Joutel made it clear in his journal that the former soldiers and the dregs of La Rochelle were not up to much at the best of times.

Joutel tried hard to maintain discipline and was tested from the beginning. While still encamped on Matagorda Island, he punished sentries who fell asleep by sitting them astride the wooden horse, a V-shaped structure that insured memorable discomfort for the rider. Some of his men plotted to kill him — a co-conspirator revealed the secret and the plotters were arrested. (Joutel does not mention their fate.) La Salle himself, as we have seen, was not unwilling to treat his men harshly. As he brooded over his failure to fulfill either of the objectives he had promised his sovereign – to harry the Spanish or to found a settlement near the mouth of the great river – his mood grew foul. Joutel tried to lift the spirits of his crew by encouraging dancing and singing in the evenings, *"pour chasser le chagrin."* La Salle, when present, put a stop to it. "La Salle did not have much reason to rejoice after so many losses and the realization that everything was not going according to his plan," Joutel observed drily in his journal. "Consequently, everyone else suffered too."

The worse things went, the more La Salle, under a spell of masochistic self-pity or depression, gave up trying to remedy the situation. In early 1686, while La Salle's attention was elsewhere, the *Belle* with all of its stores, his last link with France and the possibility of obtaining new supplies and reinforcements for the settlement, ran across a sandbank in Matagorda Bay and foundered. Robert Weddle, in his book, states exactly where the blame for the loss of the *Belle* rests: "La Salle left her loaded with the necessities of his colony, in the hands of an unskilled crew commanded by a known drunk, with a single anchor of proven inadequacy." This happened during the first of La Salle's lengthy absences from the settlement, when he was doing what made him happiest, reconnoitering a strange countryside. La Salle made two such journeys of overland exploration, each lasting for months, while Joutel was left in command of the settlement. Presumably he was still looking for the Mississippi River.

Nevertheless, the situation at Garcitas Creek was not hopeless. If little work was done on the proposed fort, at least the settlers were in no danger of starving. They had powder and shot, and the countryside was rich with game, including numerous bison. Their chickens and pigs thrived. Joutel and one of the priests tried to start a garden, but rabbits and rats ate their pumpkins and melons. They did discover turtle eggs, which, Joutel noted, "serve to thicken sauces." These were Frenchmen, we may recall, and they knew how much a good meal can fortify courage. There were even moments when they noticed that this strange country could be quite lovely, with its fields of wildflowers and the "beautiful, good grasses" of the prairie. Spiritually, they were sustained by daily mass, Joutel wrote, "as well as vespers on feast days and Sundays and common prayers every day, evening and morning." When their supply of wine grew low, unfortunately, they had to limit celebration of the mass to Sundays and feast days. On Joutel's last Christmas at the settlement, in 1686, they celebrated a particularly affecting midnight mass. Parkman wrote that as the priest "elevated the consecrated wafer, and the lamps burned dim through the clouds of incense, the kneeling group drew from the daily miracle such consolation as true Catholics alone can know." You can hear the slight undertone of condescension here, Parkman's lift of the eyebrows as he pens the sentence and thinks to himself that he personally will never experience such consolation but somehow he'll carry on.

These celebrations of the mass and daily prayers in the wilderness may also explain what we now find difficult to understand, that a little society consisting of five or six unattached women and a score or so of unattached men could exist without sexual disorder. When the company sailed for the Gulf of Mexico, everyone assumed these women would remain chaste and the men respectful – and the assumption held. Or largely held. At one point an officer named Barbier, having seduced and impregnated one of the young women, asked Joutel for permission to marry. Joutel reminded him that his status of officer placed him above the girl in question. The priests then reminded Joutel that it might be better to dispense with these social niceties in the interests of maintaining decorum. Decorum, under the circumstances, was all-important. The marriage took place. Later, a young nobleman, the Marquis de Sablonnière, asked Joutel for permission to marry a girl in the company who went by the name of Mademoiselle Paris. Miss Paris, whom Joutel called "quite young and not bad looking [*pas mal faite*]," was of unknown origins. Sablonnière was a classic case of an aristocratic roué falling for what the Victorians would have termed an adventuress. Joutel told Sablonnière to forget it and not to speak to the woman again. That these were the only cases in which Joutel seemed to have failed in his role as chaperone is a remarkable comment on the difference between twenty-first-century America and seventeenth-century France.

In October 1686, La Salle returned from his second ramble in the wilderness and almost immediately began preparations for another trip. This time he would march overland until he found the Mississippi, and then travel up the river to the fort he had established, a few years previously, in Illinois. He left in early January 1687, taking Joutel with him, along with his brother, Jean Cavelier, two nephews, another priest, his faithful Shawnee hunter, Nika, and a few others – a total of seventeen, including La Salle. That left twenty-three people at the settlement, including Madame Talon, now a widow with four children, the Marquis de Sablonnière, and Mademoiselle Paris, the object of his devotion. Since there was a priest left behind as well, it is probable that the pair were finally married in the absence of La Salle and Joutel. What would be the point of forbidding such a socially scandalous marriage now? Perhaps the marquis lasted only a few months before dying of despair or disease. Perhaps he lived long enough to enjoy some happiness with his wife. He enters the pages of history only to be characterized as profligate and dissipated – Parkman, in a footnote, tells us that "he had to be kept on short allowance, because he was in the habit of bargaining away everything given to him. He had squandered the little that belonged to him at St. Domingo, in amusements 'indignes de sa naissance,' and in consequence was suffering from diseases which had disabled him from walking." It would be pleasant to think that in the settlement near Garcitas Creek, where this apparently worthless individual finally had nothing more to lose and was joined to a woman who had never had anything to lose in the first place, he found a measure of peace. Perhaps he was even able to face with courage that early morning when he and the others were awakened by screams of terror and rage, a morning that had been long in coming. The four or five soldiers, the three young women whom Joutel had trained to do sentry duty and handle firearms, and the handful of other inhabitants could hardly hope to keep the Karankawa at bay forever, and there came a day when these Karankawa did fall upon the tiny settlement.

In his journal, however, Joutel tried to suggest these people – the remnant of two hundred original settlers – were not really in dire straits when the seventeen departed. They were not really being abandoned by La Salle. "Those who stayed at the settlement should not have to fear death by hunger because there were plenty of pigs, not less than seventy-five," Joutel wrote. "Besides that, the Indian corn that was left them was growing well, and there were still eighteen to twenty hens. Thus they only had to beware and keep a good lookout [*se bien garder et à faire bon quart*]."

How much of that last sentence Joutel actually believed is hard to say.

✤

I headed east on the highway to Houston, and then turned off to Route 111 at the town of Edna, driving northwards in an attempt to parallel the journey of the seventeen men who left Garcitas Creek on January 12. Joutel found this trip hard slogging for much of the way. For footwear, the men were clad in bison hide coverings, which when dry became hard as little iron caskets and chafed their feet, particularly when they had to walk through tall prairie grasses and "sword-like plants." (Foster suggests the latter were small soapweed yucca.) Other times they had to cut their way with hatchets through thick stretches of wood. At night, they fortified their campsites with barricades of brush, although the small bands of Indians they met were fairly peaceful. We should allow Parkman this moment to paint one of his sublime wilderness landscapes: "Here, by the grassy border of a brook, or at the edge of a grove where a spring bubbled up through the sands, they lay asleep around the embers of their fire, while the man on guard listened to the deep breathing of the slumbering horses, and the howling of the wolves that saluted the rising moon as it flooded the waste of prairie with pale mystic radiance."

La Salle generally followed the bison trails, which skirted the worst of the natural obstacles. Unfortunately, he had loaded his horses – obtained through trade with the Indians during his wanderings – with various of his goods, including clothes and linens and buffalo hides. Often the men had to widen the bison trails with their hatchets for these horses and, when fording rivers, carry the horses' loads on their own backs for the safety of the animals. Resentment against La Salle grew. Nevertheless, their progress was steady. The first river they crossed was the Lavaca, east of Garcitas Creek, which La Salle sarcastically named the Princess River, after Barbier's term of endearment for the sweetheart he had wooed on its banks, during bison hunts. That got a few laughs from the boys. Then they proceeded northwards, following the west bank of the Navidad River, and coming upon a village of Indians, not far from the present-day site of Hallettsville, on January 17. No trouble occurred.

La Salle and his men continued their weary way, fording innumerable streams and creeks, trying to stay dry and warm in the face of wind and rain, failing to light fires because the wood was green and wet. "The country was, however, quite beautiful," Joutel wrote. He never failed to note the presence of fine landscapes in the midst of their misery. For sustenance they hunted bison, turkey, deer, ducks, and other game birds, including "doves." Joutel frequently mentions, in this regard, the activity of La Salle's Shawnee friend, Nika. Joutel doesn't come out and say it, but the reader gets the strong impression that without Nika's hunting skills, the party would have been in serious trouble. One animal they killed Joutel describes as having "the appearance and color of a rat, except it has a longer snout. Beneath one side of its abdomen is a sort of sack in which it carries its young. . . . They are quite good when fat and taste like a suckling pig." The strange animal was, of course, the opossum.

Throughout their march, they continued to run across Indians. In each case, La Salle was at great pains to impress upon them that he and his men had peaceful intentions. "In truth," Joutel explains, "we were so small in numbers we had no hope of forcing our way through their country." Instead, La Salle and his men left little gifts with each group they encountered, mostly glass beads. (In return, the French received at one point some "finely dressed deer skin that was white as snow," which they made into moccasins to replace those bison hide shoes that had bloodied their feet.) La Salle did not linger at any of these villages, in part because he didn't want his men – some of whom had lost their last reserves of good judgment and self-command a long time ago, while others had none to begin with – from getting ideas about Indian women. So they kept moving. At night, in their little camp, they maintained a careful watch.

⚜

On the banks of the Colorado River, where an old bison trail that later became known as La Bahia Road crossed the river on the site of the present town of La Grange, La Salle's party was forced to wait a week for the waters to subside. Here I paused for a while too.

When I drove through the courthouse square of La Grange – seat of Fayette County – I saw an astounding sight.

A wine bar was open. By that time I had seen quite a few courthouse squares in this part of Texas and they were very similar. A magnificent old cathedral of the plains would stand proudly, surrounded by a few marginal businesses, and nobody in sight. "You know the courthouse square?" a gray-haired bartender in Hallettsville had said to me a few nights earlier. "Back in the fifties you couldn't pass by on the sidewalk it was so crowded. You had to walk in the streets, practically. There were twenty-two beer joints there. Now the only place open is the movie theater." Hallettsville, like many another town in the area, had been withering for years, sustained in recent times only by the wan hope of becoming a tourist destination. (Even that hope was gone if a town had been foolish enough to tear down its old courthouse and replace it with a modern building.) The young in these towns continued to move away and what was left of commerce gravitated to the Wal-Mart down the highway.

But here was a wine bar lighting up this particular decayed courthouse square. In a restored building first constructed in 1914, the proprietors of the Main Street Bistro had laid down a black and white checkered linoleum floor, and put in tables with black and white checkered tablecloths, and hired waiters and waitresses dressed in white shirts and black pants. They had an extensive wine list and items on the menu like gorgonzola green onion mashed potatoes. It seemed like a mirage, after days spent driving through south Texas and eating at Dairy Queens because they were less greasy than the place in town that served chicken quesadillas and fried catfish. It was like being lost in the subarctic and stumbling across a spa with a masseuse and a sauna and a good supply of cognac.

The bartender didn't blame me for being surprised at the existence of the Main Street Bistro. "It's hard enough to get a cold beer in this town," he said. He was a handsome, strapping, fair-haired youngish man who wouldn't have looked out of place in Malibu. Actually, he had spent several years in the Caribbean, guiding fishing and scuba-diving groups. Why he had abandoned that occupation to tend bar in La Grange, I had no idea. "I thought I'd join the real world," he explained with rueful irony. "Do the things grown-ups did." He missed the life, the grown-up world not being all that it was cracked up to be. Now he had a fifteen-year-old son in high school, but when the boy was a little older, he might just head back to the Caribbean.

The next day, I drove north and east to the town of Navasota, roughly following the progress of La Salle and his men after they managed to cross the Colorado River with a boat they made out of wooden poles and scraps of buffalo hide. (The hides were sewn together and the seams caulked with tallow.) La Salle's party made its way through a great forest – part of which is now known as the Post Oak Belt – with the help of a bison trail. They emerged from this into *une fort jolie prairie*, where they discovered numerous Indian tracks and saw plumes of smoke not far away. That night in camp they slept to the howling of dogs from the Indian village. The next morning, La Salle, his brother, and seven others went off to meet the inhabitants, while Joutel was left in charge of the others. It is to La Salle's brother, therefore, we owe the information that the inhabitants of this village, when the Europeans arrived, had captured a twelve-foot alligator. "The Indians, who wished to amuse themselves with it, put out its eyes and led it into a prairie," Jean Cavelier wrote. "After tormenting it in various ways for four full hours, they turned it belly up and confined it from head to tail by eight stakes, planted so that the animal could not move in any direction. In this condition they flayed him, and then gave him liberty to run, to have the pleasure of tormenting him more. This sport lasted all day, and ended with the death of this frightful beast, which they killed and gave to their dogs."

A human captive, of course, would have been much better sport, but the torture of this other creature, a creature they feared and resented, also provided enjoyment. That's the way it was in the woods and prairies of North America.

Apologists for the Indians can point out, of course, that Europeans were no strangers to cruelty. Judicial torture, in particular, was common in that era. Europeans did not regard themselves as bad people because they used the rack to break the bones and tear the sinews of suspected criminals. What they did was logical. When a man's body is in extreme physical pain, his mind lacks the flexibility to lie. The torture of captives by Indian nations also possessed a certain logic, as we shall see. But both Europeans and Indians, logic aside, took pleasure in the spectacle of grisly public deaths. "Pity is not natural to man," Samuel Johnson proclaimed. "Children are always cruel. Savages are always cruel." Johnson thought that civilized human beings lost their taste for cruelty only gradually, through the "cultivation of reason." But a century later Nietzsche reminded his fellow Europeans, "It is not long since princely weddings and public festivals of the more magnificent kind were unthinkable without executions, torturings, or perhaps an auto-da-fe, and no noble household was without creatures upon whom one could heedlessly vent one's malice and cruel jokes." For Nietzsche, the infliction of pain was the precondition for that cultivation of reason Johnson so prized. Human beings had to be tortured into forming a "conscience," a sense of moral obligation – something that their deeper instincts rebelled against. A philosopher could almost derive grim satisfaction from the spectacle – pity was an emotion indulged in by Christians and other sick animals. "To see others suffer does one good, to make others suffer even more," Nietzsche wrote, in a spirit of frank confession on behalf of the human race. "Without cruelty there is no festival."

Few people today can bear to voice such sentiments. We're all tender-hearted now. The fact that Christianity during the centuries it was dominant in the West failed in some measure to bridle the violence and brutality of Europeans is considered a heavy mark against it, but Christianity at least made it possible for people to question the routine cruelties of human existence. "We do not realize how anthropologically unique our modern attitude towards victims is," the French anthropologist René Girard wrote. "In no other culture has anything even remotely similar ever existed." Girard, who believed this modern attitude "can be traced only to Christianity," saw normal human society in much the same light as Nietzsche, as an arena of individual self-aggrandizement so intense that some drastic means of control was necessary. In Girard's view, that means had traditionally been the collective scapegoating and murder of some victim, a cathartic form of release adopted by a group when tensions and frustrations rose too high. "It is better that one man should die than that the whole nation should perish" was a classic formulation of this dynamic, articulated by the high priest Caiaphas in the Gospel According to St. John. Only Christianity, according to Girard, stood in opposition to this "founding mechanism of human society." Its god was a scapegoat who was innocent and whose torture and death were not some mythic memory but a historical event that forever condemned such violence.

Naturally the priests of Christianity who came to the New World and who did try to live by the Gospels found it hard to sell this message, especially given the behavior of their fellow Frenchmen. La Salle's band of men in their final jaunt across Texas may have been a case in point. La Salle told the Indians in this particular village that he was sent by the *plus grand capitaine du monde* and that he would fight alongside them against their enemies. It was not clear if his hosts understood exactly what he was saying. They seemed to get the gist of it, however. It was the kind of message they were attuned to hearing. This made them reluctant to see La Salle go; they had seen these men hunt with firearms and they had an idea of their military value.

La Salle was bent on reaching the Mississippi, though, and for the next few days pressed forward on his northeast course, through hilly terrain and then through a vast marsh, where his men got soaked to the skin and at one point had to backtrack. On March 14 they crossed the Brazos River near the present town of Navasota. The next day La Salle halted and sent some of the men to locate a cache of corn and beans he had buried on his expedition to this region the year before. The men found the cache, but the food, not surprisingly, was rotten. On their return to La Salle, the Shawnee hunter, Nika – the most useful member of this expedition from the day La Salle landed in Texas – killed two bison. Another member of the party was dispatched to ask La Salle for more horses to transport the meat. On the morning of the seventeenth, La Salle sent one of his nephews, named Moranget, and three others on this errand. It was a fatal choice. Moranget was an insufferably arrogant young man, and when he found the party he berated them for reserving for themselves the choicest parts of the meat and then confiscated the lot. This was the final straw for at least two of the men, a merchant named Duhaut, who had lost a younger brother and a good deal of his capital in the form of trade goods in the expedition, and a surgeon named Liotot, who had helped to save Moranget's life soon after their landing and had since been repaid with complaints and insults. With two or three other men, including a cutthroat named Hiems picked up in Haiti, they resolved upon killing Moranget, Nika, and another loyal servant of La Salle's named Saget. In the dark of night, while the three were sleeping, the surgeon took an ax to them.

La Salle spent the following day worrying about the whereabouts of his men. That evening, according to Joutel, he had a premonition of his impending death. "He asked me if I had heard of the men contriving something among themselves or if I had noticed that they had some evil plot," Joutel wrote. "I said that I had not heard anything except in certain encounters when they complained, argumentative as they often were, but that I knew nothing else." The next morning La Salle, in company with the priest Anastase Douay, went to fetch the men. Afterwards, Douay recalled that "on the way, La Salle talked with me about matters of piety, grace and predestination, mentioning all his obligations to God for having saved him from so many dangers during his years in America. He seemed to me to be much struck with a sense of God's benefits. Suddenly I saw him plunge into a profound melancholy. He was so troubled I barely knew him."

Some of this testimony may be true. His boyhood years with the Jesuits may have passed through La Salle's mind on the last day of his life, just before he walked into the ambush set by Duhaut and the other murderers hidden in the grass. They killed him with a shot to the head, stripped his body, insulted the corpse, and left it for the animals to eat.

⚜

At Navasota I had dinner at a newly opened eatery on the main street. The owners, Joe Bihms and his wife, Terrie, had distributed flyers advertising the restaurant. JOE'S PLACE *If you like Great Food, Friendly Service, and a Clean Atomosphere!! Come Eat at Joe's Place.* At Joe's Place you could choose from the following culinary styles: bar-b-q, soul food, hamburgers, Jamaican, Cajun, and boudin. I was delighted. Restaurant dinners, I must admit, had become an obsession with me since arriving in this part of the United States. To get a good cheap meal in a small south Texas town seemed as hard as La Salle and his men finding a dry, comfortable place to camp. But the flyer turned out to be truthful.

I was wondering if the place could survive, given the pitfalls of the food and beverage industry. That evening there was only a handful of people sitting at the sixteen or so tables, in the clean, well-lit room with a mural of a jazz band painted on one wall. The painting was a bit ragged, but the colors and the lines worked. They suggested frenetic energy. Joe Bihms, who was forty-two, had sketched it in pencil one night and then finished it with cans of spray paint and buckets of Sherwin-Williams enamel. "Anything I could find on sale at the Home Depot," he told me. Here was a man of parts. "I'm into designing, painting, electrical work, plumbing. Anything made I can fix it." He scurried off to do something. His wife, who was more willing to sit and relax, was easier to talk to. "It's in my heart," she said of the restaurant. "Everything else is just something to do. We've always been a hard-working family. Hard work doesn't bother me – and this restaurant business is the hardest work you can do." She looked at her husband standing behind the steam tables with the greens and the ham hocks and the ribs. "That's all he does as a matter of fact. Work."

Later Joe sat down at my table for a few minutes. When I asked where he was from, he informed me that he hailed from Louisiana and then gave me a bit of family and racial history. "My grandmother was black, but she was so white her hair was *red*," he said. "Lord have mercy. My grandad was the color of your pants, my grandma was the color of your shirt." I was wearing black jeans and a white shirt. "I've got Mexican, Jewish, French in me, you name it. People don't know what I am. They don't know if I'm black, white, polka-dot, or red. Basically, I'm a Negro." I hadn't heard anyone say "Negro" without irony for decades. Terrie, who might once have been described, like her husband, as a "light-skinned Negro," mentioned a white man who had come into the restaurant after attending the Navasota Blues Festival a few days earlier. "He was talking about the 'coloreds,'" she said. "The 'coloreds' are better blues players than the whites, he was saying. I've heard 'Negro,' I've heard 'Black,' I've heard 'African-American,' but I haven't heard 'colored' in a long time. He didn't mean any harm, though. He said he was raised in a black neighborhood in Houston, and he was brought up around the blues, and he said white guys just couldn't play blues."

The next morning I went to see a life-sized statue of La Salle on the main street of Navasota. An account of this statue can be found in a publication in the Navasota public library entitled *A History of the La Salle Monument at Navasota, Texas,* by Loyal V. Norman, Ed. D. I will let Dr. Norman describe it: "This bronze statue dedicated to the memory of La Salle represents the French Nobleman and Explorer holding, in friendly gesture, a partly unrolled map of the new world in one hand with the other hand outstretched to natives of the land he claimed in the name of the King of France. The outstretched hand was said to have been a customary gesture of friendliness recognized by the original natives of this county." The inscription below the 1930 statue called La Salle a "frontier states-man, empire builder, a nobleman in rank and character." Here was another La Salle Americans could be proud of – and Texans, in particular. "La Salle," Dr. Norman wrote, "has been classed with the Heroes of the Alamo, as a martyr to the advancement of Texas."

Of all the roles La Salle played, that surely was the least likely.

Even with this statue and this tribute, Navasota is not done with the great explorer. Off the main road, near a parking lot by a mustard-yellow Chinese restaurant called the Golden Palace, is a bust of La Salle donated to the people of Navasota by a body called the French Committee of the Bicentennial of the United States and another body called the Association France-Amérique. It was erected in 1976, and it shows a man with a large periwig, a pencil mustache, and a sneer. He looks like the judge in a pirate movie who sentences Errol Flynn to hang. He looks like a man who hadn't a clue about people skills and who made otherwise respectable and law-abiding individuals want to feed his body to the wolves.

THREE

The Great Peace

A frightful massacre • The printing press versus Gothic architecture •
Another frightful massacre • The four ways of being grieved
at another's wealth • The saint who refused to smell the flowers

In the spring of 1667, the twenty-three-year-old La Salle, fresh
from Rouen, arrived on the island of Montreal, then "the most
dangerous place in Canada," according to Francis Parkman. The
settlement stood at the confluence of the St. Lawrence River and the
Ottawa River – highway to the north, the heart of the fur trade – and
hard by Lake Champlain and the Hudson River Valley. As long as
the ownership of the continent remained in dispute this place
would be a magnet for armies.

A truce was in effect between the French and their great enemy
the Iroquois, but nobody knew when it might be broken. In the
meantime, the Sulpician Order, which then owned the entire island,
gave La Salle several thousand acres. La Salle's brother was in the
order, and he had a cousin who was a respected local merchant, but
family ties were not what the Sulpicians had in mind with this act of
generosity. La Salle's estate – called "Lachine," or "China," for reasons
I shall note later – was on the southern edge of the island, just above
the falls where visitors had to beach their canoes. If Montreal was the

most dangerous place in Canada, Lachine was the most dangerous place in Montreal, an outpost that would bear the first brunt of an Iroquois raid. The Sulpicians hoped that La Salle would bring in settlers, construct fortified houses, convert the neighborhood into a first line of defense for the island as a whole.

La Salle fulfilled his part of the bargain and brought in the hoped-for settlers. It wasn't until 1689, a few years after La Salle died, when the French and the Iroquois were back at war, that the Iroquois did overrun his old settlement. It was, Parkman assures us, "the most frightful massacre in Canadian history." Two hundred settlers, Parkman writes, "had the good fortune to be killed on the spot" during the dawn raid. Another 120 were taken prisoner. The Iroquois, who numbered about fifteen hundred and defied the military might of New France, such as it was, decided to teach the remaining Montrealers a lesson they would never forget. In their encampment across the river from Lachine, they hauled out some of their prisoners and, within sight of the French on the island of Montreal, put on a show. "On that miserable night," writes Parkman, "stupefied and speechless groups stood gazing from the strand of Lachine at the lights that gleamed along the distant shore of Chateauguay, where their friends, wives, parents or children agonized in the fires of the Iroquois, and scenes were enacted of indescribable and nameless horror." Helpless French women, it is said, were forced to turn the spit on which their children were roasted alive.

Modern historians, especially those sympathetic to the Iroquois, tend to describe the affair differently. "In late afternoon the warriors withdrew to the south shore of Lake St. Louis, where survivors in the garrisoned forts could see faint fires around which the Iroquois, celebrating their first victory in a war that would last for a decade, burned a few prisoners," writes William Fenton in his recent book, *The Great Law and the Longhouse*. That's it. Burned a few prisoners. No nameless horrors, no cruelties unprecedented in the history of mankind. French-Canadian historians, in Parkmanesque fashion, subsequently played up the event because it highlighted, in the most lurid manner, what they conceived to be the national drama of the Québécois, which is the drama of a people who are constantly under siege, constantly threatened with extinction. (The persistence of this drama in the collective imagination of Quebec helps to account for something that Americans and other Canadians find inexplicable, Quebec's modern-day "sovereigntist" movement.)

Historians of the Iroquois point out that the death toll was far lower than Parkman's two hundred, and certainly did not exceed what the Iroquois – a much more likely candidate for extinction – suffered on several occasions at the hands of the French. The currently accepted figure is twenty-four settlers killed in the first onslaught, and between seventy and ninety others carried off, some of whom eventually returned. As for the women forced to roast their own children over the spit – the story could have been like one of those World War I atrocity tales, in which the Huns were accused of spearing Belgian infants on their bayonets. Or there could have been some truth to it. The Iroquois did on occasion torture women and children. Among the many possible reasons for the Iroquois habit of ritual torture was a tactical one. The Iroquois, like other Indian nations, could not afford to lose large numbers of their warriors in pitched battles. To scare enemies with minimum loss of life, they may well have tried deliberately to terrorize their antagonists with displays like the one said to have taken place after the Lachine raid. Terror has no bottom.

Of course, it didn't work. The French, with their own Indian allies, mounted retaliatory raids, burning Schenectady to the ground in 1690. The gruesome war continued until 1701, when the French and Iroquois finally signed a peace treaty.

Three hundred years later, on the first weekend of August 2001, the city of Montreal and the province of Quebec held a historical re-enactment of that treaty, which organizers called "The Great Peace." In honor of the occasion, the streets were full of tourists. Mingling with the crowds, I was struck by the sight of two very different sorts of men who were walking around bare-chested. The ones with a bit of flab were natives playing the parts of Indian chiefs. The ones with lovingly sculptured torsos were in town for Gay Pride Week. This is an event, by the way, that Montreal does proud, with its "Lesbomonde" and "La nuit des drags" and groups like Les jardiniers ("Blessed with a ballsy rock and roll soul, a funky ass, a head for techno and the ability to laugh at themselves, Les jardiniers can freak the funk and rock the house").

Gay Pride Week comes every year, but it will be a while before the next centennial of the Great Peace rolls around. A historical event in which something reasonably positive happened between white people and Indians does seem to call for a celebration – which is why, on the Saturday of this weekend, there were, in addition to the half-naked gentlemen with fearsome face paint and feathers in their hair, men walking around with three-cornered hats and long wigs, black clerical robes, and the white and gray uniforms of Louis XIV's army. The idea was that at one o'clock, a flotilla of canoes filled with native re-enactors would come sweeping into the Montreal harbor, where they would be met by re-enactors portraying the French governor and other notables of the period. As the visitors got out of their canoes, they would be serenaded by regimental music and "Amerindian chants." The regimental music would be supplied by the Musique imperiale des cuivres et tambours de France, a troupe of amateur musicians from Paris who like to dress up in those gray and white uniforms and play military music from the era of the Sun King. The Amerindian chants would be supplied by a group from the local Kahnawake Reserve called Silver Bear and the Thunder Hawk Dancers.

As with many such events, things fell behind schedule. One o'clock came and went. It was boiling hot. The attractive Chinese-Canadian host of a program called *Timeline*, broadcast by a Toronto Chinese television station, began to fret. She and her crew were supposed to take a boat out to the harbor so they could get a good shot when the canoes came in. As it happened, there was a boat by the landing but it didn't look like it was going anywhere. "In Toronto, yes means yes and no means no," she stated. With her sunglasses and groomed-to-perfection look, she had the indestructible self-possession of her calling. If a terrorist bomb had gone off, she would have acted with cool professionalism; on the other hand, she definitely found this Gallic insouciance over details annoying. "I like discipline. Otherwise you can't control anything."

Silver Bear, meanwhile, was cool. With his drum in one hand and a drumstick in the other, he was wiggling his hips and singing, "You ain't nothing but a hound dog." Then he went up to the leader of the Tambours de France and said, "*Vous pouvez jouer Elvis?*" The leader, a scholarly looking middle-aged man with glasses, smiled and looked as if he hadn't understood the question. "*Bonjour,*" Silver Bear said. "*Buenos días.* Good day. *Bon après-midi.*" Definitely in the grip of an Elvis moment, he turned to the crowds and said, in the laid-back, faintly ironic tones of Late Presley, "Viva Las Vegas."

Finally, the canoes appeared, gliding into the harbor past the abandoned silos of the Five Roses Flour Company, the most evocative historical ruin in the city. (All the Great Lakes cities have these deserted silos and grain elevators on their lakeshores. They don't know what to do with them. Each year their concrete shells become more stained and cracked, while city planners dream of filling them with boutiques and artists' lofts.)

The re-enactors banged the sides of their canoes with their paddles to create an impressive racket and then disembarked on the landing. A squadron of students dressed up as French soldiers fired their muskets into the air. The Tambours de France played a stately air with their horns and flutes. Silver Bear and the Thunder Hawk Dancers performed their Amerindian chants. The company then proceeded to a square in the old section of Montreal and smoked a peace pipe and signed the treaty. What happened next, in 1701, was that three oxen were boiled for dinner, but no such luck this time.

Afterwards I talked to Wahiakeron George Gilbert, a Mohawk Indian portraying the Iroquois chief who signed the treaty on behalf of his confederacy. (That dignitary, in fact, had been an Onondaga – a minor detail.) Gilbert's outfit consisted solely of moccasins, a red breech cloth, and a headdress made from the feathers of Canada geese. It would not be a flattering ensemble for a lot of middle-aged men, but Gilbert carried it off, even though it was fairly clear he did not keep in trim by dancing all night to the "electrochic" of Les jardiniers. "I'm very proud that I'm still fluent in Mohawk and I had the opportunity to do this, because it's a great honor," he said, while Japanese tourists stood next to him to have their photographs taken. Gilbert, who spent twenty-five years living in the "Little Kahnawake" section of Brooklyn, turned out to be one of those legendary Mohawk ironworkers on the skyscrapers of New York. "They used to blame the ironworkers for the loss of the language," he commented, "but when we came home to Kahnawake, we were the ones who were still speaking Mohawk, because we had a community in Brooklyn and we'd always be speaking Mohawk to each other. It was the people back home who'd be watching television in English who didn't speak Mohawk."

The next day I went to 12:30 mass at Notre Dame Basilica, a remarkable building. Its architect, James O'Donnell, was given two directives when he was hired for the job in 1823. The first was that the church seat eight to nine thousand people. The second, in so many words, was that it express the latent magnificence of the Catholic soul of French Canada. O'Donnell, an Irish Protestant who had immigrated to New York City, went to work with a will. He decided to make Notre Dame the first Gothic building in Canada – a more daring move than appears in retrospect. The Gothic revival of the nineteenth century, a product of European romanticism with its renewed interest in the Middle Ages, was in part a protest against the rising tide of commercial and industrial civilization – a civilization embodied by no one better than *les anglais*, who had not only beaten General Montcalm outside the walls of Quebec City in 1759 but who, in the 1820s, were migrating to Montreal in great numbers and asserting control over the city's economic life.

The church was finished in 1829. For fifty years it was the biggest in Canada and the United States, until the Irish Catholics of New York City built St. Patrick's. For a century or so it was the most popular tourist destination in Canada, after Niagara Falls. O'Donnell, unfortunately, did not live to savor his triumph for long – it is said that he wore himself out working on his masterpiece. A sufferer from edema, he rapidly declined in health after the church was completed. The local priests labored to convert him to Catholicism before his death. O'Donnell respectfully demurred, until the priests clinched the deal with a reminder that he could be buried in his church if he accepted the faith. Two months before he died, O'Donnell assured a Montreal crowd that "it was not the solicitation of friends or others, neither could it be any worldly interest, but the conviction of his own heart that induced him to abjure heresy and make an open profession of the Roman Catholic faith." True to their word, the priests gave him a grand send-off at Notre Dame and buried him there in a crypt.

The year after O'Donnell died, Victor Hugo published a novel about another great French Catholic church in the Gothic style called Notre Dame. In this novel Hugo remarked that the printing press – invented in the fifteenth century, the same era during which his unfortunate hero, Quasimodo, was swinging like a monkey from the gargoyles of Notre Dame – was the instrument that killed Gothic architecture. It was a perception worthy of Marshall McLuhan, in which Hugo perceived that the medium, the Gutenberg press, was the message – that is, a way of outlook and an approach to life that was linear, uniform, diagrammatic. This spirit of print spelled doom for the Gothic cathedral the same way it spelled doom for the Karankawa in Texas. Prior to Gutenberg, the Gothic cathedral was the chief book of our culture. Its paintings, its stained glass windows, its statuary, its arrangement of nave and sanctuary, even the foliation on its arches and apertures, could be read as if part of a great code or hieroglyphic. Printing, a rival code, made this hieroglyphic seem crude, sprawling, obscurantist.

Hugo could patronize his Notre Dame because he was the product of a highly refined literary tradition and the inheritor of a century of virulent anti-clericalism. For Hugo and his contemporaries, Gothic cathedrals were safely picturesque. In England, too, the Gothic revival may have been an esthetic protest, but as a religious movement its claws had been pared and its teeth removed. The printing press had enjoyed too long a triumph in both countries. French Canada was different. While not medieval, it was not modern either – its Catholicism, as we shall see, was more a product of early seventeenth-century France, the France of Descartes and Pascal, where a comfortless rationalism and mysticism existed side by side.

La Salle and other early French explorers were highly literate, but the settlers who came after them were less so. French Canada simply did not have, in 1829 when Notre Dame was built, a printing press culture. This does not mean that the average French Canadian was a happy-go-lucky woodchopper who believed everything his parish priest told him – a stereotype of long duration in New England. But it is a fact that French Canada did not have a single printing press before the English conquest in 1760, as if its leaders intuited the complaint of Thomas Jefferson that "the printers can never leave us in a state of perfect rest and union of opinion." New England, on the other hand, obtained its first press in 1639 and never looked back. Almanacs, psalm books, catechisms, chapbooks, primers, broadsides, pamphlets, sermons, controversial tracts – everything from *Wine for Gospel Wantons: Or, Cautions against Spirituall Drunkenness* (1668) to *Astronomic Descriptions of the late Comet or Blazing Star* (1665) – flooded New England. It was a great literary culture, the seedbed of Hawthorne and Emerson.

There was a particularly sorry episode in the nineteenth century during which Notre Dame in Montreal acted according to

Hugo's script and tried literally to fend off the instrument of its doom. A printer named Joseph Guibord died in 1869 without the sacraments because of his involvement in a mildly free-thinking organization. The curé of Notre Dame refused a Christian burial to Guibord. The result was a legal battle that lasted for six years, ending in a court order for Guibord's burial in the cemetery of Notre Dame. Guibord's body was exhumed from the Protestant cemetery where it had lain, escorted by 1,235 soldiers to its resting place in the Notre Dame cemetery, and committed to the consecrated earth. Cement and scrap iron were placed over the coffin as protection against vandals. The day of the burial, the local bishop affirmed his intention to place the grave under interdict so that it would remain separate from consecrated ground, and stated with fine scorn, "There reposes a rebel who has been buried by force of arms."

The Gothic style of Notre Dame, then, resonated with the heart of French Canada far more than the Gothic style resonated with the France of Hugo or the England of John Ruskin. Some of that resonance may not even have to do with religion. The Gothic style, in a broader sense, lives deep in the psyche of Canada – a nation founded by two peoples who rejected the American Revolution and the French Revolution and who have thereafter tended to outward inhibition and inward brooding. One has only to compare the Gothic revival architecture of Ottawa with the Roman architecture of Washington, D.C. It is no accident that Canada's longest-serving prime minister was addicted to seances and crystal balls, and no accident either that Canadian literature is far more prone to visions of demon lovers and spirit-haunted wastes than the literature of the United States (except perhaps for the literature of the American South, another region of defeated peoples).

As a specimen of the Gothic, Notre Dame in Montreal is undoubtedly gorgeous. Even such a literate and stiff-necked New Englander as Henry David Thoreau was impressed. "It was a great cave in the midst of a city," he wrote after he visited in 1850, "and what were the altars and the tinsel but the sparkling stalactites, into which you entered in a moment, and where the still atmosphere and the sombre light disposed to serious and profitable thought?" Thoreau, as usual, was on target. To enter the church on a sunny afternoon, as I did that day, is very much like entering a stupendous cave or grotto. Facing you, at the end of the church behind the altar, is a curved wall nearly eighty feet high that glows with light and shadow and intricate patterns far beyond a dream of sparkling stalactites. Larger-than-life statues of saints, set in niches within that wall, seem to hover in the air. And everywhere on that wall are tracery and spires and pinnacles and decorated bands, a colossal accumulation of ornament that is almost too much for the eye. Yet this accumulation, as Ruskin noted in his chapter "The Nature of the Gothic" in *The Stones of Venice*, is evidence not of the grandiose, but the humble. "No architecture is so haughty as that which is simple; which refuses to address the eye, except in a few clear and forceful lines; which implies, in offering so little to our regards, that all it has offered is perfect," observed Ruskin.

The exact spiritual opposite of this embroidered cave were the two great towers that glinted in the sun and incited men to kill.

As I sat with the other small band of worshippers at this 12:30 mass – a sadly diminished group filling this great church – we were like the audience of a play that should have closed a long time ago. I didn't feel like an outlaw or an outcast, but on the other hand I did feel as if I were doing something odd that needed explaining to the horde of tourists who were crowded at the back of the church with their videocams and their Nikons and Minoltas, waiting for the mass to be over so they could come down the aisles and start shooting. What reason could I give to these tourists for my presence here? In brief: I had come to worship God and eat Christ. This is my belief, and I admit that it is strange. (But as G.K. Chesterton points out, if Christianity is a strange religion, it's because it's made to fit a strange world.) I didn't, on this day, even feel a particularly close bond with my fellow worshippers. I do not mean that there was no bond at all between the worshippers at mass, or that certain circumstances might not make it evident. But the Catholic tradition is to keep this bond undemonstrated. "If there had been fifty people there," Thoreau said of Notre Dame, "it would still have been the most solitary place imaginable. They did not look up at us, nor did one regard another."

Thoreau also talked about "a troop of Canadians, in their homespun" who entered the church and "kneeled down in the aisle before the high altar to their devotions, somewhat awkwardly, as cattle prepare to lie down." This wasn't contemptuous. "It is true, these Roman Catholics, priests and all, impress me as a people who have fallen far behind the significance of their own symbols," he wrote. "It is as if an ox had strayed into a church and were trying to bethink himself. Nevertheless they are capable of reverence; but we Yankees are a people in whom this sentiment has nearly died out, and in this respect we cannot bethink ourselves even as oxen." This is quite a handsome tribute to the Catholics of Montreal, coming from a man whose ancestors were French Huguenots. "As for the Protestant churches, here or elsewhere, they did not interest me, for it is only as caves that churches interest me at all, and in that respect they were inferior."

I wonder if some of my own forebears were among those Canadians in homespun who settled awkwardly in the pew, like cattle preparing to lie down. It would be nice to think so. There are times when I think my going to mass is a form of ancestor worship. I like the thought of sharing the same piety, say, as my great-great-great-great-great-great grandfather, Alexis Marchand, and his wife, Jeanne, in seventeenth-century Canada. What's more – while we're on the subject of strange beliefs, I might as well add this one – I do not think Alexis and Jeanne are dead. I believe they live, although not to my sight. If they now behold the face of God, I hope they remember me.

Eventually the priest stood up in front of the congregation and said, "*Passez une bonne semaine.* Have a good weekend," and the tourists were unleashed. Eight hundred thousand of them, it is said, still visit this building each year. It's the church of choice for the funeral of a prominent Quebecker, like former Montreal Canadiens great Maurice Richard, or former prime minister Pierre Trudeau. Céline Dion had her baby baptized here a week before my visit. According to press reports, nearly one thousand fans crowded the sidewalks to get a glimpse of the mother and her baby. "I think we've all gotten a lot of personal strength from her story," a twenty-year-old college student identified as Pete told a reporter. (Céline and her husband had battled infertility problems.) "Wearing a simple, grey pantsuit and large pearls," the reporter wrote of Céline, "she gave the crowd slight nods, small waves and mouthed hello and thank you."

The Catholic Church may be a shadow of its former self in Quebec, but certain rites remain important. "It's only dogs who aren't baptized," says the shocked peasant in Zola's novel *La Terre* after a disgusted priest refuses to perform the sacrament, telling his flock, "Your cows are more religious than you." Zola himself would have had a field day with the Hollywood premiere atmosphere of this particular baptism. If there was a religious feeling in the crowd that waited for Céline to arrive, it was worship of the demi-goddess in the simple gray pantsuit. To the Church, however, that mattered not at all. What was important happened at the font, where the soul of an infant, young René-Charles, was made receptive to the grace of God and the promise of eternal life.

Upon that naked infant gazed not only the wooden saints of the sanctuary, but the heroes of French Canada depicted in stained glass windows. That stained glass hall of fame was not part of the O'Donnell design; it was installed in the twentieth century, but it's worth a look, because it tells you a lot about French Canada and the kind of Catholicism that nurtured it. Three of the windows, for example, feature women. They look so serene and untroubled, these women, while they nurse the sick and teach Indian girls (who notoriously did not want to be taught). They have no equivalent in Puritan New England. Puritan New England was a patriarchy.

Quebec was and is a matriarchy. Marguerite Bourgeoys and Jeanne Mance and Marguerite d'Youville, brilliant, tough-minded women who founded hospitals and schools and religious orders in the seventeenth and eighteenth centuries, are signal instances of this. They, along with the incomparable Mother Marie de l'Incarnation, were the heart and soul of the early settlement. Their images shed a somber light in the minds of generations of French-Canadian women who, down through the ages, invoking the heavenly assistance of their saintly predecessors, would silently offer their suffering, including the memory of their numerous dead infants, to God.

And who is that dashing young man wearing a scarlet surcoat and the knee-length boots of a cavalier? The New Englanders would have recognized a deadly enemy just from the get-up. He is Adam Dollard, pledging his life to save the colony, flanked by young men raising their arms and eyes in religious exaltation, knowing they, too, are doomed. Dollard's right hand is placed over his heart, as if he's pledging allegiance, and his left hand holds what looks like an épée. He also sports a trim mustache that, together with the Three Musketeers outfit, gives him a resemblance to Douglas Fairbanks Sr. As the window was completed in 1931, it is quite possible the artist was influenced by movies like *The Black Pirate*, a Fairbanks vehicle released five years previously.

The story behind this window is that Dollard and his sixteen friends – they all confessed and received the sacrament and made out their wills – set out to intercept an Iroquois war party in 1660. Taking refuge inside a crumbling stockade at a place called Long Sault, just outside Montreal, they and a handful of Huron allies held off eight hundred Iroquois for seven days and seven nights. On the last day of the siege, Dollard, in desperation, crammed a musket with powder and lead, lit a fuse, and tried to toss this primitive grenade over the stockade into the midst of the Iroquois. Unfortunately, the musket didn't clear the stockade wall and bounced back. The explosion killed Dollard and a number of his fellows, and enabled the Iroquois to pour in and overwhelm the surviving defenders. At least one of them was tortured to death.

For three centuries, Dollard was venerated as a true Roman Catholic knight who saved his nation by his self-sacrifice. By holding off the Iroquois as long as he did, the story went, he discouraged them from carrying on their plan of wiping out not only Montreal, but the rest of New France. Of such a legend – often paired with the Lachine raid in the Quebec imagination – there is no equivalent in New England. The Puritans got a bad scare, it is true, during King Philip's War in 1675, when the Wampanoags and Naragansetts rose up in a last, desperate bid to save themselves from the white man, but there seems no doubt that the English colonists, from the day the boat landed at Plymouth Rock, knew they were in control.

The French, in contrast, had the misfortune to be opposed by the Iroquois, who were for the better part of two centuries the most powerful Indian nation in North America. Parkman called them "the Romans of the New World," which is a highly misleading analogy in most respects except for the sense it captures of how formidable they were on the field of battle. "Other colonies had their Indian wars but for none was the struggle so long or so bitter as for Canada," writes one Canadian historian. "The French who remained fought long and hard and valiantly for every inch of soil they won." In fact, the French never beat the Iroquois. The best they could do was win some of them over and neutralize most of the others, which is why that Great Peace of 1701 was so important.

The irony is that when the French first settled the St. Lawrence River valley in the beginning of the seventeenth century, luck was on their side. They found no Indians settled in the area they moved into, the stretch of river valley between present-day Quebec City and Montreal. Early explorers had encountered Indians in the region – historians call them the St. Lawrence Iroquois – but in the decades prior to 1600 they disappeared. Whether they were wiped out by disease or warfare, no one knows. In any case, the first French settlers, unlike the New Englanders, did not have to swindle or bully the locals out of their villages and their fields. The moment they strayed outside that area, however, they encountered the Iroquois war machine. This, along with other things, made for an immensely different mentality among colonial rivals. The Protestant New Englanders, in their Indian wars, invoked the God of Battles who marched with the Israelites into Canaan. They could taste their victory before they won it. The Catholic French, on the other hand, remembered Dollard, whose example told them that they would lose, they would always lose, but in embracing suffering and death they would turn defeat into something darkly beautiful, they would find a new sympathy with God Himself who had suffered as none of His creatures had ever suffered.

Needless to say, when Quebec intellectuals rejected the Church in the sixties and bitterly assailed these old religious and nationalist myths of French Canada as a nation chosen by God to convert North America to Catholicism, Dollard came in for a lot of sneers. He was a "cowboy." His military conduct was Custer-like in its impetuosity and blundering. The Iroquois on this raid, moreover, were not intent on wiping out French Canada, they just wanted revenge for previous attacks, plus a few trophies and captives. At Long Sault they got their wish.

This curling of the lip at men who endured seven days and nights of terror, exhaustion, and agonizing thirst seems a little ungenerous coming from comfortable, well-fed academics whose idea of sudden peril is a drunk sitting next to them on the subway. It betrays the same lack of imagination as turning Dollard into a stained glass swashbuckler. We can at least sympathize with half-dead Dollard throwing that musket with all his might and seeing it catch the inside tip of the stockade wall. We can sympathize with his companions, knowing the Iroquois were determined to capture them alive, the better to introduce them to a hitherto inconceivable vastness of pain. These Frenchmen had no idea why the Iroquois would want to do this. They did not know if the Iroquois would torture them in a respectful way because they wanted to test their manhood and courage (and eat their remains if they passed the test), or whether the Iroquois, in a foul mood after losing a lot of their friends, would simply enjoy the sight of them screaming and begging for mercy. It's a question of interest to historians and anthropologists, but probably not the main issue for Dollard and his men.

So Adam Dollard can stay up in that window until the end of time, as far as I'm concerned. I'm not sure, however, what I think about Jerome le Royer de la Dauversière. In his window, Dauversière looks like a well-fed bourgeois, with his sober gray clothing lit by a few fancy touches like gold rosettes on his shoes. He was, in fact, a minor bureaucrat who happened to be a member and agent of a very important organization called the Society of the Blessed Sacrament. It was the society that, in 1641, raised funds and recruited fifty settlers for the founding of a city in the New World, eventually known as Montreal. It would be a city unsullied by trade or commerce. Instead it would be wholly dedicated to the glory of God and the spread of a religious empire in the wilderness of North America.

The Society of the Blessed Sacrament is the most famous of the Catholic congregations that sprang up in Europe in the seventeenth century – groups of laymen under the guidance of Jesuits who tried to reform society on Catholic principles. It was an age suited to such an enterprise. The early seventeenth century in France, in particular, saw the revival of the Catholic Church after a century of religious civil war. Saints sprang up everywhere – St. Vincent de Paul, St. Francis de Sales, St. Claude de la Colombière, St. Margaret Mary Alacoque, St. Jane de Chantal, the Jesuit martyrs of North America. Piety was in fashion. A rich man with a conscience might well find himself recruited to a congregation like the Society of the Blessed Sacrament in order to cultivate a life of virtue and austerity.

These congregations embodied everything that was noble and also repellent about seventeenth-century French Catholic piety. "To be a member of a congregation meant above all knowing how to confess," writes the French historian Louis Chatellier. To know how to confess meant knowing how to pinpoint your failings. To pinpoint your failings meant studying a Jesuit named François De Coster, founder of one of these congregations, who wrote a manual explaining to members of the congregation the fine shades of difference in sin. Are we dismayed because our best friend has just won the lottery? "There are four ways of being grieved at another's wealth," Coster maintains.

> In the first place, if we fear that we or others will suffer as a result; and this distress is not envy but fear. Secondly, if we are annoyed not that another has something, but that we do not have it; that is jealousy. Thirdly, if we are unhappy that another has something of which he is unworthy; that is disdain. Fourthly, if we regret another's wealth because it seems to diminish our own excellence; that is envy.

Coster appeals to reason more than to the emotions in this treatment, but that's the seventeenth century for you. At least he's actually thinking about the nature of human feelings and their consequences.

There was more to life in a congregation than making a good confession, of course. Your life was bound by rules, the more rigidly adhered to for knowing the devil was ready to pounce on a moment of relaxation or inattention. You should sleep no more than six or seven hours, then jump out of bed the minute you wake up, "because," observed Father Coster, "the devil pays particular attention to the first thoughts of the day." Some rules had a tinge of the Pharisee. When the evening bells invited the faithful to say the Hail Mary, a good member should fall to his knees immediately, even if he's in a public square talking with his friends.

Men of the congregations did a lot of good work, visiting the sick and the poor and prisoners in jail. In the spirit of Molière's *Tartuffe*, however, they often made themselves extremely tiresome by imposing order on good bourgeois homes – removing frivolous books from someone else's library, for example. Worse was their attitude toward Protestants and Jews. The modern Catholic approach is to be especially nice to people who have pronounced differences with the Church. (That'll show 'em.) This was not the seventeenth-century way. The Society of the Holy Sacrament was particularly notorious for trying to break up assemblies of Jews and making life as unpleasant as possible for the Huguenots. (That the Huguenots tended to be annoyingly successful in trade and finance did not endear them to Catholic burghers, either.) But of course there was a charitable motive. If Huguenots were sufficiently harassed, they might begin to see in a new light the truths of religion that they had abjured. So members of the order tried to prevent Huguenots from setting up their hospitals and charities; they tried to exclude them from the professions and from municipal office; they spied on them and bullied them any way they could.

This is sad accounting. I do not want to add to people's reasons for believing that the Church has been a hindrance to human progress. At the same time, I am trying to note the nature of the individuals who founded Montreal: they were extremely religious men and women who did good and evil. Bigotry is one aspect of their failure to love according to the Gospels. But I am even more interested in another facet of their striking difference from us, and that is the impossible rigor of their spirituality.

Seventeenth-century France is in some ways reminiscent of ancient India, where forest hermits practiced extreme mortification of the body, the better to escape this illusory world. Like these hermits, members of the congregation fasted regularly and scourged themselves frequently, and though they did not stand on one leg for hours at a time or sit on hot rocks, naked to the blazing sun, some members did things equally remarkable, such as licking the floor of the meeting house where their brethren met. The first bishop of Quebec, the aristocratic and imperious François Montmorency de Laval, was a devotee of such extreme counter-pleasure exercises.

When he lived in France and tended the sick in hospitals, he sucked the pus from their sores. Afterwards, in Quebec, he ate rotten meat with gusto and slept in a bed where he was continually tormented with fleas.

The Catholic Church has never widely sanctioned this kind of mortification of the flesh but, again, the time and place favored it. It was the age of French baroque, when churches looked like mausoleums. It was the age when Pascal discouraged his nieces and nephews from embracing their mother. It was the age when St. Claude de la Colombière made a vow to "desire as much as I can whatever will be contrary to my natural inclinations" and "never to take pleasure in those things which of necessity I must use, such as drinking, eating, sleeping." He meant it. From the moment he uttered this vow, he went out of his way to avoid smelling flowers. He sought the most unappetizing foods. He declared war on the natural.

In fairness to the saint, he recognized that this was not the sole path to sanctity. He admitted that, throughout the history of the Church, "holy persons" had allowed themselves some "innocent pleasures." There were great saints who did, in fact, smell the flowers and enjoyed beautiful paintings and music and polished literature and even wrote verse themselves. "I do not think any the less of them," he stated. Moreover, "natural" to St. Claude is not necessarily the same thing as "natural" to us. "Natural" for us is a mysterious quality, sometimes known as "organic," that makes certain foodstuffs better than others and is always to be admired. "Natural" for St. Claude included cravings of the ego. What's more "natural" for a human being, say, than the desire to shine in conversation or to order other people around (for their own good)? Natural or not, this beast needs reining in from time to time.

St. Claude de la Colombière could point to the precedent of some of the greatest doctors of the Church – St. Augustine, for example. After his conversion, St. Augustine, mindful of the words of Ecclesiastes that "light is sweet to the eye," worried that he enjoyed the brilliant light of the Mediterranean too much.

Scrupulously, St. Augustine made an inventory of all the other human pleasures – pleasures that he relished as much as any man who ever lived – that tied a soul too closely to the world and distracted it from God. He liked his food, he informed the reader in his *Confessions*, and often ate more than strictly necessary for the maintenance of his body. "Full feeding sometimes creepeth upon Thy servant." Smell he didn't worry about too much – he appreciated nice smells as much as the next man, but thought he could do without them. ("Perchance I may be deceived.") But the delights of music and poetry! "Long have I loved thee, Beauty of ancient days, yet ever new! Too long have I loved thee!" Intellectual curiosity – no one knew the pull of that human appetite more than St. Augustine. He berated himself even for watching in fascination as a spider weaved her web or a lizard hunted flies. Fix your attention on God, he had to keep reminding himself.

St. Augustine wrote in an atmosphere of late paganism, when it seemed to Christians that the Roman world in its decadence had fouled even nature. So Augustine's contribution to Christianity, Chesterton observed, contained "a mood which unconsciously committed the heresy of dividing the substance of the Trinity. It thought of God too exclusively as a Spirit who purifies or a Saviour who redeems; and too little as a Creator who creates." In the High Middle Ages, saints like Francis of Assisi and Thomas Aquinas reunited the substance of Trinity – St. Francis of Assisi with his love of nature and music, his instinctive sense that the sun and the birds and the animals pointed Godward, St. Thomas with his theology of divine grace perfecting nature, not obliterating it. This did not mean that henceforth every Catholic was supposed to live like Friar Tuck. No one denies that the occasional fast is good for the soul, or that self-denial, even with "innocent pleasures," is salutary from time to time. We must not be slaves to comfort or appetite. As Chesterton further observed, "Asceticism, or the war with the appetites, is itself an appetite. It can never be eliminated from among the strange ambitions of Man."

Mindful of this, confessors in the Church usually moderate the austerities of their penitents. In seventeenth-century France, however, the Augustinian mood at its most rigorous had returned. Nature once again came to be viewed with intense suspicion. This was true even of secular culture. "French literature of the seventeenth century is astonishingly poor in expressions of any but a strictly utilitarian or symbolic interest in birds, flowers, animals, landscape," writes Aldous Huxley in *The Devils of Loudun*, a book that is largely an attack on seventeenth-century French Catholicism. His view of the mortifications practiced by people like Bishop Laval was that they were highly imperfect instruments of self-transcendence. "In cases where they are used with moderation, physical austerities may be made the instruments of horizontal or even of upward self-transcendence," Huxley pointed out.

When the body goes hungry, there is often a period of unusual mental lucidity. A lack of sleep tends to lower the threshold between the conscious and the subconscious. Pain, when not too extreme, is a tonic shock to organisms deeply and complacently sunk in the ruts of habit. Practised by men of prayer, these self-punishments may actually facilitate the process of upward self-transcendence. More frequently, however, they give access, not to the divine Ground of all being, but to that queer "psychic" world which lies, so to say, between the Ground and the upper, the more personal levels of the subconscious and conscious mind. Those who gain access to this psychic world – and the practice of physical austerities would seem to be a royal road to the occult – often acquire powers of the kind which our ancestors called "supernatural" or "miraculous."

Ironically, even though the Iroquois had no theological problems with "nature" – any more than fish have problems with water – they did value ecstatic trances induced through drugs and fasting, which were seen as a voyage to the other side of death, and the source of spiritual messages. (What culture, come to think of it, *doesn't* value ecstatic trances?) Many things about the Jesuits and other missionaries deeply puzzled the Indians, but they had no problem understanding the mystic transports of a Bishop Laval, induced in part through his mortification of the flesh.

In their frank embrace of death and heroic endurance, both seventeenth-century woodland Indians and seventeenth-century Jesuits stand on the same side of an immense abyss between them and us. Even conservative Catholics and Protestants nowadays emphasize self-realization more than self-denial, spiritual benefits in this life rather than eagerness for the life to come. Evangelical Christians promote a "biblical" faith, for example, but their favorite books are a mixture of therapy and an unthreatening Christianity – books like *Psychology, Jesus and Mental Health* and *The Art of Understanding Yourself.* God smiles in His heaven, and we no longer shudder at eternity.

FOUR

China

*La Salle learns to eat ants • William Carlos Williams celebrates a
Jesuit missionary • A tough hockey player • Somber thoughts
at a tomb • The Mystica Rosa • I receive a veiled threat*

After 12:30 mass, I went to visit La Salle's old estate in the middle of a working-class suburb of Montreal. A house built by one of La Salle's tenants still stands — or at least its original walls. The structure is now part of a museum, and the interior is full of Plexiglas cases containing pieces of copper kettles and lead musket balls, described in the kind of detail that makes museum-going such a fatiguing experience. However, there was a very nice young woman on staff who explained that the house was preserved from the flames of the massacre, and its lucky inhabitant able to run away before being captured or killed by the Iroquois. "It was a revenge thing," she said of the raid. "The Iroquois were . . ." (she spread her arms wide and wiggled the index and middle fingers on both hands to indicate quotation marks) ". . . the bad Indians" (she lowered her arms). "They came from the Great Lakes to get revenge for what the French did, and also for control of the land. It was a very . . ." (she raised her arms again and wiggled those fingers) ". . . non-civilized time" (she lowered her arms). "It couldn't happen today.

They're paid by the government. They've lost their independence. It's a big social issue."

She was referring to the Mohawk reserves in the province of Quebec – particularly the Kahnawake reserve, not far from where the Iroquois once celebrated their victory over the settlers of Lachine. These Mohawks – the easternmost of the Five Nations in upstate New York, and the one that bore the brunt of fighting with the French – have touchy relations with the Great White Father in Ottawa (Canadian federal government) and sometimes with Quebec City (provincial government). In turn, a lot of Québécois take a mildly cynical attitude toward the aboriginals, whose many and just grievances are not alleviated by the government funding they receive. As for the old Iroquois wars, of course, all is forgiven. For a long time, the French Canadians seemed to be the only whites in North America who felt more badly treated by the Indians than vice versa.

Certainly, when La Salle first came to the island of Montreal, he must have gotten an earful about what had happened only a few years prior to his arrival. A woman was still alive, for example, who had become a local legend after her encounter with the Iroquois. According to Father Dollier de Casson, author of a memoir entitled *Histoire du Montréal*, "a woman of virtue, called today the goodwife Primot," was attacked by three Iroquois armed with hatchets. "At this, the woman defended herself like a lioness, but as she had no weapons but hands and feet, at the third or fourth blow they felled her as if dead. Immediately one of the Iroquois flung himself upon her to scalp her and escape with this shameful trophy. But as our amazon felt herself so seized, she at once recovered her senses, raised herself and, more fierce than ever, caught hold of this monster so forcibly by a place which modesty forbids us to mention that he could not free himself." Another Montrealer, Father de Casson reports, while still breathing had his scalp removed and part of his skull by an Iroquois warrior, "which did not prevent his living for fourteen years longer, which is a wonderful thing [*ce qui est bien admirable*]."

These were very lucky Montrealers. Some of their compatriots *were* carried off and put to a long, slow, fiery death. For twenty years, nobody in this settlement could venture out of doors without being afraid a band of Iroquois might suddenly spring out of the bush. I can't conceive of living with this amount of dread. It didn't stop until the government sent over a crack regiment in 1665 to inspire a little more respect among the Iroquois for French arms. The result was the truce that obtained on La Salle's arrival.

What La Salle saw, in the summer of 1669, when he first laid eyes on his property was an impassable wilderness of white pine, spruce, cedar, hemlock, larch, and maple. To get around this part of the continent you needed a birchbark canoe. That interesting discovery was followed immediately by two more such discoveries on the part of La Salle, one pleasant, the other less so. The heartening discovery was the incredible abundance of game. You could practically knock game birds, like the wood pigeon, off trees with a stick. The waters were alive with fish. On the other hand, you couldn't walk around the neighborhood without yourself feeding hordes of mosquitos and blackflies.

La Salle's job was to bring in settlers and clear the land for farming, but something in his soul responded to the wilderness. What precise psychological reasons he had for this affinity, we will never know. We do know he did not like taking orders, and that he had no concept of "teamwork." He got along brilliantly with Indians, who also didn't like taking orders. But among his own people, if he saw that someone was depressed, he didn't go out of his way to cheer him up, he didn't go in for small talk. If others didn't cooperate with his sometimes incomprehensible plans, he became very suspicious very quickly. He would have been miserable working in an office today. If he were alive today, there's no telling what he would do. Fortunately, he found the right time and place for someone of his temperament. He wanted to go exploring, and there was the interior of North America, just waiting for him.

This leads to another mystery. Why was it that the French proved to be such geniuses of exploration in North America? At a time when the Pilgrims were carving out their first settlements in Massachusetts, the French were already traveling overland toward Hudson Bay and the prairies. And La Salle, of all the French who wandered across the wilderness, had this genius in greatest measure. Faced with the North American woodlands, a European had two choices. He could look at it as a howling wasteland, full of very dangerous humans, the sooner cleared the better – the New England way. Or he could look at it as a realm of beautiful, hard, unforgiving freedom, which was La Salle's way. So La Salle learned to paddle a birchbark canoe. "Do not begin to paddle unless you are inclined to continue paddling," advised the Jesuit Brébeuf, and in that little sentence lay the heart of wilderness wisdom. Once you put that paddle in the water, you had better be prepared for blisters and aching muscles. In the same way, La Salle learned to walk under loads fit for a horse, through snow and tangled underbrush. He developed a stamina to match that of the Indians. He learned to cover his body with grease to repel insects, he learned the art of starting fires in damp or frozen woods, he learned the art of finding direction. He learned, during the hungry time of winter, to look for the tree where a woodpecker was at work, because underneath the bark would be hordes of carpenter ants, which La Salle then scooped and ate. He learned a hundred other things, including the language of the Iroquois, a fantastically difficult and complex tongue for a European to master.

He wanted to find the fabled passage to Asia, and his ambition became so fierce it turned into a joke, which was why his neighbors called his seigneury "Lachine." But La Salle meant it, and so he turned his attention to the fur trade, which was the only way a man in his circumstances could finance a career of exploration.

What gold and silver was to the Spaniards in Peru, fur was to the French in Canada. It was a tremendously valuable commodity in Europe, where the wealthy wore hats made of long-haired felt. Enterprising men in Canada could make a lot of money trading European goods – notably brandy – for beaver pelts from the lands north of the Great Lakes. That's where the thickest, richest pelts came from. And that's why the French and the Iroquois ended up as enemies. If the French wanted those prime northern furs, they had no choice but to ally themselves with the northern Indians who were at odds with the Iroquois.

The fur trade also has been blamed for the failure of the French, despite the best efforts of Louis XIV and Colbert, to concentrate on settlement of the New World, in the manner of the English colonies. This lucrative commerce, it has been said, diverted resources and turned attention away from agricultural activity. That now seems a questionable thesis. Other things enter the picture. Good farmland in Quebec, where the land is under snow and frost half the year, is not quite so abundant as it is in Connecticut or South Carolina. But it is true that fur trading, as an economic staple of New France, shaped the French empire in North America in ways very different from the English. For one thing, it meant that the French needed the Indians. They had no interest in clearing them out of the lands they already occupied. Especially as time went on, they also relied on the Indians militarily. The French were a fraction of the population of the English and could not hope to pin the English down east of the Appalachians without alliances with various Indian nations.

This explains why the French, of all the colonizing people in North America, had the cleanest hands when it came to dealing with Indians. But there was a worm in the apple of the fur trade, and that was brandy. It was a trade good that never lost its appeal, and the markup was terrific. Unfortunately, it was also pure poison for the Indians, which is why the Jesuits, and especially Bishop Laval, were dead set against its sale. The Jesuits knew its violent effects at first hand. Famous for their courage, the black robes nevertheless made themselves scarce whenever Indians came back to their village with kegs of the stuff. Other missionaries, like the Sulpician Dollier de Casson, could bear similar witness. "In the twenty-six years that I have been in this country I have seen our flourishing and numerous Algonquin missions wholly destroyed by drunkenness," wrote this priest in 1691.

As the decades wore on, and the Jesuits began to make real progress converting the Indians, they started to imagine establishing an independent Indian nation, not unlike Paraguay, where they could shield the natives from the worst aspects of European civilization. In this dream, they would carefully limit the fur trade and make sure no brandy was sold. This is one of the reasons why the Jesuits later took a dim view of La Salle's explorations, even though La Salle had been one of their students. They saw his voyages around the Great Lakes and down the Mississippi as an end run around their own Indian protectorate and an expansion of the fur trade that would wholly undermine them.

Events shattered their dream in any case, and today the Jesuits suffer a bad press even for the work they did accomplish. Parkman, a deep-dyed New England anti-papist, always viewed them with a cold eye, and twenty-first-century historians, determined not to give the faintest benefit of the doubt to the colonizers, are even less generous. The record of the Jesuits is remarkable, nonetheless. Of all the Christian missionaries in colonial America, they were the only ones who realized that, in order to teach the Indians, so easily frightened and disgusted by the habits of the Europeans, they had to learn from them. They had to live among them, become familiar with their language, habits, way of life, outlook. "You must have sincere affection for the savages [*faut aimer de coeur les Sauvages*] ... as our brethren with whom we are to pass the rest of our lives," wrote Jean de Brébeuf to his Jesuit colleagues in his *Instructions for the Fathers of Our Society Who Shall Be Sent to the Hurons*. Among Brébeuf's pieces of advice for dealing with the Hurons: never keep them waiting; never drag wet sand into their canoes with your cassocks; never bother them while they're paddling by asking too many questions or trying to improve your command of the language; always give them a light from your tinderbox for their pipes. ("These little services win their hearts.")

The Jesuits tried very hard to find some sort of common ground with the Indians, and to change only those practices clearly at odds with the gospel of Christ, that is to say, sorcery, sacrifice to spirits, torture, revenge, excessive mourning for the dead, pre- and extra-marital sex, and a few other items. In the end, as we shall see, this policy had its own pitfalls, but on the surface anyway it was a more enlightened approach than that attempted by the English Protestant missionaries, which was "civilize" the Indians before Christianizing them. The firm belief of these missionaries seemed to be that an Indian had to wear shoes, live in a house – even though wigwams were cooler in the summer and warmer in the winter – get a haircut, and sport a first name such as Habbakuk before he could be considered a good Christian. In his "praying" towns, the Reverend John Eliot of Massachusetts carefully regulated the behavior of his native converts with a series of thou-shalt-nots. On pain of fines or a beating, for example, they were not to "kill their lice between their teeth." Needless to say, people like Eliot could get away with this because their potential converts had already lost their lands, their way of life, and the last vestiges of their pride and independence. These missionaries preached effectively when they preached to a captive audience, almost literally. The Jesuits in this regard may be said to have made a virtue of necessity, since the Indians they preached to were independent and aimed to stay that way, but nevertheless it's a tribute to their intelligence that they realized so quickly they couldn't make Frenchmen out of Hurons or Iroquois. Even someone as skilled in Indian diplomacy as Count Frontenac, governor of New France in the late seventeenth century, urged the missionaries to bring their converts to Quebec and Frenchify them. A Jesuit named Pierre de Charlevoix responded acidly that the experience of the Jesuits "has taught us that the worst system of governing these people and maintaining them in our interest is to bring them in contact with the French, whom they would have esteemed more, had they seen them less closely." There was something about the mingling of whites and Indians that brought out the worst in both groups.

The contrast between the French missionary effort and the English missionary effort was starkest in Maine, among the Abenakis, where a Jesuit father named Sebastien Rasles squared off against a succession of Protestants. William Carlos Williams's study of American history, *In the American Grain* (1925), has an eloquent chapter on Rasles. Williams begins by lamenting the "inhuman clarity" of the Puritans' Calvinist theology and its tendency to oppose the natural world to eternity. "The English appraised the New World too meanly," Williams writes. As a result, they never actually *saw* the Indians. "They never realized the Indian in the least save as an unformed Puritan. The immorality of such a concept, the inhumanity, the brutalizing effect upon their own minds, on their spirits – they never suspected."

By contrast, Father Rasles was, Williams notes, "a spirit, rich, blossoming, generous, able to give and receive, full of taste, a nose, a tongue, a laugh, enduring, self-forgetful in beneficence – a new spirit in the New World." Given the rigor of seventeenth-century French Catholicism, it might be surprising to hear a Jesuit of the era described as "a nose" and "full of taste." Wasn't this precisely what Bishop Laval was trying to mortify? Yet Catholicism at its most austere still took the human sensorium as its point of departure, which was another reason the Jesuits were more successful with Indians than the Protestants. They offered the Indians visual treats – candlelit altars, incredibly lavish churches, pictures of saints dressed in bright red and blue. They offered incense, which appealed to the nose and echoed the traditional sacrifice of tobacco. For the ear, they offered liturgical chants and hymns and tinkling bells. Even the sense of taste received recognition in the Eucharist.

Rasles himself was undoubtedly exceptional. When the Abenakis went on the warpath, they went to Rasles for his blessing and counsel. "I told them to remember their prayers and to do no cruelty, to kill no one save in the heat of battle and to treat humanely all those taken prisoners," Rasles recalled. Like all Jesuits, he never forgot these men were fighters. He didn't try to make Boy Scouts out of them. Meanwhile, he tended to the sick among them, settled their disputes, heard their confessions, in the Abenaki tongue, of course, which Rasles, according to Williams, admired for its "peculiar beauties." By contrast, the Reverend Joseph Baxter of the Congregational Church spent eight months among the Abenakis and learned two phrases: "I forgot" and "I do not care." As solace for his failure to make any converts, he invested in land, which was also characteristic. Rasles remained a stone in the shoe of the New Englanders until they solved the problem by raiding his village in 1724, slaughtering men, women, and children, including Rasles himself, mutilating his corpse and filling his mouth and eye sockets with dirt, and bringing his scalp back to Boston.

To judge the ultimate success of the French Jesuits in the seventeenth century is difficult. At the least, they converted a significant minority of the Indians they encountered, including numbers of their old enemy, the Iroquois. The latter accomplishment was extraordinary. Numbers of Catholic Iroquois removed from their old communities to Jesuit-established *reserves* along the St. Lawrence, the better to practice their faith – even as their non-Christian kinsmen, back in the longhouses in upstate New York, remained deeply suspicious, if not outright hostile to the French. The most famous *reserve* became Kahnawake, a Mohawk town for three centuries now.

⚜

After visiting Lachine, I decided to look up the "vice-postulator" of the Kateri Center at the St. Francis Xavier mission church at Kahnawake. The center is named after the "Lily of the Mohawks,"

Blessed Kateri Tekakwitha, a woman born in 1656 in present-day Auriesville, New York, who was baptized as a Catholic when she was twenty years old. Two years later, after enduring considerable abuse at the hands of her non-Christian family, she fled to a Jesuit mission on the St. Lawrence, not far from present-day Kahnawake. Her health already frail from the ravages of smallpox suffered when she was a child, Kateri nonetheless devoted herself to "extraordinary penances." She walked barefoot in the snow. She sprinkled ashes on her food. She and a friend whipped each other with briars. She put live coals between her toes, as if to show that endurance under torture could take many forms. These practices may have hastened her death at the age of twenty-three, but not before Kateri evidently attained a spiritual beatitude, a direct union with God on earth vouchsafed only to certain saints and mystics.

The vice-postulator – the man in charge of the campaign for her canonization – was a seventy-nine-year-old Jesuit named Jacques Bruyère. I met him at the Jesuit residence of the Collège Brébeuf in Montreal, a famous school where the children of the French Catholic elite of Montreal once received a classical Jesuit education. The residence itself was a brick building erected in the 1950s. Once, its gloomy linoleum-floored corridors vibrated to the hum of adolescents, but no longer. Now the only signs of life were old men appearing from time to time in the twilight, dressed in gray slacks and shirts of drab brown or blue. The fathers no longer wore their cassocks but they observed the spirit of clerical garb by not sporting any vibrant colors. Post-Vatican II reforms or no, you'll never see a Jesuit wearing a Thomas Pink shirt.

Father Bruyère, in a blue check shirt, came down a flight of stairs to greet me and lead me to a sitting room, painted institutional beige, with a window looking over a parking lot. In the corner was a wooden pole long enough to reach to the top of the window and unhook the transom. Father Bruyère, a genial soul, sat behind a table and, although not quite sure what I was after, seemed happy to answer any question I asked. No, he said, he wasn't originally from

Quebec, he started life in the prairie province of Manitoba, one of nine children born to a railroad station master and his wife, in a town called Letellier, a fifteen-minute drive from North Dakota. A lot of French Canadians went west with the railroad in the late nineteenth century, and in small farm towns, surrounded by Scots Presbyterians and Ukrainians and Icelanders and Cree Indians, they clung to their religion and language with the same tenacity as other French Canadians migrating to the mill towns of New England in the same era. "My father was a real *patriote*. Gosh, in those days all the advertisements, it was all in French. Even in the garage. *Ici Nous Vendons des Voitures*. My father made sure we all spoke French at home, too."

Most of the children eventually left home, moved to California and other places with plentiful employment and more congenial climates. "When I went back ten years ago, there was a big celebration in town and everything was in English. Lucky my father wasn't there. They would have heard about that." Father Bruyère chuckled. His father was no shrinking violet. Neither was his son, apparently. He was a notable hockey player in his youth. "Our team was called the Flying Frenchmen. The Flying Frenchmen. Imagine that. We played in Winnipeg, we played in all the towns. And we beat them all. Yeah." Father Bruyère laid his hands on the tabletop, powerful instruments that once gripped a hockey stick as if they meant business. "I was renowned as a dirty player," he said proudly. A dirty player? Like Gordie Howe, famous for using his elbows as a lethal weapon in the corners? "No, no, not the elbows. Tripping with my leg behind the skates. And they fell so nicely, so artistically, heh, heh. I really enjoyed seeing that. I remember playing a game in St. Pierre – they had a good team. I was coming up the ice when these defensemen – huge guys – but both had been drinking too much before, I guess. One of them I tripped. Down he fell. The next one I tripped. Down he fell. One guy on the left and the other guy on the right. And then I scored and didn't get a penalty! I guess they felt these guys were drunk and fell by themselves, heh, heh." He paused and looked at those meaty hands. Father Bruyère was not tall, and not particularly hefty, but getting hit by him on the rink probably felt like getting whacked by a fire hydrant. "I remember a Jesuit father said to me once, you have these two natures. Outside the ice you're a gentleman, and inside the ice you're a lion. Off the ice, you're okay, but on the ice, watch out! Yeah."

Father Bruyère was so good he considered turning pro. "I wanted to be a hockey player. The New York Rangers had an eye on me. There was a scout in my hometown. Yeah." He rubbed the fingers of one hand thoughtfully. "My father was against that." Father Bruyère paused again. His tone was matter-of-fact. "I would have enjoyed that."

Instead, in 1942, Father Bruyère joined the Jesuits. Four years later, still a scholastic (or student), he was sent to China. Unlike Robert Cavelier de la Salle, he made it to the fabulous Orient. "I was everything there," he recalled of his work in mainland China and later Taiwan. "I was a professor in the university, I taught French, music and English, I was a hospital chaplain, I was a jail chaplain, I was a choir master in the church there. I was very busy, I'm telling you. I was even a hockey coach." It must have been a sight to see, Father Bruyère on skates, wearing his cassock – Jesuits then had to wear their cassocks everywhere – knocking over defensemen like tenpins. He said his Chinese players were "pretty good skaters," but it was hard to get used to the square rinks they played in, because you could never know where the puck was going to land. The way he talked, it was clear that Father Bruyère wouldn't have traded this life even for glory in the NHL. "I don't regret anything," he said.

Now he served at Kahnawake, performing the occasional baptism and wedding but mainly hosting groups of pilgrims visiting the shrine of Kateri Tekakwitha. It was perhaps just as well that in the twilight of his earthly vocation he did not shepherd this particular flock. "You see, Indians for me, they're very much Oriental," he explained. "They're Oriental. So they have many Oriental traits.

See, when you're there, they ignore you. It doesn't mean they don't like you. Like in China, if you have not been introduced to a person and met them two or three times, you won't even be saluted. They're like that in Kahnawake."

Four hundred years ago, China and the wilderness of North America were two likely destinations for Jesuit missionaries. They seemed so far apart, these postings. One, an ancient culture – "A country that passes for being the wisest and most civilized in the universe," said Voltaire, echoing a common European sentiment – the other, a Stone Age woodland culture. But both were, in their way, very complex cultures, when you looked closely. Both were striking instances, to the highly modern Jesuits, of Otherness. Both fascinated the Jesuits, when they weren't disgusted by certain of their practices. There was a certain historical irony, then, in Father Bruyère's comparison of the Mohawks of Kahnawake to the Chinese, as if the great Jesuit missionary effort of the seventeenth century possessed an underlying unity no one suspected, and the scoffers knew better than they realized when they called the territory across the river "Lachine."

"Well, Indians are pretty unpredictable," Father Bruyère said. "I remember someone once said to me, 'When you think you have them, you haven't got 'em. When you think you don't have them, that's when you've got 'em.' And that's pretty true. Yeah. Very unpredictable. But there are a lot of nice people, and good people there. There's also a traditional movement there, going back to the old ways, which they have lost and they will never find again." Father Bruyère uttered this last comment without vindictiveness, but also without regret. Political correctness had no hold on him. "They're very touchy. You must be very careful. Like if you mention the word 'squaw' they'll punch you in the nose. And they don't like to say *'sauvage.'* Though it didn't have a bad meaning. It just meant they lived in the forests and had a natural way of living. But they're very touchy." Actually, among themselves, modern-day

Iroquois aren't quite so politically correct either. When they see people portraying Jesuits in historical re-enactments, they wink and nudge and point out the "new white meat," alluding to the fact their ancestors made a hearty meal of the occasional black robe.

"In Kahnawake, you'll hear all kinds of things," Father Bruyère continued. "They have a little cultural center and there's a video in there and they bring down the church as if we did nothing for them. We saved them! Jesuits saved them. Their language, their grammar, their history, it's all recorded in the Jesuit *Relations*. We always worked with them, we lived as they lived – we were inculturated. But they're very touchy." He chuckled. Father Bruyère was not bitter, although much of what had constituted his life, like the Jesuit Order in Quebec, had crumbled in front of his eyes in the last few decades. He tended to be philosophical about events, which was a sign of wisdom. There was no use complaining about history. History gave everybody a rough ride.

That same afternoon, I drove over the Pont Mercier across the St. Lawrence to Kahnawake, and again met George Gilbert, who was one of the traditionalists among the Mohawks. This time Gilbert was fully dressed. We sat on a park bench overlooking the St. Lawrence while the odd barge floated by, and a breeze ruffled the beech trees and the sumacs and wisps of Gilbert's black and gray hair. He gave me a photocopied booklet called *The Council of the Great Peace. The Great Binding Law, Gayanerekowa. The Constitution of the Five Nations Confederacy*. It began with a reference to the Tree of Great Peace, or the Great White Pine, the Tioneratasekowa, which was planted when the Iroquois Confederacy was formed some time in the sixteenth century. It was a culture-defining event, similar to Moses bringing down the tablets from Mount Sinai. An eagle, it was said, would perch at the top of this tree and keep an eye out in all directions. At the approach of danger, the eagle would warn the People of the Longhouse. The booklet on the whole had a highly elevated, quasi-mystical tone:

Should a calamity threaten the generations rising and living of the Five United Nations, then he who is able to climb to the top of the Tree, Tioneratasekowa, may do so. When he reaches the top of the Tree he shall look about in all directions and should he see evil things indeed are approaching, then he shall call to the people of the Five United Nations assembled beneath the Tree of the Great Peace and say: "A Calamity threatens your happiness."

Then shall the Chiefs convene in council and discuss the impending evil.

Gilbert the Mohawk steelworker certainly seemed fit enough to climb the Great Tree, although his blue eyes were not exactly primordially Iroquoian. In Montreal, when I asked Gilbert, who did the odd acting job, whether movie or television producers ever asked him to wear brown contact lenses to give him a more authentic Indian look, he seemed almost offended. "Why would I change my blue eyes?" he asked. "Everybody in the world wants blue eyes." Racial purity, at any rate, was hardly a tradition of the Iroquois, or of the French, for that matter. Given the sexual imbalance of the early French population of Quebec, and the fact that the French, unlike the English, had no taboo about marrying Indians – as long as they were Catholic, more or less – you could bet there were some Mohawks, even at the beginning of the eighteenth century in Kahnawake, who bore a striking resemblance to Norman peasants.

Gilbert's blue eyes came from some Scottish antecedents, as it happened. They didn't make him stand out in Kahnawake. "We learn here in Kahnawake how to live in two worlds," he said. "We know how to conduct business in the white man's world. We know how to be a little shady, too. We learned from the best – the French and the English." This was a reference to cigarette smuggling, a notorious source of revenue for quite a few Mohawks in Quebec and upstate

New York. It was also a reference, perhaps, to the early history of the reserve, when the Mohawks in New York suspected the residents of Kahnawake of spying for the French, and the French suspected them of spying for their Mohawk kin in New York. The colonial wars, and the diplomacy of pitting French against English, certainly sharpened wits in the longhouse.

Initially, the only common bond of the people of Kahnawake had been their Catholicism. That bond was gone. Now there was a split between Mohawks who adhered to the form of government recognized by Canadian authorities, the band council system, and those, like Gilbert, who hearkened back to the Great White Pine and the system where the only men who bore the title of chief were those who wore the deer antlers on their brow and whose families possessed the requisite strings of wampum. In this system, the traditional chiefs, not elected officials, were the ones who deliberated matters of grave importance to the Confederacy. ("The Chiefs of the Confederacy of the Five Nations shall be mentors of the people for all time. The thickness of their skin shall be seven spans which is to say that they shall be proof against anger, offensive action and criticism. Their hearts shall be full of peace and good will and their minds filled with a yearning for the welfare of the people of the Confederacy.")

Politics on the Rez. It could get murky. "Here we have three longhouses," Gilbert lamented. "The reason we have three is, I guess, because there's three different groups trying to take control. We're constantly being defeated and conquered. It's like from day one." He shrugged. "I think the only thing that keeps us together is that we have a lacrosse team. It's a great game. Being a former lacrosse player myself, I know we never talked politics. We just played the game."

The more active and politically engaged Kahnawake Mohawks, like Gilbert, tended to embrace the old ways in some form or other. Catholicism was not in fashion anywhere, and certainly not on this reserve. Yet Gilbert also casually remarked that "Kahnawake has always been Catholic – it's the way it started, as a Roman Catholic enclave – and it will always be that. I really don't expect it to change." The centuries-old dominance of the Catholic Church was symbolized by the St. Francis Xavier Mission just down the road from the main intersection in town, an imposing structure with a ceiling that, like the roof of the Sistine Chapel, was covered in biblical scenes. The sanctuary was baroque in its statuary and decor, and they hadn't spared the gilt. A larger-than-life-sized St. Ignatius of Loyola loomed high on the wall on one side of the altar, and a larger-than-life-sized St. Francis Xavier on the other. If lavish always impressed Indians, this was clearly meant to knock them dead.

But what drew me was the tomb of Kateri, off to the right of the altar. The marble tomb itself was a simple monument, with a wooden statue of Kateri above. Lit from the front, she cast a shadow on the wall, and that shadow gave her a somber depth, a suggestion of hidden life. Her face was perfectly oval and expressionless, the eyes looked slightly upwards. Her arms clutched a shawl, one hand holding a crucifix, the other a rosary. The impression was of a body held still, waiting for something. Be patient, the shrine whispered. Wait. The life you lead in the world is not your true life. Below the tomb were ceramic turtles and stuffed turtles – Kateri had been a member of the turtle clan – dried flowers, and photographs. The photographs were of people for whom devotees of Kateri were praying. There in a corner, for example, was a photograph of a man in his early twenties, wearing jeans and a white shirt and a sleeveless black sweater. He had long dark hair, broad shoulders, and his thumbs were tucked into his leather belt, as if to show he was ready for anything. He looked as if he could own the world.

Why was someone praying for this boy? Had there been a point, not long after the picture was taken, when his drinking had gotten out of hand, or someone had introduced him to crack? Had he fallen in with a bad crowd and attracted the attention of the police? Had he become infatuated with the wrong woman, who left him depressed and suicidal? Or had he been careful to stay out of trouble, but one day his friends noticed he was talking strangely, was gripped by paranoid fantasies, telling them voices on the radio were talking to him? Had he started to feel a numbness in his fingers and toes and gradually realized something was destroying his nervous system? Had he been driving late at night without a seatbelt on and met a vehicle coming the other way? Of all the numberless ways that life could destroy promise on this bitch of an earth, as Beckett would say, which one drove his heartsick parents or friends to place his photograph by the tomb of Kateri Tekakwitha?

I walked past the altar into an annex of the church where you could buy souvenirs of Kahnawake – including gold medals that had touched the bones of Kateri – and met the pastor, Father F. Louis Cyr, another Jesuit, in his office. It was now dark, and the only light in the room came from a lamp on the metal desk. The stone walls, the wooden beams of the ceiling, the wide planks on the floor – all of which hadn't changed in centuries – faded into shadow. Above Father Cyr, on a corner of the wall, was a plaster statue of a woman in cream-colored robes, her hands clasped in prayer, with three roses, yellow, red, and blue, under her collarbone. She was the Mystica Rosa, another title of the Blessed Virgin, wearing the roses that are symbols of paradise and also of martyrdom. The statue had also been in this room for a very long time. "It's not my place to take it down," Father Cyr said, although no one seemed to take much interest in it. Custom used to be that families would borrow the statue for home devotions. They would say the rosary under the eye of the Mystica Rosa. "That's the way devotions die out," Father Cyr remarked.

Death was one of the themes of our conversation – the death of the Jesuit Order, for example. "We're at the end of the line. There are hardly any Jesuit vocations any more," Cyr said, with perfect resignation it seemed. "Religious orders have come and gone in the history of the Church. We can at times outlive our usefulness." Then there was the death of the old-style Kahnawake mission, with the Jesuit priests running a tight ship and laying down the truth without hesitation. "We don't have the pretension to be the one true faith and the only door to heaven any more, all these things I grew up with in a Redemptorist parish. They have no hold any more."

With his short, heavy-set body, balding head, and goatee, Father Cyr bore a strong resemblance to the late Burl Ives. He rubbed his hands with nervous energy while he spoke softly, or moved them over the edge of the desktop as if it were a keyboard. Not for him the role of thundering Redemptorist preacher, reminding his hearers of the Four Last Things (Death, Judgement, Hell, and Heaven). Not for him even the role of his predecessor, who had been in the vanguard of Kahnawake political struggles, mobilizing his parishioners to recognize and fight for their rights. "They have done a lot of things for themselves," Cyr said of the people of Kahnawake, "and the only thing I can do is try to help persuade them that perhaps they can adopt the same tactics, the same energy, the same ambition, to their involvement with the Church. I just notice that they have been left out of the basic tenets of Vatican II. It has had its impact here, it's out there somehow, but it hasn't gone deeply inside, it hasn't penetrated the people here. Vatican II has given new directions for missions. We're in that dynamic, we're trying to work with it. So that's where I stand. I told them I was not coming here as a conductor, but that I was a good accompanist. That's something I like to do – not be the star up front or a soloist, but an accompanist who always puts someone else up front and supports them. That's the only thing I can see myself doing. It's what they want to do that I can accompany. I don't think it's up to us any more to do that sort of mental analysis of the situation and expedite and give them a direction where they should go. That would be presumptuous – although I have my own little ideas about that. But if I'm not asked I won't come forward. It's too easy to bring in a hidden agenda."

Cyr might have been particularly sensitive to the feeling of his parishioners because of his own background as an Acadian from the province of New Brunswick, a descendant of French settlers who had been overwhelmed by the English even before the fall of

Quebec in 1759. "The people here were absolutely devastated by the way they were looked down upon and preached to," Cyr said. "I witnessed some of that. I was confronted with that. The only thing that helped me here in retrospect was coming from a French minority in New Brunswick, because we were always told to shut up, too, and not defend ourselves. We at least had a language and faith that was closely protected in the home. Outside the home, we were not to protest. We were the defeated ones and that was it. But no one could tell us what to speak within the four walls of our homes, and nobody could tell us what faith to practice. I think that gave me a head start over the other missionaries here who were originally from Quebec, who would take a more look-downish attitude on the old savages. I reacted to that type of patronizing that was still extant here when I arrived, on the part of certain missionaries who didn't get it. That's all I can say. They did their best, but I could see the reaction of the people to that. They know who to respect and they know who they are respected by."

Nor did Cyr object if traditionalists among the Mohawks vehemently rejected the Church. "I don't think there's a negative in their turning their backs to the Church," he said, his hands moving over that invisible keyboard. The Mystica Rosa looked down on us with her infinitely gentle eyes. "I think they have to take that distance to discover what has been lost and what's still there and become aware of their own culture. I don't think the past is a burden. It all depends on how you look at it."

Four hundred years ago, Father Cyr's predecessors decided to live with the culture of the people they intended to convert but purge it of such obvious anti-Christian features as sorcery. Now, because that culture had become so obviously weakened and almost destroyed entirely, Father Cyr was not even concerned about the potential revival of scary stuff. "I'm not out to find things in traditional culture that are incompatible with Christian faith," he said. "That's why I haven't found any. That doesn't mean that there are none. That means that the only qualified persons to judge that would have to come from within their own culture. If they asked me, then I wouldn't refuse to say what I think – but these people have a unique way of knowing what you think, anyway. They're more observant, they have a more acute perception of who a person is than we do. That's probably ingrained in their culture. They have been dominated by our culture so long that they have been able to unmask our strategies from every conceivable angle. We can't do what we did before, insisting that they accept the faith and not ask questions. It's not a burden you carry, it's just a new step in the growth of the community."

That night I parked my car in a lot by the Mohawk Council office, got out, and walked around a bit. A cop car pulled up and the driver, a young Mohawk "Peace Keeper," asked what I was doing here. He examined my ID and asked me to open the trunk of my car. I did. It was completely empty. "Perfect," the Peace Keeper said. I suppose you have to have examined a lot of car trunks in Kahnawake to understand fully why an empty one constitutes perfection. He wished me a good night and we both drove off. I ended up at Old Malone's, a restaurant that advertised itself as "a leader in Kahnawake cuisine." This was probably true. I got a good meal at Old Malone's, and then stayed for a few beers.

The bar was crowded, but not raucous. The rows of liquor bottles underneath the mirror, with their tinted glass and eye-catching labels, reminded me of the lavish decoration and the colored lights of an old-fashioned Catholic church – like St. Francis Xavier. I like churches and bars. In both places you can sit and relax and think about your situation. Of course, in bars it's easier to meet people. I found myself in conversation with a patron standing next to me at the bar, a ruggedly built man in his forties, wearing a sports jacket. I told him about the Peace Keeper looking in my trunk, because in some ways that was the most interesting thing that had happened to me in Kahnawake. "What's your name?" he asked.

"Phil. What's yours?"

"Just call me Mohawk Man."

I gave him a look, and he told me his real name, Brian. I didn't mind Mohawk Man, though. "People see somebody walking around who doesn't belong here, they notice," Mohawk Man said. "Or somebody driving around at night. If you just come in and out, that's one thing, that's fine." He offered me a cigarette, which I reluctantly turned down. "But if you're hanging around, that's another thing completely. It's like Harlem. You're not going to hang around there, because you're not going to be comfortable. People know you don't belong. It's like, what are you doing in our neighborhood? Same here. We all know who lives in Kahnawake."

"Is that why the cop came along?"

Mohawk Man shrugged. "It's a small community. We know every car that belongs in Kahnawake. You drive around with a car people don't recognize, after a while, they're going to wonder. Some of the young guns here, they see you driving around, they'll try to beat you up. Hell, they won't try, they *will* beat you up."

"Are you serious?"

"Or they'll vandalize your car." He ordered another glass of Scotch. That last thing he said really bothered me. I wasn't afraid of getting beaten up, but I had rented a white Buick Regale for the weekend and, true to my usual practice, declined insurance for damage to the car. I could just see Budget Rent-A-Car demanding that I buy them a new Buick Regale after the boys of Kahnawake got through with the one I was driving. "As a matter of fact," Mohawk Man continued, "I think there's a bylaw. Anything happens after a certain time of night, and you don't live in Kahnawake, you can't hold anybody responsible for damage to your property."

"A bylaw?"

"Yeah, after sunset, I think. There's no liability."

"That sounds crazy." But I wondered if he was right. The Indians at Kahnawake were getting touchy, as Father Bruyère said. It was possible they were tired of strangers hanging out in their reserve and had declared open season on their persons and their automobiles after the sun went down. "What are you doing here?" Mohawk Man asked me, pointedly. I was working on a book about the French in North America, I told him. With a sidebar, as it were, on the Indians they encountered.

"You should write about the time we blocked the Pont Mercier," he said. Actually, I remembered that incident. In 1990, the village of Oka in Quebec tried to take over some disputed land near the Mohawk reserve of Kanesatake. The Kanesatake people claimed it was sacred ground. Oka said it was legally their property and just the real estate they needed to expand their nine-hole municipal golf course. The Mohawks in Kanesatake raised the barricades, and as a gesture of sympathy their fellow Mohawks in Kahnawake blocked the Pont Mercier, which thoroughly annoyed huge numbers of commuters. At one point, the Canadian army was brought in. Along the road by Lachine, on the exact spot where Parkman's "stupefied and speechless groups" once watched while their loved ones were tortured to death, Canadian armored personnel carriers lined up. Once again the Indians across the river were causing big trouble.

"Everybody here was united," Mohawk Man recalled. "Traditionalists, Protestants, Catholics. We were just Indians. No real leaders. Nobody had a plan, or a big picture. It wasn't like, this is what we got to do. We just did it. We were a collective. That was what, eleven years ago? People are thinking we should do something like that again. Kick some more ass." Mohawk Man raised the corner of his mouth, which I began to realize was a signal of oncoming irony. "A job-creation project."

"I take it, it's not that easy to get unity here," I said, remembering George Gilbert's remarks.

"Democracy. You know that word? The Americans got it from us. They say they invented it, but when they left Europe they were still in a monarchy situation. They came here, they saw the way we governed ourselves. Democracy. Everybody has a vote, everybody has a voice. That goes back thousands of years."

"But what about unity?"

"What about it? Yeah, we got the band council, we got traditionalists. We even got the pure traditionalists. There are people like that in every religion. Everything has to be done the way it was written down. So whatever the band council does, they're against it, they're against it, they're against it. They're hyper-critical. You ask them, what's your alternative, they have no idea. I tell them, look, what's the good of criticism if you can't suggest alternatives? They don't like that. I know after I leave the room they're saying, oh, he's one of *them*. He's not a real traditionalist. I come back into the room and suddenly everybody stops talking and starts whispering. Psssst, psssst, psssssst." He ordered another Scotch, and once more offered me a cigarette. Once again I turned him down reluctantly. How I used to love smoking in bars. "As if I care. The thing is, you have to adapt. What are you going to do? Burn witches? Are you going to burn 'em for playing with Tarot cards? Even the Catholic Church changes, and they go back a long way, too. How come you got your arms crossed?"

I did have my arms crossed. I think I felt a bit chilly with the air conditioning. "You got your arms crossed," Mohawk Man said. "That says you're self-protective. People see that, they'll pick a fight with you."

This time I didn't believe Mohawk Man. I've been in bars where you really could get into a brawl because of inappropriate body language, and this wasn't one of them. People were having a good time. No one was looking for trouble. Also, it wasn't as if I was nervous being a White Man. I looked as much like an Indian as anybody else. An onlooker who didn't know this was a bar in Kahnawake might have guessed it was an Irish hang-out in Queens. "Be natural, be cool. What's your name again?"

"Phil."

"Be yourself, Phil. Don't worry. I'm with you." He paused, and then that corner of his mouth lifted. "Not that that matters." Then he saw me cross my arms again. "There, you're doing it again. You don't want people to pick on you, you got to change your body language." Obediently, I uncrossed my arms. But now he seemed annoyed with me. "Were you talking with anybody before I came here?"

"No."

"That's right. You weren't. You were isolated. I gave you a lot of stuff for your book, I hope you appreciate that." He turned to talk with two middle-aged women on the other side of him. "Ricky here tonight?" he asked one of them. No, she said. It turned out she was Ricky's mother. They talked about Ricky for a while – he seemed to be a well-known person in the community. "Remember Ricky's red sneakers?" his mother asked.

"They were Converse, weren't they?"

"He loved his red sneakers." She turned to me with a delighted grin. Her son was clearly the light of her life. "He loved 'em so much he got married in them."

"Yeah, I remember. He likes those. Some of those shirts he wore, I had to put on sunglasses."

"Ricky is Ricky!"

"That is right. He's his own person. Totally outrageous."

I finished my beer and got up from the stool. "Where you going?" Mohawk Man asked.

"I'm calling it a night."

"Stick around. Why you leaving?"

"I'm worried about my car."

"Nothing's going to happen to your car."

"I'm tired, Brian. I'm calling it a night."

"Well, that's your decision," he said scornfully.

"Maybe I'll see you around."

"Probably won't remember you. I got a great memory. It just don't last that long."

FIVE

Fort Frontenac

La Salle and sexual harassment • *The Count of Frontenac* • *I see
a forbidden sight* • *A Roman Catholic conspiracy in New England* •
The man with the iron fist • *Tonty and Tonto*

In the spring of 1669, after hearing stories from Seneca visitors
about a river south of the Great Lakes that flowed westward, La
Salle made arrangements to change his life from lord of the manor
to explorer. The first thing he did was raise four thousand *livres*
capital by selling his seigneury. Exploring was an expensive business. You didn't go into the woods alone and you didn't go without
supplies, including goods to give away and to trade with. The
second thing he did was to travel to Quebec City and ask permission
from the governor, Remy de Courcelles, to do his exploring. The
fact that La Salle would be obliged to do such a thing seems strange,
no doubt, to those raised in the American myth of the frontier,
where Daniel Boone just ups and goes, asking leave of no man. But
this was New France, where the French love of bureaucracy had
already taken root. Even on the fringes of a vast wilderness, everything was regulated, everything was controlled, everything was
ultimately dependent on the will of the king, which was the will
of France.

Setting yourself up as a fur trader was a particularly tricky affair. As noted previously, Louis XIV and his minister Colbert, the bureaucrat *par excellence*, really did want to consolidate their colony, to settle it properly despite the long winters and the rocky soil. They didn't want colonists abandoning their farms to go off into the wilderness to seek their fortunes in the fur business. They turned fur trading into a government monopoly and limited the number of individuals who could participate in it.

Of course, a certain number of colonists defied this regulation and set up as freelance fur traders and *coureurs de bois*. (Franco-American novelist David Plante writes, "*Un coureur de bois* has no equivalent in English; it is purely French-Canadian. It means a man who lives in the forest, makes his living from the forest, and dies in the forest.") If these men couldn't sell their furs to somebody in Montreal, they would go to the Dutch and the English in Albany. It was better than the endless struggle to remove trees and clear off underbrush, to haul rocks out of the fields. So many colonists became lawless *coureurs de bois* in the seventeenth and eighteenth centuries that they now form the basis of a modern Québécois myth. According to this myth, the real French Canadian was not the docile farmer of nineteenth-century Quebec who was ruled by the Church and lorded over by *les anglais*. Rather the prototype of French Canada was that plucky, freedom-loving *coureur de bois*. According to a recent French-Canadian writer, the European French

> found us haughty and boastful . . . independent and undisciplined, unwilling to obey orders and disrespectful of authority. But they did see that we were indefatigable hunters, swift runners, conscientious explorers, and excellent at fighting *à l'indienne*. They also could not deny that we had a zest for life, which probably accounted for our being not too competent at farming – it is as if our spirit could not be confined to a small acreage. We played hard and for keeps, were generally good-looking and charming and pleasant to be with.

This is true. As evidence, I point to myself. It so happens that the description "good-looking and charming and pleasant to be with" fits me to a tee. I take no personal credit for this – it's all the result of the DNA passed on by my *très charmants* ancestors. I hope no other ethnic group is jealous. We all have our strong points and weak points. It's not as if the French Canadians have ever set the intellectual world on fire.

The myth of the *coureur de bois* doesn't extend in its current use to his entrepreneurial aspect. Quebec society remains far more statist and bureaucratic than the rest of Canada, itself a country far more accepting of government regulation than the United States. What the contemporary Québécois celebrators of the *coureur de bois* have in mind is more his ability to choose his own lifestyle and assert his sexuality. (Sex has replaced religion as the current obsession of once Catholic Quebec.) They certainly have historical grounds for doing so. Premarital sex presented no moral difficulty to the Indians, who sometimes considered the offer of a bedmate a natural part of hospitality. The *coureurs de bois* usually took advantage of such offers, with a sexual appetite and stamina the Indians found quite remarkable.

La Salle himself never approved of this and, as we have seen, often left an Indian village expeditiously with his men rather than have them "tamper with" the women of the place. He himself seems to have been a man of unfailing chastity. Only one man who knew him accused La Salle of sexual immorality. In his memoirs, a young engineer named Jean-Baptiste Minet, who had sailed with La Salle to Texas and then returned with Beaujeu after finding La Salle insufferable, claimed that La Salle picked out handsome young men as his servants and then forced them to sleep with him. As far as I know, no one else who knew La Salle ever claimed he was gay. Clearly, though, Minet had heard stories. My own suspicion is that these stories were like Beaujeu's tale of La Salle's cowardice in a duel, the kind of delicious – and baseless – rumors that people enjoy spreading about a superior who is arrogant and irresponsible. It is not unthinkable, however, that La Salle was what we now term a closet case, and that the tale-bearers in Texas nosed out something covert in La Salle's makeup. Part of La Salle's problems with depression and paranoia might have stemmed from his recognition that he harbored an inner enemy, a set of impulses he could not accept. Part of his harshness toward, and aloofness from, his men might have been a spillover of his own harshness toward, and unrelenting struggle against, himself.

Certainly he lived almost exclusively among men from his boyhood days with the Jesuits. In New France, where men outnumbered women ten to one, the absence of the tender passions in La Salle would not have been remarked upon. In this respect, he is no different from Samuel Champlain, the founder of Quebec, who also spent his life among men and, when he did marry, spent virtually no time with his bride. Champlain, too, is now suspected of being homosexual – a suspicion that, despite our modern-day sophistication, carries a certain sting, a little schoolboy snigger, because he's been regarded for so long not only as the great hero of French Canada but its patron saint. Revisionist historians love it.

In La Salle's case, an awareness of homosexual drives on his part might have contributed to the restless urges that the Jesuit Delanglez noted, the perpetual feeling of wanting to be somewhere other than where he was. It might, in a curious way, account for his fascination with, and ease among, Indians. Not that Indians were necessarily gay-friendly, but their exotic habits, their sheer otherness, might have relieved some of the psychic pressure on La Salle. All we know is that he had trouble living with his fellow Europeans, and trouble living with himself, but found life with Indians quite tolerable. Such a situation was not unprecedented. "It is easier to make an Indian out of a Frenchman than a Frenchman out of an Indian," the Jesuits had long observed, with a collective sigh. In North American history many white people, not just Frenchmen, found it very easy to adjust to Indian ways and become so much a part of Indian life that they hated the thought of returning to white society. The reverse was never true. No Indian ever enjoyed going white.

For the next three or four years after La Salle met with De Courcelles in Quebec City, he was off in the woods, exploring and fur trading. What exactly he did, and where he went, we have very little idea. It is likely that he did reach the Ohio, in the company of Nika, a captive Shawnee he had obtained from the Iroquois in 1669, but how far down that river he traveled is unknown. He may have spent most of his time among the Iroquois, fur trading. Then, in 1672, an event occurred that brought La Salle out from the shadows and made him a figure of lasting historical importance. A bankrupt, weathered old reprobate, the fifty-two-year-old Comte de Frontenac, veteran of the battlefields of Europe and countless boudoir intrigues, replaced De Courcelles as governor of New France.

One look at La Salle told Frontenac this man was someone he could work with. They were kindred spirits – men of action who suffered the same fate. The greater their exploits and the greater their renown, the deeper they sank into debt. Frontenac came to feel a great affection for the younger man, an emotion rare for Frontenac to experience and rare for La Salle to receive. For this and other reasons they found themselves similarly inclined to take huge risks in order to extend the reach of New France. As part of that effort, Frontenac gave La Salle the job of summoning the Iroquois to a great conference at Cataraqui, near the present city of Kingston at the eastern end of Lake Ontario. La Salle performed it admirably, and in July Frontenac led an expedition of about four hundred men down the rapids of the St. Lawrence, in 120 canoes and two large flatboats "painted in red and blue," writes Parkman, "with strange devices, intended to dazzle the Iroquois by a display of unwonted splendour." Dragging the flatboats along the shore of the rapids west of Lachine proved to be a particularly back-breaking task. Frontenac, who had been a good commander in the service of his king, did not hesitate to plunge into the water and lend his men a hand. Like La Salle, he was inclined to quarrel with his peers and colleagues and claim his prerogatives with a fierce jealousy, but unlike La Salle he got on famously with his social inferiors. He knew how to win their devotion by sharing their hardships and looking after their comfort. On this trip, he even organized games in the evening to take the minds of his men off the mosquitos.

Frontenac proved La Salle's equal, as well, in communicating with the Indians. His genius, as La Salle biographer Anka Muhlstein notes, was adapting the grand style of Versailles to the woods and to Indian life. He made a splendid entrance at Cataraqui, with the canoes and boats in formation, a band playing, banners waving. Frontenac's speech the next day, held in a tent flanked with his splendidly uniformed and drilled soldiery, was also in the grand style. "You have done well, my children, to obey the command of your Father," Parkman reports Frontenac telling the Iroquois. "Take courage: you will hear his word, which is full of peace and tenderness. For do not think that I have come for war. My mind is full of peace, and she walks by my side."

The speech seemed to go over well. Frontenac had the kind of brazen personality to pull something like this off. It didn't matter that the speech was mostly bullshit. No one loved bullshit more than Indians.

The day after Frontenac's opening speech, the French soldiers began to construct a fort according to a plan that Frontenac's engineer had outlined. "Some cut down trees, some dug the trenches, some hewed the palisades; and with such order and alacrity was the work urged on that the Indians were lost in astonishment," Parkman writes. It took them a week to finish the fort, which was the point of this whole exercise; Frontenac wanted the Iroquois not only to make peace with the Indian allies of the French and to become Roman Catholics, but to bring their furs to his new fort in this strategic location where Lake Ontario flowed into the St. Lawrence River. In this way the outpost would stop the flow of furs south to Albany and augment the revenues and influence of New

France. It would also make a lot of money for whoever controlled the fort.

With this consideration in mind, La Salle sailed to France in 1674, with Frontenac's support, to ask the king for a grant of land that included the post, now called Fort Frontenac. The request was granted, and La Salle returned in the spring of the following year with enough money loaned him by relatives to repay Frontenac's own expenses incurred in the building of the fort and to fulfill his promises to the king; that is, to rebuild Fort Frontenac in stone, to construct a church, and to maintain a garrison. All this he did, as well as — we can assume — share some of the profits of the fur trade with the governor.

⚜

In 1758, nearly one hundred years later, a force of British regulars, American colonials, and a handful of Iroquois, totalling over three thousand, descended on Fort Frontenac and set up a battery on a rising slope to the north. The Comte de Frontenac had not chosen the site for his fort very well. It was on low ground, exposed not only to attack from water but, as it proved, equally devastating attack from land. The French commander promptly surrendered and the British demolished the building. For over two centuries no trace of that fort stood. It existed only in memory. Then in 1983 an archeological team started digging. It uncovered the outlines of the old stone walls and found the inevitable ax heads and glass beads that the French traded to the Indians for furs. Like the trail of breadcrumbs through the forest, a trail of glass beads — mass-produced in places like Venice — mark the presence of the French all over North America, from Lachine to Kingston to Fort St. Louis in Texas.

When they finished digging, the team reconstructed a corner of the old wall of the fort, which stands now in a sad little island of grass surrounded by traffic in downtown Kingston. Across the street is a portion of the Royal Military College of the Canadian Armed

Forces where, it turns out, a remnant of the old wall, dug up in 1952 by a general of the Canadian army, also stands in a courtyard. I went through a gateway with a sign that read *Unauthorized Entry Prohibited / Acces Interdit Sans Autorisation* and stuck my head in the commissionaire's office to ask about the bit of La Salle's wall they owned. "Yes, it's there but it's not open to the public," said the commissionaire firmly. "I'm talking about part of the old fort," I said, meaning, I'm talking about part of the heritage of every taxpaying Canadian citizen. "Oh yeah. It's there."

"But I can't go see it?"

"Well, you can go look around the corner. Don't go beyond the area."

I peeped around the corner and spotted a bit of stone wall. It looked authentic to me. I turned and walked past the commissionaire's office, making sure he noted my exit, to set his mind at rest that I hadn't sneaked into some other part of the National Defence College, and that was it. I had viewed the only visible remains left by the French on a piece of real estate that was once the key to their empire.

"What we're actually trying to do is make sure that that aspect of the settlement of this area is not ignored," Sue Bazely, executive director of the Cataraqui Archaeological Research Foundation, told me that same day. Bazely, who had been digging around Kingston for about eighteen years, took a proprietary attitude toward her dead and buried Fort Frontenac, like an academic trying to revive the literary reputation of an unjustly neglected poet. Her work showed that the French spent a lot of time and effort keeping the fort battle-ready. They must have considered it important. "Sometimes you see it in the records referred to as a trading post, sort of another stop along the way, but I think, given what the French tried to do, constantly upgrading it and preparing for hostilities and war, I think it really did play more of a key role than some would like to suggest," Bazely maintained. Like to suggest? Out of a desire to minimize the French origins of this famously anglophile Canadian city?

"It is tricky because other than the reconstituted wall and a few place names around here, there's nothing to point to the French aspect of Kingston," Bazely said. "We have a high school named La Salle, we have a causeway named La Salle, there's all sorts of references just in place names, but there's no context for it. It's easy for everyone to ignore it. You see the buildings here, you see the fortifications like Fort Henry that are still in existence from the British period and everybody associates Kingston with that." Virtually every tourist brochure has a picture of a soldier from the Fort Henry Guard, with his rifle and his bayonet and his shako and an extremely alert look on his face, like an impatient motorist waiting for the light to change. That's what Kingston history means to tourists – redcoats.

I dropped by the Le Centre culturel Frontenac de Kingston to ask what happened to the old French families in Kingston. The director, Francis Beaulieu, a diminutive man with a scholarly air and an easy manner who gave every promise of being, like his forebears, charming and pleasant to be with, confirmed that the center's clientele were almost entirely French-speaking members of the Canadian military – the Royal Military College in Kingston is Canada's equivalent to West Point – and the faculty and students of the French Studies Department at Queen's University in Kingston. Beaulieu hoped to link these people with what he called "French-friendly" Kingstonians; that is, English-speaking residents who try to keep up their French.

I liked that phrase "French friendly." Beaulieu laughed. He had a distinctive barking laugh that, in an English Canadian or an American, would have sounded cretinous. In this native son of French Quebec, however, the laugh had an amiable, uninhibited quality, as if an outgrowth of that famous French vivacity so foreign to inhabitants of the British Isles. "It's kind of one of mine," he said of the phrase. "In French we say 'francophile.' I was trying to find a translation for that and I didn't find one, so I thought of 'French friendly.' The first time we used it with English people, they said, 'Oh, French friendly, I like that,' arrh, arrh, arrh. So we decided to use it."

Of course the phrase suggests its opposite – francophobe, or French unfriendly. Such people do exist. The history of Canada, in fact, is one long spat between English speakers and French speakers. In the 1960s, the federal government, under then prime minister Pierre Trudeau, tried to bridge the divide with a certain measure of enforced bilingualism, which included the requirement that every product in the supermarket had to be labeled both in French and English. This did nothing to satisfy the French-speaking Québécois who wanted a "sovereign" Quebec, and it proved to be a surprisingly permanent source of irritation to English-speaking Canadians. It was as if every morning over the breakfast table they were being nagged at to remember that fat-free Puffed Wheat was also known as *Blé soufflé sans gras*.

The situation of the French in the United States is, of course, very different. Like the descendants of Swedes and Lithuanians, we Franco-Americans are as innocuous as they come. There was a time, however, at the height of the great nineteenth-century migration of French Canadians to the textile mills of New England, when we stirred apprehension in the breasts of our rulers. In cities like Woonsocket, Rhode Island; Lowell, Massachusetts; and Manchester, New Hampshire, our ancestors formed "Little Canadas," ghettos in the classic sense of the term, clustered around the spires of the magnificent cathedrals they built in the midst of their slum tenements. Here they clung tenaciously to their language and religion, bolstered by their own schools, religious societies, fraternal associations, and French-language newspapers. Here they resisted assimilation well into the twentieth century, while other ethnic groups eagerly merged into mainstream America. Unlike Polish, Irish, or Jewish immigrants, they easily went back and forth between their adopted country and the Old Country – which in their case was just across the border. (That border remained remarkably porous throughout the nineteenth century.) They seemed profoundly un-American.

"The French Canadians do not give promise of incorporating themselves with our body politic," warned a *New York Times* editorial in 1889. "Comparatively few of them become citizens at all, and those who do rate their citizenship so low and understand its duties so little that the power of voting renders them much less acceptable members of the community than they would be without it." The editorial ended by proclaiming that it was "a patriotic duty for all Americans, in which the French-Canadian population is considerable, to insist upon maintaining American political principals against all assaults." Three years later, the same newspaper explored the subject at greater depth. "No other people, except the Indians, are so persistent in repeating themselves," its editorial stated.

> Where they halt they stay, and where they stay, they multiply and cover the earth. Dr. Egbert C. Smyth, in a paper just published by the American Antiquarian Society, has been at great pains to trace intelligently the extent of this immigration, and in his opinion the migration of these people is part of a priestly scheme now fervently fostered in Canada for the purpose of bringing New-England under the control of the Roman Catholic faith. He points out that this is the avowed purpose of the secret society to which every adult French-Canadian belongs, and that the prayers and the earnest efforts of these people are to turn the tables in New-England by the aid of the silent forces which they control.

Dr. Egbert C. Smyth, it is plain to see, was not French-friendly. He had a lot of company in that respect from his fellow Anglo-Saxons in the United States. Their fears, moreover, were not entirely irrational. Powerful Church leaders in late nineteenth-century Quebec openly dreamed of an independent French state in North

America, combining Quebec and New England – a state heavily influenced, if not actually run, by the Catholic Church. French Canadians, on both sides of the border, seemed good material for such a state. "The French Canadians . . . were one of the first immigrant people in the United States to challenge the myth of the Melting Pot," writes novelist Clark Blaise in *I Had a Father*, his memoir of his French-Canadian father, and the book in which I found these editorials. "They were the first whites to come to the United States with Third World values." Language, the old religion, tribal affiliations – they did not want to abandon these "values." They had already survived three centuries in their stony redoubt of Quebec, surrounded by enemies, clinging to such things. But this tenacity made them, to the editorial writers of the *New York Times*, seem like a medieval horde, barely white. Blaise once mentioned, in conversation with me, that Americans in the nineteenth century routinely referred to the "French-Canadian race" in the same way they mentioned the "Irish race" and the "Italian race." You know a group has become acceptable, Blaise remarked, when they've changed from being a race to an ethnic group. Eventually, the French Canadians of New England made this transition. It was remarkably slow in coming, however. As late as 1946, the noted author John Gunther, in his book *Inside U.S.A.*, referred to the French Canadians as "the most parochial and unassimilable of all racial groups."

That night I made my last stop in Kingston before leaving the city. I went on a "Ghosts of the Fort" tour at Fort Henry, led by a young woman dressed in a black cape, carrying a lantern. It was pure tourist fare, nothing to do with La Salle or the French or history in any real sense. Ghost tours are now a ritual of contemporary tourism, a value-added attraction for any place that's old and moldy. It was a pleasant summer night, with the lights of Kingston across the water. The British, when they constructed this fort in the 1830s, learned from the example of Fort Frontenac and placed it on high ground. Sufficiently gruesome fatalities had occurred in the years since its founding to provide material for some good ghost stories. The tour leader tried to communicate a frisson among her listeners while sticking strictly to the facts about who saw what dead man walking in the barracks. If she had been talking about charming medieval legends about saints' miracles, her tone would have been patronizing – everybody knows those are childish fabrications. About ghosts, however, she was serious. It is as if people can accept the supernatural today – but only if it is melancholy. A joyful supernaturalism is impossible to maintain, but a supernaturalism tinged with horror is all too easy to believe in.

✤

When the Iroquois gathered up their gifts and set out on their canoes back home that summer, nothing had really changed. They might patronize the new fort, but that was it. They would suffer no lessening of their status as an independent people and a military power in eastern North America. Not in the immediate future, and not for another century. They would continue to maneuver as adroitly as possible between rival European armies, fighting when necessary to maintain their fur-trading lifeline to the west. Their downfall came with the Treaty of Paris in 1783, which put an end to the American Revolution by granting independence to the thirteen colonies and thereby dooming not only the Iroquois but every Indian nation east of the Mississippi. Those nations had historically depended on European allies – first the French, and then the British – to maintain a balance of power on the continent. Now they had no one to protect them against the land-hungry Americans.

✤

For two years La Salle was sitting pretty at Fort Frontenac, buying furs from the Indians. This is why he had ostensibly come to Canada from France, to repair his fortunes. It hardly mattered that he and his partner Frontenac had outraged almost every other merchant in the colony in the process. These merchants hated La Salle's monopoly at Fort Frontenac, of course, but there was something else that embittered them — partly the personalities of La Salle and Frontenac, two men who could be imperious and abrasive, and who shared a talent for making enemies, but something else as well, the very atmosphere of New France. For some reason, small communities that feel under siege often turn out to be hotbeds of internal jealousies and petty hatreds — it's as if the tensions of being small and vulnerable and surrounded by enemies easily turn inwards. Whatever the reason, New France in the seventeenth century was divided by insane rivalries — merchant against merchant, Jesuit against Sulpician, royal official against church official, La Salle and Frontenac against everybody else.

This situation obtained even before the merchants realized that La Salle was hatching bigger plans. "As time went on," Parkman writes, "their bitterness grew more bitter; and when at last it was seen that, not satisfied with the monopoly of Fort Frontenac, La Salle aimed at control of the valleys of the Ohio and the Mississippi, and the usufruct of half a continent, the ire of his opponents redoubled, and Canada became for him a nest of hornets, buzzing in wrath, and watching the moment to sting." When the Jesuits realized La Salle's ambition, they were equally upset. As Parkman explains, the Jesuits were losing influence every day that New France became less a mission among the savages and more a colony with its own economic and social concerns. "Temporal interests and the civil power were constantly gaining ground; and the disciples of Loyola felt that relatively, if not absolutely, they were losing it," he writes. "They struggled vigorously to maintain the ascendency of their Order, or, as they would have expressed it, the ascendency of religion; but in the older and more settled parts of the colony it was clear that the day of their undivided rule was past. Therefore, they looked with redoubled solicitude to their missions in the West."

The strength of those missions depended on keeping other Frenchmen away from them. "They dreaded fur traders, partly because they interfered with their teachings and perverted their converts, and partly for other reasons," Parkman says of the Jesuits.

> But La Salle was a fur-trader, and far worse than a fur trader: he aimed at occupation, fortification, and settlement. The scope and vigour of his enterprises, and the powerful influence that aided them, made him a stumbling block in their path. He was their most dangerous rival for the control of the West, and from first to last they set themselves against him.

La Salle believed that the Jesuits, who had now established themselves as missionaries among the Iroquois south of Lake Ontario, deliberately spread rumors among these Indians that he and Frontenac were preparing war against them. Of course, to enemies of the Jesuit order, no craft or guile was beyond the "disciples of Loyola," and it is probably true that the missionaries among the Iroquois went out of their way to discourage their flock from having anything to do with that miserable fort. Whether they really were plotting to start a war between Frontenac and the Iroquois is another matter. In any case, Frontenac and La Salle, between them, managed to soothe apprehensions among the Iroquois. From then on, however, whenever La Salle met any form of hostility or non-cooperation from the Iroquois, he blamed it on the machinations of the Jesuits.

In the meantime, the vision of the magnificent country to the south and west of the Great Lakes, the portion of the earth's surface that would, in the fullness of time, become the rich, fertile, productive, potent heart of a nation richer and more fertile and more productive and more potent than anything ever dreamed of in the history of humanity, would not let La Salle rest. He might have had a glimmer of what this land meant; it couldn't have been simply the prospect of more furs, poorer in quality than the ones north of the Great Lakes, or even the prospect of a cold-weather port for New France, the St. Lawrence being shut down six months of the year, that agitated La Salle's brain. He must have sensed the real dimensions of the prize.

In the autumn of 1677 he sailed for France, once again with the backing of Frontenac. There he compared the dense forests and rocky soil and harsh winters of Quebec with the paradise in the south and west he was prepared to claim for Louis XIV – the meadows and rivers, the abundant game, the fertile soil, the potential for any kind of animal husbandry or crop that would support a large population and suit the needs of France. In addition, he promised not to interfere with the existing trade carried on between the Indians of the upper Great Lakes and New France. What seems to have caught the king's eye in all this, however, was not the realm of abundance that La Salle evoked, but the route to Mexico he would open up. Even then, it seems, the king was mostly interested in doing something about the highly annoying Spaniards. In response to La Salle's petition, therefore, the king graciously permitted La Salle to do all the exploring in this region he wanted, and to build forts along the way – "at your own cost and that of your associates," the king added, "to whom we have granted the sole right of trade in buffalo-hides." (This is the reason that La Salle would insist on loading up his horses with buffalo hides in Texas.)

Armed with this favor, La Salle proceeded to raise money for his explorations. This is a part of the story that always makes me feel tired, like reading about the blisters on the feet of La Salle's men. You could almost write a secret history of the human race on this theme. Marxists believe that the secret history of humanity is class antagonism, and Freudians believe that the secret history of humanity is repressed sex drives, and conspiracy theorists believe that the secret history of humanity is the activity of the Freemasons and the Illuminati, but the real secret history of humanity, accounting for everything from Columbus's voyages to the first production of *Hamlet*, is the history of fundraising. Poor La Salle had to do it. He approached his wealthy acquaintances and he approached his family – a cousin named François Plet, a merchant, kindly lent him eleven thousand *livres* at 40 per cent interest – and he mortgaged his seigneury at Fort Frontenac to the hilt. It was enough to take advantage of the king's gracious consent. It cost him, though, and not just in interest charges. I still think La Salle's famous ill temper was due in great part to the pressure he felt from his creditors. For a conscientious man, to be in debt is to be in a kind of prison, and La Salle, more than most, could not stand to be imprisoned.

Amidst all this, something very good did happen to La Salle while in France. He engaged the services of a man named Henri de Tonty, an Italian soldier. His father was a financier, famous chiefly for his invention of that notorious form of life insurance the tontine. Tonty senior was none too scrupulous, but his son was a wonder. One of his hands had been blown off by a grenade in battle, and he wore an iron hand covered by a glove. Parkman says he "used it to good purpose when the Indians became disorderly" by knocking out their teeth with it, which enormously impressed them. More importantly, he was utterly courageous and resourceful and faithful to La Salle. La Salle often entrusted him with difficult missions – he was the kind of man La Salle could leave in command of a fort or a group of men during his absence, and expect on his return to find his orders carried out.

Nika, too, never let him down. I know the relationship between La Salle and Nika is politically suspect these days – it savors too much of the Lone Ranger and Tonto – but I still find it sweet to read about those two men in the wilderness, teaching each other their respective languages, showing easy affection toward one another, Nika watching La Salle closely to make sure no hurt came to him, even in the streets of Paris. This shows at least that La Salle was not always a bear to the people under him. We forget the sort of people La Salle had to deal with in his expeditions – timid tradesmen overwhelmed by the wilderness, a few hardbitten types who couldn't be trusted out of eyesight, a bunch of louts and boors whose main purpose in life was to get drunk, as well as ordinary men who did not want to be heroes. Somebody like Champlain, who had a marvelous personality, could get these people to do his bidding without becoming hated in return, but La Salle, the man his Jesuit superiors had once called "Inquietus," possessed no such gifts. On the other hand, with somebody like Nika he could relax and be a human being.

In the early autumn of 1678 La Salle returned to Quebec, but various complications – more fundraising, this time among a few of his old enemies, the merchants of Quebec, who were prepared to set aside their enmity in return for an opportunity to get in on the ground floor, and a lingering fever – delayed his immediate departure for the west. In the meantime, he sent fifteen men ahead of him to trade among the Indians of Lake Michigan. La Salle had promised the king he wouldn't poach on this territory reserved for the fur traders of Montreal, but the prospect of some quick profits and front-end cash for his enterprise was too tempting to resist. At the same time he sent one of his lieutenants, a man named La Motte de Lussière, ahead of him with an advance party to build a fort at Niagara and a ship they could launch, above Niagara Falls, to sail Lake Erie and the upper Great Lakes.

SIX

The Carrying Place

A scientific experiment on two priests • Why you should believe yourself undeserving of any kind of good • What lies beneath the lawns of Baby Point • Terror by night • The lesson of two license plate mottos

La Motte and his crew of sixteen men, plus a Recollet friar named Father Louis Hennepin – famous in history for writing the first eyewitness account of Niagara Falls – set sail in a small vessel from Fort Frontenac in mid-November. The weather was rough. "They hugged the northern shore," writes Parkman, "to escape the fury of the wind, which blew savagely from the north-east; while the long, grey sweep of naked forests on their right betokened that winter was fast closing in." Their little ship found a harbor in the mouth of the Humber River, which empties into Lake Ontario where the city of Toronto now stands. That river was part of the Carrying Place, a passage between Lake Ontario and the upper Great Lakes used frequently by traders and explorers. La Salle himself used it to rejoin his men in the summer of 1680 after one of his return trips to Fort Frontenac for supplies.

Some thirty years previously, the Iroquois, at war with the Hurons over the fur trade, traveled this route to attack the main Huron settlements in southern Ontario. It was a memorable campaign. The French lost an ally – the Huron nation was destroyed – but gained a number of martyrs, including the Jesuit priests Jean de Brébeuf and Gabriel Lalemant.

The Iroquois made a point of finding out what these two black robes, members of that strange company of white men who didn't bear arms or display interest in women, were made of. They conducted the experiment with true scientific dedication. Centuries of practice had made them adept at inflicting the maximum amount of pain with minimum damage to the body, so that the victim would survive, in torment, as long as possible. With Brébeuf and Lalemant, for example, they began by ripping off the priests' fingernails. Then they cut off fingertips and tore out slices of flesh from the arms and legs, in the knowledge that the extremities of the body will take a good deal of abuse. You can spend a long time driving a human being mad with pain before getting above the elbow or the knee. The Iroquois also knew how to avoid cutting the major arteries and veins, and in fact their preferred method of torment – fire – cauterized veins and thus prevented a disappointingly early death from blood loss. When the Iroquois put red-hot coals against the stubs of the priests' fingers, for example, or performed a mock baptism by pouring boiling water over their scalped heads, they were actually helping to prolong their lives. Lalemant lived for twenty-four hours, after enduring, among other things, the wearing of a necklace of red-hot hatchets, and the gouging out of his eyes and placing of burning coals in the sockets. Somebody had to split his head open with a hatchet before he finally died.

All in all, it was a very interesting experiment, and like most scientific ventures it expanded the horizons of knowledge for the practitioners. The Iroquois learned that these gentle souls could endure torments better than the toughest warriors. That made an impression.

⚜

Three centuries later, on a sunny Sunday afternoon when I came to retrace the steps of La Salle up this river, a flotilla of sailboats and other pleasure craft stretched across the lake. In-line skaters and cyclists rolled along a bicycle path by the water. They had an air of taking their recreation seriously, with their streamlined helmets shaped like a wasp's abdomen, their Lycra shorts, their skin-tight jerseys of lime green and cherry red and other shades out of the gumball machine.

The sight reminded me of what Tom Wolfe in 1968 called the "happiness explosion," which overtook our culture in that decade. As part of the initial wave of baby boomers, I could remember the last years before the explosion, when the influence of a spiritual paratrooper such as Jean-Pierre Médaille still lingered in Catholic education. Father Médaille was a Jesuit who, in 1648, founded a religious order for women called the Congregation of the Sisters of St. Joseph (known in Catholic circles as "The Joes"). Father Médaille also wrote a book entitled *Maxims of Perfection for Souls Who Aspire to Great Virtue*, which became part of the constitution of the order. It's quite a document. There are no severe mortifications of the flesh recommended by it, but the spirit of the *Maxims* is certainly the spirit of seventeenth-century French Catholicism. The basic theme is that everything you're doing is wrong unless it has been prompted by supernatural grace, and you can never know for sure about that. God's probably given you a lot of grace, which you've frittered away. If you want some spiritual assurance, ask yourself this question: Am I suffering? If the answer to that question is yes, then maybe you're on the right track.

"Believe yourself undeserving of any kind of good and deserving of all kinds of evil," Médaille tells us, right at the start. The modern reader is shocked. Haven't we been told by Oprah Winfrey, by our therapists, by self-help gurus and motivational speakers of all descriptions that we "deserve" everything we want – money, sexual fulfillment, a rewarding job, respect from our parents? Father Médaille, from his ghostly vantage point, takes a deep breath, exhales, and shakes his head. No, he says. God wants you to ask for everything, for the deepest desire of your heart (which He will grant), but you deserve nothing. Begin by realizing that you're a mess, and it's not all your parents' fault. Cleaning up the mess is not going to be comfortable. "Grant that I may endure in my head pain proportionate to the unworthiness of my thoughts and unbridled imaginings," Father Médaille advises the penitent to pray to Christ. "It was to expiate these that your head was pierced with thorns."

In Freudian terms, this is the Superego talking. But then what do we North Americans living in the Age of Self-Indulgence know about such things as penitence? When Médaille speaks of "perfection," he means *perfection*, as in Christ's command: "Be ye perfect, even as your father in heaven is perfect." Perfection doesn't come cheap. To complain about the moral rigor of Médaille's maxims ("Detach yourself from all earthly affections. Empty your heart of them so completely that no created thing can hold it back") is like complaining about the training you have to undergo if you seriously want to win the Iron Man Triathlon. If that's your goal, you'd better be prepared to give it your all. "Do not paddle unless you are inclined to continue paddling." And don't mope, either. (That rigorous nun, St. Thérèse of Lisieux, called herself the happiest of mortals.)

The members of the Congregation of the Sisters of St. Joseph, who wore medieval clothes revealing the flesh only of their hands, wrists, and faces, and who taught me my religion, were imbued with the spirit of these *Maxims*. They have become legendary for their toughness and their strictness, this vanished breed of nun. That strictness was certainly part of the legacy of Father Médaille, who, although he urged the Sisters to be "gentle and kind," and "humble and patient," never let up the spiritual pressure on The Joes. And, yes, there were more than a few of them who were mentally ill. But we may recall that strictness was once widely considered, not just by nuns or Catholics, to be the proper mode of raising children in a hard world. For these nuns, not to be strict in the classroom was like an airport traffic controller not being strict in his directions to pilots. Laxity ensured disaster. (Mrs. Berry, the one laywoman in my Catholic high school, did not know how to be strict, and her classes were a shambles.) This was the test of the profession. My mother, who taught in a one-room schoolhouse in a New Hampshire mill town in the 1930s, can corroborate this. "Discipline was my forte," she states matter-of-factly, remembering the days when she stood up in front of children of various ages who often came from homes where there was not enough coal in the winter and not enough food on the table at any time, and who were in no mood to sit still in a classroom and learn their multiplication tables. Now in her nineties, my mother speaks with deep conviction. "Because without discipline you can't . . . teach . . . *anything*."

So my mother was strict, too. But the nuns – the nuns were in another league of strictness. "You know, the nuns wouldn't put up with anything," my mother recalls. "Families had children who were incorrigible, they sent them to the nuns, and the nuns would take care of them." Nobody at my high school was "incorrigible," as far as I can recall, and nobody needed to be "taken care of" in that way. But it was a tight ship, nonetheless.

We did not understand that it represented a dying world, a world of relative scarcity and rectitude. In that sense, we were part of the last generation that had some link, however faint, with the world of La Salle. It was a world where people saved "tin foil" for re-use, and darned socks, and joked, in their moments of financial worry, about "going to the poor house," the way people whistle past graveyards. It was a world where misbehavior had harsh consequences – homes for unwed mothers, destroyed reputations. It was a world where vigilance was called for, in the face of "the international Communist conspiracy" and other threats to the moral fiber of the country. "In fifteen years, nuns and priests will be hanging from lamp-posts," one nun informed us, on good authority. It did not seem ridiculous in 1960. Fifteen years previously, the same thing, in effect, had been happening all over Europe. (That nun would probably have been far more horrified by a vision of what actually did take place fifteen years later – fellow nuns and priests marching in anti-war demonstrations.)

So strictness was not uncalled for. Children must be made to pay attention. It was important. Once a dog barked outside the window of a classroom in which the Sister Superior, Mother Pelagia, a.k.a. "The Plague," was instructing her charges. Mother Pelagia, who told us she could gauge the state of a classroom from outside the building by seeing whether the window shades were aligned, solemnly informed the class that the dog was the Evil One, barking in an effort to distract them. Surprisingly, no such dog barked the day Sister Mary Elizabeth informed our religion class that "impure thoughts" were a mortal sin. Sister Mary Elizabeth was not cranky or ill-humored, but she was firm. She stated this firmly. And nobody said a word, but the jaws dropped on some of the boys. "You didn't know this?" she said. One or two of the boys – I may have been one of them – gave her a say-it-ain't-so look. "Well, now you know it," she said, in a tone that suggested further discussion of the topic was unnecessary.

This meant that if you wilfully entertained a sexual fantasy and were suddenly run over by a truck and killed, you would go to hell. It meant you could no longer do such a thing without pitting yourself deliberately against God and His Church. It sounds absurd, and yet, as with everything pronounced by the Church, there was a logic behind it. The appetite for sexual fantasy grows with the feeding. The only way to limit the appetite is to refuse to indulge it from the outset. Just say no. In order to impress this truth upon the faithful, the Church laid its heaviest sanctions against the practice. Such a practice could literally, the Church taught, kill the soul.

⚜

La Salle – who did not know that through his own sufferings, fortitude, and energy, penetrating the savage North American woodlands on behalf of Europe, he was helping, ultimately, to bring about a world of Lycra shorts and psychotherapy – would have come upon a Seneca village known as Teiaiagon a mile up the river. It is now a neighborhood called Baby Point, after an early nineteenth-century, French-speaking settler, Jacques Baby. Parkman says little about this stretch of territory, but a book written in 1933 by one Percy J. Robinson, entitled *Toronto During the French Regime*, fills in the gap. Robinson, a romantic like Parkman, suggested that we, in our imaginations, "weave the shadows" of the modern river "into a brief pageant of forgotten traffic along the old trail." Nothing could be easier, Robinson insisted. "A midsummer night and moonlight would be the best setting for this reunion of the ghosts of bygone days, but the trail was trodden for so many centuries by human feet on so many errands, that if anything of outworn humanity clings to our material surroundings, here at least at any time imagination may evoke the past."

Be my guest, I felt like urging Robinson. Summon those apparitions. "Along this street, when it was only a narrow foot-path in the woods, how many grotesque and terrible figures passed in the long years before and after the coming of the white man," he muses.

> War parties of painted braves; lugubrious trains of miserable prisoners destined for the stake; embassies from tribe to tribe on more peaceful errands; hunters wandering into the distant north in quest of furs; Hurons and Iroquois, Ottawas and Menominees, Shawanoes and Sacs and Foxes and last of all the debauched Mississaugas, spectators of the white man's progress and participating with him in cruel and dramatic events; raids into New York, the defeat of Braddock, the tragedy of Fort William Henry, the fall of Quebec, the massacre of Wyoming!

This will never do of course, this thrilling-pageant-of-the-past approach to history, this warmed-over Parkmanism. Robinson at one point actually describes rival Dutch and French fur traders as "these rascals from the Hudson and these lawless *coureurs-de-bois* from the St. Lawrence, wild hearts and children of the wilderness as truly as the aborigines whom they beguiled." Still, the book has good information. Robinson, God rest his soul, was a gifted painter, an amateur historian, a gentleman scholar of generous sympathies, and by no means a fool. (He knew the Huron language, for one thing.) But he really does try a contemporary reader's patience when he conjures a vision of the vanished Teiaiagon.

> There would be long-houses in place of the conical lodges of the Algonquins, and there would be the usual filthy squalor of those miserable abodes. The narrow streets would be a playground for naked children; there would be groups of women and girls gossiping or performing the simple tasks incident to savage life; there would be young men gambling in the shade and old men comforting their age with tobacco . . . coming and going there would be hunters from the woods, or old hags bringing in faggots from the forest, or braves returning from a scalping party with prisoners to be tortured; for in Teiaiagon, no doubt, were enacted those horrible scenes of torture and cannibalism which seemed to the missionaries so like their imagined conceptions of inferno.

Now, on this spot, this hilltop with a beautiful view of the Humber River valley, stand some of the nicest houses in Toronto. If La Salle could see them today he might not be startled – the stone facing of the walls, the half-timber, the bay windows, the dormer windows, all speak the language of seventeenth-century architecture. What might truly astonish him would be the lawns.

La Salle, of course, had no concept of a weed-free, insect-free, disease-free stretch of grass of uniform height and uniform color. At Baby Point, the concept is realized in all its splendor. Height is between two and two and a half inches. Color varies slightly from lawn to lawn but is generally a green with a tint of buttery yellow. Louis XIV should have so nice a front yard. But of course the North American lawn had to wait for the advent of a municipal water

supply, rubber hoses, oscillating sprinklers, potent chemical fertilizers, herbicides, pesticides, fungicides, several varieties of designer
grasses, plus a garage-full of seeders, edgers, pruners, sweepers,
cutters, and clippers. These are the advances that civilization had to
make to enable the Baby Point homeowners to lay out these lush
green carpets in front of their houses.

Beneath the grass, beneath the topsoil, lie the bones of Indians,
helping to nourish the ground on which the carpets are laid. To one
property may belong the skull of an old man who comforted his
age with tobacco; to another, the thigh bone of a girl who performed the simple tasks incident to savage life.

❧

After Teiaiagon, the waters of the Humber became too shallow for
canoes. Voyagers had to portage. Another mile or so and they
reached what is today a stretch of parkland, dutifully mowed and
maintained by Toronto Parks & Recreation workers. Here too was
once a settlement that, like Teiaiagon, has now completely vanished. On the evening of October 15, 1954, a street called Raymore
Drive stood in this park, lined by middle-class homes. Bounded by
the river on the east and the high ground to the west, the street was
a leafy enclave, the kind of small community where the inhabitants
pride themselves on their "country-style living."

The rain had been falling steadily for a week before that Friday
evening, but the residents were not particularly concerned, even
when the radio broadcast called for heavier rainfall and higher
winds that evening – the effects of a hurricane (Hazel) that had previously mauled South Carolina but was now losing its force as it
blew across New York and Pennsylvania.

It is not hard to imagine what happened later that night, to
a family living in one of those houses: they watched television, this
family, until the power went off about 10:30, and then retired to
bed, except for dad, who had fallen asleep on the sofa. At midnight

they were awakened by the whistling in the air, or by the screams of their neighbors. Dad sat up and was stunned to find his feet in water – moving water. He joined the family upstairs and watched out the window while their car backed out of the driveway at the hands of an invisible driver. That invisible person turned the car around and then, in defiance of the steering mechanism, drove the car sideways into the darkness and out of sight. By this time they felt the bumping of their furniture against the floor beneath their feet, and the father, fighting panic, led his family to the attic and then managed to smash a hole above them so they could climb to the roof. There they saw other people huddled on roofs, clinging to television aerials, pleading for help. "One group seemed to be hysterical, doing lots of screaming and crying and running about on the roof," a survivor said afterwards. "We learned later it was because somebody had drowned and was bobbing around in the water inside the house."

Help that night was hard to come by. The river, swollen to ten times its size, was too powerful. The family huddling on the roof likely knew they were going to die when they felt the house beneath them give a shudder and start to move. Thirty-six residents of Raymore Drive who never saw the dawn of Saturday, October 16, experienced something like that. All their bodies were eventually recovered and sent to a makeshift morgue where a volunteer washed the mud off the faces so that next of kin could identify them. The street itself was gone – covered with mud and rocks and tree limbs and chunks of Arborite and drywall and the odd kettle or bedside lamp. It was never rebuilt.

Some of the residents had been warned in time by people knocking on their doors before midnight, rousing them from bed. We never expect to hear that nighttime knock, that terrified shout, that rousing of a community about to be overwhelmed by catastrophe, but if there is such a thing as a collective North American consciousness, there may be a dark corner where the sound resonates. The inhabitants of Lachine heard it in the dawn hours when the Iroquois had already struck and it was too late. So did the inhabitants of Fort St. Louis in Texas. Now it emerges as a motif in movies like *The Searchers* or *Ulzana's Raid*, where the settlers' home is attacked without warning, by Indians who might simply be labeled "Worst Nightmare."

Not far from where those houses stood on Raymore Drive, on that sunny day I walked up the river, a man and a woman lounged by the banks of the Humber with fishing rods. They were oddly dressed for a Sunday outing. The woman, a blonde, seated on a plastic lawn chair, wore gold earrings, a beige skirt and jacket, as if dressed for the office. The man, who appeared to be her boyfriend, wore black pants, a chocolate brown shirt, a gray leather vest, and a gray necktie. He was spiffy, but in the manner of the musician who plays accordion at the banquet hall.

What really puzzled me was how they expected to catch anything in this part of the river, which aside from being polluted was so shallow no fish could possibly be lurking. I asked the woman what they were fishing for. She looked embarrassed. "No fish," she said. "Nutting." Her boyfriend, who was busy applying mustard to a hefty meat sandwich, looked up and grinned. "We are relax!" he said, sounding genuinely happy. The fishing rods were simply theatrical props for these immigrants, enjoying a place that was free from the nightmares of Europe.

Somewhere in the nearby parking lot stood their car with its license plate. Look upon this plate, reader, and learn a parable of Ontario. Unlike the notorious motto of New Hampshire, the motto on the Ontario license plate doesn't tell you to live free or die. It says, Yours To Discover. In other words, you can make Ontario into whatever you want, since it is still an unformed, undiscovered land – perhaps a land with no essence at all. It's a postmodernist license plate. It brushes history aside.

The motto of Quebec's license plates, by contrast, is Je Me Souviens. I remember. The French of Quebec, it seems, at least dream of remembering. Somewhere in the past is an identity, an authenticity, that only they can share, that marks them as different from other peoples on this continent. Has that authenticity been lost forever? Can anything be done with it? They do not know. But at least they do not insult the shade of La Salle with the message on their license plates.

SEVEN

Fort Niagara

La Salle pulls a fast one on the Iroquois • A historical controversy
about personal hygiene • I safeguard the life of a Jesuit priest •
The miracle of the potatoes in Trois Rivières

In late December of 1678, La Salle recovered from his feverish illness sufficiently to board the *Frontenac*, a small ship moored at Cataraqui. With Tonty and another crew of workmen and priests, La Salle set out to follow the course of La Motte and Hennepin, who had made it safely from their port in Toronto to the mouth of the Niagara River. En route La Salle stopped at the Genessee River in upstate New York, where he disembarked and paid a visit to a nearby town of the Seneca. This was a crucial diplomatic mission. La Salle was planning to build a fort near the mouth of the Niagara River, thereby intercepting a trade and military route to the west that was absolutely vital to the Iroquois, and to ease the minds of these Seneca, he tried to convince them that the only consequences of the fort would be cheaper prices for European trade goods. The role of used car salesman was becoming increasingly familiar to the merchant's son from Rouen. His auditors at least pretended to believe him – the Seneca had been doing business with him for a long time – and he managed not only to leave the settlement alive but to purchase some provisions as well.

At Niagara, La Salle found La Motte's outpost, a shelter surrounded by a wooden palisade. Inside huddled the workmen, heartily wishing they were somewhere else. La Motte was nowhere to be seen. As it turned out, he and Hennepin had gone to the same Seneca town just before La Salle, on the same errand, with less success. All La Motte had managed to do was give away trade goods in a bid to appease the profoundly suspicious inhabitants. When he heard this, La Salle was exasperated. He couldn't afford this futility. Enemies were being encouraged and energy was being wasted, which was a greater loss than trade goods. Also, why weren't these men working? La Salle led the workmen and artisans on a hike up the steep heights of the Niagara escarpment, past the falls, to the present-day site of La Salle, New York, where Cayuga Creek flows into the Niagara River. Here he decided they would build a second ship, to sail the waters west of the Niagara portage. Nika and two Mohican Indians helped the men fashion huts made of tree bark, Father Hennepin said mass over his portable altar in a tree bark chapel, and the construction of the ship commenced. Now at least the workmen had something to take their minds off their wretched state, which included cold and hunger and a diet, when obtainable, of squirrel and porcupine and other insults to the palates of good Frenchmen, Italians, and Flemings.

All of this had been barely set in motion when La Salle received bad news. His ship the *Frontenac* had anchored near the mouth of the Niagara River, and its pilot and crew, desperate to keep warm on a wet January night, had gone ashore to sleep by a bonfire. During the night a wind arose, the anchor failed to hold, and the ship was smashed against the rocks. Almost everything on board – equipment for the new ship under construction, trade goods, provisions – was lost. La Salle was going to have to return to Fort Frontenac to replace the cargo. In February, after his men had salvaged all the equipment from the other ship that had brought La Motte and Hennepin to Niagara, and had carried it on their backs up the walls of the escarpment, and after the work had well begun on the new one, La Salle took his leave.

❧

En route, he passed the two blockhouses, constructed by a work crew under La Motte, on a height of land by the mouth of the Niagara River where Fort Niagara would later stand. Those blockhouses would not long survive La Salle. After his death they fell into ruins, and the Seneca and other nations of the Iroquois Confederacy breathed more easily. In 1726, however, the French managed to persuade the Seneca to allow them to build what they described as a trading post and warehouse on the same spot. Actually, it was a fort. There it would stand, under the white flag of His Majesty's department of the marine, until the critical hour of the French empire in the New World. That came in 1759, when a force of British regulars and provincial troops numbering about 2,300 approached Niagara, accompanied by one thousand Iroquois. Exactly one hundred and fifty years earlier, Samuel Champlain, founder of Quebec City, the first permanent French settlement in North America, had joined a band of Algonquin Indians in a skirmish against the Iroquois. During that fight, he employed a weapon never before seen in those parts, the musket. The firearm helped win the day for his allies but started off French-Iroquois relations rather on the wrong foot. When after one and a half centuries the Iroquois prepared to strike their last great blow at French power, it was almost as revenge against the blast of Champlain's musket. But it had nothing to do with it. It had to do with geopolitics. The Iroquois could see the fortunes of war in the Ohio Valley tilting to the British, and they wanted to get in on the winning side and solidify their influence in that region. Their reasoning was sound, but the result was unfortunate. The Iroquois had always survived by playing off one European power against another. Henceforth, after the siege of Fort Niagara, and the surrender of Montreal the following year, there would be only one European power. The fall of Fort Niagara signified the end of both New France and an independent Five Nations Confederacy.

It all seems inevitable now. At Niagara, the British outnumbered the French two to one, which was par for the course. New France, at the time of the fall of Fort Niagara, contained seventy thousand people. The thirteen British colonies had twenty times that figure, a disparity that pretty well explains the outcome of the conflict. In war, other things being roughly equal, the bigger side wins. The real question is why there were so many English people on the continent and so few French. When La Salle breathed his last on the grasslands of Texas, France had an economy twice the size of Great Britain's, and a population three times as large.

There is an answer, but it's complicated. Pascal famously said that if Cleopatra's nose had been shorter, the whole aspect of the world would have been altered. Similarly, if Anne Boleyn's nose had been longer, the French might still be in possession of Fort Niagara. Anne Boleyn's nose, however, was of the right length at least not to detract from her other charms, a piece of good fortune that enabled her to ensnare the affections of King Henry VIII and egg him on against the Pope. Once he set himself up as supreme head of the Church in England, Henry proceeded to plunder the monasteries. Somewhere between 20 and 30 per cent of the land in Britain was owned by the Church, and it all passed through Henry's hands into the grasp of the gentry. These were men who already possessed large estates. Now many of those estates were doubled in extent, making their owners not only the social superiors of the yeomen farmers, but their economic and political masters to a degree far exceeding anything that medieval England had witnessed.

These yeomen farmers possessed small plots of land that had been in their families for generations, and for which they paid customary, often nominal, sums of rent to the Crown or to the lord of the manor. In addition, they had rights over "common land" – the right to graze their animals on common pasture, the right to gather fuel in common woodlands, and so on. Now, backed by their new-found wealth and political power, including control of the courts, the large landowners began raising rents and enclosing the common lands for their own use. Small farmers were forced off their land, to become either agricultural laborers or part of Britain's "surplus population." The wealthy, meanwhile, grew wealthier. By the seventeenth century, the mold of English politics had been cast – it was a land ruled by an oligarchy of men with great estates.

Once they had total control of the land, the wealthy owners could begin to improve it, using new methods of crop rotation, new techniques such as floating meadows (covering meadows with a thin sheet of water during winter to prevent frost and encourage early growth of grass), new efforts to drain marshes and bring "barren" land into cultivation. All this took capital, and a free hand over large plots of land, none of which would have been available had not the small farmers been dispossessed.

The yield from British agriculture did increase – sometimes to startling proportions. And it kept increasing throughout the seventeenth and eighteenth centuries as the last common land was finally enclosed and inventions such as the seed drill became widely used. Increased food production led to the doubling of the English population between 1550 and 1750 – nine years before the fall of Fort Niagara. This was not such happy news for American Indians or African slaves, because with its "surplus population" Great Britain was able to send settlers to the New World in great numbers, where they proceeded to wipe out the aboriginal populations and import slaves in the service of growing tobacco and sugar, more wellsprings of British capital.

France had no such surplus population. There had never been any plundering of the monasteries to tip the scales of power between the large landowners and the French version of yeomen farmers, the peasantry. French peasants stayed on their lands. In any case, France was not interested in large-scale settlement of its lands in North America. Great Britain had discovered the secret of wealth through capitalism; that is to say, through competitive production of goods, starting with agricultural products, and for that, large-scale settlement of its American colonies was useful. France, however, was still fixated on an older form of wealth generation – the establishment of trade monopolies. Those monopolies had been the mainstay of the great Arab Muslim empire in the Middle Ages and the source of fabulous wealth for the Venetian and Dutch empires of the Renaissance and early seventeenth century. The object of these empires was to seize control of key foreign ports and trade routes and therefore obtain the ability to buy low and sell high those goods that the rest of the world desperately craved. The French attempt to monopolize the fur trade in North America by building forts all over the Great Lakes was a classic instance of this economic strategy.

The British strategy was better – from the military point of view, anyway. The number of men they could enlist in arms on the North American continent attests to that. Moreover, all this wealth from increased labor productivity on the farm meant that the British had greater financial resources than the French. In the Seven Years War, the global conflict that decided that the future of the world would lie with English speakers rather than with French speakers, the British won basically because they could borrow money. They knew about selling interest-bearing bonds to investors. And that's why poor Captain Pierre Pouchot, commander of Fort Niagara, had no chance at all when he saw those redcoats in the woods on that day in July.

As Americans say, you can't argue with success. So unanswerable is the argument represented by success, in fact, that Protestant controversialists have often added the saga of capitalism to their arsenal of intellectual weapons against the Church of Rome. Victorian writers, in particular, were always contrasting the economic vitality, the onward march of science and technology, in the Protestant realms of Her Majesty, with the shiftless, indolent, backward, priest-ridden peasants of Catholic Europe – all those Spaniards taking too many siestas. These peasants would rather have a good time than display initiative. Something of this view, as we shall see, also attached to French-Canadian immigrants to the United States during the nineteenth century. When they weren't plotting to gift-wrap New England for the Vatican, they were just too happy-go-lucky for their own good. In the meantime, France remained perversely committed to its own peasantry despite economic logic, somewhat in the manner that present-day France supports its farmers, come what may. The French Revolution made the peasantry outright owners of their farms, free of the last obligations of feudalism, and the two Napoleons confirmed the arrangement. This disgusted Marx, who disliked farmers in general and small farmers in particular – "The system of small proprietorship," he sneered in *The Eighteenth Brumaire of Louis Bonaparte*, "has transformed the mass of the French nation into troglodytes." Another Jewish prophet had seen a day when every man shall sit under his vine and under his fig tree and none shall make him afraid, but to Marx this vision of the millennium was strictly petty bourgeois.

It took a Catholic writer, Hilaire Belloc, to come out swinging in defense of the European peasant, or the peasant as defined by Belloc – the small-scale subsistence producer working his own land. Belloc was born in France in 1870, but grew up in England and identified himself throughout his life as an Englishman. He hated rich people, and he hated progressive thinkers, whose undermining of the old truths of reason and religion he viewed as ultimately supportive of the rich. (If you have no sense of objective truth and standards of justice, you can't bring the rich, who are inherently lawless, to book.) Conversely, he loved the Catholic Church, and particularly those aspects of it that most repelled progressive people in Belloc's day – its intolerance, its rock-hard resistance to modernity, its highly formal rites and customs, its elaborate moral theology, its dry scholastic logic, its clinging to the ancient formulas of faith.

And he loved the idea of the peasant. According to this idea, the Catholic peasant was stubbornly independent, rather than servile like an English working man – the peasant owned his own means of livelihood, after all. The Catholic peasant had good local wine to drink with his lunch and dinner, celebrated the many feast days in the Church's calendar with communal merriment, observed loyalty to family and friends, and dutifully attended mass, where all the ancient human instincts for worship were satisfied.

"Certainly these people have a benediction upon them, granted them for their simple lives and their justice," he wrote in *The Path to Rome* of the Italian peasants he had encountered. "Their eyes are fearless and kindly. They are courteous, straight, and all have in them laughter and sadness. They are full of songs, of memories, of the stories of their native place; and their worship is conformable to the world that God made." To think that this had all vanished from the English countryside, thanks to that swine Henry VIII. It's enough to make you wish the French had laid a really good beating on the British army outside the walls of Fort Niagara, that summer of 1759. It would have been what they deserved. Unfortunately, I was ignorant of all this in the fourth grade, when Mrs. Drennan was scoffing at the French.

Of course, Mrs. Drennan might have replied that Belloc's description of the peasantry was rose-colored. Who knows? I don't know if there are any more Catholic peasants still singing songs and telling stories of their native place. Going by French literature, we can be sure of one thing – the French peasant, at least after the French Revolution, didn't take any *merde* from his social superiors. (This is why, incidentally, you don't hear modern Frenchmen, unlike Englishmen, still whining about their country's "class system.") Granted all this, however, granted that life in Catholic Europe is and has been more gracious than life in Protestant Britain (where would you rather live, in Tuscany and Provence, or in Herefordshire?), a serious historical question remains to be addressed. Were the British on the right track, after all? "Industrial Capitalism is a manifest evil," Belloc protested. "It cries out against our sense of justice, its products offend our sense of beauty, the society based on it is not only vile but increasingly unstable." That's one point of view.

Today Belloc could add environmental pollution and a licentious and nihilistic popular culture to the indictment. He could also add that the current fruits of capitalism – cellphones and computers and automobiles – cause as much annoyance as pleasure. But! There's modern dentistry and indoor plumbing and screen doors on the summer cottage and synthetic materials that are lighter and warmer and faster drying than wool and fur. *Voyageurs* would have killed for Gore-Tex. Setting aside nostalgic visions of the past, we have to admit the obvious: capitalism is a cornucopia, capitalism is a dynamo.

I am among those who, by temperament, tend to mourn lost Edens rather than dream of coming Utopias. Nostalgic visions of the past are a dangerous temptation for my kind, the brood of troglodytes. Yet I love that line from *Mr. Smith Goes to Washington*, when Jefferson Smith says, "Dad always used to say the only causes worth fighting for were the lost causes." Conversely, I hate Marx for making a fetish of being on the winning side of history. And speaking of Jefferson – Thomas Jefferson, I mean – I think his cause, the cause of the small farmer, is as admirable as the cause of the Catholic peasant or the English yeoman, with "petty proprietorship" being at the root of all of them. "The small land holders are the most precious part of a state," Jefferson insisted. He saw what would happen if the ideas of Alexander Hamilton prevailed, he knew that Hamilton's scheme to use debt in order to spur the growth of industry – like an injection of amphetamines to the nervous system – would eventually create an industrial and financial oligarchy similar to the landowning oligarchy of Britain and increasingly require the exportation of our industrial products and hence our involvement in endless foreign wars.

But Hamilton did win, and so we have our oligarchy and our endless wars. But Hamilton had to win. We can't do without our dynamo.

❧

"You wonder what would happen if there were an economic crash in the United States," Denise was saying, as she sewed by the light of a lantern, inside her tent. "People don't know how to rough it any more." She was explaining why she and her husband, Dan, a mechanic from Michigan, had become re-enactors. Daniel was a private in the Compagnie Le Beouf, a "unit" headed by Greg Henning, an electronics technician and high school teacher from Erie, Pennsylvania, and he and his comrades had come to the Fourth of July encampment at Fort Niagara to re-enact the siege of 1759. Like other members of their unit, Daniel and Denise had set up their tent on the grounds inside the fort. Just outside the fort were the tents of the British and provincial troops.

"I like the idea of passing on these old skills to my children so they don't die out," Denise continued. She was referring to things like repairing clothes and cooking in an iron pot over a fire. "It's also a very inexpensive way to see places. Like here. They give you breakfast and lunch, and you have a place to set up your tent and feel safe. It's not like when you go to a state park, or whatever you call them in Canada, and you end up listening to somebody's boom box all night."

I had arrived on July 2, a day ahead of the re-enactors, and looked around the place using a pamphlet entitled *Your Guide to the Fort.* In the officer's mess inside the "Castle" – the three-story building that was originally the sole structure of the fort – I read a plaque commemorating the formal surrender that took place in this room in 1759: "Of all the scenes enacted in this structure during the third of a century then past, this final ceremonial of the days of the French Wars was by no means least in significance; for here France herself quaffed a cup in acknowledgement of a conqueror to whom she was yielding an empire vaster and more potential than any statesman of that day could see or dare predict." This memorial was written by one Frank H. Severance, a man clearly under the stylistic influence of Parkman. Outside the Castle, near the wall overlooking the Niagara River as it poured into Lake Ontario, was a large upright stone with another metal plaque commemorating an "Author of Great Beginnings" and a "Dreamer of Dreams." That was none other than our hero, La Salle. "Through his courage, suffering and endurance came Christianity and Civilization," stated this irony-free plaque, which had been erected by the state of New York in 1934. I think La Salle would have been very pleased by this compliment – it wasn't just about beaver pelts and buffalo hides, thank you.

That evening I met Greg Henning, who invited me to join his family, and Dan and Denise, at Brennan's Irish Pub in Youngstown, just outside the park where the fort stands. "I married into it," Greg said by way of explaining why he had become a re-enactor fourteen years ago. "I bought a pair of shoes and that was it. I was done."

"It was in 1985," his wife, Dee Dee, said. She had a round face, red hair, and could have passed for a thirty-year-old, unlike the rest of us at the table. We were all dressed casually, like tourists – Dee Dee wore jeans and a T-shirt from the 2003 National Cherry Blossom Festival in Washington, D.C. So much the sweeter would be the moment of shedding these clothes and dressing up. In that moment, re-enactors would put distance between themselves and the tourists who ask to pose beside them in photographs. It's a good feeling, like the proud sense of difference actors feel with people in audiences, or soldiers feel with civilians. "The lady I worked with at the drugstore had been coming here to Fort Niagara for a couple years. She was portraying an upper-class Englishwoman, so she spent the day going on picnics with British officers, and because she was a rather comely woman they would fight for her affections. They would actually fight duels with each other. And then she'd bring photos back from a weekend, and I'd think, man, this looks like fun. Can't I join? So I went, and I got hooked after that first weekend. I started coming to the re-enactments as her maid. I would accompany her to all her little picnics and soirees.

"Then I got married in my real life, so that had to be re-adjusted. My interpretation had to be changed. I became, I don't know, camp cook, bottle washer. I'm now a tavern mistress. I own a tavern. When I get to the point where I can't do this any more, I have my looms for weaving. I'll become a weaver." She shrugged. "You play a part. It may not be a character who most fits your needs at that moment, but you do it and after a while it's like reading a story. You learn the names of the characters and you learn how they respond to things. It's kind of like method acting. You say to yourself, 'Okay, I'm this person. How am I supposed to react to this situation?'"

"You just have to do the research for your presentation," Greg said, "and develop your persona." You have to "stay historical," is another way of putting it. When drilling on the parade ground or marching on the field of battle, for example, Dan, a private in the *compagnie* does not speak to his friend Greg, the *capitaine*. In the eighteenth century, privates did not address officers unless spoken to. Some gentleman re-enactors take this staying historical to considerable lengths. One aristocrat, at a recent re-enactment of the siege of Louisbourg, passed by a company of soldiers and ostentatiously pressed a perfumed handkerchief to his nose, to mask the odor of the *canaille*. "We have one particular gentleman who portrays a French officer perfectly," Dee Dee said. "There was a competition at a re-enactment to see who could start a fire with a piece of steel and flint first – who could demonstrate the most authentic way to light a fire I think is how they worded it – so they gave everyone a piece of steel and flint. And this gentleman, he looked to his left, he looked to his right, and then he threw his steel and flint to a private and said, 'Make a fire.' And he won the competition. His was the most authentic way of starting a fire. He never would have gotten down on his hands and knees to start a fire. Soooo . . ." Dee Dee gave a Cheshire cat grin, "we do like to play."

But why, I asked, did the eighty-odd people from western Pennsylvania who had joined Greg's unit choose to play at being French people? I could understand why Greg, who was a retired major in the army infantry – five years on active duty, he said, and twenty years in the National Guard – would choose to be a company commander. But why a French company? Henning had some French Huguenot ancestry but was mostly descended from English and German settlers in America. "Why I chose the French? Probably because in my genealogical background I had an ancestor fight in the Revolutionary War as an American, and I never really had an interest to pursue a British interpretation. It's funny, though. When we're talking to French people at re-enactments, they really are at a loss to understand why people from Pennsylvania are doing French soldiers. They don't understand why we are so interested in their culture. I don't think they have an appreciation of how big their empire was, or that where we live now was once under French rule."

Of course, most re-enactors in Henning's neck of the woods are not interested in being either British soldiers or French soldiers. "We must have half a dozen Civil War units in our area," Greg said. For most people, "living history," or re-enactments of historical events involving men with guns, means the American Civil War. It doesn't mean F&I (re-enactor shorthand for "French and Indian War"), or Rev War, or 1812. "You can take your credit card and you can buy your Confederate or Union uniform off the rack," Greg pointed out. "You can't buy our uniforms at Wal-Mart. They don't make them like that. Our uniforms and our equipment and our interpretation, they're always a work in progress. And if you make a mistake – F&I is a very small community – that mistake's going to be broadcast very quickly to everybody else in the community. It's not like the Civil War where you have fifty to seventy thousand people. There, if you mess up you can move to another group. You can move on and remain anonymous. You don't have that luxury here – but I think that's one of the reasons why F&I is probably one of the safest groups you can belong to in terms of accidents. I also think our hobby is more educationally centered than these large Civil War events. They go for the big battle show."

We finished eating, and the waitress gave us our check, and Greg and Dee Dee kindly paid for my dinner. "When that tent opens on Friday morning," Dee Dee said, referring to the morning of the Fourth of July when the re-enactment would begin in earnest, "it all disappears." She waved her hand at a ten dollar bill on the table, as if it were something bogus, like a geranium made of organdy. "This money. Plastic cups. Yogurt containers. You just want it all to disappear. That's what we live for. It's a great fantasy."

❧

The next day, July 3, the sutlers and the French and native re-enactors pitched their tents inside the fort, while just outside the walls of the fort the British re-enactors made their encampment. "Sutlers" are retailers who sell to re-enactors and the tourists who watch their events. There were dozens at this event, offering good woolen waistcoats, rolls of fabric, candles, lanterns, wooden cutlery, cow horns, silver jewelry, reproductions of seventeenth-century muskets, beads, pottery, gewgaws and doodads of all description – almost anything that looked pre-industrial. Retailers dressed in period costume, too. I spoke to one woman wearing her eighteenth-century dress and apron and scullery maid's cap while she stirred a white gluey substance in an iron pot over a fire. It was one of the ingredients for "Scottish lye soap," on sale at her tent. "People bathed a lot more than they got credit for back then," she said. "There was none of that Walt Disney stuff about people bathing once a year. You know, they were like us. They bathed when they got the chance to bathe. They liked to be clean." To be "period correct," in other words, you didn't have to smell. "Except for the Puritans," she added. "They didn't like any activity that caused you to get naked."

"What about the French?"

"They were very clean. They were a lot cleaner than the English." I thought of Mrs. Drennan again. If only I had known. "They say the Scots were cleaner than the English, and the French were cleaner than the Scots," she continued. "The French always said they could smell the English coming. I read that in an account of a battle – they could smell the English army coming."

Greg and Dee Dee had set up the tent that housed their tavern, The Lily and the Lion – the lily being the heraldic device of the French, the lion of the English. Inside the tent were five wooden tables with benches and a bar where beverages were served. "This barrel is ale," Dee Dee said, with an exaggerated wink at the word "ale." Actually, the liquid inside the little wooden barrel was lemonade, a.k.a. "lemonale." In back of the bar were shelves with various dishes. "Is this pewter?" I asked Dee Dee of the little tankard I was drinking ice water from. It was silver and definitely looked pewterish. "These puppies, who knows where they come from," she said. "People pick them up because they look funny and they don't know who manufactured them or in what country or how many millions were produced. Eventually they get tired of them and they put the dozen or so they bought in a garage sale and we come along and buy the whole set because at an event these mugs are always walking away. This one . . ." She looked at my tankard and made a face. "Ppppfffffttttt. Looks like aluminum to me. Same thing with utensils. We don't eat with original utensils because each week we'd get stupider." I looked puzzled. "Because of the lead content."

The only problem with the tent this morning was that hordes of small winged creatures were congregating at the top. It was a situation that called for bug spray. "If a wind comes up, we'll be fine," Dee Dee said to a customer. "But you know and I know, because we've been in enough F&Is together, there ain't going to be no wind. And we're going to fry like . . ." She left the simile ominously incomplete. I noticed later that the winged creatures had disappeared from the tent, but I never did ask if it was because of bug spray. In the meantime, the heat of this Fourth of July weekend ensured that there were plenty of customers for Dee Dee's free lemonale. The Lily and the Lion was a popular place, and Dee Dee and her teenaged children, including her youngest daughter, Chelsea, were kept busy. "I've seen your tavern at a lot of events," one French soldier commented. "It's a nice touch."

"Thank you," Dee Dee said.

"It adds a lot to the ambience."

Another man dressed as a Delaware Indian, his face painted red and black, with a wicked-looking hatchet on this belt, said to me, "It's a grand thing for a unit to have something like this. It's a place where everybody can get together."

On this first afternoon of the re-enactment, most people had not yet gotten "historical." Dee Dee still wore her jeans and Cherry Blossom Festival T-shirt. A man in shorts, T-shirt, and baseball cap visiting the tavern turned out to be Daniel Roy, a French-speaking Quebecker who was a real-life major in the Canadian Armed Forces, as well as an officer in King Louis xv's army. He sipped his own ice water from another aluminum tankard and told Greg that he had just come from a re-enactment at Fort Ticonderoga. "You were at Carillon?" Greg asked. "Carillon" is how the French refer to that fort and the battle that took place there in 1758, when British forces under General James Abercrombie launched a direct attack on the French position. It was one of those fatally stupid assaults, like the battle of Fredericksburg or The Somme, against men dug in with firearms. "We kicked the Brits' butts," Roy said. He took another sip of his ice water. "They wouldn't admit it, though."

"Living history" – if only it were real history. We might see some startling results. "The Confederate army is very serious [in] what they do against the Union army," Henning said to me later. "Same with the French Canadians when they go against the British. They're very professional, they're very careful, they're very aggressive, they're really serious about it."

Another visitor to the tavern was Suzanne Tetrault, a French Canadian now living in Midland, Ontario, whose husband, Sylvain, was a regular in La Compagnie Franche de la Marine. She showed Dee Dee a photograph she had taken inside the brick walls of the old powder magazine. "I was right in here," said Tetrault, who had an exceptionally cheerful manner. She pointed to a spot outside the tent, not far from the entrance to the fort. "You see, just ahead here, you know, where the gunpowder room is? I had shivers when I went there, because I was alone. I had to bring in my camera. I thought, what are the odds? As I turned around, because I liked the way the arches are, I said, I'll picture that. But that's not what I got."

"Oh my gosh," Dee Dee said, looking at the photograph. "That is very cool. Chelsea will just . . . freak . . . *out*. Wait till she sees this."

"You see the eyes and the mouth and, like, the beard. But there's no body." I looked at the photograph. Against the red brick walls of the powder magazine floated whitish ectoplasmic shapes. "That is really cool," Dee Dee said. "I've never seen anything like that."

Later I asked Dee Dee about ghosts. "A lot of men died here," she said. "There's a lot of karmic energy." Then she gave a "don't worry we're not crackers" laugh.

At one point in the afternoon Bob Emerson, executive director of Fort Niagara and the "site director" for this re-enactment, came to the tavern to consult with Henning. Needless to say, battle re-enactments are complicated things and must be choreographed carefully. In general, this whole business would collapse very quickly if people didn't take it with utmost seriousness. Participants came to the encampment, for example, with a list of guidelines, including the following:

Participants are to be in period dress while the Fort is open to the public. No cigarettes or other anachronisms are allowed in front of the public.

Military courtesy and discipline are in effect while the Fort is open to the public.

Participants are *strongly* discouraged from bringing animals. Those who must bring pets should notify the Fort in advance. Owners should bring proof of vaccinations with them to the event. *All animals are to be kept on a leash, attended and under control at all times.*

Particular guidelines were in place regarding weapons. For safety reasons, all weapons had to be modern reproductions. No original weapons could be fired. No firearm could be pointed toward another person – visitor or re-enactor, even during battle. (Re-enactors aim their muskets slightly above the line of the enemy.) Neither side could approach the other within one hundred feet. No weapon, such as a tomahawk or knife, could be thrown at any time.

Emerson handed Henning a sheet of paper with the title "Battle Scenario." The scenario outlined the troop movements. First, the British and American Rangers and allied Indians would fire at an unsuspecting company of French soldiers, or Marines, outside the fort from the cover of a few trees. The French would return the fire, pushing the Rangers back to their cover. Then the French, sustaining a few casualties, would retreat. The Indians and Rangers would pursue them. French-Canadian militia would then emerge from a ditch outside the fort to support the soldiers. Something called a "piquet company" would also form in ranks to confront the approaching British soldiers. I am oversimplifying, but that was the basic idea. "The piquet company is going to right-about-face, and they'll volley with the British as they come on," Emerson said to Henning. "The British will easily push them back. By this point the drums in the fort will be beating and the garrison – what we think we would like to do is, before the battle, go through the normal inspection and then have everyone go into the Castle and just wait until the musicians beat the drums and then these regulars will come pouring out of the Castle and make a quick march to the port in the ravelin."

Emerson continued to outline the scenario, while Henning listened and nodded. He seemed to find it not only comprehensible but satisfying. Afterwards he told the members of his unit, "This is the battle scenario. Lots of movement. Which will be good for the public. Half the force is going into the Castle when the shooting starts, and then we're going to come pouring out.

That's good, too. It's cool in there and the guys are not going to get dehydrated."

⚜

On Friday, July 4, the eighteenth century was officially on. Every re-enactor was in period costume. Early in the afternoon, living history began with a re-creation of a conference between French officers and the Indians who were wavering in their allegiance to the British. As with the real event, the simulated gathering ended with the Indians professing alliance with their hosts. (Not that it did the French much good.) The French offered some trade goods as a sweetener for the deal, but a gray-haired man with a pot belly and a war club dismissed the bribe as unnecessary. "Forget the gifts," he said. "I do not need gifts to fight the *anglais*. I hate the *anglais*." Meanwhile, the tourists began to find places on the grass embankment overlooking the east side of the fort where the battle was about to commence.

In the middle of the afternoon, the embankment now lined solidly with spectators, the voice of Bob Emerson could be heard over a loudspeaker. "So, ladies and gentlemen, let's begin our battle demonstration this afternoon," he said. "The French and Indian War took place twenty years before the American Revolution, pitting the American colonists and the British against the French and their native allies, the French living in Canada and along the Great Lakes. . . ."

"Where is Godzilla?" a little girl perched on her daddy's shoulders asked.

"I don't know, honey. I don't think Godzilla is in this battle."

"There they are," someone said. The British and American Rangers had emerged from the trees and parking lot to the east. Shots were fired. The Marines lined up and shot back. The noise and the smoke from the guns was rousing, the movements of the troops convincing, but one thing was missing. Nobody was being hit. "How come they're not killing anybody?" a fourteen-year-old boy next to me asked his dad. "They don't want to die too early in this battle," his father said. "They got too much ammo left."

"Yeah, really. A lot of people would have been dead by now."

"The French Marines are excellent woods fighters," Bob Emerson said over the loudspeaker. "They begin to push the British and the Rangers back to the woods where they came." Suddenly two British soldiers fell down and started rolling down an embankment. "Now they're dying," the boy said. "A couple of them, anyway." The bodies kept rolling. "They're going to make the shade trees," his father said. He was right. The bodies stopped rolling at the bottom of the embankment when they got to a shady area. After that they lay reasonably still.

Drums were heard from the vicinity of the Castle, and the spectators turned to see a marching file of French soldiers, Henning's Compagnie Le Boeuf, proceeding toward the sally port on the east wall near the main entrance. They marched at a brisk pace through the grounds of the fort to the sally port, and then emerged on the outside, through the ditch by the wall, and up a grassy embankment. A couple of soldiers slipped and fell, provoking mild laughter. "I might add that the soldiers are wearing authentic leather-soled shoes," Emerson explained to the audience. "They're very difficult on these slopes." On top of the embankment, the troops lined up with well-practiced precision and for the next ten minutes volleyed furiously. More soldiers fell. "Oh, did they have it rough in those days, geez," a woman said. Suddenly the wail of an ambulance was heard. This had not been called for in the Battle Scenario. Since many re-enactors are men well into their fifties – prime heart attack territory – and decidedly overweight, I was worried one of them had fallen for real. As it turned out, however, it was a tourist, not a re-enactor, who required medical assistance. "We have more of the public going down dressed like you are than we're going down dressed in wool," Greg Henning later told me. "We're drinking water, we're staying hydrated, and wool breathes better than a lot of synthetic material." He was rightfully proud, as he put it, that "there has never been a fatality in the Hobby."

"Ladies and gentlemen, let's have a round of applause for our participants today," Emerson said. "They come to participate here with volunteers from all over the United States and Canada. We have units from California, Quebec, and from all over the continent, and they do this because they enjoy living history." The audience applauded enthusiastically. The whole event had taken half an hour – which, of course, represents a drastic compression in time of the actual events portrayed. But re-enactment, despite its attempts at "authenticity," is theater, not history. Audiences are easily bored.

The next morning, Saturday, I joined the Compagnie Le Beouf, at the kind invitation of Capitaine Henning. Helping me don the uniform was Robert, a man on the cusp of forty, dressed in what looked like a white nightshirt, with a red cloth cap – he was not a regular in the compagnie, but a member of the "milice," the French Canadian militia. He had recently graduated from a four-year archeology course, after having pursued previous careers as a chef and a registered nurse, and was hoping to get a job as an archeologist. "It's like playing army – on a different level," he said, as he presented me with my shoes, my stockings, my linen shirt, my stock – a stiff, close-fitting neckcloth – woolen waistcoat, woolen coat, tri-cornered hat, my belt with hatchet attached, my powder horn, my canteen, and of course my musket. It wasn't the most comfortable outfit on a hot July day, but I felt good when I was fully dressed. I was no longer a tourist. I was ready to play. Bob had put his finger on it. As a boy with my friend across the street I had pretended to be a soldier many times. We loved the idea of sneaking up on each other and killing each other with our cap pistols. We had our superstitious rituals – if we carried an American flag and it touched the ground, we kissed it. (Or else an American soldier would die.)

"When you get diaper rash from the wool, then you know you're there," Dee Dee said, from behind the bar of The Lily and the Lion. Another member of the compagnie pointed out that the waistcoat I was wearing was entirely covered by the outer coat. "You can lose that," he said. I took his advice and removed it. Somebody offered to go through a few of the rudimentary drills involving the musket with me, and for about half an hour I tried to master the *présentez le fusil au côté de l'épée* and other maneuvers, but with minimal success. No wonder I had never joined a real army. It was decided that I had better not try actually to fire the musket during the battle. In fact, it was decided that my role, once the compagnie had come storming out of the sally port, was to detach from the unit and stand by the Jesuit who was giving last rites to the wounded. I would be his bodyguard, so to speak. It was not very "historical," but it gave me something to do and kept me out of everybody's way.

At mid-afternoon, we lined up for inspection outside the Castle, as per the Battle Scenario. One of the sergeants made sure I filled my canteen with water. After yesterday's stricken tourist, everyone was very conscious of dehydration. We did a few *présentez le fusil* maneuvers, including one with the ramrod that you employ to stuff the powder into the barrel of the musket. "Use the other end of the ramrod," the sergeant said to me. "Try not to hit anybody, please." I was relieved when it was over. Then the head sergeant, a French Canadian, stood in front of our ranks and delivered a harangue in French, of which I could catch the phrase *tuer les anglais*. He switched to English. "You are here to kill the English," he shouted, "as many as you can. You are not here to wave at them, or give them a kiss. You are here to kill as many of them as you can. For that, I am your leader and you will listen to my commands. And after the battle you will pay the sergeant a beer who has taken such good care of you."

We filed into the Castle and milled around inside the stone vestibule while the initial stages of the battle raged outside the fort. Behind us was the room where the French had quaffed the cup of surrender, but we were pretending that had not yet happened. Then the sergeant barked an order and we stood in ranks again. Daniel Roy, who portrayed a superior officer, pronounced a few final inspirational words before our rush to battle: "Kick some British butts. Enjoy yourselves. *S'amusez bien*." With that, we began our march, proceeding in quick step across the grounds of the fort with the drummers beating their drums and the tourists lined up on either side of us – oh, taste of martial glory – to the sally port and outside and up the embankment. With my "authentic" leather soles, I was fearful of falling on my own butt, to the derision of the crowd on the walls behind me. Later I found out that Greg Henning had rubber soles on his eighteenth-century shoes. "It's not period correct," he admitted, "but it's safety correct." With some sliding, I managed to get up the embankment, whereupon I separated from the unit and stood by the Jesuit father, a retired police officer from the Niagara region who told me he was a Lutheran.

All writers who describe battles will tell you that it is mostly chaos and confusion. "Is this a real battle?" Stendhal's hero Fabrizio asks a sergeant in the middle of Waterloo. So don't ask me for salient details of this particular engagement. I remember somebody beside me playing a fife, and a lot of smoke and noise, and a few Indians and militia yelling and screaming and taking the occasional shot with their muskets – one of the Indians mooned the British ranks, which I think was "historical" – and my friend the Lutheran in the black robe holding a big wooden crucifix over a couple of wounded and dying men sprawled on the grass, who looked up with sneaky grins. Then suddenly we were going down the embankment again – *mon Dieu*, those leather soles were slippery – and back into the fort. The battle was over. I was sorry it hadn't lasted longer. Time passes more swiftly for a re-enactor than for his audience.

But it was not quite over. We formed into ranks again in front of the Castle, and Greg Henning assured us we had made a good account of ourselves. "You're outstanding soldiers, every one of you." I felt a slight pang – a Vietnam-era draft dodger in real life, a French regular who couldn't be trusted to fire a musket in re-enactment life, I certainly deserved no such praise. The shadow of some reality seemed to fall over us. A year and a half later I heard that Henning had been re-activated and sent to Iraq, where soldiers carried guns with real ammunition and the battle scenario was as yet unwritten.

"You did very good work today," our French-Canadian sergeant said. "But there's one thing that I didn't hear you do and that was to say the angelus. What kind of Christian soldiers are you? Tonight at six I want you to join the good father and say the angelus." The angelus is a beautiful prayer that, in Catholic countries, used to be publicly recited every morning at six, at noon, and six in the evening. Belloc's Catholic peasants would stop their labors in the field as the bells of the angelus tolled, and someone would say the first verse, "The Angel of the Lord declared unto Mary," and they would respond, "And she conceived of the Holy Spirit," and so on, until the end of the prayer: "Pour forth, we beseech Thee, O Lord, Thy grace into our hearts, that we to whom the Incarnation of Christ Thy Son was made known by the message of an angel, may by His Passion and Cross be brought to the glory of His Resurrection." Battle-hardened soldiers would also say this prayer, as our sergeant reminded us, which is why they are now in heaven and we, here on earth, remain in doubt of our salvation.

We were then dismissed, our military duties over. For the rest of the afternoon I wandered the grounds of the fort, taking a look at the wares inside the sutlers' tents, roaming the areas where the native re-enactors had pitched their tents — how many of them were genuine aboriginals, how many white people I had no idea, but the men all looked convincing in their war paint and breech cloths and shaved heads. The Delaware Indian attached to our unit, I soon discovered, was a white man, a civil servant from Pennsylvania. He explained to me that the red on his face was actual brick dust laid over a layer of Vaseline. The rest was of various substances, including the makeup used in theater. "Getting it off is the real trick," he said of his war paint. "I use waterless hand cleaner —

the kind with lanolin in it, not grit. You rub it over your arm until it looks like butter, and then you take a paper towel, and off she goes. At least a majority of it. After that you get regular soap and do some serious scrubbing."

A troupe of Iroquois – not Silver Bear and the Thunder Hawk Dancers, but Seneca and Tuscarora performers from western New York State – did a few dances near the Castle. An Amish family stood with rapt attention among the spectators. "The Amish are fascinated by Indians," Bob Emerson said to me. I went over to talk to them, but when I got there they were already in conversation with a tall young man entirely naked except for his breech cloth. His name was Ken, and he turned out to be a white man who was portraying an Ottawa Indian. He had gone over to talk to the Amish because he was worried they might think the Iroquois dancing was "devil worship," and he wanted to set them straight. Who knows what conclusions these austere Christians might be jumping to? But the Amish – an older man with his wife, two daughters, and a son, who was also bearded and wore suspenders and a wide-brimmed straw hat – were not scandalized. They asked Ken numerous questions about his face paint, for example, and Ken gave them a complicated history lesson about Ottawa Indians and war paint, which seemed a little dubious to me, but what do I know about "oral tradition." After Ken left, I asked the family their impressions of the Indians, and the older woman, in her plain gray dress and her white cap, smiled and said, "They're an interesting people. They have strong reasons for what they do, and so do we." These Amish were probably even more successful than the Indians in distancing themselves from the dynamo. They seemed to be in a good mood, being here – it was one of the rare occasions when they could be in public and not feel self-conscious about the way they looked. "Yes, they have traditions, just like we do," the patriarch said. "Of course, the basics are different." Pacifism is not a notable Indian tradition, for starters.

Later I shared dinner with members of the unit in The Lily and the Lion while a rainstorm swept over the fort. It soon cleared, however, and the evening was beautiful. The last of the tourists left the fort at seven-thirty, the gates were closed, the doors to the gunpowder magazine locked – the ghosts inside now free to cherish their sad memories, undisturbed by the living. In the declining rays of the sun, white re-enactors performed complicated eighteenth-century minuets on the grass to the music of a flute and a drum, while native re-enactors played a vigorous game of lacrosse. Out of nowhere appeared a file of seven Scottish Highlanders, in their kilts and uniforms and muskets, spaced carefully a few paces apart, led by a sergeant. They were on evening patrol. They marched silently to a spot near the lacrosse players and then halted and stood still for ten minutes or so while the sergeant casually walked about casting an eye on his surroundings. It was a military ritual – an evening reconnaissance. The sergeant, satisfied with what he saw, issued a terse command and the Highlanders turned a half-step and marched, with grave deliberation, to a spot near the wall of the fort overlooking the mouth of the Niagara River. Again they halted. Their silence as they stood there motionless, silhouetted now against the evening sky, was a statement of immense dignity. This was not part of the theater of re-enactment. It had not been planned according to some scenario laid down by a site director. These men were doing this for their own satisfaction – a species of play-acting as serious as you can get, this side of delusion. "They live for their sergeant," a re-enactor said to me.

I went into the Castle, to the second floor, and leaned out an open window to watch the sun set. Across the lake could still be seen the fading towers of Toronto, like a mirage. The red sun disappeared beyond the lake, and all that was left was the black water and a trail of cirrus clouds, still lightly touched with pink. A boy with serious, deep brown eyes joined me at the window. I had seen him earlier in the vestibule of the Castle, with his Indian outfit and war paint and shaved head with ridge of hair in the middle, reciting to a small audience what appeared to be an Indian legend. "I heard you telling a story about a woodpecker," I said.

"That's a good story. I've got another one about why dogs always sniff each other's tails. The dogs were all at a prayer meeting, in the house of purity, for a healing. . . ."

"I know that one. They hung their tails on the wall, and somebody yelled 'fire' and they all grabbed a tail as they ran out the door, but they got them mixed up. That's why they sniff each other's tails, to see if they can find their real one." I recalled this story from third grade in Pittsfield.

"No, at first they all took the right tails, but then there's a part where the cats get into it, and that's why the dogs couldn't find their tails." I was sorry I had interrupted his story. I should have let him tell it. "I like that story," the boy said. "I got it from a Creek storyteller in Georgia."

Almost directly below us, the waters lapped at the breakwater. Off to our left we could see the lights of houses across the river, in Canada. "I play the flute and tell stories," the boy explained. "Last year I made twenty-seven dollars. Most of that was in quarters. Six of it was in dollars. I bought a silver earring with the money, and a bell and cone. That bell and cone I got real cheap. Some of them I know cost eighteen dollars, but this man let me have it for the six dollars I had that weren't in quarters." The last light had now disappeared from the sky. "My daddy's a storyteller, too," the boy continued. "He's Cherokee. We live in Ohio now but his family used to live in the Appalachians. When they came to take the Cherokee away, his family, they just went up into the hills and lived there, and by the time they came down everybody just thought they were white people. I like storytelling, but I'm getting too old for it."

"How old are you?"

"Twelve. I'd like to pass it on to my brother and do something else."

"Like what?"

"Wampum. Bead work. I been doing that for a while now. It's good work but I don't have patience a lot of times and I don't know whether that's a good thing or a bad thing. I'm pulling the thread back and the bead breaks, I get this close" – he held this thumb and forefinger an inch apart – "to throwing the whole thing away."

"Is your dad here?"

"Oh yeah, we like these re-enactments. My mom doesn't, but next year my dad and I are going to the three big ones, Fort Necessity, Fort Ticonderoga, and Fort Niagara. That's the two-hundred-and-fiftieth anniversary of the beginning of the French and Indian War. What do they call it, the Seven Years War? Next seven years now, you won't have to look at the calendar, you'll know what year it is 'cause of all the anniversaries."

"Is that brick dust?" I asked, indicating the red on the lower part of his face.

"Oh, it's just paint. Some of the people here, they shave and do the full body paint. All red with black designs – that's real good. My daddy said he'd do it if he could. Trouble is, it's hard to get it all off. I can't do it. My mom wouldn't stand for it."

We chatted for a while longer – he said he had heard Canada was so "clean," and he wanted to see for himself. Finally we parted. Later that night I saw him dance around a roaring campfire, and he was every bit as good as the Tuscaroras had been earlier that day, or the Thunder Hawk Dancers, but I wondered how long the world would accommodate this remarkable boy and his single-hearted dedication to archaic pursuits.

⚜

Before I left that night, I made a final stop at The Lily and the Lion to return my eighteenth-century clothes and to say goodbye to Greg and Dee Dee. In the course of our conversation, we talked about muskets and about how many expressions we still use today derive from those old weapons – "flash in the pan," "half-cocked," "lock, stock, and barrel." "I was reading about muskets in Stephen Ambrose's book about the Lewis and Clark Expedition, *Dauntless Courage*," one of the re-enactors in the inn said. "He tried to describe how they worked. It was terrible. It was so bad, it was so inaccurate, I just put that book down and I haven't been able to pick it up since."

Historians beware. Detail is not taken lightly by re-enactors. For their part, historians often think of re-enactors as mere anti-quarians who view "history as a storage room for costumes," in Nietzsche's phrase. You have your F&I costume, your Rev War costume, and so on. But then academic historians have their sins to atone for, quite apart from the question of accuracy in describing flintlock muskets. One of these sins – speaking of Nietzsche – is the extent to which they have allowed that philosopher's twentieth-century adherent, Michel Foucault, to exercise such a malign sway over the discipline. I probably shouldn't even mention this subject, it's such a can of worms. Let's just say that at least re-enactors believe, contrary to Foucault, there's a truth outside language we can actually get in touch with. Re-enactors, contrary to Foucault, think we can actually learn something about, and from, the past. That's dangerous talk in the academy, these days. "It is possible to tell several different stories about the past and there is no way, finally, to check them against the fact of the matter," a historian has recently pronounced. "The criterion for evaluating them is moral or poetic." What's your favorite myth? There's your criterion.

Mind you, no one ever said it was easy, even with the best will in the world, to check stories "against the fact of the matter." That soap-maker from the fort is a case in point. I mentioned her comments about how the French could smell the British coming to an acquaintance who happened to be writing a book on the history of personal hygiene. She told me – surprise – that the English of the period said exactly the same thing about the French. I don't know if any histori-ans have seriously investigated this matter. If the records can't tell us for a certainty who smelled worse, the French or the English, how can we hope to get to the bottom of more serious historical controversies? "I believe that the problem is not to make the division between that which, in a discourse, falls under scientificity and truth and that which falls under something else, but to see historically how truth-effects are produced inside discourses which are not in themselves either true or false," Foucault tells us. Does that help?

❧

The next morning, Sunday, I woke up at my friend's house in Niagara-on-the-Lake, across the river in Ontario, where I had been staying while visiting the fort. It was time for my Hobby, which is the practice of Catholicism. Sunday mass beckoned. This practice of Catholicism, like living history, has its odd demands, however, beyond mere attendance at mass. My friend wanted help that morning in putting up a store-bought gazebo, an affair of plastic tubes and a canvas covering, in her backyard. I was happy to oblige, but a thought occurred to me: the Church has always forbidden "servile work" on the sabbath. Did this assembly of the gazebo not constitute such labor?

The issue, oddly enough, cropped up often enough, in my sojourn through the ghost empire of La Salle, that I began to think the old prohibition had a particular resonance with the French in America. In Detroit, I met a man named Al Trudeau, who told me about his grandmother from Trois Rivières, Quebec. As a boy, Al heard from his grandmother a cautionary tale about a Trois Rivières farmer. "The farmer was planting his potatoes on Sunday when everybody was going to mass," Trudeau recalled. "People were saying, 'You shouldn't do that,' but he insisted that he had to get these potatoes planted right away. Well, he had a bumper crop. And when he pulled them out of the ground, they were all rocks." Trudeau laughed. "My grandmother swore the story was true." (Call it a truth-effect inside the grandmother's discourse.) Later I heard about a town in Quebec called Rigaud, just west of Montreal, where they not only told the same story about a local farmer but actually showed visitors the very field where his unholy potatoes had turned to stone.

My own maternal grandmother told my mother that if you knit on a Sunday you would unstitch every stitch with your nose in purgatory.

It was a difficult issue for my father. He would sit in Sacred Heart Church on a Sunday morning, listening to the priest thunder in the pulpit about the mortal sin of servile labor on the sabbath and then after mass change into his work clothes and take out his tools and start renovating his new house, just across the street from the church. He may have felt he had an out – he loved working with his hands. It wasn't really servile work, it was recreation. But I'm sure he felt guilty. That new house, the first house he ever owned after years of scraping by in the Depression, meant a great deal to him. It would have been torture for him not to work on it when he had the time to do so.

As far as the gazebo was concerned, I could hardly say no to my friend. It was the least I could do to repay her for putting me up. Anyway, it only took us half an hour to get the thing standing, and we didn't exactly break into a sweat while doing it. I trust that mitigated the offense. If not, I hope for the intercessory prayers in heaven of my more scrupulous grandmother.

Shortly afterwards I said goodbye to my hostess and headed once more for the American border, en route to La Salle, New York, just outside the city of Niagara Falls. I wanted to make one more trip before returning home. (Where I would attend evening mass.) I wanted to see the spot where La Salle's men built their ship.

Construction on that ship proceeded during the winter while La Salle was away, under the supervision of Tonty. Trees were felled, timbers hewed, and the ribs of the vessel laid out under the care of a master carpenter named Moise Hillaret. Meanwhile, all of Tonty's nerve and steadiness were called upon. The Iroquois were not friendly. "They loitered sullenly about the place," Parkman writes. "One of them, pretending to be drunk, attacked the blacksmith and tried to kill him; but the Frenchman, brandishing a red-hot bar of iron, held him at bay till Hennepin ran to the rescue, when, as he declares, the severity of his rebuke caused the savage to desist." Still, the work went on, including the carving of a griffin, that beast with the head of an eagle and the body of a lion, for the prow. By spring, the ship was finished. "The friar pronounced his blessing on her," writes Parkman, "the assembled company sang *Te Deum*; cannon were fired; and French and Indians, warmed alike by a generous gift of brandy, shouted and yelped in chorus as she glided into the Niagara."

Further progress had to wait for the arrival of La Salle, however, who was in the middle of legal battles back in New France. As soon as he had returned to Fort Frontenac, he discovered that his creditors, spooked by rumors of disaster at Niagara and abetted by his older brother, the ever-useless Jean Cavelier, had initiated proceedings to seize La Salle's furs stored in Montreal and Fort Frontenac as a way to recoup their money. Here again was fuel for La Salle's paranoia. He had to sign over Fort Frontenac temporarily to a subordinate in order to prevent creditors from picking over any more of the bones of his property. By the time he returned to Niagara, in the company of three more friars – La Salle, as we have seen, never ventured into the wilderness without men under Holy Orders – it was already August.

On August 7, the new ship, named the *Griffon*, with twenty-five men aboard, and five cannon on deck, and the *fleur-de-lys* flying, set sail for the upper Great Lakes. "A fresh breeze sprang up; and with swelling canvas the *Griffon* ploughed the virgin waves of Lake Erie, where sail was never seen before," Parkman writes. It was a turning of the hinge of history, a foreshadowing of centuries of commerce across the Great Lakes, a moment when the cities of Detroit and Chicago and Milwaukee became conceivable. The Iroquois were right to be suspicious.

After crossing the border that Sunday afternoon I headed south to Niagara Falls and eventually found myself on Buffalo Avenue, westbound for La Salle. I drove down Buffalo Avenue, dodging potholes and noting the weathered look of the neighborhood and the absence of pedestrians on the sidewalks, until I turned off the avenue to the dirt parking lot of a boat-launching area on the Niagara River. According to my calculations, this was the site where La Salle's crew shivered in their bark huts and kept guard all night because the Iroquois had threatened to burn the ship under construction. A few people were maneuvering boats with inboard motors into a narrow, sluggish, green channel that emptied into the main body of the Niagara River just ahead. On the other side of the channel was a small island with bungalows and compact two-story houses with neat, well-watered backyards and patios with potted flowers. They were the kind of houses a man making a good wage at the plant might own.

Beside this boat-launching area was a miserable little park wedged between the highway, the river, and the channel. It was definitely a park and not simply a vacant lot because there was a playground area for children. But the playground was empty on this sunny afternoon on a Fourth of July weekend. Since there was no water fountain and no trees to shade children from the sun, which had already withered the grass, I was not surprised. Only one person was enjoying the park – a man in a bathing suit lying on his back on top of a picnic table. Perhaps he was only a few yards away from the spot where Tonty and his men did their own boat launching, firing their cannon and singing *Te Deum* and passing around the bottle. The sunbather could have been asleep – there was no noise here, except for the odd eighteen-wheeler on the highway. Then, as I watched, he slowly raised himself and leaned on one elbow as if he was trying to decide whether to continue tanning. After a brief moment, he made his decision and lowered his back to the table.

EIGHT

Detroit

When Detroit was an earthly paradise • Reflections on the grandmother of Christ • An Iroquois Indian who didn't know how to quit • A very aggressive chicken and a dog who could leap thirteen feet

On the morning of the fourth day of sailing, the *Griffon* entered the strait of Detroit. It would be another eighty years before a sailing ship appeared in those waters again. Meanwhile, the French admired the scenery. Hennepin noted groves of black walnut and chestnut and apple and wild plum trees, grapevines entwined around oaks, and game in abundance – flocks of swans and wild turkeys, herds of deer, and bear so fat they practically begged to be killed. One such animal was shot and butchered. According to Hennepin its flesh was "more delicious than fresh pork." In a prophetic strain he wrote, "Those who will one day have the happiness to possess this fertile and pleasant strait, will be very much obliged to those who have shown them the way."

Possessors were not long in coming. In 1701 a French officer named Antoine Laumet de Lamothe, Sieur de Cadillac, arrived on the spot with fifty soldiers and almost as many *coureurs de bois* to construct a permanent fort and trading post. Peace with the Iroquois had just been signed in Montreal, clearing the way for a new French presence in this strategic location athwart the east–west trade routes. It was the beginning of an emerging French strategy. With the discoveries of La Salle, with the reasonably successful conclusion of a long war with the English – the War of the Grand Alliance, as it was named in Britain, or King William's War, as it was known in the English colonies – and with its recent understanding with the Iroquois, New France had come as close as it ever would to dominating the continent. Detroit was the first step in a gradual process of building forts and outposts along the western Great Lakes, in the Ohio valley, and down the Mississippi to New Orleans, that would pin the English between the Allegheny Mountains and the Atlantic Ocean. (Fort Niagara would follow shortly.)

In October of 1701, Cadillac wrote a letter to his superiors describing the locale. From the first sentence of the letter, you can tell that the man, like La Salle, has been given a proper training in grammar and rhetoric. "Since the trade of war is not that of a writer," he begins, "I cannot without rashness draw the portrait of a country so worthy of a better pen than mine; but since you have ordered me to give you an account of it I will do so." He then describes the banks of the Detroit River as

so many vast meadows where the freshness of these beautiful streams keep the grass always green. These same meadows are fringed with long and broad avenues of fruit trees which have never felt the careful hand of the watchful gardener; and fruit trees, young and old, droop under the weight and multitude of their fruit, and bend their branches towards the fertile soil which has produced them. . . . Under these vast avenues you may see assembling in hundreds the shy stag and the timid hind with the bounding roebuck, to pick up eagerly the apples and plums with which the ground is paved. . . . The golden pheasant, the quail, the partridge, the woodcock, the teeming turtle-dove, swarm in the woods and cover the open country intersected and broken by groves of full-grown forest trees – groves forming a charming prospect which of itself might sweeten the melancholy tedium of solitude.

Cadillac was laying it on so thick because he was still selling the idea of Detroit. But in so doing he was using a vocabulary Europeans found familiar. For two centuries they had been searching the western hemisphere for the last traces of Paradise. Columbus thought he had found the Garden of Eden in his third voyage to the New World. As he neared the equator in that voyage, he believed, because of a series of mistaken navigational calculations, that he was sailing uphill. The shape of the world, he later wrote the king and queen of Spain, was not perfectly round. "It has the shape of a pear, which is all very round, except at the stem, which is very prominent . . . as if one had a very round ball, on one part of which something like a woman's nipple were placed." When he reached Trinidad, where the rivers of the Boca del Drago, the River of the Dragon, emptied into the Gulf of Paria, he believed he had arrived at the nipple. He was on top of the world, where man was closest to the heavens. It was an easy mistake to make. The air was balmy, the sky clear, the breezes soft, the landscape green and fruitful and "as beautiful as the orchards of Valencia in April." The waters of the Boca del Drago were majestic – surely they were an outlet for the fountain near the tree of life. "I am completely persuaded in my own mind that the Terrestrial Paradise is in the place I have described," he concluded. He did not attempt to explore the interior to prove it, of course. God had forbidden man to set foot in Paradise.

Some of the Indians Columbus met were so handsome and intelligent and good natured, it was easy to believe they lived next door to Eden. They became famous in Europe for their primitive simplicity and sweet manners. Peter Martyr, the Italian Renaissance intellectual who was an avid student of scientific reports from the

New World, wrote about Indians of the Caribbean living "without weights and measures, and most all without the fatal curse of money, living in the golden age, without laws, without false judges, without books. They lead a life content by nature, with never a care for the future." A generation later, Montaigne, who had witnessed all the horrors of religious and civil warfare in France, drew from Martyr's observation for his essay "On the Cannibals," which was really a broadside aimed at the religious zealots of his own land.

Cadillac, however, was not tapping this vein of New World mythology in his letter. He was drawing on the theme of the richness and power of nature herself. The New World had a fecund beauty that the Old had lost. The New World was a rejuvenation and a restoration. "Our cattle are said to be born fatter there, and turn out much bigger, on account of the lush pastures," wrote Peter Martyr. Up north, it was hard to make a claim for lush pastures and fat cattle, but the French early on noticed an animal that was nearly extinct in Europe but flourishing abundantly in the streams and lakes of Canada – the beaver.

"It is only the opponents of the truth who are the enemies of this settlement," Cadillac ended his visionary letter, "so essential to the glory of the King, to the spread of religion, and to the destruction of the throne of Baal." Who were the adherents of Baal in this case? They were familiar figures – the merchants of Montreal, quick to see in this new outpost the ruin of their trade, and, above all, the Jesuits, who foresaw correctly that the outpost would draw away their native parishioners from Michilimackinac, where they had been ministering to Indians for thirty years and which they had hoped would be the capital of their new Paraguay. Their protests were in vain. Detroit had a future. In 1706 Cadillac brought settlers – two hundred soldiers, whom he hoped would intermarry with the natives, and forty families, with domestic animals, grain and seeds, carpentry tools, and so on. Cadillac subdivided the land he had been granted as a seigneury into plots along the Detroit River of the "ribbon" kind characteristic of the farms along the St. Lawrence River in Quebec. That is, they had narrow fronts on the water – a seventh of a mile, characteristically, so that every farmer had access to fish and water transport – and extended back from the banks of the river about ten times that length. This division of the land meant farmhouses were set close together along the river – a much more sociable style of settlement than the traditional American farm. In exchange for their land, the farmers paid rent and some other charges to Cadillac. It was a medieval arrangement rather than a modern one; as long as the farmer paid his feudal dues, which were not onerous, he had a sure title to his farm. The average Englishman at the time would have been delighted with the deal.

Mass had been said at Detroit from the day Cadillac first arrived, and, even more propitious, the soil in which the Church would grow had been watered with the blood of at least one martyr. A devoted priest named Constantin Delhalle was shot by an Indian during an outbreak of inter-tribal warfare in 1706, just before Cadillac's settlers arrived. "Neither the tragedy of his death nor the memory of his kind and saintly life were ever forgotten by the French inhabitants of old Detroit," writes Father George Paré in his 1951 history *The Catholic Church in Detroit.* "He was enshrined in their traditions, and there grew up around him a cult which disappeared only when alien races, ignorant and contemptuous of the past, became dominant." And who might those "alien races" be, who helped wipe out the memory of French Detroit? Whoever they were, you can bet they were Protestants. But I am ahead of myself. Let us return briefly to the Sieur de Cadillac. In 1708 he supervised construction of the first real church in Detroit, a ten-foot-high structure built of logs, thirty-five feet long and twenty-four and a half feet wide, with a green carpet for the sanctuary, an altar of French walnut, and a bell to toll the angelus.

⚜

Three hundred years after the beginning of Detroit, I drove into the great, ruined city and headed for the spires of Ste. Anne de Detroit, a Gothic revival church in downtown Detroit and the successor to the log chapel with the green carpet. That chapel had been the first of six wooden churches, some lost to fire and war, all destroyed eventually. The seventh church was called the Stone Church. It was torn down in 1886 and the present St. Anne's built on its site – the eighth, and no doubt the last church of St. Anne de Detroit. It's a handsome monument to "living history," if ever there was one. "St. Anne's is the oldest European institution between the Alleghenies and the Mississippi," states the guidebook to the church, written by Father Leo Reilly, C.S.B. (Congregation of St. Basil). This excellent little book is worth a look, if only for its outline of the social changes in St. Anne's parish. "By the 1920s, the Irish had become the dominant group, although French Masses continued to be said until 1942," Father Reilly writes. (Surely the Irish were not Father Paré's "alien race"?)

Under the heading "The Collapse of the City," Father Reilly cites a familiar American tragedy – the flight of the middle class to the suburbs after World War II, the resulting strain on inner-city schools and public services, the carving up of the downtown by new interstate highways, the razing of inner-city houses under the rubric of Urban Renewal. "A new slavery of enforced ignorance and disadvantage was imposed on the city leading to exploitation by the rich, the terrible effects of concentrated child poverty for the poor, and a false sense of entitlement for the majority, while minorities wrongly blame themselves for their own problems," Father Reilly states. We seem to be straying quite far from altars and stained glass windows and statuary. But it's all context. "The parish changed during this time from a relatively stable neighborhood, first to a transitional housing zone in the 1950s, providing good, affordable housing for newcomers, and then to being part of the general process of depopulation, abandonment and ruin."

So bad had things gotten that in 1965 the archdiocese ordered the parish to be closed for lack of parishioners and money. A campaign to save it ensued. Foundations and governments supplied funds, the church underwent a major restoration, and new waves of Mexican immigrants revitalized the parish. Today, the economy is also perking up, although severe social problems remain. In response, the church has helped to found a non-profit association that is currently building homes in the parish and has re-opened a parochial school that had been closed for thirty years. It's now a charter school, partly funded by General Motors and something called the Empowerment Zone.

There is a continuity between the Mexican immigrants who currently worship at St. Anne's and the French who attended mass at the log chapel that preceded it. Not only were both Catholics, but both were attached particularly to the maternal side of the Church. The early French Canadians, for example, had a particular devotion to St. Anne, the mother of the Blessed Virgin Mary and the grandmother of Jesus – hence the name of their church in Detroit. Of course, if you listen to a stout Protestant or a modern Catholic, you will quickly be informed that she is a legendary figure. There is no mention of her in scripture. Her name, as well as the name of her husband, Joachim, comes from an early apocryphal (that is, fanciful) work called the *Protevangelium of James*. This need not perturb us. We can assume that Mary had a mother, and that this mother very probably was a saint, that is to say someone who loved greatly. Why should we not grant both assumptions? "Eagles have eaglets," a psychotherapist once said to me, meaning that you can't escape, even if you desperately want to, your resemblance to your parents. This resemblance can be explained by nurture or nature, but it comes to the same. "Henceforth all generations shall call me blessed," Mary correctly prophesied after the visit of the angel announcing her impending pregnancy, and among her blessings must surely have been a mother who helped mold her luminous character. This mother presumably lived to see her unmarried daughter become pregnant and nevertheless did not add to her difficulties in that extremely delicate situation. Let's say her real name is lost to history, but she will answer to "Anne" in your prayers.

❦

The first time I met Gail Moreau was in a French-Canadian archive in a small town near Windsor, Ontario, just across the border from Detroit. Moreau, who lives north of Detroit, is vice-president of the French-Canadian Heritage Society of Michigan and editor of their quarterly journal, *Michigan's Habitant Heritage*. She spends a lot of time in archives, doing genealogical and historical research. She had recently been to Kingston, Ontario, for example, to root around in their archives, but did not have the happiness to meet any of Francis Beaulieu's "French-friendly" Kingstonians. "You mention the word 'French,' and it's a dirty word there," she recalled. "They say, 'Oh yeah.' I tried to find what I could on the French and see what information they had, and nothing. You can't get a thing out of them."

Moreau, fifty-nine, was wearing a purple sweater and a silver *fleur-de-lys* pendant. A former schoolteacher, she has a tendency to deliver summary judgments, a tendency often found in veteran members of that profession, whose patience for nonsense has worn thin over long years in the classroom. French descendants in Michigan who evinced no interest in their heritage – like a certain parish priest she knew – had no excuse, in her eyes. "These priests like Father Lacroix – *beautiful* French-Canadian name – he could care less," she said. "I just ignore him now."

Given her passion for French heritage, I was startled to learn that she was born Gail Schreiner – Moreau is the name of her first, deceased husband – and was mostly of German descent. Her French-friendly attitude came from her years teaching in Michigan public schools. "I taught French and I loved it," she said.

She has not given up hope of finding some French in her own family. "I have a great-great-great grandmother from Saarbrucken, whose name was Andres," she said. "That name could have gone either way, French or German, depending on its precise spelling and accent. It's probably German, unfortunately. I won't know until I get to some real records."

No wonder she was impatient with people like Father LaCroix, who didn't appreciate the sublimity of being French.

I asked her what the members of her society, aside from the pleasure of tracking down ancestors, got from their interest in their heritage. "They understand the food concept," she said, citing their tenacious fondness for the *tourtière*, a meat pie – the national dish of French Canada, if you want to call it that. As a third-generation French Canadian living in the United States, I must confess that *tourtières* and my family were strangers. In my father's time, the main French-Canadian food concept was baked beans. Pots of navy beans or yellow-eyed beans or pea beans, flavored with salt pork, would be boiling all day Saturday in French-Canadian households across New England, in preparation for the Saturday night baked bean dinner.

For Michigan French Canadians, however, the *tourtière* was the major culinary link – perhaps the only link – with their old *habitant* forebears. "Pork pie is a big thing – that's one thing everybody can come up with their own version of," Moreau said. "We've published a million recipes of that in the journal over the years." She gave me a couple of issues of the journal to look at. I was impressed with the articles, which were meticulously documented histories of local French parishes and families, among other items. "If you really look for a good history of Detroit from the beginning, you don't find one," Moreau said. "That's what we're doing in the journal, is putting good solid information in there. I've gotten some criticism for being too scholarly in my choice of articles, but if somebody else wants to do this job – for which I'm not being paid, heh, heh – they can go for it."

If nothing else, my jaunt across the continent in the footsteps of La Salle was giving me a new appreciation of amateur history in North America, which ranges from Judge Krischke's one hundred and sixty monographs on local cemeteries, to some re-enactor making sure the design and material of the buttons for his uniform were exactly the right kind, to members of the French-Canadian Heritage Society of Michigan ruining their eyesight on microfilm machines going over old parish records to prove that so-and-so was the real wife of so-and-so. These people were certainly not inhabitants of what Gore Vidal calls the United States of Amnesia.

I next met Gail Moreau a few weeks later, when there was a special mass at St. Anne's for people of French descent. It was part of a "novena," or succession of nine evening masses, dedicated to various ethnic groups. Aside from the French, masses were celebrated for Croatians and Ukrainians, African Americans, Native Americans, Italians, Poles, Irish, and Latinos. (The ninth mass was for "healing," a specialty of St. Anne's; the great shrine of Ste-Anne-de-Beaupré in Quebec City is famous for its cures.)

The mass began with a procession of the Fourth Degree Knights of Columbus Color Corps down the main aisle followed by a few dozen men and women dressed in French period costume. Gail Moreau was there, dressed in the white cap and dress of an eighteenth-century *châtelaine*, or lady of the household. This time she wore silver *fleur-de-lys* earrings. "Tonight we welcome the French community of Detroit," a monsignor began by saying. Then he invoked the saint in whose honor the church had been built. "St. Anne is and was much loved by Jesus," he said. "All children love their grandparents. *Chaque enfant aime ses grandparents.*"

The actual sermon was delivered by the "presider" – an awful word, currently employed by the American Catholic church instead of "celebrant," to describe the priest officiating at the mass. He was a Basilian named Father George Beaune. "Everywhere we are surrounded by French influence, subtle though it may be today," he said in his sermon. Well, yes. There's the Hotel Ponchartrain, and Grosse

Pointe and Livernois Avenue and other French names that few people in Detroit even realize are French, which is a very subtle form of influence, like Mohican influence in my hometown of Pittsfield, Massachusetts, where we had place names such as Wahconah Park and Pontoosuc Lake. He was on firmer ground when he turned to the church itself and talked about its French Gothic architectural style. "It's extremely busy," he noted. "In fact, in later times other architects or artists criticized this style because they thought it was too busy, but if you remember, in the Middle Ages, people like you, people like me, could not read. We couldn't read the Bible, we couldn't follow the missal, and so what we read were pictures. And the cathedral was filled with pictures. This church is just filled with symbols of our faith, symbols of the sacred figures of the saints, and biblical figures." Father Beaune did not mention that the same post-Vatican II approach that replaced "celebrant" with "presider" had little use for "busy" churches that employed pictures and statuary to impress the faithful. Five hundred years after Luther and Calvin used the printing press as a battering ram against the Gothic Cathedral – and against Rome itself – the Catholic Church has given in. No longer will any Catholic church look like the chief book of our culture. The television age has put the final nail in that coffin.

After the mass, the Knights of Columbus led a procession out of the church, carrying on a litter a statue of St. Anne, who was holding her young daughter in one arm and raising the other in benediction. Both figures wore white and gold robes, the younger with a crown to signify her status as Queen of Heaven. We walked slowly in procession around the square in front of the church, saying a decade of the rosary, and then back to the front door of the church, where I kissed, with other worshippers, a reliquary containing the relics of St. Anne.

The worshippers then gathered under a canopy beside the church for some refreshments *à la française*. There were no *tourtières* or pots of baked beans, but there was red wine served in paper cups and some *bonbons* from the *pâtisserie*. I met Gail Moreau's son,

Jean-Pierre, visiting with his girlfriend, Kyle, from Indiana. Jean-Pierre was a smiling young man with a goatee. "He's looking more and more French every day," Gail Moreau said to her friends. "Is that a disease?" one of them joked. "Yes," she replied. "A French disease. *Mal à la tête.*" She laughed. It was clear nothing could delight her more than her son looking French. How I wish she had been present in that fourth grade classroom with Mrs. Drennan. I think Mrs. Drennan might have learned something.

I also met Al Trudeau, a sixty-nine-year-old native of Detroit whose French forebears had come to Michigan in the late nineteenth century. Trudeau's grandmother from Trois Rivières was the one who reported the negative miracle of the potatoes. Al Trudeau's particular pride was his descent from a certain Étienne Trudeau, a master carpenter who came to New France from La Rochelle, France, in the seventeenth century. Apparently, his crossing of the Atlantic had been particularly rough, which was considered an ominous beginning for Étienne Trudeau's new start in life. But in New France, Étienne Trudeau and his wife proceeded to have fourteen children – thirteen boys, one girl. From that brood has descended virtually every person named Trudeau in North America, including the late Canadian prime minister Pierre Trudeau and Doonesbury creator Garry Trudeau. "As my cousin says, 'We're as numerous as fleas on a dog,'" Al Trudeau remarked. Blessed patriarch Étienne Trudeau. The ancient Israelites would have identified him as God's favorite. "Thou shalt know also that thy seed shall be great, and thine offspring as the grass of the earth," Eliphaz promises Job in the midst of his wretchedness, as if that promise made up for any sorrow. Alternatively, you can also view this man as a Darwinian hero, obeying the call to reproduce his kind with remarkable fidelity. Either way, Étienne Trudeau could not say his life had been purposeless.

❧

One of the first things the French in Detroit did, after building their fort and their church, was to persuade the Hurons, who had been living near Michilimackinac, to remove to this new settlement. They didn't need much persuasion; the Hurons, dependent on trade with the French, had nowhere else to go. In the whole bitter history of New France, no story is more tragic than the story of these people. Based largely in southern Ontario at the time of the European arrival, the Hurons were closely related in language and culture — the culture of hunters and corn farmers — to the Iroquois, their southern cousins and inveterate foes. Nearly as populous as their enemies, at probably twenty thousand in the early seventeenth century, the Hurons held their own for many years. Land and resources were not the issue in this struggle; the Hurons and the Iroquois were engaged in traditional warfare, the aim of which, according to Bruce Trigger, the noted authority on the Hurons, was "to preserve one's enemies as a group in order to be able to go on fighting with them indefinitely." The Indians, a French observer noted, "do not make war to invade the lands of their neighbours nor to plunder them. . . . It is solely for the pleasure of killing men."

The first European to write about the Hurons at any length was a Recollet priest named Gabriel Sagard, who visited them in 1623 and later wrote about his experiences in two books, the *History of Canada* and the *Long Journey to the Country of the Hurons*. Sagard never forgot that the Hurons were uncivilized, shockingly immoral in many ways, and in dire need of the gospel, but he also portrayed them with surprising sympathy, particularly in *Long Journey*. To begin with, they were much better physical specimens than the Europeans. "They are as a rule well shaped and proportioned in body, and without any deformity, and I can say with truth that I have seen among them as fine children as there could be in France," Sagard wrote. "There are none indeed of those big-bellied men [*gros ventres*], full of humours and fat, that we have here." Even the aged were *forts et robustes*, and the women so strong they gave birth practically without assistance. Some of their cultural practices were equally pleasant to behold. Sagard praised the great generosity and hospitality of the Hurons, as exemplified by their "pious and charitable" custom of making sure every member of their village was adequately lodged and fed, and their habit of providing for wayfarers. "They reciprocate hospitality," he noted, "and give such assistance to one another that the necessities of all are provided for without there being any indigent beggar in their towns and villages. And they considered it a very bad thing when they heard it said that there were in France a great many of these needy beggars, and thought that this was for lack of charity in us, and blamed us for it severely." The general rule was that native Americans were far more generous to their own than Europeans; on the other hand, they were far more ruthless to outsiders than were Europeans.

Sagard was revolted by sexual promiscuity among the Hurons, but he also had to admit that, despite their working harder than the menfolk, Huron wives were more affectionate toward their husbands than their French counterparts. "They have more love for one another," he concluded of the Hurons, "than we who call ourselves better." Certainly they were more indulgent toward their children. Fathers "love their children dearly, in spite of the doubt that they are really their own, and of the fact that they are for the most part very naughty [*très mauvais*] children, paying them little respect, and hardly more obedience; for unhappily in these lands the young have no respect for the old, nor are children obedient to their parents, and moreover there is no punishment for any fault." Some years later a young Huron called Savignon by the French, the first of his nation to be received at the French court, returned and warned his fellow Hurons not to send their children to France if they wanted to see them alive again. He was shocked by the Europeans' habit of cuffing and manhandling children. Huron parents did not even speak a harsh word to their children lest they grow up to be weak and timid. Savignon was also disgusted by Frenchmen who quarreled and gesticulated with their arms without actually coming to blows. These verbal spats were unmanly.

The *Long Journey to the Country of the Hurons* and the *History of Canada*, both published in the 1630s, had an enormous impact on France in the seventeenth and eighteenth centuries. Like the sixteenth-century work of Peter Martyr, these books aroused the tormented conscience of Europe – a conscience that grew ever more tormented as time passed with the wars of religion, the ferocious persecution of the French Protestants after the revocation of the Edict of Nantes in 1689, the ongoing pillage of the New World, the piratical nature of wealth and privilege in the capitals of Europe. By contrast, Sagard's Hurons appeared to be free, natural, generous spirits, doing what they pleased and obeying nature's laws in the wilderness. Rousseau, who, in his hatred of the artificial and the authoritarian and the hierarchical, founded the cult of the child, took notice. His child-rearing program breathed the Huron spirit – no physical restraints, no tyranny of book learning, no over-stimulus of the imagination. Voltaire took notice, although he was no lover of the primitive. The hero of his 1767 novella *L'Ingénu* (*The Innocent*) is a white man raised by Hurons in North America, suddenly transplanted to Bourbon France. Like Sagard's Hurons, and unlike Frenchmen, the Innocent is far too polite to interrupt other people when they're speaking. Like the Hurons, he sees no reason not to "marry" the woman he wants without going through all sorts of civil and ecclesiastical rigmarole. Like the Hurons, he is a reliable support to his family and countrymen. "I lived among the Hurons for twenty years," he tells a fellow prisoner in the Bastille, where he ends up after offending various high personages. "People call them barbarians because they take revenge on their enemies, but they have never oppressed their friends." Most importantly for Voltaire, the Huron-raised Innocent has not been indoctrinated from birth with European prejudices. Therefore, though a savage, he is a nascent philosopher.

The idealization of the North American Indian has not diminished since Montaigne and Voltaire, and in fact is probably more influential in western culture than ever before. It is impossible now to portray a bullying or oafish Indian on television or in the movies, and this prohibition extends to all members of tribal societies, past and present. Even academics are prone to what Bruce Trigger refers to as "the Garden of Eden syndrome," which he defines as a tendency "to attribute static qualities to simpler cultures and see in their equilibrium evidence of a successful adaptation to their environment, and to one another, that contrasts with the conflict and confusion of modern industrial societies." We still need, in short, to see the Indians as redemptive in some way.

It goes without saying that North American Indians have displayed no notable tendency to idealize Europeans. The Hurons that Sagard met, for example, were sometimes wary and fearful of the French, sometimes fascinated by them, but often contemptuous. They didn't like the way French merchants haggled over the price of beaver pelts, for example, which was not the way allies were supposed to treat each other. They were very aware that the French were shorter and scrawnier than they were and that they also wore beards, which the Hurons regarded as repulsive. (Was that what made the French so stupid on occasion, their beards?) On the other hand, they were quite taken with the domestic cats the French brought with them. The Hurons thought these animals possessed powerful spirits.

Given all this, it was a tall order to convert the Hurons to Christianity, a task the Jesuits took over from the Recollets after 1634. The latter had intended to Frenchify the Hurons before converting them. The Jesuits, as we have seen, had a very different approach. If the Hurons never learned French, that would be fine – the Jesuits could do their talking for them, back in Quebec. But the ostensibly enlightened attitude of the Jesuits toward non-interference with Huron culture may have actually led to more harm than good. Because the Hurons lacked formal religious creeds and institutions, the Jesuits assumed they had minimal religious beliefs, and that it would be easy simply to remove the un-Christian parts of their culture. But supernatural views and rituals underlay virtually every aspect of Huron life. Huron hunters were careful not to let the fat from their catch fall into the fire, for example, lest the soul of the animal be offended. They were also as mad for charms as were medieval Christians – that is, theologically unsophisticated medieval Christians – had been mad for relics. "Some were purchased at great price from the northern Algonkians who, because of their reputation as hunters and fishermen, were believed to possess very powerful charms," Trigger writes.

Faced with this reality, the Jesuits realized Huron culture was less benign than they thought and found themselves opposing a multitude of rituals and practices inspired by the Evil One. On their part, many Hurons regarded the black robes as sorcerers bent on the destruction of the Huron nation. Not surprisingly, the Jesuit missionaries made little headway. They were very ambitious to think they could turn Huronia into a Christian commonwealth within a few decades; it took centuries for the Church to convert the Franks and the Visigoths. But how hard they tried. One of the most touching examples is the story of Father Noel Chabanel, who came from the sunny hills of Garonne in France to the North American wilderness in 1643, at the age of thirty. A letter written by a fellow Jesuit after Chabanel's death tells us how the good father "burned with desire for the conversion of the Savages." The first step was to learn the Huron language, a language Chabanel was confident he could master because he had "for some years successfully taught Rhetoric in France." He had also mastered Greek, Latin, Italian, and Spanish. To his mortification he found Huron impenetrable – after five years of study, he could barely ask the person next to him to pass the bowl of cornmeal.

But then every aspect of living with the Hurons "did such violence to his entire nature." There was the awful food he could barely bring himself to eat, the absence of wine as a digestive and fortifier of spirits, the sleeping on bare ground, the lice, the long-houses full of smoke and bad smells, and perhaps worst of all the absence of that new European luxury, privacy. Father Chabanel could not repair to some quiet spot in the longhouse and do a little reading without being surrounded by crying children and barking dogs and men and women in animated conversations. (Was that laughter at his expense?) It didn't take long for the Hurons to notice his sensitivity, and of course they took delight in aggravating it. Once, when a hunting party returned, they invited him to join in the feast of good, fresh meat. After he had eaten his fill, they pulled a human hand out of the kettle to show him he had eaten of an Iroquois prisoner. They then howled with laughter as the priest bent over and vomited.

That wasn't even the worst of it. "It appeared that God, in order to make his Cross heavier, deprived him of visible graces by aban-doning him to disgust and to sadness," a fellow Jesuit wrote. "Is not this a great trial, especially if it lasts five or six whole years?" No wonder the Devil began to speak to him. Why not return to France? Why waste his talents here in the wilderness? He could be just as zealous in saving souls there as here, and probably a good deal more successful. In response, the depressed and fearful Chabanel made a solemn vow to stay where he was until his dying breath and continue to work for the conversion of the Hurons. "I conjure you, therefore, O my Savior, to be pleased to receive me as a perpetual servant of this Mission, and to make me worthy of so lofty a min-istry. Amen." A few years later he perished alone in the wilderness, murdered by a renegade Huron. "No man ever gave up more for Christ than Noel Chabanel," says a fellow priest in Willa Cather's novel about early Quebec, *Shadows on the Rock*. "Many gave all, but few had so much to give."

By Chabanel's time, both the Iroquois and the Hurons had become dependent on the fur trade for the tools and weapons that gave their possessors an overwhelming economic and military advantage. But the supply of furs was limited. Warfare between the Iroquois and the Hurons, therefore, ceased to be traditional in form and became genocidal, as both nations struggled to retain their hold on a now vital resource. Initially fortunes of war swayed back and forth. In 1638 a combined force of three hundred Hurons and Algonquins ran into a band of one hundred Iroquois. Most of the Iroquois wanted to run for their lives, but a headman named Ononkwaia opposed them. "He argued that such cowardice was possible only if it were night-time or if the sky was overcast," Trigger writes, "but that since the spirit of the sun could see what was happening, it was necessary for each man to fight as bravely as he could." The Iroquois were overwhelmed, and about eighty taken prisoner, including the resolute Ononkwaia. The Jesuit fathers, according to Parkman, "could not save his life, but, what was more to the purpose, they baptized him. On the scaffold where he was burned, he wrought himself into a fury which seemed to render him insensible to pain. Thinking him nearly spent, his tormentors scalped him, when, to their amazement, he leaped up, snatched the brands that had been the instruments of his torture, drove the screeching crowd from the scaffold, and held them all at bay, while they pelted him from below with sticks, stones, and showers of live coals." The crowd managed to seize him finally and throw him back into the fire, but once more he leaped out and ran. He was wrestled to the ground anew, his hands and feet cut off, and thrown back again into the fire. On his elbows and knees he crawled out of the flames, still defiant. Finally, they cut off his head.

This is the kind of tale that, in other circumstances, would have been told for generations in the Iroquois and Huron longhouses. If the Iroquois had been ancient Greeks, they would have woven it into an epic poem and made one of Ononkwaia's parents a god, like the mother of Achilles or the father of Hercules. Of course, in real life you wouldn't necessarily want Ononkwaia in your war party, any more than, if you were a trooper in the Seventh Cavalry, you would want your commanding officer to be George Armstrong Custer.

Eventually the Iroquois, well armed with Dutch muskets, got the upper hand. The Jesuits, according to Trigger, may have inadvertently contributed to the Huron defeat by insisting that only Christian Hurons receive French arms; the Jesuits hoped that the French would take care of the Dutch and the Iroquois so the Hurons wouldn't have to. That was a delusion. The French were far too weak militarily; in fact, during the decade of the 1640s, it sometimes seemed that the Iroquois were poised to wipe out New France as well as Huronia. Adam Dollard's last stand in 1660 is testimony to the desperate straits of the French. A poorly armed Huron nation, then, was left to fight virtually on its own. In addition, the Hurons had to devote more of their men to trading with the French, given the greater territory encompassed by their trade routes; by contrast, the Iroquois had easy access to the Dutch.

"Their true superiority was a moral one," Parkman says of the Iroquois. In the same way that he believed the English were a more forceful nation than the French, he believed the Iroquois simply outclassed the Hurons. The Iroquois, Parkman wrote, "were in one of those transports of pride, self-confidence, and rage for ascendancy, which, in a savage people, marks an era of conquest." The Hurons could not stand up to this rage for ascendancy. With every year that passed, the Iroquois grew bolder and penetrated farther into the territory of the Hurons. Martyrdom became an ever more probable destiny for the Jesuit missionaries. "Not the most hideous nightmare of a fevered brain," wrote Parkman, "could transcend in horror the real and waking perils with which [the Iroquois] beset the path of these intrepid priests."

One such intrepid priest was an Italian Jesuit named Joseph Bressani, captured by the Iroquois in the spring of 1644 while canoeing up the St. Lawrence. For days he was tortured, on and off, by his captors – mangled, burnt, and lacerated. "I could not have believed that a man was so hard to kill," he later wrote his superior, after the Iroquois spared his life and sold him to the Dutch. "I do not know if your Paternity will recognize the handwriting of one whom you once knew very well," he apologized. "The letter is soiled and ill-written; because the writer has only one finger of his right hand left entire, and cannot prevent the blood from his wounds, which are still open, from staining the paper. His ink is gunpowder mixed with water, and his table is the earth." Liberated by the Dutch and placed on board a ship for France, Bressani was restored to his continental brethren that fall, only to return to the wilderness in the following spring, to continue his work among the Huron.

The most spectacular martyrdom, of course, was that of Brébeuf and Lalemant a few years later, when the fortified village of St. Louis in the heart of Huron territory fell to an army of a thousand well-armed Iroquois warriors. "All was over with the Hurons," Parkman writes of that calamity in the spring of 1649. "The death-knell of their nation had been struck. Without a leader, without organization, without union, crazed with fright and para-lyzed with misery, they yielded to their doom without a blow. Their only thought was flight." Starving as well as terrified – Iroquois raids had prevented them from cultivating their fields – the Hurons aban-doned their towns and scattered. "The Hurons, as a nation, ceased to exist," Parkman writes.

Many were absorbed into the Iroquois Confederacy. Of those who resisted such absorption, one group found a lasting home in La Jeune Lorette, ten miles outside of Quebec City, where their descendants live today. Another group – the true remnant of the Huron nation – became the Hurons at Michilimackinac that Cadillac summoned to Detroit. In the early eighteenth century these Detroit Hurons, numbering a few hundred, were praised by French observers for their industry in farming and hunting, their courage, their fidelity to the French, and their religion. "The Hurons are all Christians," a visiting Jesuit noted in 1721. The dream of Brébeuf and Chabanel had at last been fulfilled, after nearly a century of unspeakable human suffering. Alternatively, one can view this development as the last indignation visited upon a help-less remnant of a once mighty nation.

Who knows? The Hurons seemed to be very sincere Christians. We can't be too sentimental, either, about "native spirituality," which the Hurons presumably could have clung to if they wanted. There's a point where a human society has got to stop eating the roasted flesh of prisoners who have been tortured to death. Christianity played a role in discrediting such a practice. This much should be granted, even by people who think the Hurons would have done better adopting a philosophy that combined the best of Sitting Bull and Bertrand Russell.

❧

It was one of their Jesuit pastors, Father Pierre Potier, who tried to stop the Hurons of Detroit from joining the greatest Indian uprising in North American history. That uprising occurred in 1763, two and a half years after the British arrived at the gates of Detroit, in November of 1760, to demand its surrender. By then the last French commander in Detroit, a man named Captain Belestre, had heard of the surrender of Canada in Montreal, and knew the game was up. The flag of the French was hauled down, the thirty-odd French soldiers under Belestre's command escorted back east, and the local French-Canadian inhabitants given the choice of clearing out or swearing an oath of loyalty to the English king. Almost all of them took the oath. For seven years of war, they had endured hunger and penury and the hazards of war. The British promised to leave them pretty much alone, and, for once, a wartime promise was kept. The French of Canada, in Detroit and Montreal and Quebec City, soon went back to farming and hunting and trapping and attending mass, which is why their numbers steadily increased in the next two centuries and why, in the fullness of time, I was born in a New England town to Catholic, middle-class parents who possessed a vestigial memory of the French language.

The Indians weren't so lucky. Almost immediately after the French surrender, the British commander in North America,

Jeffery Amherst, instructed his officers to cut down on the distribution of gifts among their Indian allies. It was the flow of British largesse, combined with the choking off of French gifts and trade goods in the latter years of the war, that had finally broken the old French and Indian alliance in the heart of the continent. But now the French were gone for good, and, in the eyes of the British, other measures were called for. "Services must be rewarded; it has ever been a maxim with me," Amherst declared early in 1761. "But as to purchasing the good behavior either of Indians, or any others, that is what I do not understand; when men of what race soever behave ill, they must be punished but not bribed."

Amherst was a classic case in the annals of the British ruling class. He was not stupid. He had enough intelligence and determination successfully to carry out a good plan that required not much imagination, and so he won a continent with his superior armies. But he had no wish to appreciate his true situation. He could not understand that the Indians expected gifts from the British almost as their right, because the British were making free use of their land, for one thing, and also because many Indians had died fighting for the British and these dead must either be avenged or paid for. French officers and Jesuit priests had no trouble understanding this attitude. They stopped giving gifts to the Indians only when they lost the power to do so. Amherst, on the other hand, thought the French had spoiled the Indians. He assumed that if the Indians weren't given a lot of gifts they'd go back to hunting and fending for themselves and staying out of trouble. Idle hands, and so on. Besides, Britain was deep in debt. Expenses had to be cut.

Naturally the Indians began to wish for the return of those *charmant* French, who had adopted many of their ways and married many of their women, as opposed to the stiff-necked English, who had little tolerance of their ways and who merely prostituted their women. And surely the French would return. "Englishman, we are informed that our Father, the King of France, is old and infirm; and that being fatigued with making war upon your nation, he is fallen asleep," one Chippewa chief told a British trader in 1761. "During his sleep you have taken advantage of him and possessed yourselves of Canada. But his nap is almost at an end. I think I hear him already stirring and inquiring for his children, the Indians; and when he does awake, what must become of you? He will destroy you utterly."

With Amherst's policy of minimal gift-giving in effect, and with English-speaking settlers increasingly invading their lands, an Ottawa war chief named Pontiac decided to force the hand of the French and wake their king from his nap. So in April of 1763 he launched an attack on the British fort at Detroit with about 460 warriors. The fort held out against the surprise assault, and Pontiac settled into a siege. By midsummer, his force had doubled. Meanwhile, seven British forts in the west fell to Pontiac's allies. Two others were abandoned. From western Pennsylvania to the Mississippi, from the northern tip of Michigan to the Ohio River, Indian nations rose in defiance of Amherst and the British.

The Hurons were divided on the question of whether to join Pontiac – a majority was in favor, but a significant minority, swayed by the arguments of Father Potier, who well knew the hopelessness of trying to oust the British, hesitated. Potier, tall and gaunt, was remarkable even among the Jesuits for his scholarship. He never traveled anywhere without making meticulous records of the people and landscape; more fortunate in linguistic studies than Father Chabanel, he composed a Huron grammar and dictionary. Apparently he lacked easygoing warmth and never entirely won the hearts of his Huron flock. But he was respected. He would have kept at least a part of the Huron nation away from war had not Pontiac paid a visit to their settlement and threatened to kill those who did not join him. It was a persuasive argument. The neutralist faction joined the pro-war faction of the Hurons, which in turn prompted Father Potier to threaten to withhold the sacraments from the rebellious Hurons. That, too, was a persuasive argument. The result was that the Potier-influenced faction of Hurons fought for two days and then removed themselves far enough from Detroit to wait out the rest of the war.

For a few months in the summer of 1763, that war went very well for the Indians. Several hundred English were killed or captured, while Indian casualties remained minimal. Once again, the land west of the Appalachians belonged to its woodland inhabitants, the Shawnee and the Chippewa, the Delaware and the Miami, the Ottawa and the Potawatomi, and even the few hundred Hurons living outside of Detroit, who had no claim to this land but also nowhere else to go. Outraged, Amherst made himself infamous in history by proposing that blankets infected with smallpox be distributed among the Indians. Fortunately it never came to that. British expeditions successfully relieved the two forts still under siege – Fort Pitt and Detroit – thereby making it clear they would not be driven out. Indian enthusiasm, along with their supplies and ammunition, began to wear thin. The crushing blow to their uprising occurred when they learned that the French, who had signed the Treaty of Paris in February 1763, renouncing their North American empire, would never be returning. The old king would never waken from his nap. In October of that year, a French soldier named DeQuindre brought the heartbreaking news to Pontiac and his warriors. "The great day has come at last, whereupon it has pleased the Master of Life to inspire the Great King of the French and him of the English, to make Peace between them, sorry to see the blood of men spilt so long," DeQuindre told them. "What joy you will have in seeing the French and English smoking with the same pipe and eating out of the same spoon and finally living like brethren. You will see the roads free, the lakes and rivers unstopped. Ammunition and merchandise will abound in your villages."

The heirs of Pontiac, however, would never enjoy this vision of free and prosperous Indians smoking the same pipe and eating out of the same bowl with their French and English brethren. In the years after the Treaty of Paris, and the murder of a powerless Pontiac by a disaffected Indian, the British Crown did its best – to its credit – to keep the Indian lands west of the Appalachians from white invasion, but the only reward it reaped for its efforts was the American Revolution. The Hurons of Detroit, meanwhile, lived as best they could in their mission, located now on the Canadian side of the Detroit River, opposite the growing city. In 1767 that mission officially disappeared when the Church created a new parish, Assumption parish, that would henceforth serve both Huron and French-Canadian Catholics. It would be headed by Father Potier.

This bit of ecclesiastical housekeeping serves as well as any other event to mark the final demise of the Huron nation in its old domain. Groups of Hurons would continue to live in the settlement near Quebec City, and in a small reservation in Oklahoma, where numbers of the nation settled in the nineteenth century, but the last living community in old Huronia was now a memory. Father Potier, too, represented the end of the road. In 1773, Pope Clement XIV, under severe pressure from European monarchs, suppressed the Jesuit order. No longer would Jesuit priests come to Canada from France and Belgium to wander the wilderness. Father Potier stayed at his post and watched the last of his Jesuit colleagues in America die, and then in July 1781 his own frail body was found in front of his fireplace. His intellect, Father Paré tells us, might have brought him fame and distinction under other circumstances. Instead he "spent thirty years in the service of a rude and often ungrateful flock."

I presume that means the Hurons. Given their history, it is understandable they were not profoundly grateful to any white man, no matter how well intentioned. Still, whatever we know of Potier indicates he was deeply dedicated to the spiritual and material welfare of these people. His pastoral style was hardly that of Father Cyr, the "good accompanist" rather than conductor. You knew who was in charge in those days. It was the man in the pulpit. For thirty years, Potier conducted his ragtag orchestra according to his best lights, for the love of God and neighbor. A century and a half earlier his Jesuit predecessors, as Parkman writes, "surveyed a field of labor whose vastness might tire the wings of thought itself; a scene repellent and appalling, darkened with omens of peril and woe. They were an advance-guard of the great army of Loyola, strong in a discipline that controlled not alone the body and the will, but the intellect, the heart, the soul, and the inmost conscious-ness." Brébeuf was among the numbers of this advance guard, paddling his canoe until his arms burned with fatigue. After him came others, equally heroic. But when the exhausted seventy-three-year-old heart of Pierre Potier finally gave out, in his home near the banks of the Detroit River, there were none to follow.

⚜

In 1796 a detachment of sixty-five American soldiers appeared before Detroit to remind the British garrison that the fort was the property of the United States, according to the 1783 treaty ending the Revolutionary War. After that, American settlers poured in. For a while, however, Detroit took its tone from the French inhabi-tants. The British rulers of Detroit had found this *habitant* to be "a lazy, happy-go-lucky sort of fellow, contented to satisfy his stomach in a moderate way and let the world take care of itself," in the words of Henry M. Utley and Byron M. Cutcheon, authors of *Michigan as a Province, Territory and State, the Twenty-Sixth Member of the Federal Union*, published in 1906.

Why bring in these two fools? Isn't one condescending Yankee, in the person of Francis Parkman, enough? We all know nineteenth-century American histories leave something to be desired in their treatment of non-Anglo-Saxon populations. Why belabor the issue? The reason is that Utley and Cutcheon at least have something to say about the French of Detroit. When it comes to chroniclers, those early French settlers are less fortunate even than the Huron and the Iroquois, who had indefatigable Jesuits writing down notes about them from the moment introductions were made. The Jesuits were not disinterested, to put it mildly, but they did believe in keeping their eyes open. No one had any particular interest in the *habitants*, however, except for the first British governors who wanted to make sure they were of a peaceable disposition. When they proved to be so, they disappeared from history.

So what do Utley and Cutcheon have to say about the average French peasant in Detroit, whom they name, with amiable condescension, "Johnny Couteau"? (*Couteau* means "knife." How this ethnic term came into being, I have no idea.) "He had no ambitions beyond his modest sphere in life," Utley and Cutcheon write of Johnny Couteau. "As a farmer he was indifferent." According to our authorities, Johnny Couteau was so shiftless he worked with crude farming implements, failed to feed his animals properly during winter, raised razorback hogs because they could forage for themselves, and instead of horses rode tough little ponies, who also foraged for themselves. He was virtually illiterate. "He did not take kindly to new fangled notions. He preferred to plod along in the old-fashioned way."

On the plus side, and in distinct contrast to those hard-drinking, randy *coureurs de bois*, the French settlers "were devoted to the services of the church. Their moral characters were above reproach. They married early and reared numerous children." They also knew how to have a good time. Observe this charming scene painted by Utley and Cutcheon:

> The long summer evenings were spent in the open air. Canoeing upon the river was naturally a favorite pastime. Gallantry towards ladies has always been a French characteristic, as have social festivities generally. So, young men and maidens were likely to be found in each other's company either upon the river or upon the lawns. Barbecues were a form of recreation in which the elders indulged themselves. The open-air roast furnished a hearty feast, washed down with generous potations of home-made wine or cider.

Somebody always brought out a fiddle. Winter did not interrupt the good times either. Pony racing on the frozen waters of the River Rouge was very popular. "Every Johnny Couteau had a pony of uncertain speed," Utley and Cutcheon write. After Sunday mass, the crowd would gather, the ponies and riders would line up, the bets would be laid down. According to Utley and Cutcheon, this custom continued on the Rouge River almost to the end of the nineteenth century, when larger crowds became unruly and spoiled the fun. "The rough element which imbibes freely and proves itself a noisome nuisance was made up wholly of Americans," Utley and Cutcheon assure us. "Johnny Couteau is naturally of a somewhat excitable nature, but he still behaves himself and relishes the sport for the excitement and uncertainty there is in it."

Good old Johnny Couteau. Ethnic stereotypes, as we all know, derive from some basis in reality. The French did know how to enjoy themselves, and still do. There's no comparison between "social festivities" held by Irish Catholics, say, and French Canadians. I've been to both and believe me the latter are more pleasurable, relaxing, convivial. A social scientist will demonstrate this beyond doubt one of these days. It is a matter of historical record, meanwhile, that back in colonial days when young New Yorkers or New Englanders were kidnapped by French and Indians and taken to Canada, they often refused to go back, even when freed – life among the French was more easygoing than among Dutch merchants and New England Puritans. As a descendant of those French, I like that. But it is still galling to see your ethnic group being portrayed in history as not very bright.

The picture of fun-loving, unambitious Johnny Couteau still carries a sting because French immigrants to the United States generally – and especially in New England – have remained collective underachievers. If you take all the newcomers to North America who didn't come over on the *Mayflower*, and you put the Jews at one end of the scale – the incredible success-story end – and the Blacks at the other – the persistent legacy-of-oppression end – then

Johnny Couteau is much closer to the Blacks than he is to the Jews. In the old South, white morons used to say, "If you could be a nigger on a Saturday night, you'd never want to be anything else." Maybe if you could be Johnny Couteau, "a lazy, happy-go-lucky sort of fellow, contented to satisfy his stomach in a moderate way, and let the world take care of itself" for a few days, you wouldn't want to be anything else, either. Hand that Johnny a slice of watermelon.

Back in 1968 a radical firebrand named Pierre Vallières, member of the Front du Libération de Québec (FLQ), that province's rather feeble version of the IRA or the Weathermen, actually wrote a book entitled *Les nègres blancs d'Amérique*, which was translated into English as *White Niggers of America*. Vallières claimed that the French-Canadian proletariat occupied the same social and economic position as Blacks. The book made a stir. It spoke to the condition of French-speaking taxi drivers and welfare recipients in the gritty east end of Montreal, and also to generations of French-Canadian mill workers in New England. In his memoir *American Ghosts*, David Plante tells the story of his aunt, employed in a laundry, handling an undershirt filthy with blood and pus that a black woman refused to touch. Not only did his aunt handle it, she pressed it against her face. (Shades of Bishop Laval.) "Well, who else would do such dirty work, who else but one of us French?" Plante recalls her saying. "We're not called white niggers for nothing."

Yet this is a far cry from Johnny Couteau. We really don't know much about Johnny, when all is said. Get past the patronizing tones of Utley and Cutcheon, it's even possible to speculate that Johnny and his kind really were among the happiest people on the continent at the time, and not just because they were lazy and happy-go-lucky. Fortified by the sacraments and observances of their church, secure in the ownership of their own land, invigorated by physical work that was demanding but not monotonous or exhausting – Johnny Couteau was not *that* lazy – comforted by the variety and depth of their family ties, stimulated by their bonds to a lively community, and, yes, frequently refreshed by "social festivities," they might have been happier than most of us are. They probably didn't worry as much. Racing a pony on the ice was probably more thrilling than playing video games, and dancing all night under the winter stars to the music of a fiddler more satisfying than watching television. It's possible.

❧

That old culture, of course, has vanished, although not without leaving some traces. After my visit to Detroit, I went south to Monroe, a town about half an hour's drive from the city and the heart of French Michigan. Before heading out, I read a scholarly article by Dennis M. Au, former assistant director of the Monroe County Historical Museum, entitled "The Mushrat French." In this article, Au gave a brief history of the French in Detroit and southern Michigan, and the slow erosion of their culture. The 1930s, for example, was the last decade in which French was spoken in Monroe County homes, according to Au. French folk songs and folk tales have just about disappeared from this part of America, preserved only in Au's cassette tapes; he and Professor Marcel Beneteau, an ethnologist at the University of Windsor, on the Canadian side of the Detroit River, have made strenuous efforts in recent decades to preserve hundreds of these French folk songs. They acted none too soon. Many of the grandfathers and grandmothers whose voices were captured in the tape recorders of Au and Beneteau have since passed on. No one now will ever sing their songs late at night in a bar, or in a hut in the marshes, waiting for the ducks to appear. No one now will tell stories to her grandchildren about the *loup garou*, the hairy creature who haunts farmhouses at night.

What then remains of the old French culture? The answer is simple: food. As Gail Moreau pointed out, the descendants of the French still like to prepare their *tourtières*, as well as their pork *boulettes* (meat balls), their *galettes carées* (square cakes), and other delicacies from French Canada. The oddest of these items is muskrat, or "mushrat." Refer to the animal by the former term, Au assures the reader, and the locals will know you're from out of town. Apparently this is one dish the Indians passed on to the French settlers, the muskrat being a frequent dweller of the swamps near Lake Erie. The muskrat had another advantage as a culinary item. Since it was an aquatic animal, the local French Catholics reasoned, the muskrat could be eaten without sin on Fridays, the traditional day of abstinence from meat. In fact, eating muskrat on Fridays became something of a ritual in Catholic homes in Monroe. "*Ora ramus* – God bless dee mushrat, she's a fish!" sang out old Pip Laboe, as the muskrat was brought to the table (according to his son Jack Laboe, who recalled this ritual years later to Dennis Au).

So closely associated did the local French become with the muskrat that they became known as "mushrats" themselves. It wasn't mean, like the term "Coon" for Blacks or, for that matter, the term "Pepsi," which English Canadians often apply to their French brethren, supposedly because of their fondness for that brand of soft drink. (A term to be used with extreme caution in Quebec bars.) Certainly "Mushrat" is a lot more endearing than "Frog." The local French used it freely in conversation. "*Comment ça va*, you mushrat you?" Only on occasion was the term used less than affectionately. In 1894, for example, the Monroe baseball team and its fans were called "Frenchmen, Dudes and Muskrats" – a trio of insults – by opposing fans. ("Dude" in 1904 meant a fop and may have been a contemptuous reference to what Utley and Cutcheon term the "characteristic French fondness for dress.") On the whole, however, the Yankees were rather indulgent toward the Mushrat French, especially the swells who came, at the turn of the century, in special railroad cars from Chicago and Detroit and Toledo to hunt and fish and sail their yachts. They were fond of their grizzled French guides and gamekeepers, who spoke in a colorful patois straight out of popular books of humorous French dialect poetry, like *French-Canadian Verse* by William Baubie. Baubie's lines to the muskrat are worth quoting:

De fine citay laday put de musk hon for style
But offen shees go widout bath for a while;
But le bon Dieu was make de poor mushrat dat way,
So he carry hees musk, but he wash every day.

In 1903 the Monroe Yacht Club put on a muskrat carnival at the Michigan National Guard Armory, organized by its founder, the local cedar baron, Commodore W.C. Sterling. Four hundred and fifty guests consumed seven hundred muskrats, while a delegation from the Toledo Yacht Club, led by the mayor of Toledo, marched into the armory singing naughty sailing songs. It was the beginning of a tradition of public muskrat dinners in Monroe at places like the local VFW, the Rod & Gun Club, the two Catholic churches in town. (Monroe Protestants do not identify so much with this tradition, but have been known to consume a dish or two of *rat musqu'au maïs* – muskrat in corn – when the public dinners are at their height.)

This fine custom was threatened on Ash Wednesday, 1987, when the *Detroit Free Press* ran a story about Kola's Food Factory, a restaurant just south of Detroit, serving muskrat. Apparently a lot of Catholics enjoyed muskrat dinners on that day, on the old theory that muskrats were fish. Abstinence from meat on Ash Wednesday is still taken seriously by the Church, and the Archbishop of Detroit became concerned somebody was misleading his flock. At the same time, the story caught the eye of the Michigan Department of Agriculture. Officials from the department promptly placed a ban on the meat because it had not been inspected.

The good citizens of Monroe rose in anger. Bumper stickers with the stirring motto "Let them eat muskrat!" appeared, along with T-shirts and buttons proclaiming "Muskrat Mania." Petitions were circulated. At a public meeting of the Monroe County Board of Commissioners, 150 citizens cheered the defiant words of County Commissioner Richard Reed: "I think it's a sad commentary when a bunch of bureaucrats has nothing better to do than regulate muskrat dinners out of existence. We'll have less bureaucrats and more muskrat dinners." The Department of Agriculture backed off. At the same time, the Archbishop of Detroit was informed that Church officials had already looked into the matter. In 1956 the local bishop had decided that eating muskrat on days of abstinence was an "immemorial custom" of the local church, and therefore it was permitted by canon law. That ecclesiastic may have thought eating muskrat was penance in itself.

"Muskrat was the line in the sand for them," Dennis Au writes of the descendants of the French in Monroe. "While they lost the battle to preserve their language, they were not going to have muskrat taken from them without a fight." It was the last stand of a three-hundred-year-old French culture on the American side of the Detroit River. And the stand held. "What we have here is a unique and vibrant expression of French culture that has evolved in isolation and that has stood remarkably well against the Herculean forces of American acculturation," Au concludes. "Here . . . is a French people *not* defined by language – as they are all too much in Canada. French on the American side is defined by historical connections and an affinity with and a love of a foodway."

When I arrived in downtown Monroe I hoped to find a restaurant that would serve muskrat. I settled on McGeady's, an upscale beer and burger joint with an exposed brick wall. When I asked about a "mushrat" dinner – mindful of Au's comment about outsiders – the waitress stared at me in incomprehension. I had to settle for a Cajun burger. Then I went to see the current assistant director of the Monroe County Historical Museum, Ralph Naveaux. Naveaux was a native of Monroe who had spent most of his life in that town and had no regrets about it. "Every other generation leaves Monroe," he said. "But they always come back." That was one thing I was learning in my travels. Sooner or later people do come back. All over this continent retired people are building second homes in the neighborhoods they left in the days of their youth. Naveaux, meanwhile, honored his eighteenth-century forebears in exemplary fashion, not only by staying in Monroe but by learning French. He tuned in every morning to the French-language television station in Windsor, Ontario, for the news and weather, and every once in a while practiced conversation with members of the Alliance Française in Toledo, Ohio.

He drove me out to what is known as the Navarre-Anderson trading post site on the bank of the River Raisin, just outside of town. The site contained a number of old buildings, more or less faithfully preserved – a nineteenth-century trading post, country store, barn, and so on. Naveaux organized yearly lantern tours of the site in October, with guides dressed up in period costumes and re-enactments of farm activities. As we passed over a bridge crossing a stream, Naveaux said one year the *loup garou* hid under the bridge during a lantern tour. At a strategic moment, he popped out and ran howling away. In legend, the *loup garou* was often a man transformed into a werewolf at night for his sins. He was somebody who missed his Easter duty, or made a pact with the Devil, or planted potatoes on Sunday. When attacked by a *loup garou*, one's best response was often to throw a rock at him, or wield a knife – if you succeeded in drawing blood, the werewolf would disappear in a cloud of smoke and a foul smell, and in his place would be your brother-in-law or somebody else you had always suspected of dubious behavior. "We've got one fellow in the lantern tour who specializes in the *loup garou* howl," Naveaux told me. What does a *loup garou* howl sound like, I asked. "Pretty scary."

Afterwards, he gave me directions to Kola's Food Factory, since I was bound and determined to get a muskrat dinner before I left town. "I think it tastes great," he said. "It is an acquired taste, however. A lot depends on how it's prepared. Some of the old trappers actually liked that old musky taste, but when it comes out good, it tastes like turkey – like dark meat. If you fry it up with onions, it sometimes tastes like beef. One person compared the taste to a very aggressive chicken." He shook his head. "Actually, I don't think it tastes like any of those things."

I drove north toward Detroit, turning off Route 75 to Fort Street in the town of Riverview. Fort Street was one of those endless suburban divided highways, with auto parts stores and industrial parks and fast-food restaurants. At first sight, when I saw the Kola's sign and the nondescript building, it looked just like any other fast-food joint. Inside there were Arborite tables in a dining room as clean and bright as a McDonald's. But it wasn't McDonald's. Small American flags stuck out of the condiment containers, and twenty-eight stuffed game birds hung from the ceiling – mostly ducks, but also pheasants and a Canada goose and one seagull. This was promising. Unfortunately, the waitress advised me that they had run out of muskrat.

"Try Dom Polski," one of the customers said. "They serve muskrat." Dom Polski's was only a ten-minute drive away. It could have been an American Legion Hall, with a darkly lit interior and a linoleum floor and a few regulars, seated at tables with their glasses of beer, who didn't look like they were in a hurry to go anywhere. The waitress, Susie, could not help me. The last of their muskrat was served a week ago. And no, they knew of no other place that offered it. The summer, I was reminded, is not the best time to eat muskrat. It's the time of the year when the animals are mating and the musk glands are at their muskiest. Otherwise, Susie pointed out, the flesh of this rodent is just fine. "It's the cleanest meat you can eat," she told me. "They don't put anything dirty in their mouths, they wash it and wash it before they eat." She mimed a muskrat scrubbing a morsel in its little paws. *So he carry hees musk, but he wash every day.* "Not like chickens. You think about chickens, what they eat."

I seemed destined to failure. I was still hungry, however, and decided to drive back to Kola's Food Factory and have a corned beef sandwich. When I got there and told the waitress my story, she commiserated. "Wait a minute," she said. "I'll call Johnny." This was the owner of the restaurant and the author of a cookbook, which I later obtained, entitled *Cookin' Wild with Johnny: A Wild Game*

Cookbook by Johnny Kolakowski Chef & Proprietor America's Premier SmokeHouse. On the cover, Johnny was smiling. He wore a white pleated shirt, a big black bow tie, a jacket with black and orange swirls, and a matching top hat – the kind magicians use to pull rabbits out of. Inside the book were recipes for Stewed Coon, Possum, Bambi in a Blanket, and Wild Boar Goulash. His recipe for Muskrat Saute began, "To prepare muskrat, begin by skinning, removing all visible fat with your thumb and a paring knife. Open up the hind legs along the thighs from the base of tail to knee. Spot the musk sacks and remove."

Fortune smiled upon me. Johnny told the waitress about a stash of muskrat somewhere in the depths of their freezer. "You want salad or cole slaw with your rat?" the waitress asked. I ordered cole slaw. In fairly short order the waitress appeared with my dinner plate. It contained mashed potatoes with gravy, and hunks of meat that looked like pot roast on a bed of sauerkraut. Johnny's approach to muskrat owed more to eastern Europe, it appeared, than to the cuisine of old French-Canadian trappers. This is how cultures evolve.

I wish I could say I enjoyed it. The meat, however, was stringy, and full of little bones, and there was a hint of blood in the taste – the kind of flavor people usually refer to as "gamy." This chicken was very aggressive. I couldn't clean my plate. "He's a bony little critter, ain't he?" the waitress said cheerfully, as she removed it. "You definitely have to like your rat."

⚜

That same evening I drove south on Route 125 until I came to the La Salle Bar, which was the only indication I was in the town of La Salle, Michigan. Inside, a half-dozen men and women sat at the bar. It was very dark, providing good contrast for the glowing lights behind the bar, and I was reminded of Thoreau's remark about churches as caves. This was a cave, too. Were the bears inside friendly? I took a seat at the bar, under a sign that read *La Salle is too small to have a town drunk so we all take our turn.* Beside me was a man in his twenties whose name I didn't get. He was dressed in running shoes, jeans, a T-shirt, and a bandanna that covered the top of his head. Beneath the bandanna, dreadlocks fell to his shoulder.

I told him I'd come down from Canada. "Why aren't you drinking Labatt's Blue?" he asked. A good question. "I like Canadian beer," he said. "But it's too expensive for me right now." The notion of Labatt's Blue as a premium beer was startling to me. In response I mentioned a local delicacy. "I hear you can get good turtle soup in this part of Michigan."

This statement was not so out of left field as it might sound. I had just heard him tell the man on the other side of him a story about how his brother, hauling in turtles from his underwater trapline in a canoe, got bit by one and had to have his hand sewed up. "Oh yeah, you can cook it pretty good."

"What about muskrat. You ever eat muskrat?"

"I won't eat nothing with the word 'rat' in it. Not unless I have to. Not unless I'm starving." We sat in silence for a few minutes, drinking our Budweisers. He was not a talkative man, at least with strangers. "My dog got one of them muskrats the other day," he finally volunteered. "He gets muskrats, woodchucks."

"What kind of dog is he?"

"He's a pit bull. A big baby. Like a lap dog. I call him a pet bull." He gave me a thin smile. "It's just other animals he doesn't like."

"Do they still trap muskrat around here?"

"No, we don't trap muskrats any more. You can get money for coyote furs, though. Not furs. Hides."

"Who pays for hides?"

"Whoever. Man, those coyotes are everywhere now. You should hear 'em at night if a train whistles. They start howling. Like a pack of hyenas. Just like hyenas."

"Dogs afraid of them?"

"Not my dog. My dog, he can leap thirteen feet. You put something on this ceiling he wants, he'll get it." He turned to a man on the other side of him. "My brother and I, we were out deer hunting last winter, we saw one of those coyotes big as a German shepherd. You know that gun I have, it has the scope and then the sight below it?"

"Twenty-two mag?"

"Yeah."

"What kind of mag?"

"Remington. I thought I had him dead in my sights, man, I got off a good shot." He shrugged. "He just disappeared on us. My brother couldn't get it either. It was weird. We looked for blood on the snow, and everything. Nothing."

I was about to ask him if there had been a full moon that night, but thought better of it. I had the feeling this man had never heard of the *loup garou*. Instead I asked him about the neighborhood, if more people were moving in to La Salle and nearby towns, because I remembered Ralph Naveaux saying this part of the state was getting more populated, with people moving south from Detroit and north from Toledo. "Yeah," he said. "I do concrete here. I'm putting concrete in what used to be the middle of nowhere now. I don't like it. But I guess people have to have somewhere to live."

"A lot of people moving from Detroit?"

He gave me a look. At first I thought it was because I put the emphasis on the second syllable of Detroit, as a kind of homage to its French founders, which might have struck him as pointy-headed affectation. Around here, of course, everybody put the emphasis on the first syllable. But as soon as he spoke I realized that "people from Detroit" meant one thing for him: African-Americans. "You see any coloreds in this bar?" he asked. No, I didn't see any colored people in the La Salle Bar. "This ain't the town for that." He took another swallow of Bud. "They ain't all bad. They're lots of white people just as worse. But different people, you stick with your own kind."

❧

Before I left the Detroit area, I underwent one other pilgrimage, this time to the other side of the river, the Canadian side. There, almost literally under the shadow of the Ambassador Bridge between Windsor and Detroit, was the Church of Our Lady of the Assumption. This is where the Huron Mission first established by St. Jean de Brébeuf and other Jesuits of the early seventeenth century was finally laid to rest. The Hurons are now gone. None of their descendants, so far as is known to the present pastor of the church, worship here. The building itself, constructed in 1846, is a mighty piece of Gothic architecture – the steeples, the buttresses, the spires, the long, narrow windows ending in a pointed arch, all speak of a soaring, and yet massive and weighty spiritual *imperium*. That *imperium* flattened Huron culture.

I stood outside the church and looked up at the Ambassador Bridge. An endless line of trucks, bound for Detroit, had come to a temporary halt. You could hear the rattle, the ping, the sigh, the snort of the vehicles with perfect clarity as they stood idling on the bridge. In the twenty-first century, just as in the seventeenth and eighteenth centuries, this spot was a strategic point in a far-flung continental trade route. Now it was part of a highway connecting Canada, the United States, and Mexico. The line of trucks was testimony to how necessary this highway had become to North American prosperity.

At the beginning of the twenty-first century, nearly everybody has acquiesced to the idea that free trade is a key ingredient in economic growth. But if the ghost of one of those last surviving Hurons from southern Ontario who ended up in this spot could speak to us, what would he say? Would he whisper from the beyond that his people, too, had once experienced a burst of prosperity from joining a vast trading network? Iron hatchets and blankets and firearms, and, yes, the brandy that made fear and anxiety disappear for a time, represented incredible advances in material well-being. No Indian civilization could do without them, the same way we can no longer do without oil. At the same time, however, this dependence brought forth unheard-of levels of violence. The violence consumed the Huron people.

It is no accident that most of the trucks on that bridge belong to a nation heavily armed beyond any precedent in history.

NINE

Saint Ignace

The man who built a time machine • *The man who thought Jesus Christ was a French name* • *The greatest scoundrels the world ever knew* • *Ladies' Night Out at the Bear Dance* • *The Jesuit who killed Abraham Lincoln* • *Treachery at Fort Michilimackinac*

After La Salle's *Griffon* left the straits of Detroit it entered Lake Huron, where it soon encountered a storm so violent La Salle and his crew fell on their knees to beg deliverance from God. La Salle even promised to build a chapel to St. Anthony of Padua, patron saint of mariners, in the event his life was spared. Only the ship's pilot refused to join in the supplication. Instead he cursed La Salle. Evidently the man was upset at the idea of drowning in the middle of a lake instead of the ocean, like a true salt. Some day some biographer really should explain this enmity between La Salle and his pilots. He was always saddled with bad ones, he knew they were bad, and yet he sat back and allowed them to sink his precious ships and destroy his prospects of success. It is very strange.

Fortunately St. Anthony heard La Salle and his crew, interceded on their behalf before the throne of God, and the winds abated. A week later the *Griffon* appeared on the waters off St. Ignace, the Jesuit mission on the north bank of the Straits of Mackinac, where the waters of Lake Michigan pour into Lake Huron. La Salle fired a cannon, Parkman writes, "and the Indians yelped in wonder and amazement." Parkman's Indians, the reader may have noticed, are always yelping. This time they had good reason. In a part of the world that had never seen any craft larger than a birchbark canoe, the ship was an astonishing sight. Even the Jesuits were impressed. Before this day in history, no one had come from the east to the Straits of Mackinac except via the Ottawa River, or the Humber River carrying place. That La Salle had pioneered a new route, and introduced a sailing ship to the waters of the Great Lakes, was profoundly bad news to the Jesuits, who wanted no more Frenchmen in this part of the world, and to the fur traders and *coureurs de bois*, who welcomed no competition from La Salle.

The air was thick with ill-will toward the man. On his part, La Salle was anxious to find out what had happened to the fifteen men he had sent ahead to trade in furs. He suspected, probably rightly, that they had been encouraged to abandon that enterprise by the inhabitants of St. Ignace and to make personal use of La Salle's trade goods. Sure enough, near St. Ignace he found four of his delinquent employees, who had spent his capital with no furs to show for it. La Salle arrested them and dispatched Tonty to round up some others he had heard were skulking about in the vicinity of Sault Ste. Marie.

⚜

When La Salle arrived, the mission of St. Ignace consisted of the Jesuits, a village of Ottawa Indians, a settlement of Hurons, and the fur traders and *coureurs de bois* who came and went. The latter group, who loom large in the mythology of French America, partly because they struck so many European and American observers as being more Indian than white, remain an enigma to us. "Wearied from their long journey, these *voyageurs* devoted themselves wholeheartedly, at its end, to enjoying themselves," wrote the Baron Lahontan in 1684, observing a group of them return to Montreal after spending eighteen months in the wilderness. "They immersed themselves up to the neck in riotous pleasures – women, drink, gambling, you name it. You'd be amazed at how much money they threw away. When it was all gone, they sold their lace, their gold embroidery, all their fancy duds."

This comment establishes a number of themes that persist over the centuries in descriptions of the French who lived and traded in the wilderness: they were dudes who loved to dress up, party, and gamble. They did not believe in saving for retirement. This vein of commentary continued in the nineteenth century when the French fur traders lost their independence and became employees of outfits like the Hudson's Bay Company and the American Fur Company. (From that point they were referred to more often as *voyageurs* – that is, boatmen – than as *coureurs de bois*, or woodsmen.) Washington Irving, visiting the Straits of Mackinac in 1810, wrote, "Here *voyageurs* frolicked away their wages, fiddling and dancing in the booths and cabins, buying all kinds of knick knacks, dressing themselves out finely, and parading up and down, like arrant braggarts and coxcombs."

Fortunes were made on the backs of these "arrant braggarts and coxcombs" – the *voyageurs* were legendary for their hardihood. An official with the United States Bureau of Indian Affairs named Thomas McKenney observed in the 1820s the killing pace at which *voyageurs* paddled all day – to the rhythm of a man singing in the bow, hired for that purpose – and remarked, "No human being but the Canadian French could stand this." During portages they carried two hundred pounds of cargo on their backs, and oftentimes considerably more – "What only a horse in our country would be expected to carry," McKenney wrote. They also endured swarms of blackflies and mosquitos while retaining their sanity. An American Fur Company employee in 1818, after making the standard comment that "the *voyageurs* were fond of fun and frolic," observed further that the Canadian French "were the only people fitted for the life they were compelled to endure; their cheerful temperament and happy disposition made them contented under the privations and hardships incident to their calling."

As the nineteenth century wore on and the fur trade declined, the jobs of the *voyageurs* became increasingly obsolete, but as is the case with many an outmoded class of people, tourists loved them. It was their lingering aura of hardihood that prompted the British to recruit these French-Canadian *voyageurs* when they needed some tough boatmen to man an expedition up the Nile and rescue General Gordon at Khartoum. And when the historian Arnold Toynbee witnessed as a boy the celebrations of Queen Victoria's Silver Jubilee in 1887, it was not the kings and the princes that he longed to see but the *voyageurs*. It may have been this boyhood memory of French-Canadian vigor that prompted his reflection, shortly after World War II, "I would prophesy that there is a future in the Old World for the Chinese, and in North America for the *Canadiens*. Whatever the future of mankind in North America, I feel pretty confident that these French-speaking Canadians, at any rate, will be there at the end of the story."

⚜

My first stop in Michigan was at the home of the man who more than anyone else has devoted his life to fleshing out the enigma of the wilderness French. I first met him at the re-enactment at Fort Niagara, where he presented a striking sight. He wore a long white shirt over deer-hide leggings and moccasins, a bone necklace and conch shell gorget, and a black, broad-brimmed felt hat with one side of the brim folded up and attached to the crown, like Teddy Roosevelt's hat when he charged up San Juan Hill. The hat was decorated with colorful feathers. Talk about finery. Most striking of all, however, was his wiry black hair. It was like a helmet of hair, or a Mediterranean Afro, sticking out about five inches or so on top of his head and behind his ears. This man played trumpet for the Chicago Symphony Orchestra, and when he performed patrons wrote irate letters to the management demanding that he get a haircut, it was that distracting.

His name, when he wasn't Timothy J. Kent, was Silver Fox. His wife, Doree Manion, a former high school sweetheart, went by the name of Sunning Otter, and wore a deer-hide dress. They were "an early French trader and his native wife."

Seven months after I met them at Fort Niagara, I crossed the Straits of Mackinac and drove southward on Highway 23 along the western shore of Lake Huron to their home in Ossineke, Michigan. They lived in a two-story frame house set back from the highway, a few hundred yards past a tourist attraction called Dinosaur Gardens, which also featured an eighteen-foot-high statue of Jesus Christ. The figure, nicknamed Jesus with a Basketball by the locals, held a globe in one outstretched hand.

When I arrived, Doree served a lunch of moussaka and tabbouleh salad. "If you said 'moussaka' here, people wouldn't know what you were talking about," she laughed. Ossineke is a fine place to be, in other words, if you like outdoor activities and are not worldly in your outlook. The Kents seemed fairly content living here, though few people in town had a clue as to what Timothy Kent did, or why he did it. Ossineke was where he was born, in 1949. He returned in 1996 after spending almost two decades with the CSO and moved into this house, which his father had built, and which was a perfectly natural place to serve moussaka since his father was of Greek descent. For that matter, Doree could also have served a *tourtière* or roasted muskrat given that Timothy's mother, the source of his blood ties with the old fur traders, was a French Canadian named Bouchard.

After lunch Kent and I adjourned to a pair of rocking chairs in a sunroom, with a gas fireplace flaming in one wall. Kent was much more casually dressed than the last time I saw him. He was still wearing a pair of moccasins, but these were not Silver Fox's moccasins, made of deer hide and sinew thread from dried elk tendons, and treated with bear oil, but a pair you could pick up at Wal-Mart.

Beside us was a stack of Tim's books – a two-volume, 1,154-page work entitled *Ft. Ponchartrain at Detroit: A Guide to the Daily Lives of Fur Trade and Military Personnel, Settlers, and Missionaries at French Posts*, a two-volume, 686-page work entitled *Birchbark Canoes of the Fur Trade*, and two smaller books, *Tahquamenon Tales: Experiences of an Early French Trader and His Native Family* (the Kents), and *Paddling Across the Peninsula: An Important Cross-Michigan Canoe Route During the French Regime*. This was a mountain of scholarship, and it represented only a portion of Kent's work; he was about to publish equally massive studies of daily life at the Straits of Mackinac under the French regime and an exhaustive work on dugout canoes. He has also been, for many years, researching 725 of his direct French and French-Canadian ancestors.

It is very rare that the man of signal accomplishment in unusual pursuits gives much credit to his high school, that bad memory of sensitive adolescents everywhere. But at nearby Alpena High, where Kent played lead trumpet in the school band and his future wife played the French horn, he learned something. "The standards of that era were excellent, the teachers were excellent, and the school was excellent," he said. "We were pre-television era, before the standards became less book oriented and less geared to a high level of excellence, so I've been able to base an entire historical writing and research career on just the foundation of a high school level of English literature and grammar – and a grand total of one North American history course – the basic requirement one had to have to get a high school diploma in the United States."

It also helped being indefatigable. "What I didn't realize at the time was that the training it took to become an extremely high-level symphonic musician was the best kind of training for any kind of drive for perfection," he said. "In the orchestra, you learned the total falsehood of the old saying that practice makes perfect. That's only at a medium level of performance. When you reach the level of symphonic music, there's no such thing as true perfection. At the end of the day you know you could always have done more to hone your craft. It's the kind of occupation where you can never do enough."

Still, music never consumed his life entirely. The other great passion – the passion for exhuming the past – he encountered at the age of twenty-two, on a visit home to Ossineke. A neighbor who operated a bulldozer for a living and had unearthed many an Indian artifact under his scoop showed Tim his collection. "I never had a shred of interest in history or archeology, but I was bitten," he recalled. For the next ten years, he filled his spare moments with the pursuit of pre-history and its remains buried in the North American earth. "I did that at a level of seriousness as if I were in a doctoral program," he told me. Then his interests took another turn after he met his mother's relatives. That led to genealogical studies of his French ancestors, which evolved into a particular interest in those – a considerable number – who had been involved in the fur trade. Silver Fox and Sunning Otter were born.

All re-enactors are amateur historians of a sort, but the difference between the research of your average re-enactor and the research of Tim Kent is the difference between playing trumpet in the local dance band and playing in the brass section of the CSO. His role model was a man named Edwin Tappan Adney, who was born in Athens, Ohio, in 1868. Adney became a New York journalist and covered the Klondike Gold Rush of 1897 for *Harper's Weekly*. He wrote a book about it, *The Klondike Stampede*, which was published in 1900 and is still in print. His chief claim to fame, however, is "saving the art of the birch bark canoe construction from oblivion," in the words of a biographer. Adney was one of those numerous cultivated gentlemen of the late nineteenth and early twentieth centuries who couldn't get over their fascination with Indians. In Adney's case it took the form of lifelong research into Indian birch-bark canoes, conducted at a time when some old men still knew how to make them. He himself built more than one hundred scale models of these canoes. If you're ever in Newport News, Virginia, you should visit the Mariners' Museum and take a look at them.

Adney also left his papers with the museum, which were edited by the curator of transportation at the Smithsonian Institution, one Howard Irving Chapelle, and published by the institution in 1964 under the title *The Bark Canoes and Skin Boats of North America*. In his introduction, Chapelle lamented that not one single full-sized fur-trade canoe had been preserved in a museum. Adney had spent decades looking for a decent surviving specimen of these great trading canoes and failed to find one. Tim Kent took up the challenge. It was as if Kent vowed to appease the restless shade of Tappan Adney, who died in 1950 and is buried in the Canadian maritime province of New Brunswick. "All of those years while I was practicing and honing my craft as a symphonic trumpeter – that taught me to work for decades without being known by anybody else and without getting credit from others," Tim said. "I carried that same approach over to decades of research and gathering materials and traveling all over the United States and Canada, entirely content to be unknown and unfunded. The model of Tappan Adney was exactly parallel. My goal was to live long enough to actually produce my books, which unfortunately Adney, in his case, never lived to see. I'm going through all of his original correspondence, and I can see that he was plagued by that terrible thought that all of these many decades of work would never result in publication in his own lifetime."

Eventually Tim was able to find four full-sized trading canoes in the United States, Canada, and England. One of them had somehow gotten into the possession of the British Royal Family and was loaned by Queen Elizabeth to the National Maritime Museum in London in 1957. When the CSO played in London, Tim seized his advantage. "We would play a concert in the evening and then I would go back to the hotel and sleep for a couple of hours and then in the wee hours of the morning I would go to the back door of the museum and ring, and the night staff would let me in," he recalled. There he spent hours studying the canoe. Some people would call it obsessive – noting every last detail on a twenty-nine-foot canoe, while the night gradually turned into morning and the morning into afternoon. But then those people would not know what it was like to play a trumpet for hours every day, either. You can never practice enough as a symphonic musician? Well, you can never do enough research into birchbark canoes. You can never say to yourself, that detail is too tiny to bother with. When Kent self-published *Birchbark Canoes of the Fur Trade* in 1997, he devoted fifty-eight pages to his meticulous examination of Queen Elizabeth's canoe. A characteristic paragraph from this chapter would begin, "The combined width of the inwale (¾ inch) and the outwale (⅝ inch) is ¼ inch less than the width of the gunwale cap. But the bark wall and the reinforcement bark strip sandwiched between the inwale and the outwale add as much as ¼ to ⅜ inch thickness to the combined gunwales. Also, the degree to which the inwale and the outwale were squeezed against the bark elements and each other when they were all nailed and lashed together varies in different areas."

Every sentence reads like that. Kent's purpose was to enable anybody to build an exact replica of the canoe using only the book's data and drawings and photos. Five hundred years from now, if this book survives and if anybody is still reading printed English, an individual who studies the volume can make himself a birchbark trading canoe fit to hold eight jolly French-Canadian paddlers and a few thousand pounds of beaver pelts. Somewhere, with the publication of this book, Edwin Tappan Adley felt better about his earthly life. The work of that life had been carried on.

"About suppertime I would catch a cab back to the Royal Albert Hall, practice my trumpet a little, and suit up in my tails," Kent recalled. "After the concert, the whole routine would begin again. I remember once, one of the members of the symphony said to me, 'I couldn't sleep last night' – we were all jet-lagged – 'and I went out in the lobby and saw you taking a taxi. Where were you going at three in the morning?'"

To look at a birchbark canoe, of course.

Kent's passion for historical exactitude carried over to his vacation time. For ten years he and his family would spend a week in June, camping out in the wilderness of northern Michigan and northern Ontario, doing "living-history research," trying to live in the manner of a seventeenth-century French fur trader and his native family. They couldn't absolutely recreate this life – they had to bring with them cameras and notebooks and watches in order to record the absolutely minute details, and three times a day Kent had to go off some place in the woods to practice his trumpet – but they did their best to create what Kent called their time machine, the great goal of all re-enactors or living-history buffs. Kent acquired a genuine French wheel-lock pistol from the early seventeenth century, had craftsmen forge harpoon heads and fish hooks and other items according to specifications from excavated objects of the period, and engaged the services of glass blowers and potters and birchbark canoe makers for similar purposes. "All of my unusual animal parts I got from a firm in northern Idaho which is one of the largest fur buyers in North America," Kent told me. "If I wanted a buffalo bladder to make a container, or deer ankle bones to make conical ornaments, or a porcupine tail to make a hairbrush, or a skunk pelt with the claws and paws intact to make a fire bag, I would have them spread the word among their trappers and hunters."

A reader interested in the various expeditions of the Kent family time machine – including sons Golden Eagle and Red-tailed Hawk (Kevin and Ben) – would be advised to consult *Tahquamenon Tales*, available from Silver Fox Enterprises, in Ossineke, Michigan. Written in the third person, the narrative recounts in detail such episodes as the experiment in contrasting native with French cooking methods. What worked better, heating your stew in a wooden trough with hot stones, or using copper or brass pots? According to this experiment, copper and brass pots won hands down. Kent writes, "After the family had completed their several days of experiments with the traditional native cooking methods, they filled the following string of warm, sunny days with further explorations of the river, as well as fashioning birchbark containers, braiding trade line into cordage, feasting, telling stories of the ancestors around evening fires, and singing their ancient *chansons*."

If the time machine had really worked, if it had slipped the family through a crack into the past and Silver Fox had met one of his French forebears in a canoe, the idea was that the seventeenth-century Frenchman wouldn't have a clue he was encountering a descendant from three centuries in the future. (Unless Silver Fox forgot to take off his watch.) That's the dream, anyway, of re-enactors, the great fantasy. It's as if one day, if their representation is faithful enough, they might actually return to the past and escape this lousy modernity. The Kent family no longer went on these June vacations – the boys had grown, for one thing – but the lure remained. "For me, it's so easy to be transformed into that period," Kent told me. "On a camping trip, I swear that within ninety seconds of pushing the canoe off into the river, I am totally consumed. I am a *voyageur* on the river."

Don't call it escapism. There's a lesson here. "Our predecessors lived in eras of often far greater physical labors and discomforts than ours," Kent writes in his introduction to *Tahquamenon Tales*. "However, they also lived in times when many more aspects of life, learned by example and done by hand, could bring satisfactions. It would behoove us all to look back more often at the old days, and ponder the value of those things which have been abandoned." This is the moral of *Tahquamenon Tales*. "For every thing that is given something is taken," Ralph Waldo Emerson observed. "Society acquires new arts and loses old instincts."

But this talk about it behooving us all to look back more often at the old days is suspect to academic historians. It's language they don't entertain in their discipline and it reinforces their belief that re-enactors and living-history researchers have moral or philosophical agendas. It suggests that these amateurs willfully ignore contextual issues. (Not that the professionals don't happily expropriate whatever they find useful in books like Kent's.) Kent, of course, was ready to defend his approach. "I'm not presumptuous to say that there are not other scholars who are doing good work about the French period, but this interest in daily living, in the small detail, it probably wouldn't be a stretch to say that my work is very pioneering from that angle," he told me. "My approach is one of the micro-vision, in contrast to the macro-vision, which traditionally has been a global, economic approach."

Get enough of the small details right, and you might actually find an answer to the bigger questions, ranging from whether the French or English bathed more frequently, to what the Indians really thought of the missionaries. That's the promise of the micro-vision. Heaven knows, the macro-vision has its own problems. You don't have to be Michel Foucault to see how much these sweeping narratives of history have brushed aside. Look at all those yelping savages written off by Parkman. Look at the French. "In the United States and Canada very strong emphasis is placed on British activities and accomplishments, and those of the Frenchmen – French people, I should say – who preceded them are very much not acknowledged," Kent said. "In the United States, history is a fantasy and a myth that our country was populated solely along the eastern seaboard, and that these brave people bravely pushed further and further into the west, and it's as if there were no French regime at all when they got there, that the French did not have a huge economic sphere in place, and military operations, and bona fide communities there." Daniel Boone, in this myth, crossed the Alleghenies and found himself in the great virgin wilderness of Kentucky. It was just him and the Indians and the bears. And then a trickle of hardy pioneers followed, and settlements were built where previously there had been nothing but wigwams – and that's the story of America. But the French had been there long before.

The French were in Michigan when the English colonists were still huddled along the coastline of New York and Virginia. But signs of their presence are muted today. The restored Fort

Michilimackinac in Mackinaw City, on the south shore of the Straits of Mackinac, is a case in point. The fort was built by the French in 1715, seized by the British in 1763, and then, after Pontiac's rebellion, moved to a more secure site on Mackinac Island by the British in 1780. Now the restored fort in Mackinaw City is known as "Colonial Michilimackinac." In the summer, tourists witness re-enactments featuring British redcoats and American Revolutionary soldiers. "The term 'colonial' is a marketing tool," Kent said to me. He was right. In the language of tourism, "colonial" means Williamsburg and ye olde New England taverns with waitresses in mobcaps. "The fort has been reconstructed," said Kent, "but it's from the British period, and tours of the site, and demonstrations of weapons, are done by museum staff posing as British soldiers. The tip of the cap that's done toward the French is mostly done by talking about the stupid but happy singing *voyageurs*, the minimum wage employees of the clever British entrepreneurs. They can be nice fellows, these *voyageurs*, but you don't think of them as clever entrepreneurs. So even today, people visiting the absolute center of the world during the French fur-trade era receive a dosage of British history."

Just as bad, in Kent's view, was the emphasis on Father Jacques Marquette, founder of the St. Ignace mission, and the man celebrated in a memorial and a park in St. Ignace, a monument in Mackinac Island, and at numerous other sites. Why this flurry of Marquettes? "The tip of the hat to the French period still consists of just a few famous figures, and with every repetition of these same names they become more and more famous, like La Salle, who was so hated he was shot by his own men, and Father Marquette," Kent said. "I'm hoping that my work will replace all these macro-visions, like the myth of Marquette, who spent a grand total of two years at the straits, and frankly made minimal conversions. The best thing he ever did was die of dysentery or some similar disease and become a martyr. You want to take this down, Phil – it's a quote from a nineteenth-century historian, Joseph Ernest Renan: 'To forget and to get one's history wrong are the essential factors in the making of a nation.' He hit it so on the head. And this is going to be the last sentence of the introduction to my book on the Mackinac Straits. 'Let us remember correctly and get our history right, when we explore the deeds of those before us.'" Kent sat still in his rocking chair while tears formed in his eyes, and he pondered the point of his labors, of so much of his life devoted to "unknown and unfunded" research. "Getting it right is critical to me," he said.

⚜

The next morning I visited Steven Brisson, chief curator of the Mackinac State Historic Parks, at his office not far from Fort Michilimackinac, which was closed for the winter. "It's always a challenge when you have a place that existed from 1715 to 1780, at one point under French control and later the British," he said when I mentioned Kent's criticism of the fort's overemphasis on the British era. "How to present that richness and variety to visitors can be a challenge. The reason why we interpret the British period is because the British had the fort last. The excavations uncovered the fort's final form, and that's what we based our reconstruction on. If we had tried to go back further than the British conquest, we would have had to take down this fort and build a new one. We would have had to destroy some of the structures in there that the British built."

Brisson himself was of French descent – not fur-trader French, but from the line of French-speaking lumberjacks and miners and farmers who came in the nineteenth century. Born in the upper peninsula, Brisson remembers his paternal grandfather, wholly French in blood but no longer speaking the language – except on his death bed, when he muttered his prayers in French. "Religion was French, Jesus Christ was a French name," writes David Plante in *The Family*, his novel about a French-Canadian family in Rhode Island. Of his protagonist, Plante observes, "Jesus Christ in English always sounded to him, no matter how pious the intention, like blasphemy." Brisson's grandfather did not want to go into eternity talking to a strange God.

As a child, Brisson became keenly interested in his French heritage. "I remember even as an elementary school student being more interested in French Canada, and La Salle, and Jean Nicolet – they just fascinated me," he told me. "You *felt* this connection to that history because you knew it was part of your heritage. You read about the Pilgrims in American history and you had this vague sense of, no, this is not my history. These Protestants coming to New England – no, no, no. I'm a *voyageur*."

Afterwards, I flew from St. Ignace to Mackinac Island with four other passengers in a Piper Cherokee to see some of the historic sites. My starting point was "downtown" on Mackinac Island, which looked like any tourist destination upon which the spirit of Walt Disney breathed – all those pretty shops selling fudge and candlesticks, with fan lights over the doors and gables on the roof. I walked up Astor Lane to Market Street to see Stuart House, a handsome three-story building built in 1817 and named after the island manager of the American Fur Company, a man named Robert Stuart. Next to it was a former warehouse of the company, now a building called Community Hall. It seemed to me that this was a much more sacred and important spot in the history of the American republic than, say, Plymouth Rock.

The American Fur Company was founded by John Jacob Astor, a German who landed in New York City in 1784 and soon smelled money in the fur trade. He made contacts with the men who would be his principal rivals, the fur-trading partners of the Northwest Company of Montreal, learned the business, and, in 1808, incorporated under the laws of the state of New York his own outfit, the American Fur Company. It was the first great American corporation. It would serve as the model for all the Cornelius Vanderbilts and John D. Rockefellers who came after and followed Astor's example of destroying competition with a combination of business shrewdness, brass-knuckle tactics, and currying favors from the government. During the War of 1812, for example, Astor was shameless in soliciting the government to protect his fur-trading investments, war or no war. But then Astor, who also was a pioneer of the China trade, knew and practiced globalization on a grand scale, before any other corporate magnate in American history. National boundaries meant nothing to him – except when he found them convenient, as in 1816, when the federal government, at his behest, passed a law prohibiting Canadian fur traders from operating in American territory. (Astor made sure this law did not prohibit his employing French-Canadian *voyageurs* – they were indispensable.)

After his death in 1848, Astor, then the richest man in America, passed into legend as the quintessential American Scrooge – grasping, avaricious, penny-pinching, mercilessly foreclosing mortgages on widows and orphans during his latter career as real estate developer in Manhattan. Delicious stories spread about the fabulously wealthy Astor in his dotage, drooling, bedridden, suckling milk at the breast of a wet nurse when he could no longer eat. The American Fur Company also grew in legend as the most hated organization in the west, the company that robbed Indians, terrorized competition, and maintained an iron control over the fur trade. President Zachary Taylor, whose frontier service in the army had familiarized him with American Fur Company men, called them "the greatest scoundrels the world ever knew."

Recent historians have tended to chip away at this legend. True, Astor was a war profiteer, a slumlord, a purveyor of opium to the Chinese and liquor to the Indians, and a tough nut, but he wasn't *that* bad. He helped solidify American control over the west and expand American commerce. He was a true business pioneer. Thanks in no small part to those impossibly robust *voyageurs*, those light-hearted and penniless French Canadians, he built a financial empire and spawned American corporate capitalism, which has gone on to bestride the world. And here, in this modern-day tourist town, which was once the headquarters of the American Fur Company, its center of operations for the interior of North America, still stand the buildings where the foundations of modern America were laid. No historian has yet fully reckoned what this trade in the pelts of animals meant to both Canada and the United States.

The old headquarters and the old warehouse were handsome, well-proportioned buildings, trim as the lines in a ledger. They had limited interest. I continued walking eastward along Market Street until I came to Marquette Park, where the statue of Marquette stood on the slope of the hill, overlooking the harbor and the docks of downtown Mackinac. Father Marquette arrived at this island with his Huron flock in the spring of 1671. It seemed a fitting place to launch a new mission – the island gave promise of safety from enemy raiding parties, whether the Iroquois to the east or the Sioux to the west. The soil proved too thin for cultivation, however, and before the year was out they moved to the mainland north of the straits, to the spot they called St. Ignace.

Marquette seems to have been everybody's ideal Jesuit missionary. He spoke six Indian languages. He was described by his superior as a man "of sound health and strong body, of excellent character and tried virtue; and because of his wonderfully gentle ways, most acceptable to the natives." So agreeable was his temperament that he charmed even Parkman. Normally, you can detect the beginnings of a sneer on Parkman's face when he refers to anyone's devotion to Our Lady. In Marquette's case, however, he was indulgent. "A subtle element of romance was blended with the fervor of his worship, and hung like an illuminated cloud over the harsh and hard realities of his daily lot," Parkman wrote. "Kindled by the smile of his celestial mistress, his gentle and noble nature knew no fear. For her he burned to dare and to suffer, discover new lands and conquer new realms to her sway."

Of course, by today's standards, Marquette was culturally insensitive to an abominable degree. He believed that, left to themselves, the Hurons would fall back into the clutches of the Devil. Why else would someone like Marquette, fitted by nature to be a college professor, charming his audience in the lecture hall and the common room, be out there in the woods, feeding mosquitos and teaching Huron children their catechism? Nonetheless he exemplified the Jesuit ideal of "going in by their door in order to come out by ours." He was willing to tolerate any native cultural practice that wasn't obviously sinful and to maximize the good in it. "I cheerfully attended their festival of squashes, at which I instructed them and called upon them to thank God, who gave them food in abundance while other tribes, who had not yet embraced Christianity, had great difficulty in preserving themselves from hunger," he wrote. On one occasion, some of his flock at St. Ignace asked him what dances he prohibited. "I replied in the first place that I would not permit those which God forbids, such as indecent ones; that as regards the others, I would decide about them when I had seen them." Having seen them he observed, "Every dance has its own name; but I did not find any harm in any of them, except that called 'The Bear Dance.'" A sick woman, he wrote, invited several friends to participate in the Bear Dance. They covered themselves in bear skins, growled like bears, and performed other bear-like gestures. Marquette is reticent on this point, but it appears some nudity and lewd behavior were involved.

It was hard to know exactly what went on in such dances. Trigger mentions a Huron healing ceremony called the *andacwander*, which greatly scandalized the earlier Jesuits, although, like Marquette, they never spelled out what was so outrageous about it. Fortunately for ethnologists and for curious readers, Father Sagard watched the ceremony through a chink in the wall of a Huron longhouse, and our knowledge of Huron culture is the richer for it. "To perform this ceremony," Trigger writes, "the unmarried people of the village assembled in the sick person's house and spent the night having sexual intercourse with the partner of their choice, while the patient watched and two shamans shook their tortoise shell rattles and sang. Sometimes a sick man might request a young girl to have intercourse with him."

My suspicion is that the Bear Dance was a burlesque of the old *andacwander*. For a burlesque of this orgiastic ceremony, what better joke than to have women dressed up as bears – an animal so venerated for its masculine potency that in some tribes of the northeastern woodlands, girls and unmarried women were literally not allowed to show their faces when a slain bear was brought into camp. (The early twentieth-century anthropologist A. Irving Hallowell, wrote a treatise entitled *Bear Ceremonialism in the Northern Hemisphere*, about how Indians tended to anthropomorphize bears. They were easy animals to anthropomorphize, according to Hallowell. They masturbated a lot, "at least in captivity," and their turds resembled human turds, "only considerably larger.") Burlesque or not, Marquette was firm. "I tried to induce some Huron women not to be present at any of these dances, which generally lasted a good part of the day; but they told me that they had only that time in which to divert themselves, and that, moreover, I had not explicitly forbidden them to dance."

The tone of Marquette's report on his experiences with the Indians of the St. Ignace mission was generally positive. He prepared many of them for confession, for example, and was pleased by their tender consciences. "I would not have believed that savages could render so exact an account of all their lives," he wrote. "They begged me not to give them absolution until they had said all. Some women spent two weeks in examining themselves." Marquette was particularly pleased when the hunters returned laden with game. "God has aided in a special manner the Hurons who went to hunt, for He led them to places where they killed a great number of deer, bears, beaver and bobcats," he wrote. "Several bands failed not to observe the directions that I had given them respecting prayers. Dreams, to which they formerly had recourse, were looked upon as illusions; and if they happened to dream of bears, they did not kill any on account of that; on the contrary, after they had recourse to prayer, God gave them what they desired."

Of course by the time Marquette arrived, the Hurons had been exposed to Christianity for decades and grown used to the authority of black robes; it is not clear how favorably other tribes, such as the Ottawas, responded to missionary efforts. As Timothy Kent pointed out, Marquette did not stay long enough to attempt a true experiment along those lines. In May of 1673, he and the explorer Louis Jolliet departed on the expedition that would make Marquette famous. With five companions, the two paddled down the Mississippi as far as Arkansas, seven hundred miles north of the sea, far enough to establish that the river flowed into the Gulf of Mexico instead of the Pacific Ocean or the waters off the coast of Virginia.

Fearing the Spanish, they halted and returned to the Jesuit mission at Green Bay, Wisconsin. Marquette remained there for another year, trying to rally his health, which had suddenly begun to fail. In October of 1674 he felt well enough to go to Illinois, where he had long desired to establish a mission. He began such a mission but never fully regained his strength, and in the following spring determined to return to St. Ignace. En route, by the shores of Lake Michigan, in May of 1675, the missionary breathed his last. Two years later, a band of Indians Marquette had once evangelized on the western shores of Lake Superior searched for his grave and found it. They dug up his body, which they later testified was still intact, cut away and scraped off the dried flesh and organs, washed and dried the bones, and laid them in a birchbark container. "Then," writes Parkman, "in a procession of thirty canoes, they bore it, singing their funeral songs, to St. Ignace of Michilimackinac. As they approached, priests, Indians, and traders all thronged to the shore. The relics of Marquette were received with solemn ceremony, and buried beneath the floor of the little chapel of the mission."

That, in brief, is the story of Marquette. It's a remarkable story, but hardly sufficient to explain why he has become so legendary. In fact, for nearly two centuries after his death he remained a fairly obscure figure. According to historian Steven Brisson, Marquette's reputation bloomed only when Midwesterners began chafing at "eastern jibes that the west had no history." Having a history is a psychic necessity for people, like having some form of art. In response, Midwesterners looked to the earliest years of European exploration and found white men who were roaming Michigan and Wisconsin at the same time that the Puritans were founding the Commonwealth of Massachusetts and the Virginians were learning to cope with swamp fever. The history of Green Bay, Wisconsin, it turned out, was just as venerable as the history of Boston.

"By the end of the nineteenth-century numerous towns, counties, a river, iron range and railroad were named in Marquette's honor," Brisson writes in an article in *Mackinac History*. Wisconsin sent a statue of Marquette to represent the state in the U.S. Capitol. An even more monumental statue of the Jesuit missionary was erected in Marquette, Michigan. The one I was looking at in Marquette Park was unveiled in 1909. It showed a man of noble brow, thoughtful air, and serene temperament − just like the Marquette reported by his contemporaries. It is easy to forget, gazing upon that figure, that the commemoration of Marquette ran into severe opposition the moment it started. The first enemies of the memory of Marquette weren't those who viewed him as a patriarchal, European imperialist trying to crush native culture. The first enemies were staunch Protestants, who couldn't care less about Indians. An anti-Catholic lobby group called the American Protective Association vehemently protested the inclusion of the statue of "the Jesuit priest" in the nation's capital, right next to "the Immortal Lincoln, stricken down by the hand of the Jesuit." (That would be John Wilkes Booth, S.J.)

A good deal of that old Anglo-Saxon, Bible-believing, No Popery Here sentiment lingers in the United States, joined by anti-Catholic fervor from a number of new quarters. Catholicism wouldn't be Catholicism if it weren't hated by disparate groups of people. There will be no new monuments to Marquette. On that subject, we can only be certain that Father Marquette doesn't give a hoot.

After paying my respects to the statue, I walked up Fort Street to the top of the hill, where Fort Mackinac stood. The British had abandoned Fort Michilimackinac and removed here in 1780 after a disastrous experience in Pontiac's war. An eyewitness account of this episode comes from a trader named Alexander Henry, one of the first Englishmen to try to take advantage of the French defeat and horn in on their trading territory. It was an audacious move, and the Indians were suspicious – it was as if they sensed he was the forerunner of the American Fur Company.

He was there at Fort Michilimackinac on a sunny day in June 1763 when the Ojibwa were playing a game of lacrosse outside the fort. The commander had opened the gates and was sitting nearby with his men, enjoying the spectacle. A player hit a ball through the gates and a group of other players ran inside after it. Then somebody gave a signal, and the Indians drew their knives. "I saw several of my countrymen fall, and more than one struggling between the knees of an Indian, who, holding him in this manner, scalped him while yet living," Alexander Henry wrote. Henry ran up to a garret in the fort. "Through an aperture, which afforded me a view of the area of the fort, I beheld, in shapes the foulest and most terrible, the ferocious triumphs of barbarian conquerors. The dead were scalped and mangled; the dying were writhing and shrieking under the unsatiated knife and tomahawk; and from the bodies of some, ripped open, their butchers were drinking the blood, scooped up in hollows of joined hands, and quaffed amid shouts of rage and victory."

The reader will note that Henry made sure whatever happened did not suffer in the telling. This was not a garden variety massacre he had survived, this was savagery at its most savage. Doubtless he had a grim time of it. His own life was spared by a friendly Indian, and he was taken captive, along with a handful of soldiers. For two days, food was withheld them. On the third day, Henry wrote, their captors "had a loaf, which they cut with the same knives they had employed in the massacre, and knives still covered with blood. The blood they moistened with spittle, and rubbing it on the bread, offered this for food to their prisoners, telling them to eat the blood of their countrymen." Henry does not say if they did.

After this, the British were determined that their presence in the Straits of Mackinac would never again be so vulnerable. Hence the new Fort Mackinac. In 1796 they had to haul down the Union Jack and hand the fort over to the Americans, in what amounted to the final episode of the Revolutionary War. They soon took up, however, where they had left off. The first episode of the War of 1812 was a surprise British attack on the fort, which surrendered without a shot. It looked like the British were suddenly in command of the entire Midwest again. Down south in Detroit, the American commander, Isaac Hull, was terrified at the prospect of a horde of enemy soldiers and Indians descending upon him. He withdrew his own army from Canada and huddled inside the gates of the city, which in turn he promptly surrendered to the British – perhaps the most disgraceful episode in American military history.

In 1814 American forces attempted to recapture Fort Mackinac, but were repulsed. No one knew it at the time, but this minor engagement amounted to the last serious bloodshed in the Straits of Mackinac. With the conclusion of the war in 1815, the fort fell back into American hands for good and remained an American military installation until it was finally closed in 1895. For centuries, since the Hurons at St. Ignace built a log stockade in 1673, this area had been continuously fortified. No other place in the United States, with the possible exception of the Spanish presence in St. Augustine, Florida, had been guarded by walls and armaments for so long.

Now, of course, the place is for tourists. On that sunny day I walked past the main entrance – like Fort Michilimackinac, Fort Mackinac was closed for the winter – and made my way on a road along the north side of the fort. Somebody had left a gate open in that wall, and I passed through it and entered the grounds. A snowmobile was parked in a corner, but not a soul was in evidence. The only sound came from two or three crows perched on a stand of tall cedars, and the only movement snow blown off the branches of those cedars, like a shower of dust, by a light breeze. The white particles drifted for a few seconds before falling on the bright, glazed surface of the snowy parade grounds. I was glad the fort was empty. I was content not to see interpreters dressed up as Yankee artillerymen, demonstrating to crowds of tourists how the cannons were fired, or re-enactors pretending to be members of Company B of the 16th Michigan. The message of the silent fort was simple: the soldiers are gone. They will not come back to us.

I left the fort and walked the East Bluff Road toward the overlook where there was a tablet commemorating Jean Nicolet, a young man who was a trusted interpreter and explorer for Champlain. I found it at the top of a wooden stairway near the edge of the bluffs overlooking Lake Huron and Bois Blanc Island. Clearing the snow off the tablet, I read: NICOLET WATCH TOWER IN HONOR OF JOHN NICOLET WHO IN 1634 PASSED THROUGH THE STRAITS OF MACKINAC IN A BIRCH-BARK CANOE AND WAS THE FIRST WHITE MAN TO ENTER MICHIGAN AND THE OLD NORTHWEST. He had come this way at the behest of Champlain, who had heard stories of a great river flowing to the west and the Pacific Coast. Not only that, but some Indians around Lake Superior had talked of beardless men, not Indians, who came from the west on trading expeditions. Who else could they be but Orientals?

The tablet was unveiled in 1915, and the main speaker was a Jesuit priest named Thomas Campbell, author of a book entitled *Pioneer Priests of America, and Pioneer Laymen of America.* "The memorial tablet of Jean Nicolet which has been affixed to the rocks of the Island of Mackinac, is not only the record of a notable historical event, but is also the declaration of a doctrine," Campbell began his oration. He was right, of course. Every memorial tablet, every statue, every plaque on a heritage building, is the declaration of a doctrine – which is why I have sometimes lingered on them. What was the doctrine of this piece of stone? "It is a protest against a philosophical theory prevalent at the present day, which makes man the creature as well as the victim of his environment – a theory which assails the dignity of human nature, by robbing it of its freedom of will," Father Campbell declared.

Nicolet defied this theory. As one of the first *coureurs de bois*, he had spent some fifteen years among the Indians, learning their culture and language. An impressionable youth, he might have been expected to learn their morals, as well. "The aborigines were far from being the noble creatures depicted by Fenimore Cooper and other romancers, but were steeped in the foulest vices," Campbell told his audience. Nicolet, however, kept free of them. He remained pious, chaste, and dutiful. "He is a man whose virtues may be proposed to the youth of the country as an example and an inspiration," Campbell said. We shall meet Nicolet again, this friend of the Indian and friend of the missionaries.

⚜

For some years after Marquette's death, St. Ignace continued to embody the Jesuit ideal in the New World: a mission to the "aborigines" relatively undisturbed by European influence. French fur traders were not as yet sufficiently numerous to disrupt the work of the missionaries. This is why the Jesuits were so unhappy at the sight of the *Griffon*. Why could this man La Salle not stay put at Fort Frontenac, where he had a perfectly good situation? Why must he always be raising the ante in the fur-trading business? (They could not know about his wanting perpetually to be somewhere other than where he was.) Sure enough, a few years after La Salle's visit, French soldiers came and built their own fort, called de Buade. In 1696 the Sieur de Cadillac arrived to command the garrison. He was everything the Jesuits feared. A forceful, intelligent, sharp-tongued soldier, he won the admiration of Parkman, who, when all was said and done, could never rid himself of his bedrock conviction that the

Jesuits were a sinister organization. For that matter Cadillac, in common with many Frenchmen of the era, had no high regard for Jesuits either. (The Jesuits educated the elite of France – how much of a high regard do any of us have for our teachers?) But it was the liquor trade that brought Cadillac into violent collision with the Jesuits of the St. Ignace mission. Cadillac thought such trade should be tolerated, for all the usual reasons – if the Indians didn't get their French brandy, they'd get their English rum.

His chief antagonist in this controversy was Father Étienne de Carheil, who had a sharp tongue of his own. At one point, he personally accosted Cadillac for winking at the liquor trade and the free use of Indian women by his soldiers. Cadillac gave his side of the story to his superiors:

> I answered that this was seditious language that smelled to heaven and I begged him to desist. Again he told me that I was not obeying the orders of the King, and that I was putting on airs, and at the same time he shook his fist under my nose. I tell you, Monsieur, that I almost forgot he was a priest, and was on the point of breaking his jaw. But, thanks be to God, I contented myself with taking him by the arm, and leading him out of the fort, telling him to stay out of it in the future.

Carheil, meanwhile, was writing his own letters to the governor of New France:

> The missions are reduced to such extremities that we can no longer maintain them against an infinite multitude of evil acts – acts of brutality and violence, injustice and impiety, lewd and shameless conduct. To such acts the infamous and baleful trade in brandy gives rise everywhere without restraint. . . . In our despair there is no other step to take than to leave our missions and abandon them to the brandy traders, so they may establish their trade of drunkenness and immorality.

Cadillac was soon recalled, for reasons not necessarily connected with his fight with Carheil. Back in France, he pursued his scheme of settling Detroit as an alternative to St. Ignace. Building a fort and a town there, Cadillac argued, would give New France greater control over the fur trade, stymie the English and Iroquois, and encourage the native inhabitants to learn French, become farmers, and adopt a civilized manner of life. This was, as we have seen, counter to the Jesuit strategy, but not the less appealing to Cadillac, and many other Frenchmen, for all that. Give these children of the forest, who already followed *les pures lumières de la Nature*, the additional graces of French language and culture and – voilà – you would have excellent subjects of His Most Christian Majesty. The process would be reinforced by intermarriage between the French and the Indians.

It was a policy advocated by French leaders going back to Champlain. Everyone knew, for a variety of reasons – including the absence of a dispossessed agricultural population – that France was not going to export hundreds of thousands of its people to Canada. But if you could get the small number of French males in Canada to generate a new, mixed Indian-French population, that might be the next best thing. At the very least, this new French-speaking population wouldn't need Jesuits to run their lives and interpret for them.

Cadillac, as we know, got his settlement at Detroit, and successfully drew the Hurons and other Indian nations away from St. Ignace. In 1705, the Jesuits, with almost no flock left to shepherd, burnt their church and residence and returned to Quebec. Michilimackinac, however, was too strategic a location to abandon for long. The authorities in France ordered the re-establishment of a mission in that region, and a solitary Jesuit, Father Joseph Marest, dutifully returned to the Straits of Mackinac the year after St. Ignace was abandoned. Marest probably shifted his operations to the south shore of the straits, in present-day Mackinaw City – it was there, at any rate, that the French built their new fort in 1715, and where they remained in force until the British arrived in 1761.

✤

The French and the British are gone now, but the Indians, or at least the Chippewa (Ojibwa) tribe, remain. Referred to as the "Chips" by other residents of St. Ignace, they are often indistinguishable from non-Chippewas. No one would guess, for example, that James Boynton, a Jesuit brother who had written a sixty-seven-page book entitled *Fishers of Men: The Jesuit Mission in Mackinac 1670–1765*, published by St. Anne's Church on Mackinac Island, was a card-carrying member of the Chippewa tribe. Boynton, who taught at a Jesuit school in Detroit, had blue eyes, but he was one-eighth Chippewa, and that was more than enough to qualify him for the card. He reminded me of George Gilbert, the blue-eyed Mohawk.

The visible minorities in today's St. Ignace are the Jamaican immigrants who work the resorts every summer, and the 40 per cent of the Catholic priests in the region who come from southern India. "There are no limits to the irony of history," Friedrich Engels remarked – but the fact that the new fishers of men in this territory are literal "Indians" indicates that history relishes not only irony but word play and puns of the most dubious kind.

TEN

Green Bay

*The story of three paintings • D.H. Lawrence makes a
false prophecy • Sex and the Indian • A slave owner becomes
lord of Green Bay • A vanished civilization • Two interesting
pairs of footwear at a political rally*

In early September La Salle set sail for Lake Michigan, although
Tonty had not yet returned from searching the environs of Sault
Ste. Marie for those men who had absconded from St. Ignace – the
two would rendezvous later. He shortly arrived at the Jesuit mission
in Green Bay, where – surprise – the rest of the men he had sent
ahead of him to trade were waiting for him. They had proved loyal
and had accumulated a small fortune in furs. La Salle was not used
to things working out this well, and like a man afraid of his good
fortune, he botched it. He decided he would free himself of his
creditors by sending the *Griffon* back to deposit the furs at Niagara,
where they could then be sent on to Fort Frontenac. He removed
four canoes from the ship and kept with him fourteen men and
their tools. Among those tools was a portable forge, useful for
repairing all sorts of iron implements and therefore an infallible
means of obtaining the goodwill of Indians wherever they went.
He also kept a few trade goods. The rest was in the hold of the

Griffon, now captained by La Salle's pilot, a man of proven unrelia-
bility and ill will. On September 18, the ship sailed back eastward,
while La Salle readied his men for paddling down the shores of
Lake Michigan.

Forty-five years earlier, Jean Nicolet, after becoming the first
white man to set foot in the state of Michigan, had become the
first to set foot in the state of Wisconsin, by continuing his voyage
at the behest of Champlain westward from the Straits of Mackinac
into Lake Michigan and Green Bay. Never was a more capable
envoy sent into an unfamiliar world. From what we can gather of
Nicolet's fifteen years among the Indians, he lived as comfortably
among them as any European in history. Whether he seriously
thought the Indians he was about to encounter – formerly called the
Winnebagos, and now known as the Ho-Chunks – had contact with
beardless Orientals, or retained ancestral legends of trading with the
Chinese, we will never know, but he prepared himself. Landing not
far from the present city of Green Bay, he made a great entrance.
"He wore a grand robe of China damask, all strewn with flowers and
birds of many colors," the Jesuit *Relations* tell us. "No sooner did
they perceive him than the women and children fled, at the sight of
a man who carried thunder in both hands – for thus they called the
two pistols that he held. The news of his coming quickly spread to
the places round about, and there assembled four or five thousand
men. Each of the chief men made a feast for him, and at one of these
banquets they served at least one hundred twenty beavers."

About fifteen miles north and east of downtown Green Bay, in
an area known as Red Banks, a memorial stands on top of the bluffs
overlooking the bay. Below this memorial is the spot where Nicolet
is said to have landed. Nobody knows for sure, but the spot was the
site of a traditional Ho-Chunk gathering place, and so it is as likely
as any other place. Birches and cedars and oaks and boxwood elders
cover the slope of the bluffs, which rise from a shoreline one
hundred feet above the water. I stood near the edge of those bluffs
on a winter day, with the bay frozen, but I could easily imagine a

Ho-Chunk in the late summer surveying the blue waters, and the dark green of the opposite shore, and seeing Nicolet's canoe approach. Nicolet had sent emissaries ahead of him to notify the Ho-Chunks of his coming, but even if he hadn't, it is doubtful he would have arrived unnoticed.

When I first read about this period of history, it amazed me that people kept running into each other in the vast wilderness of North America. Eventually I realized that it was much easier to hide yourself in modern America than in seventeenth-century America. Back then you could wander off in the woods, to be sure, but in order to survive you eventually had to fall in with an Indian band or a European settlement – and news of strangers spread quickly among the villages and forts strung along the trading routes. The Jesuits, in particular, provided an extremely efficient courier service for messages and information, a service La Salle himself used.

Moreover, given the absence of roads, there were only certain routes that travelers could take, and those were on water. This is worth pondering for a moment, because if you want to understand the French in America you have to understand water routes. In the opening chapter of *Shadows on the Rock*, Willa Cather writes that north and west of Quebec City,

the forest stretched no living man knew how far. That was the dead, sealed world of the vegetable kingdom, an uncharted continent choked with interlocking trees, living, dead, half-dead, their roots in bogs and swamps, strangling each other in a slow agony that had lasted for centuries. The forest was suffocation, annihilation; there European man was quickly swallowed up in silence, distance, mould, black mud, and the stinging swarms of insect life that bred in it. The only avenue of escape was along the river. The river was the one thing that lived, moved, glittered, changed – a highway along which men could travel, taste the sun and open air, feel freedom, join their fellows, reach the open sea . . . reach the world even!

This is strongly put, but it gives you the idea. If La Salle, and other Frenchmen like him, could regard the wilderness as a tonic, rather than the playground of the Devil, as the New Englanders did, it was because within it they could get in a canoe and go places. The innumerable lakes and rivers made bearable Cather's suffocating forest, Kerouac's "utterly hopeless place to which the French came," Whitman's "extreme of grimness," Wyndham Lewis's endless tundra "dotted with the eternal fir tree." And the French, unlike the English, who were hemmed in by the Allegheny Mountains, had full access to rivers and lakes. "From Montreal it was possible to travel by canoe to the Rocky Mountains, to Hudson Bay, or the Gulf of Mexico by way of the St. Lawrence, the Ottawa, the Great Lakes, the Mississippi, and their tributary rivers and lakes," wrote the Canadian historian W.J. Eccles. "Not only were these river routes accessible to the French, and to no other European colonies, but the best means to travel along the rivers was also available to the French and to no other Europeans." That means was the birchbark canoe – easy to carry, easy to make, easy to repair. The raw material of that canoe, the birch, also grew in abundance only in areas dominated by the French. (The Iroquois often had to make do with much less handy and durable elmbark canoes.)

This system of inland waters made it harder, however, for travelers to travel unnoticed. You couldn't hide yourself in a lake or a river. On one occasion La Salle, who had temporarily returned to Fort Frontenac, heard news that some of his men in Illinois had deserted. He realized they would be trying to return to Quebec, and so he lay in wait along the shores of Lake Ontario. Sure enough, before too long the deserters came paddling by and were duly arrested by La Salle.

The Ho-Chunk, then, had plenty of warning somebody of great importance and interest was dropping in for a visit. That was one thing I learned at Red Banks. The most important thing I learned about Nicolet, however, I learned later. The lesson began when I visited the Brown County Courthouse in Green Bay and saw a mural, unveiled in 1910, of Nicolet's landing by a German-born Milwaukee artist named Franz Rohrbeck. It was a lively painting, but unfortunate for a number of reasons. "Rohrbeck confessed to having a number of rather stout German burghers . . . as models for the figures represented in the painting," a contemporary newspaper account of the unveiling stated. "As a result, the dozens of savages who greeted the French explorer are pictured as short, obese persons, in sharp contrast to the well proportioned, lithe beings other artists and photographers have shown." Nicolet, in his Chinese robe, firing his pistols in the air, looks like a drunken cowboy shooting up the Long Branch Saloon. Rohrbeck painted him bug-eyed with excitement – the effects of too much brandy, or the transport of being a *visionnaire*, perhaps, like La Salle.

The next day I ran into another mural depicting Nicolet's landing. This was in the Neville Public Museum, and it was completed in 1937 by one Anna Lou Matthews Bedore, a local artist and sculptress who was commissioned to do the piece by the Works Progress Administration. This showed Nicolet sitting cross-legged in the center of a group of Indians. He had put his pistols away, removed the damask gown (now fastened around his neck like a cape), and was firmly grasping a peace pipe. The Indians were also sitting cross-legged, facing the viewer. They were appropriately lithe and well-proportioned. Everybody's face, including Nicolet's, was an expressionless mask – except for one young Winnebago, on the edge of the group, who seemed to be giving Nicolet a suspicious, sidelong glance. Did he know something the others didn't, or was he simply lacking in the facial control of his fellow Ho-Chunks?

The third depiction of Nicolet's landing I saw was in the Green Bay Public Library. It was supposed to be hanging in a prominent space on the wall but had recently fallen and cracked its gilt frame. A helpful librarian in the local history section named Mary Jane Herber brought it out of temporary storage to show me. It was by an artist named Edwin Willard Deming, and it was the most famous of the Nicolet paintings, having once been used on a three-cent stamp, issued by the Post Office in 1934 to commemorate the tricentennial of the landing. Actually, the library's painting was not the finished product – it was a model or sketch for the finished product, a larger-scale version of the painting now displayed at the state Capitol at Madison. "The reason why this picture is interesting is because it's uncensored," Herber told me. It didn't take me long to spot the uncensored part. A savage maiden in the background was topless. Otherwise, this 1904 portrait was the same as the one in Madison, with Nicolet once again dressed in his Chinese robe firing his pistols in the air. Deming managed to steer midway between the extremes of Rohrbeck's wild-eyed Nicolet and alarmed Winnebagos, and Bedore's expressionless figures. That is to say, all parties looked lively but retained their dignity.

In 1925, Henry Fairfield Osborn, director of the American Museum of Natural History in New York City, wrote an interesting pamphlet on Deming's work. He compared Deming to such nineteenth-century portrayers of Indians as George Catlin, Paul Kane, Seth Eastman, Baldwin Mollhauser, Rudolf Friedrich Kurz, and Clark Wimar. Deming, it turned out, was another cultivated white man obsessed with the Red Man. "From early childhood Deming associated with the Red people of the Winnebago tribe, and learned to love them as brothers," Osborn wrote. "He would sit around the camp fires of these (even to this very small boy) most interesting people listening to their stories and learning the customs of these friends." In his adult career as a painter, Deming turned out a series of sublime, dramatic portraits of Indians, with such titles as *The Vow of Vengeance* and *Prayer to the Great Mystery*. "In our many meetings and conversations," continued Osborn, "I have always been impressed with his deep sympathy for the mystical and supernatural side of the Indian life and his admiration for the many fine characteristics of this great and fast vanishing race."

No wonder there was a market for the work of people like Deming and Mollhauser and Kurz in the late nineteenth and early twentieth centuries. The Indian had always been picturesque, but now that he was vanishing he was even more so. Now his portraitist could tint the canvas with a glow of romantic pathos. By the twenties, everybody knew the American Indian was dying out. So sad – and yet probably better for all concerned. Even D.H. Lawrence looked forward to the Red Man's demise, for reasons of his own. "Within the present generation the surviving Red Indians are due to merge in the great white swamp," he wrote in his 1924 *Studies in Classic American Literature*. "Then the Daimon of America will work overtly, and we shall see real changes." Osborn himself was a deep-dyed racist who strongly believed in the practice of eugenics to eliminate "worthless race types." Although the Red Man had "many fine characteristics" and was certainly no worthless race type, Osborn knew that this branch of humanity had no future and could be safely mourned in advance, like the eohippus or the wooly mammoth.

Osborn's pamphlet was an interesting back story to the Deming painting. What I realized from these paintings, however, was that the paintings themselves didn't matter. What mattered was the public appetite for the paintings. The courthouse, the museum, the library – major public buildings in Green Bay, and all graced by portraits of Nicolet meeting the local Indians. What was it about this subject that so interested the citizens of Wisconsin and Green Bay? "It's the beginning of Wisconsin history," Jerrold Rodesch, history professor at the University of Wisconsin, told me. "Every culture needs a genesis story."

Perhaps not every culture. The woodland Indians, who lived in a world where change was always a fearful and disturbing phenomenon, would never turn a historical event such as Nicolet's landing into a cherished genesis story. But Westerners love to be told, this was when the curtain rose and the drama began. This was the birth.

The artistic celebration of Nicolet's landing assures the people who are doing the celebrating that they have a history. It assures them that the events subsequent to the landing have not been random or meaningless, but rather that these events have been part of an unfolding narrative – a narrative, moreover, that's going some-where. This is true even though no one can prove that Nicolet, in fact, ever set foot in Wisconsin, given the vagueness of the geogra-phy in the *Relations*. In the 1980s a Canadian historian named Marcel Trudel claimed that Nicolet actually landed on the shore of Lake Superior instead of Green Bay – a thesis met with some dis-belief in Green Bay. "The fact that there is such slight historical recording supporting the whole thing – either the site of Nicolet's landing, or the story – suggests how important it is for people to have some sort of beginning point," Rodesch commented. The story of Nicolet's landing, as Timothy Kent might say, is pure macro-vision.

As genesis stories in North America go, it is a relatively cheerful one, even from an Indian point of view. "For some reason or other, the French and the Ojibwa peoples and other Great Lakes tribes got on very well," Denise Sweet, professor of American Indian Studies at the University of Wisconsin, told me. "To me, the story is a nar-rative of survival, of trade, of a sense of shared respect. Whether or not Nicolet and the French had ulterior motives is not for me to say. I do know there was a buck to be made here. And Indian people understand very well this notion of trade. We had something they wanted, and they had something we wanted."

Certainly it's happier than other, highly emblematic stories of early colonial beginnings – Pocahontas saving the life of Captain John Smith, the Indians joining in with the Pilgrims at the first Thanksgiving dinner. When I was a boy, pictures of these semi-mythological events could be displayed, and their narratives told in the classroom, without embarrassment. But that's gone, because we are too aware now that within a few decades of these happy stories the Virginians and the Massachusetts men were doing their best to exterminate the people of Pocahontas and the turkey-bearing dinner guests. By contrast, for two centuries after Nicolet's landing things went reasonably well in Green Bay.

When the British army conquered Quebec in 1760, its officers discovered, somewhat to their surprise, that the French Canadians along the banks of the St. Lawrence were quite an agreeable set of people. As historian Kerry Trask points out, British officers were imbued with the ethos of the landed aristocracy. They detested the commercial class, including the British merchants who descended on Montreal to get their slice of the fur trade. General James Murray, Governor in Chief of Canada, called these entrepreneurs "ignorant, licentious, factious men." The *habitants*, on the other hand, were honest, churchgoing, polite, unambitious farmers with a gracious way of acknowledging hierarchies. The basic structure of Quebec society was, as we know, feudal, a feudalism that was worn very lightly – the economic and social gulf between *seigneur* and tenant was narrow. Yet the notion of *seigneur* was still honored. No grasping bourgeoisie – no bourgeoisie of any sort – had taken hold in this community. General Murray, in the spirit of Arnold Toynbee two centuries later, called the population he ruled over "perhaps the best and bravest race upon the Globe."

But this same aristocratic ethos, as Trask points out, gave rise to diametrically opposite opinions of the French half-breeds running loose in the woods in places like Green Bay. The British despised them. (This is one reason why modern Québécois have clung to the myth of the *coureurs de bois* as embodying the true soul of the race.) Murray's colleague, General Thomas Gage, termed the French fur traders "as wild as the country they go in, or the [native] people they deal with, and . . . far more vicious and wicked." They lived a semi-nomadic life, paid no taxes, did what they pleased, and most odious of all, encouraged whatever resentments the Indians felt toward the British. The generals and colonial administrators in London entertained schemes of removing every one of these *coureurs de bois* from the northwest – they might have done it, too, had not more pressing events intervened.

What would we give to know more about these people, who seemed to exist somewhere on a sliding scale between native and European culture? They were French-speaking Catholics who had little contact with priests and frequently offered tobacco as a sacrifice to the *manitous*. They made the sign of the cross and prayed to St. Anne, and whistled through the wing bones of an eagle to calm an impending storm. They sang the songs of medieval France and painted their faces with colored clay and charcoal. They built houses of Norman design, and covered the walls and roofs with bark. And they took wives among the Indian bands they traded with.

Who else would they marry in the wilderness? Indian women knew how to do the tasks, such as preparing furs and sewing clothes, that were essential to their work. Marriage with an Indian woman also solidified business and political alliances with her kin. As for Indian women, they too had incentives for taking Frenchmen as their partners. Inter-tribal wars killed a lot of eligible men. And late at night there might have been ribald talk in the wigwams about the sexual appetites of those *coureurs de bois*. It's not that Indian males didn't enjoy sex – but they had certain attitudes that we, who live in a consumer culture that encourages self-indulgence, find hard to understand. They thought it was more manly to refrain from sex than to behave like a stud. That was in keeping with the entire tenor of their existence in the world, where the key to functioning was endurance, not the pursuit of comfort and pleasure. In this world, you just had to make up your mind to rise superior to cold, hunger, and fatigue – not that you had much choice in the matter. Your choice, if you can call it a choice, was either to be a miserable weakling or make a virtue of necessity. (Courage at the torture stake was the extreme of such forbearance.) At least some rewards came with this toughness, however, spiritual power being one of them. A man didn't want to lose his familiarity with spirits because he spent too much time pleasuring a wife.

This was not a scruple that bothered the French, and it may have been a reason why Cadillac claimed that Indian women "always prefer a Frenchman for a husband to any savage whatever." In any case, by the beginning of the nineteenth century, a long-established community of Metis fur traders in Green Bay stood as proof that Indian culture and white culture were not irreconcilable opposites. Green Bay demonstrated that the encounter of these two worlds did not have to result, as it resulted everywhere else in North America except New France, in the eventual crushing of Indian nationhood.

Unfortunately, it was not a very visible demonstration. For Americans, at the dawn of the nineteenth century, anything west of Lake Huron was a howling wilderness, inhabited only by scattered Indian tribes and therefore, in effect, empty space. When the first Americans came to Green Bay after the War of 1812, they discovered an actual town populated by people of mixed blood who spoke French, built houses, planted gardens, observed Lenten fasts, and, à la Detroit's Johnny Couteau, played the fiddle, danced the night away, and in winter bet on horse races on the ice of the Fox River. It was not as literate as New England, but it was a permanent settlement with distinct cultural amenities, a social hierarchy – the town was dominated by a few highly successful trading families – and a population generally with much better manners than the Yankee newcomers.

The symbol of this makeshift civilization might have been Charles Langlade, who moved to Green Bay in 1765 and initiated its growth as a permanent settlement. He was born in 1729 at Michilimackinac, of a French fur-trading father and a mother who was a full-blooded Ottawa woman. His education, like his parentage, was a perfect mixture of cultures – European modernity, as exemplified by his Jesuit instructors, combined with native lore. When Langlade was ten, his Ottawa uncle, a chieftain named La

Fourche ("The Pitchfork") by the French, dreamed that a war party he was organizing against the Chickasaw would enjoy success only if the boy accompanied it. The young Langlade duly left with the war party, after his father gave him these parting words: "You must go with your uncles – but never let me hear of your showing any signs of cowardice." In later years, Langlade would tell his grandchildren that the subsequent battle seemed to him like an elaborate game. (In its origins, such fighting probably *was* an elaborate game.) He also discovered it was a game for which he had a pronounced liking.

He grew up, as a result, to be a pre-eminent guerrilla fighter in the woods of North America. His greatest success occurred in 1755, when British General Edward Braddock led more than 2,200 troops, including a regiment of Virginians under the command of George Washington, against Fort Duquesne, on the site of present-day Pittsburgh. Langlade and a French captain named Beaujeu, leading a force consisting mostly of Indians, ambushed Braddock in the hills near the fort, killing the general and routing his men. Partly because Braddock embodied a fatal British arrogance – he scorned the services of Indian allies – and because the cool-headed Washington was credited with helping save the remnants of the army, the defeat became famous in American history. It was one of those dramatic stories that seemed, in retrospect, to reveal the deep design of things. Edwin Willard Deming even contributed to the legendary quality of the event with a particularly stirring portrait of the battle – Langlade and the Indians firing from cover while the mortally wounded Braddock, vulnerable in a clearing of the forest, bathed in light, reared back on his horse.

Langlade went on to fight many more battles in that war. He was like Confederate cavalryman Nathan Bedford Forrest; if his military superiors had made better use of his barbarous talents, they might at least have prolonged their hopeless struggle. But the defeat came, and Langlade went back to the business of fur trading. When the Revolutionary War broke out, he served his new British masters faithfully, and when that war was over returned to Green

Bay, presiding over the settlement with his family and employees and slaves (Indians from west of the Mississippi captured in war) as the lord of the manor. Every May 1 he would appear in his red British uniform, with his sword given to him by King Louis XV, while the townspeople fired their guns in salute to the *seigneur*. Legend reports him as saying, shortly before his death in 1802, that he could remember fighting in ninety-nine battles and regretted only that he was unable to round off that number to an even hundred. That story alone should have made him better remembered in the country where his bones lie. He deserved fame. In the wilderness or the senate chamber, it is obvious, he could have eaten Davy Crockett for breakfast. But it would not do to make an American icon out of a man who tried to kill George Washington.

At least he was spared the sight of what happened to his people after the War of 1812. American troops were sent to Green Bay in 1816 and tyrannized the population. Businessmen and land speculators followed. The fur traders were told only American citizens could pursue that occupation, and when they asked for American citizenship they were refused. The French-Canadian fur traders were forced to deal exclusively with the American Fur Company, which drove them into debt and, by the mid-1830s, out of business entirely. At the same time, the traders lost their land, to which they never had a clear title anyway. The Metis began to disperse – many ended up in the Canadian prairies, where they still form a large element of the population. But in Green Bay they disappeared. The memory of their culture and their settlement faded with the passing decades, and the great myth, cited by Timothy Kent, that American pioneers from the east pushed ever westward into virgin wilderness, untamed by man, took deep root.

⚜

My last evening at Green Bay I found myself at the University of Wisconsin talking to Bill Meindl, publisher of a magazine called

Voyageur: Northeast Wisconsin's Historical Review. Meindl mentioned that in half an hour there was going to be a campaign appearance by Senator John Edwards in a campus lounge – it was shortly before the Wisconsin Democratic primary. I went over and got a seat in the lounge, next to a man in jeans and a jacket with a Local 2376 UAW logo on it. His name was Jason Borden, he was thirty-three, a Gulf War veteran, and he had come from Sheboygan, where he worked in a Lear Corporation factory, to see if Edwards was some-body he could support. The big issue in Borden's mind was the loss of jobs because of free trade. "There's more Made in China prod-ucts in this country than Made in America products, maybe a ten to one ratio," he argued. "Just go to any store, try to find products made in America. I do my best but it's tough. I mean, shoes. Find a shoe that's made in America. I wear my combat boots now because I know at least they're American products." I looked down at his feet. They were encased in big shiny black boots – boots that had trod the dust of Iraq. "It makes me sad. You go to buy an American flag and it says Made in China."

We waited for the candidate to appear. True to form in these matters, he was half an hour, forty-five minutes late. "The only reason we won World War II was because we had an industrial base," Borden said. "We were just able to produce more and faster. That's the only reason we won. Now look. We may have the strongest mil-itary in the world right now, but you can't sustain it if you don't have the industrial base to manufacture weapons and equipment. You got to have replacement parts. The reason the Germans took off and were able to take over half the world was because they had the best factories in the world at the time. We can't wage a war like that again, because we don't have the factories any more." Perhaps the sit-uation of the United States, in this regard, was not so different from the situation of the Great Lakes Indians four hundred years ago. They grew in wealth because of the new trade goods but lost their own industrial base. Their home territory could no longer sustain them, and the fur trade became a tiger they dared not dismount.

There was a stir at the entrance of the lounge. Edwards was now visible, shaking hands as he made his way to the microphone. "I hear you have a couple of basketball teams that are doing okay," he began his speech. "Is that right?" Behind me, a woman nudged her companion and pointed at Edwards. "Somebody gave him a pair of boots." He had come prepared for the snowdrifts of Wisconsin, in a pair of hiking shoes that I'm sure had the latest waterproof and breathable Gore-Tex membrane, shock-absorbing air-sole, and internal speed plate shank to enhance torsional rigidity, but they looked funny with his dark blue suit. "When I got up this morning, in the Milwaukee paper I saw in the headlines on the front page five hundred jobs gone to Mexico," Edwards said. "Here we go again, same old story with the Bush administration."

"Boo," Borden said. We were sitting three rows behind Edwards, who was at the center of a ring of seats. It gave me an excellent view of the back of his head, which was an extremely impressive sight – not the tiniest hint of a bald spot. I noticed this, I might add, even before Senator Edwards's hair became a campaign issue in the upcoming presidential election. My gaze took in his brown hair, a quarter of an inch over his immaculate white collar, and his dark blue suit and his pants hanging perfectly – except for the cuffs, which were hiked up over those complicated shoes. They say maître d's in expensive restaurants size you up by looking at your footwear. In that case, Edwards was definitely not in the running for a good table. (But then Edwards's point was that few Americans were in the running for a good table.)

"I'll tell you something, think about this," Edwards went on. "It wasn't that long ago we made most of the automobiles and steel in the whole world. Not any more. We used to make most of the jet-liners for the whole world. Not any more. We were the ones who perfected radio and television. Now we don't make them any more. It isn't just jobs going overseas, it's whole industries. . . . We've had enough of free trade, it's time to think a little about fair trade."

"Amen," Borden said. This was music to his ears. It made me realize why people were so upset about the loss of industrial jobs. It was because they were the kind of jobs that enabled a man to retire to the country after thirty-five years and tend his lawn and his garden, and fill his three or four freezers with half a beef, and sit with his rifle in a hunting shack on his own land waiting for a lordly stag to appear. Was all this to be lost to the Mexicans and Chinese, who paid their workers shit and happily polluted the environment?

Edwards was really talking about the Daimon of capitalism, however, Creator of Wealth and Destroyer of Cultures. Edwards was saying he could help tame this powerful spirit. Father Carheil had tried to do the same thing with his bitter denunciation of the trade in brandy at St. Ignace, and the medieval Churchmen with their condemnations of usury, and many another spiritual and political authority over the centuries, and their conspicuous lack of success did not bode well for Edwards's promises.

ELEVEN

Kankakee

La Salle teaches a lesson to some sneak thieves • A mysterious church looms over the soybeans • The hobbits of North America • Abraham Lincoln revealed as a paranoiac • An urban legend in nineteenth-century Kankakee • The dangers of being too accommodating to ghosts • The darkest episode in the history of La Salle • Giant catfish lurk in the depths • The gay soul of the Illinois habitant

The trip down Lake Michigan proved to be a nightmare for La Salle and his party. Storms lasting for days swept the lake, leaving the men shivering under blankets on the shore. While waiting for the weather to improve, they ate the last of their scanty provisions. By the time they were prepared to venture their canoes in the water, they were famished. Twelve days after they had set out from Green Bay, on October 1, they sighted a village of Potawatomis. Some of the villagers ran down to the shore making signs of friendship. La Salle's men, not for the first time or the last, wanted to kill their leader when he insisted, instead of buying food right then and there, that they keep paddling and disembark a few miles down from the village. Aside from everything else, another storm was brewing. But La Salle was not being perverse – he knew it was a bad idea to have a band of men desperate for food clambering out of canoes while he tried to manage the situation with the Indians. So they went their way, while the wind and the waters rose, and made another miserable landing with the waves breaking over their heads as they pulled the canoes on shore. Some of them nearly drowned. La Salle had his men construct a makeshift fort of logs and brush, and then sent three emissaries to negotiate properly with the Potawatomis. At first, the three found the village deserted – the inhabitants had been frightened by the worrying disappearance into the woods of the white men. But the emissaries carried with them a calumet La Salle had obtained at Green Bay, a long-stemmed pipe of great symbolic importance. It signified peaceful intentions. When the Potawatomis caught a glimpse of it, their attitude changed again, and they supplied the voyagers with food in exchange for La Salle's gifts.

For the rest of the month, La Salle and his men continued to make their way southward in face of rough weather and the back-breaking necessity, every night when they made camp, of carrying their canoes up steep bluffs that rose from the shoreline. One night, near the end of October, a sentry glimpsed some Fox Indians lurking about their camp. When challenged, the Indians stepped forward and explained they were exercising caution because they thought the French were Iroquois but now were pleased to see their mistake. The next morning, when it was discovered a coat was missing, La Salle determined to retrieve it from the Indians. There'd be nothing but trouble ahead if they got away with this.

La Salle obtained leverage when he ran across a lone Fox warrior in the woods and captured him. Unfortunately, the Fox Indians had already cut the coat into pieces, and when La Salle showed up in their village to demand its return – on pain of never seeing their fellow warrior alive – they were unable to give him satisfaction. Instead they resolved to free the captive. Some 125 warriors soon confronted twelve Frenchmen armed with flintlocks in the woods, but, being deficient in guns and ammunition themselves they thought twice about forcing the issue, and eventually negotiations resumed. The Indians gave La Salle beaver pelts in reparation for the theft, and politeness reigned once more. In the course of conversation, someone told the French that the Illinois had gotten word of an impending Iroquois attack and were now on a war footing. Not only that, but the Illinois blamed the French for stirring up Iroquois hostility and were ready to kill any Frenchman on sight. La Salle believed that the Jesuits and rival fur traders were responsible for the piece of misinformation. He told the Fox that he could handle the Illinois just fine, thank you, but the morale of his men, on hearing the news, sank even lower.

⚜

On November 1, La Salle's party landed at the mouth of the St. Joseph River, in what is now southwestern Michigan, where there were enough wild grapes for the resourceful priests to make Communion wine before stting out for the country of the Illinois.

Today the country of the Illinois is the country of corn and soybean and Holstein cows. On a sunny early summer afternoon I cruised past bright green fields of corn shoots and found myself in the small town of Beaverville — just a bump on the highway, as the natives would say — with a downtown consisting of grain storage silos, a hardware store, the Iroquois Farmers State Bank, a coin wash, a post office, and a bar and grill. Just before I found myself back in the fields of corn, I saw a prodigious sight, a massive Romanesque church, looking like it had been transported there by mistake from some old, ethnic neighborhood of Chicago or Montreal. In the middle of nowhere, it just stood there.

I got out of the car and walked up the front steps of the church, which was set well back from the highway, as suited its dignity. Then I received my second surprise. The door opened when I pulled it. In this age of vandalism, keeping the doors of a church unlocked when nobody is around is unheard of. I stepped inside and in the twilight of the interior was startled to see somebody standing in front of me. A split second later I perceived it was an angel, about four feet high, holding a font of holy water. I made the sign of the cross with the holy water and walked down the center aisle, genuflected, and sat in a pew. To the left of the altar a red light was burning, and I realized why the church door was unlocked. It was shortly after three on a Friday afternoon, the first Friday of the month of June, and the red sanctuary light signified the presence of Blessed Sacrament, the consecrated communion host, on the altar.

The faithful were invited to enter the church and adore the sacrament; that is to say, to adore the body, blood, soul, and divinity of Christ. The invitation was particularly extended on the first Friday of every month, because traditionally Friday was the day of the death of Christ; the faithful were urged to receive Communion on nine first Fridays in reparation for sin. In the years during and just after the Second Vatican Council, it seemed as if these traditional devotions would die out – the same way that the custom of Father Cyr's parishioners borrowing the statue of the Mystica Rosa and taking it home to say the rosary in front of it was dying out. Catholic theologians of a reforming bent, particularly in those years, seemed to agree with Protestants that such devotions smacked of superstition and idolatry. First Friday adorations, Stations of the Cross, Novenas in honor of Our Lady of the Miraculous Medal – they'd all be swept away in a general housecleaning, to be replaced by more relevant forms of spirituality, such as social justice activism.

Forty years after the council, however, these devotions stubbornly persist, along with such medieval concepts as indulgences, which caused all that fuss in Germany five centuries ago. (In traditional Catholic theology, sins that have been forgiven still entail some temporal punishment – you might say bad karma has to be dealt with, even after guilt has been removed. Indulgences remit part or all of that punishment.) Why this is, I am not sure. I myself felt mildly guilty that I kept looking about this church like a tourist, rather than remaining attentive to the presence of Christ. But it was a very interesting church. I read the inscription at the bottom of one of the beautiful stained glass windows: *A La Mémoire De Dame Hilaire Lambert, Don De Son Epoux.* As improbable as it seems, this part of Illinois used to be a French enclave. French-speaking families had come from Quebec to live here with their religion and their language, in the heart of the United States of America.

They almost seemed to have disappeared. The great church – the cornerstone said it was erected in 1909 – was like some monumental edifice or temple left behind in the outback of Australia or the African veldt by a mysterious race of people. Perhaps this is why Norman Mailer, in his 1968 book *Miami and the Siege of Chicago*, could begin his hymn to Chicago – an hour's drive away from Beaverville – with a rhapsodic recital of virtually every ethnic group in the city except the French. In that book, he wrote of "the neighborhoods [that] hint of eastern Europe, Ireland, Tennessee, a gathering of all the clans of the Midwest, the Indians and Scotch-Irish, Swedes, some Germans, Italians, Hungarians, Rumanians, Finns, Slovaks, Slovenes – it was only the French who did not travel." You would never know from this comment that the city was founded by the French. These French who did not travel roamed across the continent and laid out the first streets of Detroit, Milwaukee, St. Paul – even Juneau, Alaska. Such brave, resolute, resourceful people. But their minds were shadowed by an awareness no other European arrival to North America had to contend with; namely, that they had come here and built a nation and an empire and then seen it overwhelmed by invaders and lost to them. They were a conquered race, not in the Old World but in the New World. Even the Mexicans had proudly maintained the heart of their country against such powerful invaders as James K. Polk and Napoleon III. They had not lost that core of independence. But the French Canadians had.

Something in them, as a result, was resistant to the American Dream, something made them keep their heads down and fade into the landscape like hobbits.

⚜

La Salle and his men waited nearly three weeks for Tonty – presumably finished with his task of rounding up deserters in Sault Ste. Marie and now paddling down Lake Michigan – to show up at their agreed-upon rendezvous. In the meantime, La Salle ordered his men to build a fort at the mouth of the St. Joseph River. Like the building of the *Griffon*, the construction of a fort would at least distract them from the cold and the bad food. Then they could move on. It didn't matter to La Salle's plan that winter was fast approaching – in fact, it was better, since winter was the season when the Illinois split up into hunting parties and therefore presented a less formidable front to intruders. Tonty, meanwhile, arrived with the deserters but bearing no news of the *Griffon*. La Salle's heart sank. That ship represented financial salvation. Still, his men finished the fort and La Salle, at the beginning of December, gave the order to proceed up the St. Joseph River. At the southernmost curve in the river, near the present site of South Bend, they disembarked from their canoes and started looking for westward-flowing water that would take them to Illinois.

On this occasion, something happened to La Salle that I find incredible, although I do not doubt the truthfulness of the account. Their Indian scout, a Mohican, was off hunting, and in his absence the French were wholly at a loss to find the portage they were looking for. La Salle went off by himself to search for it. By nightfall he had not returned to the camp. Late the next afternoon, he finally re-appeared before the worried Tonty and Hennepin, with two dead opossums hanging from his belt. (He had literally whacked the animals off a tree with a stick.) La Salle had gotten lost, he told the two men, but had managed, even after nightfall, to find his way back to the St. Joseph River. He fired his gun as a signal to his men, but heard no reply. Following the bank of the river, he saw the gleam of a campfire, which he assumed belonged to his men. When he got there, however, he found only the fire and the impression of a body on a bed of grass. Clearly an Indian, who may or may not have been waiting to ambush somebody, had just fled. La Salle called out in various Indian languages, and when no response came, he shouted that he was going to sleep in this recently vacated bed. Then, as Parkman writes, he "piled a barricade of bushes around the spot, rekindled the dying fire, warmed his benumbed hands, stretched himself on the dried grass, and slept undisturbed till morning."

Say what you want about La Salle, he had nerve.

With the return of the Mohican scout, the party managed to find the portage. It led to a series of half-frozen swamps. Somebody named Duplessis, driven nearly mad by this cheerless march, was about to shoot La Salle in the back when another member of the party grabbed the gun away from him. (Neither La Salle nor any other chronicler of this expedition saw fit to say more about this disquieting incident.) Finally, in the midst of this icy wetland, the men found a stagnant stream twisting through the ooze. It was the Kankakee River. They followed it until it broadened into something they could recognize as a river, although it was a river that looped so tortuously through impenetrable brush tangles that progress was difficult.

Then they were in the prairies, a country of grass and the occasional stand of tall oaks. All around them the ground was charred – the Illinois set fires at carefully chosen locations to force the buffalo to run past groups of hunters, who then slaughtered the herds. This method of killing buffalo on a large scale does not exactly support the reputation of native Americans living in harmony with Mother Earth. Carcasses were left scattered on the ground for wolves and ravens – a foretaste of the great slaughter of the buffalo in the nineteenth century. As they paddled down the river, the French saw the bones and skulls of these animals lying in great heaps. At one point they spotted a huge bull mired in mud at the river's edge. It took twelve men to kill the beast and haul him up from the riverbank, but their efforts were repaid with a rare feast.

They reached the point where the Kankakee flowed into the Illinois River and continued westward. The month was almost gone when they arrived at a great Illinois village not far from the present town of Utica. Four hundred and sixty lodges stood empty. La Salle and his men found pits in the earth where grain was stored, helped themselves to a quantity of it, and continued down the river. Just below the present city of Peoria, they encountered another, somewhat smaller, Illinois village. This one was occupied. Now La Salle would find out first-hand just what the disposition of the Illinois nation was toward the French. He ordered the eight canoes to line up abreast on the river and the men to lay down their paddles and pick up their rifles. They let the current carry them past the village; if the Illinois really were spoiling for a fight they would know the French were ready. Surprise was always the deadliest part of wilderness conflict. This is exactly why, despite their superior numbers, the Illinois in this instance found themselves at a disadvantage. Somewhere between one and two hundred warriors in this village stood opposed to thirty-odd Frenchmen in canoes, but they were not prepared for the sight of the armed and resolute strangers at their doorstep.

La Salle's party found a landing spot below the village, beached the canoes, and stood ready to repulse an attack. The Indians collected themselves and approached the French with a calumet; La Salle displayed his own. In an instant it was decided that the visitors would enjoy the hospitality of the village. The French were feasted, and speeches were made, and gifts given to the villagers in return for the "borrowed" corn. La Salle declared his intention to build a fort and stay the winter in the area, and to help make that idea palatable he brought out his iron forge and demonstrated its use. He also told them of his intention to travel down the great river to the sea.

This would benefit the Illinois, he said, because through this new trade route valuable goods would come to them. They would grow prosperous and powerful through trade with the French, and the French would ensure such an outcome by providing protection against the Iroquois. La Salle's master, the great king of France, would see to that.

In short, La Salle outlined to his hosts the prospects of a commercial and political alliance between the French and the Illinois that would dominate the heart of the continent.

⚜

La Salle was penetrating a region where other French – fur traders, Jesuits, a handful of farmers – would shortly settle. Two centuries later, however, there was a further, very different wave of French immigration that would come to Illinois. A few miles south of the Kankakee River, where La Salle and his men passed through in December of 1679, these nineteenth-century French-Canadian immigrants settled the pleasant town of St. Anne – and coincidentally launched one of the more curious episodes in the history of American religion.

It began in December 1850, when the Catholic bishop of Chicago wrote a letter to a priest in Quebec named Charles Chiniquy. (In Illinois, pronounced *SHIN a kee*.) The bishop, the Right Reverend James Oliver Van De Velde, urged Chiniquy in his letter to help the great cause of attracting "immigrants from the French-speaking countries of Europe and America, till they cover the whole territory of Illinois with their sturdy sons and pious daughters." Chiniquy went to Illinois, saw the promised land, and returned to Quebec an evangelist for the cause. That, in turn, aroused the ire of the bishop of Montreal, Ignace Bourget. The subject of immigration was a sore spot for someone like him. He and his confreres had always encouraged the high birth rate among French Canadians in Quebec but were never sure how to deal with the reality that Quebec could support only a limited population on its existing farmland. As the nineteenth century wore on, the diaspora of French Canadians from Quebec increased, and it was deeply troubling to Bourget and other church leaders. Lord Elgin, the British governor-general of Canada, observed in 1848 that these leaders were forced to watch their flock emigrating "annually in thousands to the States, where they become hewers of wood and drawers of water to the Yankees and bad Catholics in the bargain." (It is another irony of history that these emigrants proved better Catholics in the long run than the French of Quebec.)

The Bourget solution was to urge French Canadians to settle and colonize the uninhabited regions of their own province before leaving the country. When Quebec became fully industrialized in the twentieth century, the exodus did indeed come to an end – until that time, however, jobs in the textile mills of New Hampshire and Massachusetts remained more appealing than back-breaking labor as a lumberjack or farmer in the backwoods of Quebec. The bishop of Chicago's solution was different – mass emigration to selected parts of the United States. Concentrate enough French-Canadian immigrants in one area, and they could be prevented from "scattering any longer among Protestants." Illinois could be turned into Nouveau Québec.

Chiniquy, the bishop decided, was just the man to set this scheme in motion. The priest had proven himself an able and charismatic figure, the founder and head of a temperance society in Quebec that claimed two hundred thousand members. He was a born crusader. In November 1851 he returned to Illinois, selected a site for the new colony where the town of St. Anne now stands, oversaw the construction of a log-cabin chapel, and welcomed the first French-Canadian families. By the end of that decade, the town's population was well over a thousand, not including French settlers to offshoot communities such as Beaverville.

Like many crusaders, however, Chiniquy had problems getting along with people, particularly authority figures. He engaged in a long legal battle over the title to the land at St. Anne with Anthony O'Regan, the Bishop of Chicago, who had succeeded Bishop Van De Velde in 1853. Chiniquy claimed that he owned the land. He also engaged in legal battles over ownership of land in St. Anne with a land developer named Peter Spink. It was in the course of this litigation that Chiniquy employed the services of a lawyer and politician eminent in the state of Illinois, Abraham Lincoln. Lincoln did his usual professional job in representing Father Chiniquy against Spink. (The parties reached a compromise solution.) According to Chiniquy, he and Lincoln got along like a house on fire. No records indicate that Chiniquy ever saw Lincoln again, however. It didn't matter. Chiniquy had established his Lincoln connection, which he would draw upon in the future.

Meanwhile, in between the two trials, Bishop O'Regan suspended Chiniquy from his duties. The reason for the suspension was not made explicit, and Chiniquy, who continued to exercise his priestly office, claimed that the bishop had been misinformed on certain delicate matters by Chiniquy's enemies. The bishop subsequently excommunicated Chiniquy, and priests were sent from Canada to save the flock from its discredited pastor. Chiniquy's hold over his parishioners remained firm, however, and most followed him when he finally announced his decision to leave forever the Roman Catholic Church and become a minister of the Presbyterian Church. The Church of St. Anne became the First Presbyterian Church of St. Anne, which Chiniquy headed until his retirement in 1891. While serving as pastor of that church, Chiniquy married, fathered two daughters, and embarked on a series of speaking tours in the United States, Europe, and Australia, thundering against the godless and depraved Church of Rome.

In 1886 he published *Fifty Years in the Church of Rome*, a massive, 832-page memoir in which he painted the Catholic Church, particularly the French-Canadian church he knew intimately, as a nest of drunkards, hypocrites, schemers and liars, Bible-snatching idolators, and sexual profligates. Catholics were not slow to respond.

Chiniquy's entire career came under an unfriendly spotlight, and it was reported, with some accuracy, that he had been detected in numerous instances of personal immorality dating back to his years in the seminary. The suspension by Bishop O'Regan, for example, was said to be prompted by instances of Chiniquy's violent and immoral behavior. Chiniquy, on his part, maintained that O'Regan tried to get rid of him because the bishop wanted to hand over all the French-Canadian churches in Illinois to the Irish. (This suspicion, I might add, would have struck a chord in more places than St. Anne. Across North America, it was often said that the worst enemies of French-speaking Catholics were Irish bishops.)

In his memoir, Chiniquy played the Lincoln card for all it was worth. According to that memoir, Chiniquy visited the president in the White House, where Lincoln told him, "A few days ago, I saw Mr. Morse, the learned inventor of electric telegraphy; he told me that, when he was in Rome, not long ago, he found out the proofs of a most formidable conspiracy against this country and all its institutions. It is evident that it is to the intrigues and emissaries of the pope, that we owe, in great part, the horrible civil war which is threatening to cover the country with blood and ruins." Lincoln offered Chiniquy a job as secretary in the American embassy in France, in which capacity he could visit Rome and investigate the conspiracy. "As you have been twenty-five years a priest of Rome, I do not know any man in the United States so well acquainted as you are with the tricks of the Jesuits, and on the devotedness of whom I could better rely," Lincoln told Chiniquy. "And, when once on the staff of my ambassador, even as one of his secretaries, might you not soon yourself become the ambassador? I am in need of Christian men in every department of the public service, but more in those high positions. What do you think of that?"

Amazingly, Chiniquy turned down the job offer. "The honor you want to confer upon me is much above my merit; but my conscience tells me that I cannot give up the preaching of the Gospel to my poor French Canadian countrymen, who are still in the errors of Popery," Chiniquy replied. "For I am about the only one who, by the Providence of God, has any real influence over them. I am, surely, the only one the bishops and priests seem to fear in that work. The many attempts they have made to take away my life are a proof of it." Chiniquy thus remained true to his mission. You can talk all you want about Brébeuf and other heroic Jesuit martyrs among the Iroquois – here was a man willing to give up a diplomatic posting in Paris to remain in a one-horse town in northern Illinois, preaching to French-Canadian farmers, and risking day and night a sneak attack by some murderous Irish Catholic, inflamed jointly by the Bishop of Chicago and the nearest grog shop.

Chiniquy succeeded in creating a profound rift in the town of St. Anne, a bitter hostility between those who followed Chiniquy out of the Catholic Church and those who stayed. Horror stories about Chiniquy circulated among Catholics. It was said that whenever the bread truck came around, *Le Vieux Charles* would consecrate all the bread in it. It was said, after his demise, that on his deathbed he begged for a priest, but his wife refused to listen.

On my visit to St. Anne, however, I discovered that relations between St. Anne's Church and the First Presbyterian Church in the town of St. Anne had grown very cordial indeed. In the 1960s the Catholic priest, Father Naughton, and the pastor of the First Presbyterian Church, the Reverend Reinhold Heinrich, became good friends and golfing buddies. Reverend Heinrich assisted at a Catholic wedding involving a Presbyterian girl from an old pro-Chiniquy French family and a Catholic boy from an old anti-Chiniquy French family. Parishioners from St. Anne's even brought their hammers and saws and helped Presbyterian workmen complete renovations on the Presbyterian Church. These good relations have since continued. Recently, the Presbyterians held a pork roast dinner as a fundraiser, and the pastor of St. Anne's, Father Fanale, let them use his own parish hall, free of charge, for the event. In his grave, *Le Vieux Charles* rotated another 360 degrees.

"Any feelings of hostility still around are from people outside the community," Dean Tolly, a church elder at the First Presbyterian Church, told me. "Like yourself, there are people who come from all over the country who are curiosity seekers. There was a gentleman from California who called me several months ago. He had read Chiniquy's book and he was contacting me to know a little about our church and hoping we were keeping with the spirit of what Father Chiniquy wrote." Tolly shrugged. "I haven't read Father Chiniquy's books." The gentleman from California will certainly not be the last person to call, or drop by, the First Presbyterian Church of St. Anne in homage to Chiniquy. His memoir has now been published in comic book format and advertised on the Internet by Jack T. Chick, the indefatigable crusader against all forms of heresy and godlessness, but chiefly Roman Catholicism. He's produced a kind of Classics Illustrated version of *Fifty Years in the Church of Rome*. At one point in the memoir, for example, Chiniquy writes that twelve Jesuit priests attended his trial against Peter Spink, hoping to see him thrown in the slammer. To illustrate the episode, Chick drew a row of twelve scowling men dressed in black, staring directly at the reader. The reader could practically see these Jesuits contemplating the assassination of Abraham Lincoln. This sort of lunacy will not die. Centuries hence nobody will recall the name of Freud or Marx, but the name Charles Chiniquy may well be preserved by pockets of true believers in North Dakota or Togo or Uzbekistan.

❧

I met Leland Ponton, retired factory worker, musician, law-enforcement officer – among other former occupations – in the kitchen of his bungalow, which was full of Holstein cows, in the form of refrigerator magnets, lighting switch covers, wall decorations, even a clock. Holstein cows are a common motif in these parts. It was Ponton's great-grandmother, one Euphemie Reno, who, with some other members of the parish, wrote a letter to the Bishop of Chicago asking for the removal of Chiniquy. This was after Chiniquy had been caught in bed with his housekeeper, according to Ponton. "The old woman was telling the truth," Ponton said. "She was not lying. And they didn't want to hear that." *They* meant Chiniquy's supporters. "They knew we were related to the Renos," Ponton said. "That meant automatically we got a cold shoulder." Ponton was reluctant to elaborate. "That's a lot of water under the bridge," he said. "You don't like to kick an old dog too hard."

The story he preferred to tell was what happened to Euphemie's son, Calix. One autumn night in 1859, the nine-year-old boy spotted the light of a lantern hanging from a cottonwood tree not far from where Ponton's bungalow now stands. He moved closer and saw a man and a woman digging a hole. When they stopped digging, they hauled a large object he couldn't recognize from their buckboard, threw it in the hole, covered it with earth, put out the lantern, and then rode off. Calix never told anyone what he saw until sixty-six years later, in 1925, when he reckoned that anybody who might have been involved in this incident was dead, and then he told his daughter, Ponton's mother. He was that frightened. His supposition was that the man and woman had murdered a cattle drover for the money in his pocket. There used to be a trail past the Reno farm that the cattlemen used to drive their herds to Chicago, and a tavern catering to the drovers at the top of the hill, visible from Ponton's house. The tavern was run by shady characters. One of them might have been the woman involved in the murder and burial.

In the years since then, the light of a lantern had been seen from time to time floating along the top of the hill where the tavern once stood. Ponton reckoned he himself had seen that lantern about twenty-five times. "It was a bluish-auburn light," he said. "It was like – well, it was like somebody carrying a lantern." He also saw the ghost of the murdered drover when he was seven years old. "My mother and I and my sister were working in the garden,"

Ponton told me. The garden was on the same property as the bungalow. "It was in the spring of the year. I looked up and saw this man, this big, tall, lanky guy, wearing a long black rider coat – you know what a rider coat is, the cowboys used to wear them. They would come down almost to your shins. Anyway, I looked up and saw this guy. And my mother, who was right there, she grabbed me and said, 'Let's get out of here.' I turned around and looked behind me, and he had disappeared. The one thing I remember is that you couldn't make his face out. Or his hands."

Ponton saw the man in the rider coat a second time, in 1988, but he doesn't expect to see him again. He told the story of the murdered man to a reporter for the *Kankakee Journal* in 1988. "Here's my theory," Ponton said. "Let's say you were in an area you had never been to before, you were just passing through, and you were murdered there. What would be your dying request, knowing you could never go home? It would be for someone to know at least where you were buried. Wouldn't you feel that way? My thought was this – if it had been me, I would want somebody to know where the hell I was buried. The man who was killed needed to be publicized of his death. He needed recognition to know where he was at. The little brief story about it in the newspaper made his dying wish come true. That's all he wanted."

There were certain complications following the publication of the article. "That opened a big can of worms for me," Ponton said. I asked him what he meant. "Have you ever given a dollar to a drunk?" Ponton said. "The next thing you know, you got seven or eight of them lined up with their hands out. That's about the same kind of deal. Good Samaritans, they hear about you." I still didn't know what he meant. "If this was true that these guys were there, then there surely must be others," Ponton said. "There had to be others." He wouldn't say anything more, but at that point I thought I got the drift of what he was saying. There was more blood crying out from the soil, there were other restless spirits who wanted to send a message to the living.

Ponton had even written a song about what his grandfather saw. A superb musician, Ponton had been taught to play guitar by his father, and for the last thirty years, with a band called the Country Combination Committee, he had entertained people in the area with his pride and joy, an electric guitar he named Thelma Lue. He showed me the guitar with the worn fretboard. "Every one of these holes is for somebody," he said. He meant that, over the thirty years, he and Thelma Lue and the band had played innumerable musical benefits for people needing help. They had raised money for medical bills and emergency assistance and all kinds of sore needs that people had. It was something he was understandably proud of. He played the song about what his grandfather saw. It had a nice B minor chord running through it. He had written lyrics to the song, he told me, but he wasn't sure where they were. I asked him what the title was. He thought for a moment and then said, "Pale Rider."

Afterwards he showed me the depression in the ground where he believed the cattle drover was buried. It was where his gravel driveway circled around a willow tree. It wasn't a highly visible depression – you had to stand back ten feet or so to perceive the slight dip in the surface of the grass. I asked him the obvious question. Had he ever thought of digging on that spot and seeing if the bones of the man were really there? But Ponton, like the witchers in Texas, had no appetite for testing suppositions about where bodies were. "I thought about it," he said. "But I don't like stirring the shit. Leave it alone."

⚜

The very night of La Salle's speech to the Illinois, a band of Miami Indians from west of the Mississippi arrived in the village. They could see in a flash that these Frenchmen, if successful, would supplant them as middlemen in the fur trade between the sources of fur in the northwest and the traders east of the Mississippi. While La

Salle and his men slept, they told the Illinois they were fools to welcome the French. The leader of these intruders, the tall, outspoken one, was a friend to their enemies the Iroquois, as everybody knew. If he did succeed in establishing himself in the lower reaches of the Mississippi, he would arm the people there, and the Illinois would be crushed between the Iroquois and these Indians from the south. Having delivered this message, the Miami party slipped out of the village before dawn.

La Salle got wind of this visit from an informant among the Illinois and was prepared, the following evening, when the Illinois invited them to a feast and their spokesman proceeded to tell them that a trip down the Mississippi was quite out of the question. He spoke of river monsters, and ferocious, warring nations along the riverbanks, and treacherous waterfalls that suddenly appeared without warning beneath a man's canoe, and the mysterious terminus of the river where it flowed into a giant hole in the earth into which no man had ever entered and returned. This story was the only way the Illinois figured they could stop the French. The alternative was to try to kill them all, but that was no easy matter; these Frenchmen were not careless and stupid, and they had weapons about them. In reply, La Salle said coolly that he and his men could handle whatever perils they might encounter on the Mississippi. Then he took the bull by the horns. "We were not asleep, my brother," La Salle told the headman, "when these Miami came to tell you, under cover of night, that we were spies of the Iroquois.... If they told the truth, why did they skulk away in the dark?" La Salle, the old student of rhetoric, no doubt paused for a moment to let that sink in. "If we meant to make war on you, we should need no help from the Iroquois, who have so often felt the force of our arms." The headman of the Illinois grunted in response. As usual, La Salle had given the Indians something to think about.

Unfortunately for La Salle, six of his men — including Monsieur Duplessis, who had already tried to kill La Salle — took the Illinois story about the perils of the Mississippi to heart. That night, they deserted. They didn't necessarily believe the Illinois, but they chose not to disbelieve them, and to take their tall tales as a good excuse to remove from the neighborhood. They had had enough. It wasn't just the uncertainty about ever getting a good meal again, or a warm and dry place to sleep, or the nightmares about being tortured to death by these unpredictable *sauvages*, or the bone-deep weariness of paddling canoes and trudging through the snow, or the constant scolding they got from this man who never joked with them or gave them a friendly arm around the shoulder, who didn't seem to realize they weren't used to this misery, that they never in their lives had to put up with these constant demands to do this, do that. (Of course, La Salle pushed himself harder than he pushed anybody else. But he was going to reap whatever glory and profits came from this endless wilderness trek, not them.) It wasn't just these things. It was also that they couldn't even lighten their woes with brandy or express their feelings with manly obscenities or look twice at an Indian woman. Fur traders, they had heard in France, could fornicate to their heart's delight in these Indian villages – and wouldn't that help make up for sore muscles and filthy rations? But not with La Salle about. Who did he think he was? More to the point, where were the men at arms to enforce his dictates? The man had only his force of character to rely on. "I will not tolerate blasphemy, drunkenness, impudence, or any sexual license [*libertinage*] that is incompatible with the kind of order needed for success," he wrote to a friend about his unhappy crew. "Also, I am a Christian and do not want to bear the burden of their crimes."

What the six deserters should have realized was that they were putting their comrades who stayed behind in grave danger. If the Illinois realized that men were running away from La Salle, they would rethink their hospitality. Cautioning his remaining followers to show no anxiety (the official story for the benefit of the Illinois, in case they inquired about the missing men, was that they had been sent on an errand), La Salle moved a few miles downriver from the Illinois village and set about building another fort, located on a height of land above the river, set between two deep ravines. La Salle called it Crevecoeur – Fort Heartbreak.

Throughout construction of this building, the Illinois remained peaceable. They were never a bloodthirsty or particularly formidable military force at the best of times – or at the worst. They seemed to bear out the Indian notion that what the French call *jouissance* is bad for a man. "They are very passionate towards women, and even more so towards boys," Tonty wrote of the Illinois. "They become almost effeminate from soft living and indulgence in pleasure. Either from the influence of the climate or in consequence of their perverse imaginations, one finds many hermaphrodites among them." Whatever the reasons for their accommodating attitude, it must have afforded La Salle bitter reflection. Never in his career had he been betrayed by a *sauvage* – only by his own countrymen.

Sensing that the Illinois had made up their minds to leave the French alone, La Salle was emboldened to split up his men. He sent Father Hennepin and two men down the Illinois River. Once they reached the Mississippi they were to turn to their right and proceed north to the headwaters of that river. There they would establish a mission to demonstrate to the Indians, the Jesuits, and other French fur traders in that region that La Salle was back in business – a business whose reach would henceforth extend from the Gulf of Mexico to the far north of Canada.

On February 28, 1680, Hennepin and his companions duly set off on this daunting mission. A month later they were captured by hostile Sioux in what is now the state of Minnesota and kept prisoner for months before being rescued from possible torture and death by a party of Frenchmen led by Daniel Greysolon du Lhut. Hennepin eventually returned to Europe, where his account of his adventures, *Description de la Louisiane*, became a bestseller. Like many another neophyte writer who scores big with a memoir, Hennepin didn't know when to stop. Subsequent editions of his writing became increasingly fanciful and preposterous, so that this basically decent man ended up with a terrible reputation as a liar.

La Salle, meanwhile, decided he needed to go back to Fort Frontenac and Montreal, to soothe his creditors if possible, to find out what had happened to the *Griffon*, and to return with more trade goods and equipment if the news about the *Griffon* was indeed bad. The day after Hennepin left, he departed with five men: Nika and four Frenchmen. Tonty was left literally to hold the fort with about fifteen men. It was a terrible time of year, very early spring, to embark on such a journey. Food was hard to come by – March was the month that many aboriginal groups starved to death – and conditions on the ground were difficult for travelers. There was still enough ice on the river to make canoeing all but impossible, but not enough to walk on. The snow, melting and then freezing again, was too soft and heavy for snowshoes. When the snow didn't threaten to immobilize the men, the half-frozen, half-liquid mud did. It took them three and a half weeks to reach their fort at the mouth of the St. Joseph River.

When they arrived, they found two *coureurs de bois*, who had been dispatched the previous autumn to rendezvous with the *Griffon*. Of that ship, they told La Salle, they had seen not a trace. It now became clear to La Salle that it was lost with all its cargo. As always, the sole recourse was to make the best of things, which in this case meant continuing to Fort Frontenac and Montreal to let everyone know that his project was still on. Before continuing, however, he sent two men back to Tonty with a recommendation that he begin fortifying the top of a sandstone cliff a few miles east of the Grand Village of the Illinois. History would know the place as Starved Rock. It was a commanding site that would be much easier to defend than Crevecoeur.

Because the waters of Lake Michigan were still icy, La Salle decided not to return the way he had come. Instead of retracing his route up Lake Michigan to Michilimackinac and then down Lake Huron to the straits of Detroit, he would cross southern Michigan by land, with his three remaining men and the two *coureurs de bois*. This trip was another ordeal. The woods, La Salle wrote, were "so interlaced with thorns and brambles that in two days and a half our clothes were all torn, and our faces so covered with blood that we hardly knew each other." After a few days of this, they emerged into more open, but no less daunting, country. It was a no man's land fought over by various Indian nations. Men not looking for a fight were well advised to give it a wide berth. But La Salle had no choice if he wanted to reach the straits of Detroit in reasonable time, so he and his men pressed onwards. One morning they lit a fire to thaw their wet clothes, which had frozen overnight, and sure enough a band of Miscoutin Indians showed up. They seemed ready to attack, but then told the French they thought they were Iroquois, and since this was happily not the case they would go on their way. We will never know exactly why these Miscoutins decided not to press their advantage. We only know that even the most "warlike" of men require strong motivation for blood-letting, nine times out of ten, and this just wasn't one of those occasions.

In early April, the exhausted party – some of whom, racked with fever and inflammation of the chest, were spitting blood – reached Detroit. On the twenty-first of that month, they reached the fort La Salle had built on the Niagara River. Leaving his men to rest there, La Salle took three of the men who had been staying at the fort in Niagara and continued up Lake Ontario. Finally, on May 6, La Salle, more dead than alive, arrived at Fort Frontenac, where his creditors, displaying their usual largeness of spirit, were fighting over his pelts. La Salle subsequently made an appearance in Montreal and succeeded in obtaining more supplies on credit – he may not have been the most popular man in New France, but it was clear to creditors that nobody else was going to recoup their investments. Like it or not, everything still depended on La Salle.

La Salle was at Fort Frontenac, preparing to return to Illinois, when two men from Tonty arrived, on July 22, with devastating news. While Tonty, with three men, had been scouting Starved Rock in accordance with La Salle's instructions, the rest of his crew had burnt Fort Crevecoeur, destroyed virtually everything in the fort they couldn't carry with them, and fled. One of them had written a message on a piece of wood: *Nous sommes tous sauvages*.

No more resonant statement has ever been recorded in the history of this continent. It was an utterance of the late seventeenth century that seems more of a piece with the twentieth, when civilized nations proved they could indeed nurture and display savagery unparalleled in human experience. It seemed to have come from the mouth of the dying Kurtz, in Conrad's *Heart of Darkness*. Of course, as Father Bruyère pointed out, the French word "*sauvage*" did not necessarily mean "savage" in this sense of wild or bestial or bloodthirsty or hopelessly primitive. It just meant, as he said, people who "lived in the forests and had a natural way of living." These French deserters could relate to that. They noticed that nobody told the Indians what to do. Nobody laid down the law, like La Salle. Indians were free. Why couldn't they be free?

That was one meaning of the statement. Those of us in the twenty-first century can hardly begin to divine all the meanings of the sentence. It evokes, for one thing, our own profound unease about civilization. One of the reasons we now find North American Indians such sympathetic figures – more attractive, more noble, more rich in integrity and simplicity of heart than we – is because we sense the terrible price we have paid for the accomplishments of civilization, and in particular for the dynamo of capitalism and technology that was already gathering steam in La Salle's day. Not just our freedom, but our need for quiet and repose has been sacrificed to that Molech.

Before capitalism and industrialism was the invention of the phonetic alphabet, which is the defining moment for civilization as we understand it in the West. Even Socrates sensed that the phonetic alphabet and literacy were a tyranny. Written words, he complained in Plato's *Phaedrus*, "seem to talk to you as though they were intelligent, but if you ask them anything about what they say, from a desire to be instructed, they go on telling you just the same thing forever." This hectoring medium was a huge leap in the direction of the abstract, which the *sauvages* were spared. This medium was also a weapon. It did not escape the notice of these deserters that La Salle was a letter writer. Who knew what was in those letters?

There was another of our civilization's burdens that these deserters may have wanted to cast off. "The price we pay for the advancement of our civilization is a loss of happiness through the heightening of the sense of guilt," Freud wrote. Where did he think this guilt comes from? The need to curb innate human aggression and to suppress certain manifestations of sexuality. The *sauvages* felt shame keenly, but not guilt, possibly because their instinctual life was less repressed. So that was something else the deserters were, in effect, saying: we are all creatures of appetite and instinct. We do not need a god of morality, passed on to us by the Jews and then institutionalized in the Christian Church. The Indians get along perfectly well without one.

Nous sommes tous sauvages. Those words could have been incised, of course, in a spirit of horror, rather than of defiance or sardonic amusement. The man who made that statement might have discovered some instinct or appetite within himself that he could not live with. In deserting, he may have been running away from himself, as much as running away from La Salle, and wishing that he had never ventured into this wilderness where spirits of cruelty exercised dominion.

After the desertion, Tonty and his remaining handful of men took refuge in the Grand Village of the Illinois, to which the inhabitants were now returning. It was an extremely uncomfortable refuge, since their ammunition was running low and the Illinois villagers remained suspicious and unfriendly. There they would wait, however, until La Salle returned.

In mid-August, La Salle left for Illinois with a new band of some twenty-five men, taking the Humber River route to the upper Great Lakes rather than portage at Niagara. Reports that the Iroquois were preparing for an invasion of the west had reached La Salle, and he may have felt it more politic – and safe – to avoid contact with his old trading partners. Both parties at this point had too much to explain to each other. Best to leave that reckoning when La Salle had a fort and a committed band of Indian allies behind him. After reaching Michilimackinac, La Salle followed his previous route down Lake Michigan to the St. Joseph River. Leaving the rest of his men behind him, he set out, in early November, for the Grand Village of the Illinois with seven followers.

As they proceeded down the Kankakee and then the Illinois River, they were alternately pleased at the abundance of game – hunger was always a possibility in the wilderness – and anxious about the absence of Illinois hunting parties. The Indians should have been in these parts hunting buffalo and deer for the coming winter. They soon found out why they were absent. As they approached the Grand Village of the Illinois, they saw one of the most macabre scenes ever recorded in American history – a scene surpassed in horror only by another one they would shortly encounter. The entire settlement with its cornfields had been burned to the ground, and in its place stood charred lodgepoles decorated with human skulls. La Salle and his men had to chase away wolves and scavenging birds from the site – the Iroquois had dug up the graves of the Illinois and scattered the remains of old human carcasses. La Salle, fearing the worst, examined every skull – but they all had remnants of Indian hair sticking to them.

He and his men spent a dismal night in a camp not far from the scene of the holocaust, listening to the howling of wolves. The next morning, he told three of his men to conceal themselves as best they could and keep watch. He and the four remaining men pressed on in their canoes. All along the river they saw the abandoned encampments of the Illinois on one side and the Iroquois on the other – it was clear that a large body of Illinois had fled downriver, closely pursued by its enemies. They reached the remains of Fort Crevecoeur and discovered the reverberant message left by one of the deserters. Still they kept on, finding more opposing camps until they finally reached, not far from where the Illinois flows into the

Mississippi, a meadow where the Iroquois had fallen on seven hundred women and children evidently abandoned by the men in their flight. Half of them had been tortured to death at stakes or roasted over slow fires. La Salle and his men stayed long enough to absorb the sight of the charred bodies still bound to the stakes and to discover copper kettles full of half-eaten arms and legs.

La Salle went as far as the mouth of the Illinois River, where it flowed into the Mississippi, as if to fix in his mind that notable juncture, and then turned back. Still there was no sign of Tonty and his men. At the burnt-out town of the Illinois, he found the men he had stationed there in his absence. That night a curious thing happened. A huge comet streaked across the sky – the "Great Comet of 1680," as it later became known. Parkman noted that it sent a thrill of foreboding throughout Europe and New England, frightening even sophisticated observers such as Increase Mather, the Massachusetts divine, with its message of dire events to come. "It is characteristic of La Salle," Parkman wrote, "that, beset as he was with perils, and surrounded with ghastly images of death, he coolly notes down the phenomenon, not as a portentous messenger of war and woe, but rather as an object of scientific curiosity." Parkman always did want to emphasize the modern-man aspect of La Salle. He wanted a La Salle unburdened by a lot of seventeenth-century religiosity, whether Jesuit or Puritan. Not frightened of a prodigious comet, was our hero. But in measuring the height of the comet from the horizon with his astrolabe, and making precise notes about its characteristics and time of appearance, La Salle was behaving exactly as his Jesuit instructors, who were dead keen on astronomy and science, had trained him. In many ways, La Salle never ceased being a child of the Jesuits.

La Salle and his reunited party continued to make their way back to the fort at the mouth of the St. Joseph River. That was another freezing, bone-wearying journey. The cold was so severe, La Salle later wrote, "I never knew a harder winter, even in Canada. We were obliged to cross forty leagues of open country, where we could hardly find wood to warm ourselves at evening, and could get no bark whatever to make a hut, so that we had to spend the night exposed to the furious winds which blow over these plains." If La Salle, no man to complain about the hardships of nature, said it was cold, it was cold. It took him and his men the better part of two months finally to stagger into the fort. La Salle, as usual, did not take long to recover. The terrible blow that had befallen the Illinois nation was a blow to his own ambitions, but he saw a way out of this. He would build his fort at Starved Rock and use it as a rallying point for the remnants of the Illinois and other Indian nations in that region. Armed by, and allied to, the French, they would stand fast against the Iroquois, settle down as good Christian subjects of the king – taught by the Franciscans, not the Jesuits – and grow prosperous.

To start with, he recruited a band of about thirty Indians who had been driven from their homes in New England by the Puritans and had attached themselves to the French. In the spring of 1681, he made another expedition down the Kankakee River to seek out remnants of the Illinois. He met one band, gave them presents, and urged them to make peace with their neighbors, the Miami Indians, who had recently allied themselves with the Iroquois. He himself, he assured the Illinois, would come to live with them and help them resist any further invasions of their territory. His listeners seemed to take heart and promised to convey his message to their compatriots. Afterwards, La Salle journeyed to a village of the Miami Indians, erstwhile allies of the Iroquois. Since their victory, the Iroquois had carried themselves very high, and the Miami were already experiencing what Mafiosi call a lack of respect. Arriving at the Miami village, La Salle ran into three Iroquois warriors who had been deriding the French and generally making themselves obnoxious. Never better than in these situations, La Salle dared the three men to repeat to his face what they had said about the French. To the delight of the Miami, they skulked away and disappeared that night from the village. Shortly afterwards, at a grand council of the Miami, La Salle stood up and delivered a brilliant oration. "You ought," he told them, "to live at peace with your neighbors, and above all with the Illinois. You have had causes of quarrel with them; but their defeat has avenged you. Though they are still strong, they wish to make peace with you. Be content with the glory of having obliged them to ask for it. You have an interest in preserving them; since, if the Iroquois destroy them, they will next destroy you."

The speech had the desired effect; the Miami pledged peace to their neighbors, the Illinois, and allegiance to the Great King of France. That task accomplished, La Salle had one more chore to perform, infinitely more difficult – making his own tribe under-stand him. He had to go back to Canada one more time, listen to the complaints of his creditors, squeeze a few more *livres* from them, stock up again on trade goods and equipment. This would be his last attempt to go down the Mississippi, and he had to do it right. At the beginning of the summer, then, he paddled back to Michilimackinac en route to Fort Frontenac and Montreal – and there, at Michilimackinac, to his great joy he found Tonty alive and well.

His old lieutenant had a story to tell. In the Grand Village of the Illinois he had spent the previous summer, waiting for La Salle's return. That summer passed without incident. Then, on a warm day in early September, a friendly Shawnee came paddling down the river in a desperate hurry, with news that an army of five hundred Iroquois was headed their way. Panic struck the Illinois – as it hap-pened, most of their warriors were away on a hunt, and fewer than five hundred were left to face the Iroquois. Women and children were evacuated downriver, and the warriors braced themselves for a fight. "All night long fires blazed along the shore," Parkman writes. "The excited warriors greased their bodies, painted their faces, befeathered their heads, sang their war-songs, danced, stamped, yelled, and brandished their hatchets, to work up their courage to face the crisis. The morning came, and with it the Iroquois."

Suspicion fell on Tonty and his men that they had brought this force upon the Illinois, and some enraged warriors surrounded him in a highly threatening manner. Tonty declared he would fight by their side, which appeased them a little. At any rate, they didn't have time to think over the matter. They decided to take a run at the Iroquois rather than wait for their attack, which would be hard on their nerves. Tonty watched them cross the river in their canoes, run through the woods, and join battle in an open plain. Unfortunately for the Illinois, the Iroquois were not only more redoubtable warriors, they were better armed. "Tonty saw that it would go hard with his allies," Parkman writes. "It was of the last moment to stop the fight, if possible."

He did one of the bravest things I've ever read about. He walked alone through the battlefield to the Iroquois, holding up a wampum belt as a sign of truce. "With his swarthy complexion and his half-savage dress, they thought he was an Indian, and thronged about him, glaring murder," Parkman writes. "A young warrior stabbed at his heart with a knife, but the point glanced aside against a rib, inflicting only a deep gash. A chief called out that as Tonty's ears were not pierced he must be a Frenchman. On this, some of them tried to stop the bleeding, and led him to the rear, where an angry parley ensued, while the yells and firing still resounded in the front." Tonty tried to outface the Iroquois by declaring that the Illinois were under the protection of the Great King and the Iroquois must cease their attack. One of the chiefs of the Seneca demanded this insolent Frenchman be tortured to death, while an Onondaga chief, who had been a friend of La Salle's, insisted that no harm come to him. Tonty brazenly declared, further, that the Iroquois would be smart to listen to him, because the Illinois had twelve hundred warriors at their disposal, and sixty well-armed Frenchmen in the village. "This invention, though not fully believed, had no little effect," Parkman writes. "The friendly Onondaga carried his point; and the Iroquois, having failed to surprise their enemies, as they had hoped, now saw an opportunity to delude them by a truce."

Several days followed in which Tonty tried to keep the Iroquois and the Illinois apart, but it was clear that the Iroquois were not going to go home without accomplishing what they had set out to do, which was to eat Illinois flesh. They were still at peace with France, and had no wish to provoke Onontio (the name by which the Iroquois and their neighbors personified the French regime); but they could not allow the Illinois to control the fur trade in this region. That would leave them in an economic backwater. That would leave them naked to their enemies. So they quietly surrounded the village after the Illinois had accepted their truce, and the Illinois, knowing very well the next step in this maneuver, managed to slip away and rejoin their women and children downstream. The Iroquois then proceeded to desecrate every grave and every Illinois corpse they could find, and to burn the village. And by the way, they remarked to Tonty, we don't see those sixty Frenchmen you were talking about. Tonty could tell they were preparing another attack against the Illinois, and when the Iroquois informed him and his friends they had better leave, he didn't need a second warning. He and his men lit out. All that bravery, for nothing.

The Iroquois followed the Illinois as they moved down the river. By now, Illinois courage had vanished, sapped by hunger and the nightly spectacle of Iroquois campfires across the river. Various bands made off in different directions fleeing for their lives. One band, a tribe within the Illinois nation called the Tamaroas, got themselves caught near the mouth of the Illinois River by their pursuers. It was their women and children who were captured and tortured to death. Tonty and his companions, by that time, were headed in the opposite direction, north to Lake Michigan. When they reached it, they continued to walk northward along its western shore. It was one of those incredible wilderness trips, undertaken without food or shelter or warm clothing, which remind us of how elastic the limits of human endurance are. In fact, Tonty and his men very nearly starved to death. They avoided that fate only because some friendly

Indians discovered them by the shore of Green Bay, perishing from hunger, and took them in.

After rejoining La Salle in Michilimackinac, Tonty accompanied him back to Montreal. More business negotiations followed. By the time La Salle left, he had renewed supplies, and more French workmen and *voyageurs* in his employ. At this point, it probably would have taken him two lifetimes to pay off all his debts. There was nothing for it, however. This was his third start for the Mississippi, and one way or another, it would be his last. La Salle once again took the Humber River portage, passed through the Straits of Mackinac, paddled down Lake Michigan, and arrived at the St. Joseph River in early November. Accompanying him were twenty-three Frenchmen and eighteen Indians from New England, ten of whom had brought their wives.

⚜

From Kankakee I drove westward until I came to Starved Rock, which is now a state park. The plaque near the visitors' center, while still laudatory, presented a French explorer more palatable to contemporary sensibilities.

> La Salle was a man of vision and courage. He established contact with Native Americans and brought European culture to this area, while acting as a peacemaker in his actions with local Indian peoples. His explorations were responsible for expansion of the Western Frontier into this area of Illinois.

In that visitors' center was a scale model of the fort La Salle's men built on top of the cliffs here on their return from the voyage down the Mississippi, in the winter of 1682. It showed Iroquois warriors besieging the fort, now called Fort Saint Louis des Illinois, during their second invasion of Illinois, in January of 1684. In command of the fort at the time was Tonty. Short of food and ammunition, he

and his twenty-two soldiers, and an equal number of Shawnee
refugees from the Iroquois, faced another formidable army of five
hundred Iroquois. Fortunately, the fort was impregnable. When the
Iroquois exhausted their own rations, they were forced to with-
draw. The Europeans' victory meant that the French claim to an
empire extending from Canada down the Mississippi Valley hence-
forward had to be taken seriously.

That this claim proved ultimately untenable Parkman believes
was due to the Iroquois and their wars against the French. These
wars, it is true, did come to an end with the Great Peace of 1701.
There were some Mohawk raids on Canada during King George's
War (known in Europe as the War of the Austrian Succession, waged
from 1744 to 1748), and, as we have seen, some Iroquois participation
in the siege of Fort Niagara in 1759, but after 1701 the Iroquois basically ceased being a mortal antagonist to New France. Parkman's
point, however, is that by 1701 this no longer mattered. The Iroquois
had already fulfilled their mission in history by crippling the early
growth of New France. If it had not been for the long war with the
Iroquois, the French, Parkman suggests, "would have occupied
the West with traders, settlers, and garrisons, and cut up the virgin
wilderness into fiefs, while as yet the colonies of England were but a
weak and broken line along the shore of the Atlantic."

In this way, the Iroquois prevented the continent from falling
prey to "the principles of Richelieu and of Loyola" – that is, the
principle of royal absolutism and Catholicism. "Liberty may thank
the Iroquois, that, by their insensate fury, the plans of her adversary
were brought to nought, and a peril and a woe averted from her
future," Parkman wrote.

> They ruined the trade which was the life-blood of New
> France; they stopped the current of her arteries, and made all her
> early years a misery and a terror. Not that they changed her des-
> tinies. The contest on this continent between Liberty and
> Absolutism was never doubtful; but the triumph of the one

would have been dearly bought, and the downfall of the other incomplete. Populations formed in the ideas and habits of a feudal monarchy, and controlled by a hierarchy profoundly hostile to freedom of thought, would have remained a hindrance and a stumbling-block in the way of that majestic experiment of which America is the field.

I do not believe, by the way, that the French in America posed a stumbling block to "Liberty" and "freedom of thought." The bit about Richelieu, in my opinion, is a red herring. As for Loyola, a little of his spirit would have done that New England gang of Calvinists, Deists, Transcendentalists, and Pragmatists some real good. But let it pass. The question is whether the Iroquois can take the credit for the ultimate failure of the French. It is a difficult one to answer. The French, at the time of La Salle, had two options open to them. They could have consolidated their hold on their possessions along the banks of the St. Lawrence; emphasized agriculture, fisheries, and other local industries; and tried to lessen their dependence on the fur trade. By not provoking war with the English colonists over her forays into the Ohio Valley and the Mississippi Valley, France might have retained her Canadian possessions.

The other option was the La Salle option, of seizing and holding the Mississippi and Ohio and Missouri waterways and thereby pushing the English and the Spanish to the margins of what is now the United States of America. This might have succeeded, even given the shaky beginnings of New France, had the mother country been willing to invest a great amount of money in military and naval expenditures in North America, in building forts and maintaining strong native alliances through lavish gifts and other forms of bribery. It could have been done. But it cost too much money. It cost too much money for what it was worth, in the ultimate judgment of the court of Versailles. Instead of pursuing either option, then, the French chose an uncertain middle course that doomed their empire to defeat.

For a while, however, the fate of the continent did seem to hang in the balance. This is what made that scale model of Starved Rock in the visitors' center such an interesting object. It showed a small-scale battle with potentially huge consequences. It is also our last glimpse of this great Indian nation, the Iroquois Confederacy, whose members played, it seems, a historical role benefiting everybody except them. Francis Parkman was not the only one who thanked their memory. His contemporary, a Rochester businessman and lawyer named Lewis Henry Morgan, grew up, like Parkman, roaming the woods and fantasizing about Indians. As a young man he formed the Grand Order of the Iroquois with some other young men in 1843. They sat around council fires in the woods, wore Iroquois leggings and moccasins and headdresses and tomahawks, conducted initiation rituals, made speeches in which, according to Morgan's biographer Carl Resek, they said things like "The tall pine in the young forest has not spoken with forked tongue."

Morgan wanted members of the order to visit real Iroquois settlements, attend real Iroquois ceremonies, and thereby learn about their customs and institutions. He wanted the order, in other words, to conduct anthropological fieldwork. In 1851 he summarized his own fieldwork in *The League of the Iroquois*. According to Resek, it "still remains the most comprehensive single volume on the New York Indians." It really was an attempt to take an objective, scientific look at an Indian nation, to break from a long American tradition of viewing Indians either simply as depraved heathens or exotics descended from the Ten Lost Tribes of Israel (an opinion adopted by the Mormons) or the Visigoths or some other colorful strain.

With this book and *Systems of Consanguinity and Affinity*, published in 1871, Morgan described what he understood as the clan system of the Iroquois, a system that fostered, in effect, group marriage (subject to rigid incest taboos). While scandalous to Morgan's Victorian friends, this system, in Morgan's view, made for a remarkable degree of equality within the clan. "It would be difficult to describe," Morgan wrote, "any political society in which there was less oppression and discontent, more of individual independence and boundless freedom." What's more, Morgan thought a revival of the Iroquois clan system "in a higher form" would lead to "the next higher plane of society," with the full fruition of "democracy in government, brotherhood in society, equality in rights and privileges, and universal education."

Marx and Engels took notice. In 1884, three years after Morgan died, Engels published *The Origin of the Family, Private Property and the State*, his classic commentary on Morgan. Like Morgan, Engels felt a little wistful when contemplating the lost harmony of life among the Old Iroquois. "The glimpses into the quality of interpersonal relations that we are afforded from accounts of North American Indians and peoples in the rest of the world before they had experienced the alienation from the produce of their labor, and the divisiveness of being placed in fundamental competition with their fellow men . . . do indeed make us somewhat envious," he wrote. "There did seem to be an underlying sense of self-respect and an ability to draw great satisfaction from work and personal relations. Perhaps most bitter to industrial man is the divisiveness which permeates relationships with those most dear, and the enmity between husbands and wives, parents and children."

The bourgeois family – how Engels hated it. "The dehumanization of conjugal relationships, caught as men and women are in a network of fear and confusion; the brutalization and petty dominance of the man; the anger and bitterness of the woman; the nature of marriage, all too often a constant battle – all this is only too well known," he observed. Was he supposed to be morally indignant because the Iroquois practiced group marriage instead of the noble ideal of monogamy? Don't make him laugh. "If strict monogamy is the height of all virtue, then the palm must go to the tapeworm, which has a complete set of male and female sexual organs in each of its 50 to 200 proglottides or sections, and spends its whole life copulating with itself."

Engels joined a long tradition of sophisticated European intellectuals rhapsodizing over primitives. Montaigne started the tradition with his essay "Of Cannibals." The cannibals, Montaigne wrote, had "no name for governor or political superior, no practice of subordination or of riches or of poverty, no contracts, no inheritances, no divided estates. . . . Among them you hear no words for treachery, lying, cheating, avarice, envy, backbiting or pardon." Engels, three hundred years later, was still going at it:

> No soldiers, no gendarmes or police, no nobles, kings, regents, prefects, or judges, no prisons, or lawsuits – and everything takes its orderly course. All quarrels and disputes are settled by the whole of the community affected. . . . There cannot be any poor or needy – the communal household and the gentes [clan] know their responsibilities toward the old, the sick, and those disabled in war. All are equal and free – the women included. . . . And what men and women such a society breeds is proved by the admiration inspired in all white people who have come into contact with unspoiled Indians, by the personal dignity, uprightness, strength of character, and courage of these barbarians.

These "barbarians" suffered no "alienation from the produce of their labor." They made what they needed or wanted, and that was that. "They knew what became of their product; they consumed it; it did not leave their hands."

This Eden, like all Edens, had to be left behind, eventually. "The power of this primitive community had to be broken, and it was broken," Engels wrote.

> But it was broken by influences which from the very start appear as a degradation, a fall from the simple moral greatness of the old . . . society. The lowest interests – base greed, brutal appetites, sordid avarice, selfish robbery of the common wealth – inaugurate the new, civilized, class society. It is by the vilest

means – theft, violence, fraud, treason – that the old classless . . . society is undermined and overthrown. And the new society itself during all the 2,500 years of its existence has never been anything else but the development of the small minority at the expense of the great exploited and oppressed majority; today it is so more than ever before.

Here, in a nutshell, was the great paradox of Marxism. The lowest interests, the vilest means, were truly low and vile and base and brutal and sordid and selfish – but according to the iron laws of history, they were actually a Good Thing. They destroyed a beautiful society and paved the way for a truly ugly society, but that was all right because they pushed humanity farther along the road to an even more beautiful society. Eden had to be corrupted so that a better Eden, somewhere far ahead in the future, could arise. A poor Iroquois who protested against base greed, sordid avarice, and so on – who wanted nothing to do with Count Frontenac, full of peace and tenderness though he was, or the fur trade in general – was not playing his proper historic role. He might have been ten times nobler than Frontenac, or La Salle, but Frontenac and La Salle were on the right side of the iron laws, and he was on the wrong side. It goes without saying that the Jesuit who tried to prevent the fur trader from selling this Iroquois brandy was also a retrograde character.

Marxist revolutionaries have always been elated at bad news and depressed at good news. The worse things get, the clearer the road to revolution. And after the revolution – then what? Good Marxists are not supposed even to speculate what the wonderful socialist millennium will be like. But then that's the odd thing about the future, as readers of sci-fi know. Visions of the future, no matter how technically advanced or paradisal, always seem curiously meager and colorless compared to the richness of the past. In fact, the great revolutions in Western history, prior to Marx, had been driven by people who were not trying to concoct a "world of the future," but rather revive a state of things that had disappeared a long time ago. This is what drove Marx crazy. In *The 18th Brumaire of Louis Bonaparte*, he noted scornfully that the 1848 revolutionaries pretended they were re-enacting the French Revolution of Danton and Robespierre all over again – but then Danton and Robespierre themselves, in their heyday, hearkened back to the ancient Roman Republic, which they thought they were restoring, and before them Oliver Cromwell and his revolutionaries hearkened back to the people of Israel driving out the Philistines, which they also thought they were re-enacting. "The tradition of all the dead generations weighs like a nightmare on the brain of the living," he wrote. Marx's whole life was an attempt to wake up from that nightmare, everything he wrote was an attempt to grab the sleepwalker known as human society and give it a shaking. "At the very time when they seem to be engaged in revolutionizing themselves and things, when they seem to be creating something new," Marx wrote of those heroic and half-blind revolutionaries of old, "in such epochs of revolutionary crisis, they are eager to press the spirits of the past into their service, borrowing the names of the dead, reviving old war-cries, dressing up in traditional costumes, that they may make a braver pageant in the newly-staged scene of universal history."

Leave the dead generations in peace, Marx protested, and build the new world, which has nothing to do with Rome or Jerusalem. But this desire itself was an illusion, protested G.K. Chesterton in his own revolutionary manifesto, *What's Wrong with the World*. "For some strange reason," Chesterton observed, "man can only find life among the dead. Man is a misshapen monster, with his feet set forward and his face turned back. He can make the future luxuriant and gigantic, so long as he is thinking about the past. When he tries to think about the future itself, his mind diminishes to a pin point with imbecility."

Who was right, Marx or Chesterton? Here's a clue: the Puritan Revolution of the seventeenth century, and the French Revolution, made by men and women thinking of the past instead of the future, had huge and enduring results, both good and evil. The Russian

Revolution, made by men and women looking solely toward the future for their inspiration, had no positive results whatsoever. It left us nothing the human race can remember with pride, except perhaps a few films by Eisenstein and Dovzhenko, and Yuri Gagarin's space flight – but who wouldn't gladly have burned up all the film prints of *Potemkin* if it meant we could have had poor, stupid Nicholas II back instead of Lenin and Stalin?

Marxism was never so close to being vital and human as when it looked back in longing toward the Iroquois. "Doesn't it make you want to go out and lift dead Indians tenderly from their graves," wrote William Carlos Williams, "to steal from them – as if it must be clinging even to their corpses – some authenticity."

✤

If he had wanted to, Williams could probably have done his grave robbing at Starved Rock. From the visitors' center a trail led to a wooden stairway up that sandstone bluff, notable for its size and its yellow hue, derived from iron deposits. Here another group of defenders, a band of Illinois Indians, held out against an army of Potawatomi, Kickapoo, and Miami Indians shortly after Pontiac's Revolt in 1763. According to legend, the besiegers were seeking revenge for the assassination of Pontiac by an Illinois brave. I say "according to legend," because one historian, Fred Anderson, in his book *Crucible of War: The Seven Years' War and the Fate of Empire in British North America 1754–1766*, states flatly that "no one – not even his own sons – felt obliged to avenge Pontiac's murder." (In politics, who cares about a loser?) The legend, true or not, tells us that the defenders resisted until they finally starved to death. Hence the name of this landmark.

The stairway ended in a boardwalk that circled the summit of the rock. No trace of the fort remained. Below was the Illinois River, surrounded by bluffs on both banks. The view was splendid.

It did not lend itself to romantic fancies about the old wilderness fort, however. Vaporous clouds arose from a mill on the other side of the river, the light of a radio tower flashed, and storage tanks, silos, and other geometric shapes dotted the horizon. There was also a lock just east of Starved Rock, constructed in 1933 by the U.S. Army Corps of Engineers. Those engineers had transformed La Salle's Illinois River into the Illinois Waterway, a highway of commerce. "More than 45 million tons of coal, gravel, silica, soybeans, grain, fertilizers, petroleum, iron products, and chemicals are locked through here each year," a sign informed me. It was a reminder that I was standing in a great industrial and agricultural heartland supplying the needs of America – until such time as we get all that stuff cheaper from China.

I sat on a bench by the boardwalk and watched a stream of visitors go by. A surprising number of them were speaking Spanish. In fact, below the bench, on the surface of the rock, where I imagined that a man's blood had once dripped from the hole created by a French or Iroquois bullet – you could almost see the thin trickle of red – somebody had carved a message that read, "Te amo Carlos." What would Parkman have thought of a United States of America rapidly becoming Latinized by immigrants from the Spanish-speaking parts of the New World? Not much, you could be sure. I wasn't sure myself. We were here first, I wanted to say to Hispanic America, we who were your prototypes. "French Canadians are as Latin American as Mexicans," Clark Blaise insisted in *I Had a Father*. He could make sense of his father's life, Blaise wrote, the life of a man transplanted to the United States from a backward, Catholic, economically wobbly neighbor, only by seeing him as one of the first wetbacks. "It has helped me see my father's boxing and boozing and marriages; his harmonica playing, tap dancing, and crooning charm; his women and his police record as discards in his gringo-izing," Blaise wrote. My grandparents, who were the same generation as Blaise's father, were not such flashy, disreputable figures. They were hard-working, church-going citizens. (Just like most Mexicans, who don't usually come to us straight from Tijuana nightclubs.) But they, too, had to be gringo-ized, a process that required a much more rueful sacrifice of historical memory than required of other immigrants.

Not far from the park was a little town called La Salle, where I stopped for a drink at a place called Doc's Pub. A woman in jeans and a strap-style T-shirt – a picture of a motorcycle with a halo on the back, and the inscription Doc's Angels – was dancing on the bar when I entered. She could have been in her twenties or thirties, a nice-looking woman getting a little thick in the waist. I sat down at the bar and ordered a beer, but it was hard to feel relaxed because the boots of this woman, whose name was Mary Lou, were now about a foot away from my bottle of Bud Light. She was gyrating her hips and threatening to unzip her pants in front of another woman sitting next to me, and to tell the truth, I was afraid to look up at her. I didn't want to draw her attention. (I'm a bit shy about these things.) To my relief, she jumped off the bar, and then she and a man two barstools down from me began kissing passionately, like Ingrid Bergman and Cary Grant in *Notorious*. I glanced at the sign above the door. It said: Bikes Babes Beer.

Mary Lou would not stop. She and another young woman, dressed in identical jeans and Doc's Angels T-shirt, grabbed a young man and pulled him up on a little stage by the front door, a stage that had a stripper's pole. They pushed him against the pole and stood on either side of him and rubbed their crotches against him. I couldn't tell whether he was having a good time or not, because I didn't want to be caught staring at them. "You're next," the bartender said to me, with an evil smirk on his face. That'll teach you to come into a biker bar, the smirk said, when you look more like an off-duty viola player in a string quartet than a man with a Harley. It is true that I have what might be called an un-biker-like appearance. I wished that at least I had remembered to pack a T-shirt and baseball cap before I left home, so I could have observed the same dress code as everybody else in America, and not end up wearing a stupid polo shirt in a biker bar.

Mary Lou, who had a big voice, leaned in the direction of a woman to my left, and shouted, FUCK, I KNOW YOU! The woman to my left didn't look any more like a biker mama than I looked like a biker. She was middle-aged with dark, curly hair and a lean, sensitive, intelligent face, who could have been a high school English teacher or the assistant manager of a health food store, except she had tattoos all over her forearms. Not surprisingly, Mary Lou did know her. They started chatting, and I relaxed a bit and ordered another beer. After a while Mary Lou started horsing around again with the young woman in the identical jeans and T-shirt. The two got on top of a table and simulated sexual intercourse, with Mary Lou on top.

More people came into the bar, none of whom looked like a member of a string quartet. Mary Lou greeted one woman with her booming voice. HERE'S MY BITCH! She grabbed her bitch by the rear end and I finished my beer and left.

The next day I continued to follow the route of La Salle down the Illinois River. Just south of Peoria, I turned off the highway to a place called Fort Crevecoeur Park, which included camping grounds, hiking trails, picnicking area, nature sanctuary, museum and gift shop, and historical monument. The monument was a full-scale reconstruction of the original Fort Crevecoeur, built by the U.S. Army Corps of Engineers in 1980, set in a corner of a grassy area where the RVs parked. I had no idea what La Salle would have made of this structure, had he come back from the grave to see it. He might have wondered about the paint job.

Mike Bohanon, a board member of the non-profit organization in charge of the site, was sitting in front of a tent with a man named Ken. Ken was a retired military man who had an authentic backwoods look – his face was bronzed and wrinkled from years spent in the sun, and his hair hung down in ropy strands from underneath his baseball cap to the bottom of his shoulder blades.

They were having a beer to mark the end of the annual Memorial Day "Rendezvous" at the fort – an event that included, according to a flyer, "a black powder shooting competition, tomahawk and knife throwing contests, historic crafts that the visitor may purchase, and a chance to witness camp life as it would have been for the early Indians, French and Buckskinners of the time." The flyer also stated that "food and refreshments are also sold during the Rendezvous, including buffalo burgers, and the famous Fort Crevecoeur Spicy Buffalo Chili. This chili is not for the timid!"

Bohanon told me that the money raised by the Rendezvous was earmarked for improvements to the site. "We're slowly but surely trying to build it up," he said. "One of the biggest projects is getting that campground up and running full force so it will bring income for the park. Right now, it's funded by private donations and the Rendezvous event. I think the next project that's on the drawing board is trying to get something done with that fort. It needs some repairs. And my dad wants to get it closer to what it was when La Salle built it. Like the gate. The original fort, from what I understand, had ladders to get in. And the actual fort wasn't one hundred per cent square, like you see there. It actually had a taper to it." This is not to mention the question of where the original fort actually stood, a matter of perennial controversy. In the late nineteenth century, for example, claims were made for nine different locations. "Peoria wants the site on their side of the river," Bohanon said. "The town of Crevecoeur wants it here, right where it is."

I mentioned a man I had seen earlier fishing in the polluted Illinois River. Bohanon laughed. "Yeah. You can catch fish with five heads and tails that glow in the dark." He took another sip of beer. "I heard some divers working on the lock of the dam say there are catfish down there big enough to swallow a truck." I didn't know if he was serious or pulling my leg, but I recalled the river monsters that the headman of the Illinois told La Salle about. It seemed monsters still lurked in these rivers, even if they never materialized in the light of day. That didn't matter. We always have a place for monsters in our imagination.

❧

This time there would be no more building forts or waiting for news that would never arrive about a ship. La Salle and his men headed straight for the Mississippi River. On February 6, 1682, after passing the ruins of Fort Crevecoeur and the ghastly meadows where the women and children of the Illinois had fallen into the hands of their enemies, La Salle reached the junction of the Illinois and the Mississippi. The Mississippi River was still choked with ice, but after a week of waiting, a thaw enabled them to proceed, and La Salle and his party of forty-three men and ten women guided their canoes into the southbound current. The attempt to seize the heart of America for the King of France and the spread of the gospel of Christ had begun.

Behind him, La Salle left an Illinois still uninhabited by whites. That would very soon change. The next year, La Salle's devoted enemies, the Jesuits, established a mission on the shore of Lake Michigan at a spot they called Chicagua. A fort was built there at the same time, and another great American city was born under the sign of the Cross and the *fleurs-de-lys*. French fur traders followed immediately, violating La Salle's monopoly and following the pattern established elsewhere of intermarrying with the native population and creating small, settled communities of mixed blood. In 1703 the Jesuits founded another mission at a place where the Kaskaskia River flowed into the Mississippi. Alongside the mission grew a small town inhabited by the local Kaskaskia Indians and the French and Metis fur traders. Like Cadillac extolling the beauties of Detroit, the French viewed this area as an earthly paradise, with excellent timber, including stands of oak, walnut, cedar, hickory, chestnut, and pecan trees, as well as apple, pear, plum, peach, and cherry, and enormous grape vines. It also had rich soil and a temperate climate. For once, the French in North America had come by some good farmland.

A little over a century later the town became the first capital of the state of Illinois. That honor didn't last long. One year later, the capital was moved to a city named Vandalia. Kaskaskia was born under a star other than Chicago's, and their fates were diametrically opposed. Rather than grow in the nineteenth century, Kaskaskia faded away. Throughout the eighteenth century, however, it remained the heart of French Illinois. Its first spurt of growth spurred in 1718, when it fell under the control of the Mississippi Company, an outfit founded by a Scottish financier, John Law, who had found favor with the French court. The company received a monopoly of the fur trade and the newly discovered lead and copper mines, in return for assuming the job of governing the territory, posting officials and military personnel, importing mining engineers and African slaves. The company also encouraged the development of agriculture, to help feed the company's home base, Louisiana.

Growth even then was relatively slow, partly because French Illinois remained the target of Indian raids. The chief scourge were the Fox Indians, otherwise known as Outagamies or, as they referred to themselves, the Musquawkies, which, according to Parkman, meant "red earth," the color of the soil near their villages. Whatever their name, they were by far the toughest gang on the block. They continually fought, harassed, and displaced other Indian nations in the prolonged competition for dominance in the fur trade. They gave the French endless grief. In 1720 they were finally cornered by an allied army of French and Illinois at a fork in the Vermillion River in Illinois and virtually wiped out. A few hundred ended up on the western side of the Mississippi. In 1832, under the leadership of Chief Black Hawk, a band crossed the river to reclaim some of its ancient territory in Illinois. The subsequent war is notable in American history mostly for providing Abraham

Lincoln with his only military experience. The Fox were utterly defeated, of course, but that was not the end of their curious history. James Fenimore Cooper's Leatherstocking Tales, published beginning in the 1820s, and continuing for two decades, had begun the process of romanticizing the American Indian. A year after Black Hawk's defeat, the artist Charles Bodmer painted the Fox Indians in all their colorful regalia, including scalp locks, eagle feathers, and war paint. The eastern public loved it. A troop of Fox Indians were brought to Boston, where on the common they danced a war dance in full gear. Among the rapt audience was a fourteen-year-old boy named Francis Parkman.

Despite these vicissitudes, French Illinois did expand, sustained by its mining and agriculture. In 1767, when the British arrived, they found about six hundred white inhabitants of Kaskaskia, plus half that number of blacks. That made it an impressive frontier settlement. Like the early French settlements in Detroit, and throughout the frontier, the most striking characteristic of the Kaskaskia population was its devotion to the graces of life. "The Illinois habitant was a gay soul," wrote Natalia Maree Belting in her classic 1948 study, *Kaskaskia Under the French Regime*. "He seemed shockingly carefree to later, self-righteous puritans from the American colonies. He danced on Sunday after mass, was passionately attached to faro and half a dozen other card games, and played billiards at all hours. He gossiped long over a friendly pipe and a congenial mug of brandy in the half-dusk of his porch or in the noisy tavern. And every conceivable occasion he celebrated with religious rituals and pagan ceremonies." (Belting counted twenty-seven Catholic holy days in the Kaskaskia calendar, each one an occasion for stopping work and having a good time.)

As Belting suggested, all this represented a deplorable work ethic and lack of seriousness to the American newcomers. Their attitude was confirmed when they saw the *habitants* farming with primitive equipment and methods, just like Johnny Coteau of Detroit. (They didn't even fertilize their fields.) A clue as to why this was so is provided by the testimony of Louis-Antoine de Bougainville, aide-de-camp to General Montcalm and future explorer of the South Pacific. Bougainville noted that the French Canadians were tireless at hunting and fur trading, but "lazy at cultivation of the land." The French *habitants* of Kaskaskia, like those of early Detroit and early Montreal and Quebec, were still at heart hunters and trappers and fur traders rather than agriculturalists. It was only when the fur trade in Canada was taken over by the English that farming in Quebec became a serious affair – which is why the mid-nineteenth-century French immigrants in Bourbonnais and Kankakee proved to be fully as good farmers as their English-speaking neighbors.

It wasn't the substandard agricultural practices that really aroused the contempt of American newcomers toward their French predecessors, however. It was their language, their religion, and above all their free and easy attitude toward racial miscegenation. "For them the Catholics were enemies, as they had been on many a battlefield of the Old World," wrote Illinois historian Clarence Alvord. "The French lived on good terms with the Indians; the pioneer knew no good Indian save a dead one. With unremitting and relentless watchfulness they waged that war of extermination until the Indian was driven from the coveted prairies."

Among those Indians driven from the coveted prairies were, of course, the Illinois. These aborigines cut an unusually poor figure, even for Parkman. It is important to remember, however, that the events of 1680 and 1681, as recorded by the French, showed nations like the Illinois and the Iroquois at their worst. Before they met La Salle, for example, the Illinois had already suffered serious losses in the fur-trade wars, with deeply shaken morale as one result. To focus on their behavior in this period, especially in relation to the Iroquois, another highly stressed people, is like focusing on central Europe during the Thirty Years War or Japan during the Great Depression. These people were more than the sum of their weaknesses. The Jesuit priest Pierre-François-Xavier de Charlevoix, for example, was profoundly impressed by their intelligence, and particularly by their imaginative life. "Their speeches are filled with luminous bursts which would have been applauded in the public assemblies of Rome and Athens," he wrote. Coming from a Jesuit, an expert in history and rhetoric, this was a high compliment. "It would be surprising if with such a beautiful imagination they would not have an excellent memory," Charlevoix added. "In fact, their narration is clear and precise, and although they use many allegories and other figures of speech, it remains lively. . . . Their judgement is straight and strong, they go right to the point, without pause, without deviation, and without accepting substitution."

St. Jean de Brebeuf noticed much the same thing with his flock. You rarely met an Indian, he said, who was "incapable of conversing or reasoning well." Europeans had developed hierarchies and bureaucracies, with their strong tendency to make people stupid. If a Huron on a war party had a bright idea, on the other hand, he had to persuade his comrades to come around to it; he couldn't just issue an order. This requirement naturally led to a high degree of skill in that greatest of human technologies, language.

All this beauty and vivacity of language and thought that Charlevoix noted is now utterly lost to us, unfortunately, just like the gay soul of the Illinois *habitant*. In the negotiations with Great Britain toward the end of the Seven Years War, the French tried to retain Illinois as a kind of neutral Indian buffer state, but without success. The area was ceded to Britain, and then to the Americans after the Revolution. Following the War of 1812, the American newcomers – viewed by the French as a rough, lawless bunch – overwhelmed the *habitants*, as they overwhelmed the Metis settlers in Green Bay. The French were particularly vulnerable to land swindles, because they often lacked precise records of ownership, had never had their lands surveyed, and were ill adept at legal haggling – especially in English. A few French families who learned to co-exist with American interests survived, but as a community French Illinois disappeared.

TWELVE

Sainte Genevieve

A visitor is impressed with the slaves of Upper Louisiana •
A generous hangman visits Ste. Genevieve • Rumors of bloodshed
blot a fair escutcheon • The legend of Box Car Emily •
Other atrocities committed in Ste. Genevieve

Late on the first day of their expedition down the Mississippi, La Salle and his party passed the mouth of a tributary from the west. Its powerful waters swept chunks of embankment, including trees, into the mainstream and turned it muddy and treacherous. The *voyageurs*, skilled canoeists, kept close to the banks of the river and away from whirlpools and counter-currents. That night they camped beside a village of Illinois Indians, who told them that the river whose mouth they had passed, the Missouri, was as wide and as long as the Mississippi and arose from a great mountain several days' journey to the west. The inhabitants of this country, the Illinois Indians told La Salle and his men, used horses to hunt buffalo and war on their neighbors.

❧

No one knows precisely when the village of Ste. Genevieve, the first permanent settlement in the state of Missouri, was established by the French, south of that junction of the two great rivers, but we do know that there were settlers there by 1752. As with Kaskaskia, the chief attraction of the area was its incredibly rich alluvial soil. The land was eventually divided into the same kind of ribbon farms characteristic of French settlement along the Detroit River and the St. Lawrence River – narrow fronts along the river, stretching back many times the width of that front. In the case of Ste. Genevieve, the farms stretched back across the flood plain to where the foothills of the Ozarks rose. (The word "Ozarks" derives from the French *Aux Arcs*, a phrase that means, more or less, "in the territory of the Arkansas Indians.") On this land, Ste. Genevieve farmers grew the best wheat in North America, an excellent variety of corn, and plentiful tobacco.

Their principal neighbors were the Osage. It is not quite true to say neighbors, in this case, got along famously. The Osage enjoyed stealing horses from the French. Actually, stealing horses constituted one of the graces of life generally among Indian nations west of the Mississippi, a delightful and honorable and near-universal activity, like cattle rustling among the Scottish Highlanders. In Ste. Genevieve a kind of etiquette developed to prevent bloodshed – if caught in the act, the Osage usually gave up their booty without a fight. Such restraint was characteristic. Even when lead mining developed in the hinterlands, and farmers encroached on Indian land at the end of the eighteenth century, very few whites from Ste. Genevieve were killed. It wasn't the French these Indians hated. The historian Carl J. Ekberg, in his book *Colonial Ste Genevieve: An Adventure on the Mississippi Frontier*, quotes a Frenchman, Bonnevie de Pogniat, who was traveling in this region in the mid-1790s. Pogniat claimed that the Indians were "fond of the French; they say that the English deceived them and that the Americans steal their land. The French alone are their true friends."

That the French were different from other whites in North America in their relations with the aborigines, and more benign, is by now one of history's truisms. "Spanish civilization crushed the Indian," Parkman stated. "English civilization scorned and neglected him; French civilization embraced and cherished him." Parkman overstated the case, as he overstated everything. Pogniat also overstated the case. The French were not exactly true friends of the Indians. The French used the Indians. They left the Indians their land because they didn't want their land, and they formed alliances with them for their own commercial and military and religious purposes. It is true, however, that quite a few Frenchmen did end up having a sincere affection for *les sauvages*, as Jean de Brébeuf insisted – a state of mind uncommon among the English, to be sure.

The French, of course, took it for granted that Indians were inferior. This was not because the French were infected with the virus of racism, as were their English counterparts along the Atlantic seaboard. The French adopted this attitude because of certain manifest deficiencies in Indian life, such as their inability to cook a decent meal or sing in the opera or observe the true religion. In that respect, the Hurons and Potawatomis and Choctaws and Osage were in the same boat as that nice Methodist couple from San Diego taking in the Champs Elysée on their tour of Europe. Many Frenchmen, as we have seen, thought that these deficiencies of their Indian friends could be remedied without resorting to drastic measures. Intermarriage and proper instruction would do the trick.

The same holds true of the French attitudes toward Blacks. They were not racists, the French, even though 40 per cent of Ste. Genevieve settlers owned at least one black slave. Slavery at that time was simply taken for granted, the way Americans now take the Pentagon for granted. It was nothing personal, it was just business. If nothing else, business dictated that slaves be taken reasonably good care of. "In regard to health, diet, standard of living, and longevity the black slaves of colonial Ste. Genevieve were perhaps as well off, relative to their white masters, as any slaves on earth during the eighteenth century," Carl Ekberg writes. He also quotes an American journalist, Edmund Flagg, who stated that the slaves he had seen in the French communities of the Mississippi Valley in the 1830s were "a sleeker, fleshier, happier-looking set of mortals" than any he had seen elsewhere in the west.

As with the Indians, we know very little about the views of the black slaves, but it can be safely doubted they were overcome with gratitude toward their French masters. We do know, however, that their condition was not the same as that of slaves in the English colonies and the American South. Much of this is reflected in the *Code Noir*, the set of laws laid down for Louisiana in 1724 by the French government in an attempt to regulate slaves and slave-owners. The code had nothing to do with those twentieth-century catch words humanitarianism and human rights – as Ekberg and other historians note, the set of laws was intended to make sure that slavery, an economic institution presumed to be of benefit to the French state, really did operate to the benefit of the French state. This involved preventing abuses by slave-owners as well as controlling slaves – and the code was unambiguous in asserting that a slave, while property, was a human being and not the equivalent of a plow horse. The later Anglo-Saxon practice of justifying slavery on the basis of the racial inferiority of slaves was entirely alien to the spirit of the *Code Noir*. Of course the French also viewed black slaves as social inferiors – but, as in the case of Indians, they were inferior because of circumstance, not biology. Ekberg cites the example of a wealthy Missouri lead miner named Pierre Viriat, who freed a mulatto slave in 1801 and two days later married her. The marriage was witnessed by the social elite of Ste. Genevieve, who apparently had no problem with this signal instance of racial miscegenation. Once the bride-to-be was freed by her owner, Ekberg notes, "she was not stigmatized by her race or by her late position as a slave."

Proper treatment of slaves was laid out in the code. Slaves, including those too old or infirm to work, had to be adequately housed, clothed, and fed. They could be punished by whipping, but not mutilated or seriously bloodied. They could not be worked before sunrise or after sunset, or on Sundays or religious holidays. Slave families could not be broken up by the selling of children or the separation of legitimate spouses. Female slaves could not be sexually exploited. All slaves were to be baptized and instructed in the Catholic faith. They had the right to take their owners to court if their masters violated any of these provisions.

Those last two items of the *Code Noir* were more or less dead letters. Religious instruction of slaves was spotty, and slaves did not take their owners to court, although many of them, doubtless, had grounds to do so. Slave-owners in Louisiana and Ste. Genevieve were as brutal to their workers as they felt they had to be – the motivational techniques of slave-owners were always starkly limited. But the code in general laid the legal groundwork for a more relaxed slave-holding environment, in which slaves could own their own property and businesses, borrow and lend money, and purchase their freedom with greater ease than in the rest of America. Sometimes, in fact, the slave-holding environment became entirely too relaxed in the opinion of officials in Ste. Genevieve. From the edicts of one such official cited by Ekberg, we get the picture of Ste. Genevieve slaves roaming freely at night, thieving, drinking, and partying with irresponsible whites, and committing other "disorders." Not only that; these slaves were in many cases fully armed.

Despite, or because of, this relative laxity, there never was a threat of slave rebellion in Ste. Genevieve. A successful rebellion would scarcely have improved matters much for the town's black slaves. This was true under the French, and it was true under the Spanish after King Louis xv, in 1762, handed over Louisiana and Ste. Genevieve to his esteemed cousin King Carlos iii. (The transfer of sovereignty was part of the complicated horse trading ending the Seven Years War.) The transfer meant little to Ste. Genevieve. It remained French in language and culture, and racially diverse – a town where, as Ekberg notes, white, black, and Indian children played together in the streets. The onset of the Americans, after the Louisiana Purchase in 1803, changed everything, however, including the problem of undisciplined slaves. It was no surprise to the enterprising and vigorous Americans that the French didn't know how to handle their slaves. The geologist and explorer Henry Schoolcraft – future author of the six-volume *Historical and Statistical Information Respecting the History, Condition, and Prospects of the Indian Tribes of the United States*, a literary monument to something or other – passed through the area in 1818 and noted that "the French constitute a considerable proportion of the whole population, and it is but repeating a common observation to say, that in morality and intelligence they are far inferior to the American population."

Inferiority in morals meant that the French were Roman Catholics. Inferiority in intelligence meant that they were not as quick to embrace technological change and not as literate as their American counterparts, which was generally true. The French in Ste. Genevieve had amusements other than reading and seeking out the latest in plows, just like their brethren in Kaskaskia and elsewhere. And they enjoyed their food. One observer of the French of Ste. Genevieve in the 1790s, quoted by Ekberg, makes them sound like precursors of today's healthy-heart gourmets. "With the poorest French peasant, cookery is an art well understood," this observer noted. "They make great use of vegetables, prepared in a manner to be wholesome and palatable. Instead of roast and fried, they had soups and fricassees and gumbos . . . and a variety of other dishes."

Perhaps Henry Schoolcraft would not have regarded this culinary expertise as contributing to morals and intelligence. The road to frivolity is paved with tasty gumbos. But Willa Cather knew better. In *Death Comes to the Archbishop*, her character Father Vaillant, a French missionary to the American Southwest, is tough as nails but still loves a good French soup with fresh greens. His bishop, also a Frenchman, understands. "Time and time again," Cather writes of the bishop when he hosted Father Vaillant at his table, "the Bishop had seen a good dinner, a bottle of claret, transformed into spiritual energy under his very eyes." Perhaps even Bishop Laval and St. Claude de la Colombière, two men who made a point of eating awful food for the purposes of mortifying the flesh, would have understood.

For the ordinary resident of Ste. Genevieve, good cookery was simply part of a normal life, along with music and dancing. No wonder visitors – with the possible exception of Henry Schoolcraft – found them to be an amiable bunch. "It seems fair to describe the townspeople of colonial Ste. Genevieve as a civil and relatively (relative, say, to the New England colonists) cheerful and light-hearted group of people," Ekberg writes. The New Englanders, of course, might have answered that though they weren't great fiddle players, they at least weren't governed by despotic Bourbon monarchs, like a certain town on the banks of the Mississippi. They didn't sing silly love songs on New Year's Eve, and maybe that was a shame, but at least they were too self-reliant and independent to bend the knee to some French count or Spanish grandee.

The French in Ste. Genevieve were not politically oppressed. Royal officials interfered minimally in the life of the town. Within Ste. Genevieve there were class divisions – one family, the Valles, dominated for decades – but there was no great gulf between the wealthy individual and the average townsman. The farmers of Ste. Genevieve, who formed the bulk of the population, were as economically independent and socially self-respecting as any in Stockbridge or Framingham. Local political issues were discussed at public gatherings in Ste. Genevieve as fearlessly and intelligently and peacefully as they were at New England's famous town meetings.

Of course, there was slavery. But there was slavery in New England for most of the time Ste. Genevieve was French; the institution was not abolished in Massachusetts until 1781. More to the point, there was no place in America, in the eighteenth century, as promising in its prospects of a racially egalitarian society as the French settlements along the Mississippi. But that was before the Louisiana Purchase. Until that epochal event, Ste. Genevieve served, in effect, as an alternative prototype of America, a prototype that would have repaid the attention of a Jefferson or an Adams.

❧

The corner of Third and Market, near the heart of downtown, is a good place to stand if you want to get an idea of twenty-first-century Ste. Genevieve. On the northeast corner is a courthouse built in 1885, with elegantly contrasting red brick and white stone. On the southeast corner is the Old Brick House, built in 1804 of hand-fired bricks. Just a little way down from the southwest corner is the Southern Hotel, built some time around 1811 with very similar weathered old red bricks. There are a lot of buildings in Ste. Genevieve made of old red bricks. Old red bricks and dormers and friezes and arched window heads, and other attractive features, which is why Ste. Genevieve is a magnet for tourists.

The Women's Club of Ste. Genevieve, Missouri, produced a pamphlet forty years ago entitled *Historical Highlights of Ste. Genevieve 1735–1963* that tried to explain the *esprit* of Ste. Genevieve. Two paragraphs are worth quoting in full:

> Sainte Genevieve has been referred to, and rightly so, as a rare jewel nestling in the filigreed setting of the rolling foothills of the Ozarks. For here has always been found a village of unusual interest, inhabited by a gracious and cultivated people.

> From the beginning of our little city, we have been blessed with a population devoted to the finer things. Here the arts have flourished almost without our knowing it, for they are so much a part of that great French heritage which gave us founding fathers whose very nature was an artistic one, nourished as many of

them had been by the golden age of France's greatness, when her citizens learned to love not only that Gallic zest for joy but to appreciate all that was good and admirable in the field of arts.

In other words, Ste. Genevieve wasn't your average philistine American burg. Frenchmen with their Frenchified taste for the "finer things" had built it, and now its residents were reaping the benefit in tourist dollars.

Art Papin, born in 1929, a retiree who had worked in various enterprises throughout his life, including owning and operating a One Hour Photo Lab franchise, was one of the Ste. Genevieve residents proud of his descent from the French founding fathers. His family was originally named Pepin. (He now pronounces his name *PAPE in*.) He wasn't entirely French, however – his father had married a woman of German descent. German farmers had settled in these parts in the early nineteenth century and eventually they outnumbered the French. "That's why I'm tall," he said. "I got her height. The other five kids in the family are short." His remark reminded me of the old wooden crucifix I had seen in the 1785 Bolduc House, perhaps the town's most significant historical building. Christ, in this eighteenth-century carving, had short, stubby legs, like a Frenchman of the period. The average height of these Frenchmen, the guide at the Bolduc House informed me, was five feet. (The average height of Frenchwomen was four feet, eight inches.) There was historical support, then, for the "swarthy, stunted Frenchmen" of novelist Kenneth Roberts's imagination.

Fortunately French males had other qualities than sheer height that might attract a German woman like Art Papin's mother. "Here anyway, the French were easy-going, fun-loving people," Papin told me. His father loved to dance, and so did *his* father, and so did *his* father, and so on, back into the mists of time. There was a long family tradition of shoving the furniture back and dancing the night away at somebody's house. Papin's mother also happened to be crazy for dancing, which is why she chose to marry Papin's father, despite certain ethnic and socio-economic differences between her German family and his French family. "She lived right down the street, a block away from my dad," Papin said. "And being Germans, they had a really fine home, a two-story frame house. My dad lived in a log cabin – he was born in this log cabin down by the creek. My mom said her mother told her he was a lazy Frenchman. She'd chase my dad back to his house so many times when he came courting."

Henry Schoolcraft would have approved. But chalk one up for "Gallic zest for joy," which can work its magic even among the Germans. Papin's father won over not only his sweetheart but eventually her mother. He became her favorite son-in-law. "My mother had three sisters and two brothers, and her sisters especially were jealous, because their German husbands never took them out," Papin recalls. "They would just sock away cash. My dad, he would spend all his. They spent it all on a good time. And my mother's sisters were all jealous because they never had a good time."

Papin had inherited another pleasant family tradition – leading *La Guignolée*. This New Year's Eve revel, which had its origins in medieval France, and was transported to the Mississippi Valley via French Canada, saw young men dressing up in grotesque costumes and going to the homes of young women and clowning around and singing at the top of their lungs: "We're not asking a lot, just your oldest daughter, to cheer her up and warm her feet . . ." Papin's uncle, when he served in France during World War I, asked about the custom in that country. "He could speak good French, my uncle," Papin told me. "He sang *La Guignolée* over there and nobody had ever heard of it." Nevertheless, the custom was still celebrated in Ste. Genevieve and one or two other towns in the region. Every New Year's Eve, then, twenty-five or so individuals would gather in the American Legion Hall in Ste. Genevieve to perform the venerable rites. Papin and four other leaders would dress up in tuxedos, and the other men would don various costumes.

"People used to make their own costumes," Papin said. "Then I guess about fifteen or twenty years ago the lime company out here, they bought costumes for us. Nice costumes. Trappers, clowns, early French soldiers. They also used to furnish the bus. But two years ago they quit sponsoring us – they're cutting back. They have a new president. Last year we sold tickets around town for a draw to pay for the bus."

At the American Legion Hall, at the start of the evening, Papin and the other leaders would rehearse the song, and then they would climb into the bus – a relatively new wrinkle in the rites, but this is the age of road checks and Breathalyzers. Another new wrinkle was that they didn't stop at private homes any more. Their first stop would be the Valle High School gym, and then to local retirement homes and care centers. "We go to these places first because every other place you go, you get a drink," Papin explained. "You want to be sober when you go to these places." Papin and the other leaders would sing the song, and the other twenty-five people would waltz around them in a circle and repeat it. Then they would shake hands with everybody and wish them a happy New Year. That was just about it. Then it was time to repeat the performance at various local bars and restaurants. "A couple of girls, they go ahead of the bus and they go into the bar and they give the bartender a list of our preferred drinks," Papin said. "Before we even go into the bar, or while we're singing our song, they're making our drinks for us, so when the song is over our drinks are ready for us. Right in a row on the bar." Papin rapped the table where we sat, to indicate the smartness and efficiency of the operation. "Everybody gets half-loaded. You just have a good time. All the places are just jammed with people waiting to see us – I guess that's what they're waiting for, because they always have a good time."

Unfortunately, since French is no longer spoken in these parts, those who wish to memorize the song have to do so phonetically. Bone swarr le may truh eh la may tress/ Eh two le moaned doo low gee. ("Bon soir le maître et la maîtresse,/ Et tout le monde du logis.") It's not the song they sang in Papin's grandfather's time, but it will do.

✧

Papin has other historical memories of Ste. Genevieve that are not quite so pleasant. One winter morning in 1937, when he was seven years old, he was playing in the schoolyard at recess when one of the kids shouted, and they all rushed to a corner of the fence. Just below, on Third Street, a man was walking in chains, surrounded by the sheriff and other officials. He was a thirty-one-year-old man named Hurt Hardy, Jr., and he was being escorted from the jail at the corner of Third and Market – the same building with the elegant red brick and white stone – to the County Poor Farm on Main Street. Hardy had once worked at the Peerless Lime Company in Ste. Genevieve, where he became friends with a quarry foreman named Fahnestock. Hardy spent many evenings at Fahnestock's farm, in the charming company of his blond, twenty-year-old daughter, Ethel. He grew fond of her, but Miss Ethel Fahnestock did not return his affection, in part because he drank heavily on occasion. The young man, driven insane by love, and by the thought of another man succeeding where he had failed, hid himself in the Fahnestock barn one morning and fatally shot her with a 12-gauge shotgun as she entered to milk the cows.

"My friend Alvin Petrequin, who was editor of the *Fair Play*, said this fellow Hardy had syphilis," Papin said. "He said he wasn't all there." No mercy was extended Hardy by a jury of his peers, however, and he was condemned to die. On the grounds of the Poor Farm they built a gallows and a sixteen-foot stockade to enclose it. The sheriff, it was said, charged a dollar a head for admission. "My mom's brother, he got an invitation for this hanging, but he had a flat tire on his way over and missed the whole show," Papin said. Another thousand spectators, according to local newspapers, gathered outside the stockade to witness the hanging.

To make sure the execution went well, local authorities obtained the services of a hangman from Illinois named Phil Hanna. Hanna, according to the newspapers, had supervised over one hundred of these affairs. He also accepted no payment for his services, outside of traveling expenses. His sole motivation, he said, was to make sure the hanged man did not suffer. "This guy was supposed to be a super-duper expert," Papin said. "They weigh you up before they hang you, and measure you, and calculate the drop and make sure everything's fixed up correctly – what the hanging's supposed to do is separate your neck from your spinal column right away. But this guy goofed up. The poor man strangled to death. He kicked for about fifteen or twenty minutes."

Newspaper accounts confirm this. The trap door was sprung at 1:56 p.m. At 2:15 p.m. Hardy was finally pronounced dead by attending physicians. The spectators inside the stockade had certainly gotten their money's worth. First they heard a speech from the condemned man. "Friends, I am proud to admit my personal trust in Jesus Christ," Hardy was reported to have said. "This belief and trust has been a great comfort to me during my long months of imprisonment. I feel no malice toward anyone, not even against those who have been so bitter against me. I am prepared to meet my Master on the other side, and my golden-haired darling." That speech wasn't bad for a syphilitic whose nerves were presumably none the better for his infirmity. And then came his prolonged agony.

Apparently, the gruesome spectacle served a purpose. Hardy was the last man to be executed by hanging in the state of Missouri, perhaps because of the behavior of the crowd enjoying the show. A St. Louis newspaper editorialized, "Ste. Genevieve – Missouri's oldest community and heir to centuries of French culture – has proved as primitive as the rest of us when humanity is allowed to be exposed to the raw." The sentence betrays an ill-concealed tone of satisfaction, which often emerges when Americans detect a hollow ring to all that talk about "centuries of French culture." Something raises American hackles when good people like the members of the

Women's Club of Ste. Genevieve go on about how "devoted to the finer things" they are because of their "great French heritage." Well, in 1937 these heirs of artistic and cultivated France turned out to see a man dance at the end of a rope.

That same decade, another disturbing episode took place in Ste. Genevieve. It began on a late Saturday night in October 1930, when two Ste. Genevieve men, looking for a little excitement – white men, married, with families – dropped in at a party some Blacks were having in a shack by the railroad depot. Two black men – Lonnie Taylor, a sporting type from nearby Crystal City, and Columbus Jennings, known as "C.J." – and a black woman named Vera Rogers, offered to pay the two men, Harry Panchot and Paul Ritter, a dollar-fifty if they would drive them a few miles out of town to where a craps game was in progress. Panchot and Ritter accepted. Before they reached the craps game, however, something happened – the black men tried to hold up Panchot and Ritter, as Panchot claimed in his dying statement to the police, or one of the white men made advances to the woman, as Taylor and his friends claimed. The result, in any case, was that Lonnie Taylor shot and killed Panchot and Ritter. He, C.J., and Vera were arrested later that Sunday and questioned by the sheriff in the Ste. Genevieve jail. After a crowd gathered in front of that jail, the sheriff deemed it prudent to remove the prisoners to a county jail in Hillsboro. From there, for their further protection, they were sent to a jail in St. Louis.

That evening, according to a Ste. Genevieve newspaper, *The Fair Play*, "a number of men quietly visited the negro settlements and informed all negroes to leave town before 5 p.m. the next day. This ruling affected about 200 negroes and Monday morning the exodus began. The banished negroes left by car, train and some walked out of town." These two hundred Blacks were what the other Ste. Genevieve newspaper, *The Herald*, called "an undesirable itinerant element . . . from the extreme southern limit of the country." They were black migrant workers in other words, from parts of the Deep South, who had come to Ste. Genevieve to work in the lime plants and stone quarries. Nervous, with good reason, about a possible lynching, the sheriff asked the governor to call in the National Guard, and two companies arrived late Monday to protect what Blacks remained in town. By that time, however, only two or three families, long-time residents of Ste. Genevieve, were left to protect.

After the National Guard departed on Tuesday afternoon, a group of armed vigilantes stopped by the home of Louis Ribeau, a rural mail delivery man. Ribeau was hardly one of those undesirable itinerants, but the vigilantes wanted him out of town. Ribeau managed to get away from them, word of the incident spread, and once again the town was agitated and crowds started to gather. The National Guard returned. Finally, on Wednesday, at a public meeting, the American Legion offered to help support the sheriff and patrol the streets of the town to ensure law and order. On Thursday afternoon, the National Guard, satisfied that things had calmed down and that the Legionnaires were capable of handling the situation, departed a second time. "Thus ended one of the most serious situations ever experienced in Ste. Genevieve," reported *The Herald.*

If *The Herald* and *The Fair Play* accurately reflected local feeling, what agitated the citizens of Ste. Genevieve, after the dust settled, was not that two hundred Blacks had been driven away, but that the "gracious and cultured people" of Ste. Genevieve, the descendants of "founding fathers whose very nature was an artistic one," were being accused of acting like barbarians. On this occasion, as on the occasion of the public hanging, the citizens of the town were being judged "as primitive as the rest of us," by non-French outsiders. *The Herald* reported that citizens were receiving long-distance calls from friends and relatives asking if there really was rioting and bloodshed on the streets of Ste. Genevieve, among "many other ridiculous and preposterous questions." According to *The Herald,* "Much of this was no doubt caused by the many exaggerated statements published in the daily newspapers, reporters for which evidently drew on their prolific imaginations to paint as black and revolting a picture as possible. . . . Ste. Genevieve has an enviable reputation for peace and quiet and fine hospitality, and any effort to darken her fair escutcheon will be resisted to the limit."

It is certainly true that leading citizens were appalled at what had happened. The pastor of Ste. Genevieve, Father C.L. van Tourenhout, addressed a meeting of local businessmen shortly after the disturbances and called for an end to mob violence and racial antagonisms. "Ste. Genevieve has always boasted openly of its good name and of its law-abiding citizens," he told his audience. "If this is true, it is now their duty to curb, in every way possible, this spirit of racial animosity that has been expressing itself during the last few days." Father van Tourenhout, it should be said, wasn't just talking. On that Monday when the threat of violence hung over the head of every black resident in town, he sheltered a black family, long-time parishioners, in the church.

Most inhabitants of the town, however, were probably just as happy that the migrant workers had been chased out for good. In the 1950s and 1960s, some homeless Blacks did end up back in Ste. Genevieve, living in shacks north of the town. They, too, were chased out by persons unknown. "I know somebody went up there and burned those shacks down," Art Papin told me. "I don't know who. I don't know anything about that. I've heard rumors, which I wouldn't repeat. I just know the Blacks all moved."

⚜

The thirties weren't all bad for Ste. Genevieve. One happy thing did take place. In 1932, two St. Louis artists named Bernie Peters and Jesse Beard Rickly rented a house with studio space in the town and spent the summer painting there. They were joined by a third St. Louis artist, Aimee Schweig. This was the nucleus of the Ste. Genevieve Artists' Colony and Summer School of Art, which lasted a decade, until World War II, when gasoline rationing made driving from St. Louis to Ste. Genevieve impractical. It was an attempt to emulate the success of other notable American art colonies that had been founded around the turn of the century – art colonies such as Provincetown, Massachusetts; Taos, New Mexico; Old Lyme, Connecticut; Woodstock, New York; and the MacDowell Colony in New Hampshire. The art colony was a bright American idea. If America lacked Europe's salons and *ateliers* and Academies of Fine Art, it had lots of scenic outdoors.

Schweig and Rickly and Peters thought there was no reason artists in the Midwest had to journey east to have an art colony experience. All they required was an outdoors setting just far enough from the big city to make it seem like a real retreat. But this setting couldn't be just any hick town. It had to have esthetic appeal. It had to be as mellow as Old Lyme or Woodstock. And what better place, in that regard, than Ste. Genevieve? Ste. Genevieve "is a quaint village possessing a unique combination of characteristics that appeal to artists who have a sense of the picturesque," writes art historian James G. Rogers, Jr., in his 1998 monograph on the Ste. Genevieve art colony. "Little changed by the passage of time, it boasts the largest collection of eighteenth century French Creole structures in North America. With a central square dominated by its steepled church, it retains a European flavor unusual in Middle America."

Like many art colonies – Old Lyme, for example, was a nursery for American Impressionists – the Ste. Genevieve Artists' Colony promoted a certain strain of art. That was American Scene Painting – or, as it was more widely known, Regionalism. Perhaps the best-known American Regionalist of the period was Missouri painter Thomas Hart Benton, who came to the Ste. Genevieve colony and gave it his blessing. I visited the Ste. Genevieve post office, where Aimee Schweig's daughter Martyl had painted a mural entitled *La Guignolée* in 1941. It was a fine example of American Scene Painting in my opinion. The horny-handed tillers of the soil, on this New Year's Eve, were wearing floppy hats and dancing with their women to the tune of a fiddler, and there were a lot of interesting peripheral figures, like a red-robed priest and a man in costume – he was wearing a mask and what looked like a dunce cap – and a woman with low décolletage standing in the light of the doorway. The painting didn't seem to be making any Statement. Everybody in it seemed to be having a good time, which was the point of *La Guignolée*, and the point of the painting, I assumed.

Martyl was the last survivor of the Ste. Genevieve art colony, along with her younger brother Martin, who was a boy when the colony flourished and who had gone on to run the family photographic studio in St. Louis. I spoke to Martin first. He lived in a gentrified area of St. Louis, in a brick house that reminded me of the Venable family mansion in Tennessee Williams's play *Suddenly Last Summer*. To enter, you passed a gate and walked a path that ran through a semi-tropical garden, with dwarf hemlocks and dogwood trees and hibiscus plants and ferns. Inside the house, I did not hear the "harsh cries and sibilant hissings and thrashing sounds in the garden as if it were inhabited by beasts, serpents and birds, all of savage nature," that Williams describes in the Venable mansion, but there were three parrots in a greenhouse whose voices were startlingly loud when they spoke, and a pool full of large koi in the back garden, and grotesque plants scattered about – a tall, slender Pachypodium, and Euphorbia plants from Madagascar, and gnarled cacti of various sorts. "In the last few years I've gotten interested in succulents," Martin said. "I want to collect plants that look like sculpture."

He was also proud of his collection of clocks from the Morbier area of France. They were tall, stately devices, with decorative pendulums and fine wood exteriors. "The French had the best clocks for a long time," Martin said. "But the English finally beat the French because they developed more accurate timepieces. They were much more complicated mechanisms than these French clocks. That's why they could get their ships to port faster and more accurately." Here was one more clue to the disposition of human events. The English had better clocks than the French. The thought occurred to me that history was an endless dark house, full of crazy corridors and unexplored rooms. Occasionally you could find a match and light it, like this information about clocks, and the small light shed by the little match went surprisingly far, illuminated vast areas of darkness – but there was so much darkness beyond.

Martin, who had what Englishmen of the seventeenth century would have called amiable manners and pleasing conversation, confessed that he had been too young in the 1930s to remember much of the art colony. He remembered what any boy would remember, odd and vivid presences, like a painter at Ste. Genevieve named Emily Pheleps. No amount of scholarly excavation and argument will ever resurrect Emily Pheleps. She left so shadowy an artistic reputation behind her that it is doubtful she ever made the full transition up the ladder of fame from being "unknown" to being "obscure." (The rung after that is called "minor.") But this woman, known as "Box Car Emily" because of her fondness for the drink of that name, survived in the memory of at least one living person. "I remember her because she wore black and she smoked cigars," Martin said. He shook his head. "If a woman did that today, it would be far more noticeable. Even though we're supposed to be more sophisticated these days, some of these eccentric people were accepted much more readily back then. I don't think there was this big fascination with who was gay and who was not gay and all that bullshit. It existed then but it didn't seem to faze anybody."

Martin also remembered, of course, the "European flavor" of Ste. Genevieve, with all those old French houses. "Very few people knew about the town then," he said. "It wasn't a very prosperous place. People were too poor to tear their houses down. If there had been a lot of money around, there wouldn't have been anything left."

After I left Martin Schweig's house, I phoned his sister, now Martyl Langsdorf of Chicago. Of all the painters who spent summers at Ste. Genevieve, Martyl Langsdorf, born in 1918, had proven the most successful – currently she was one of the most admired and exhibited painters in Chicago. "The thing about

Ste. Genevieve, it was a French settlement, which had its charm, which is why the art colony was there – because of the ambience," she said to me over the phone. "But there was this German farm culture superimposed upon it, which was antithetical to the French in every way." I complimented her on her *La Guignolée* in the Ste. Genevieve post office. "I wanted to do something significant," she said. "I knew that was very important and that would relate to the community. It also had nothing to do with the German farm culture, and that's why I chose the subject."

The pastor of Ste. Genevieve church, Father van Tourenhout, embodied the finest of the French ambience, despite his non-French name. Francis J. Yealy, a Jesuit priest who wrote a history of Ste. Genevieve in 1935, called van Tourenhout a man of "scholarly tastes" and "cultivated mind." These qualities, according to Yealy, "crystallized and intensified the refinement observed in the people more than a hundred years ago." As well as being racially progressive, he was an ardent supporter of the art colony. "He was a wonderful man," Martyl said of this intellectual priest. "He and my mother used to drink sacramental wine together." Aimee Schweig was a member of the Ethical Culture Society, a liberal, humanist organization opposed to all notions of the Deity, but that raised no barriers between them. "If my mother liked Father Van, you can be sure he was okay."

When the war came, and money began to flow into the community, the ambience suffered. Esthetic atrocities were committed. "My mother tried to stem the tide of this destruction," Martyl said. "Every year we would go down there, spring, fall or summer, and some terrible thing had happened. A statue in a niche on the outside of the church that had this nice patina, a beautiful green, we went down one summer and it had been painted with silver radiator paint. Then they cut down these trees, hundred-year-old trees, so they could park their cars all around the center of the town. Then they tore up the flagstone sidewalks and poured concrete instead."

Fortunately prosperity in Ste. Genevieve was sufficiently delayed so that many of the old buildings – the Louis Bolduc House and the Joseph Amoureux House and the Jean Baptiste Valle House and the Bequette-Robault House and the Pierre Dorloc House and the Charles Gregoire House and the Hubardeau House and La Lumendière House and the Petrequin House – were still more or less standing when the heritage and restoration movement came to the rescue in the 1960s. The French ambience was saved – barely. Be thankful, America. "I do love the French," Martyl Langsdorf said to me. "We long for the French."

⚜

Observers tended to view the French inhabitants of Ste. Genevieve as under-achievers. (Just like us New England Franco-Americans. Irish and Italian immigrants hit the ground running when they came to New England, while we avoided making a stir, watching them with a mixture of envy and contempt. We were here before you, was our attitude. We'll be here when you're gone.) Father Yealy, in his history, thought this under-achievement of Ste. Genevieve Frenchmen was a fine thing. "To such as these, the vulgar, aggressive, mercenary spirit of the age was a thing abhorred," he wrote. In Ste. Genevieve, Jeffersonian economics still prevailed. "Saint Genevieve has avoided the arrogant materialism of booming towns and the unhappy extremes of fortune which prevail in great cities," he wrote. "The wealthiest is assessed at less than a million, and some of the poorest have a garden and a pig."

Yealy wrote this in 1935, during the depths of the Depression. It was a time when desperate people in big cities would have been happy with a garden and a pig. World War II and post-war prosperity made that a joke, like the image of a hillbilly with a squirrel-hunting rifle. Abhorrence of a vulgar, aggressive, mercenary spirit began to look like simple lack of gumption. Shunning the arrogant material-ism of booming towns began to look like acceptance of decay. "A stranger visiting Ste. Genevieve today might very well see it as a town which has lacked initiative, has lost its vitality, and like so many other small towns now finding it difficult to compete successfully with large industrial cities, has succumbed to an attitude of indifference," wrote a landscape architect named Neil H. Porterfield in the late sixties. He saw rubber tires floating in the streams around Ste. Genevieve, the heaps of junked cars, the dusty display windows of marginal businesses, the houses needing paint and new roofs. He saw the historic buildings falling apart.

"Fortunately, there are many people in Ste. Genevieve who recognize that the town's single, most important asset is its unique history, and the fact that there still exist today many physical elements which reveal and portray this history," he wrote. These forward-looking people were by then picking up certain signals. They could hear dimly the hum of future recreational vehicles on the highway. They could see those dusty display windows struggling to transform themselves into the neat facades of candle shops and quilt shops and stores selling all varieties of chocolate. They could sense their town was about to be remade by the great new cultural force of mass tourism.

THIRTEEN

Fort Assumption

La Salle bestows a curious honor on one of his party • A rare instance of an aboriginal nation fondly regarded by the English • Reflections on a modern Dionysus • A mysterious message from a Super 8 Motel

The next morning La Salle, as Parkman tells us, embarked anew "on the dark and mighty stream," and "drifted swiftly down towards unknown destinies." It was pleasant journeying. The French even experienced one of those rare occasions when Indian cuisine met their approval. From swamps the Indian women gathered highly edible roots, a food source so plentiful, La Salle observed, it made the local Indians a little lazier than was usual for inhabitants of this continent. Some of the roots were as thick as a man's arm. "They dig a hole in the ground where they lay down a bed of red hot stones, followed by some leaves, then a layer of roots, then a covering of red hot stones," La Salle wrote. "Then they cover the hole with earth and let it roast for a while. The roots can be eaten unseasoned or with a little oil – it's quite a good meal [*une assez bonne nourriture*], as long as the roots are thoroughly cooked."

Three days later La Salle and his party passed the mouth of the Ohio. A week after that they camped a little northward of the present city of Memphis, where the heights of land known as the Chickasaw

Bluffs overlook the river. La Salle called a halt and sent out hunting expeditions. One of his party, an armorer named Pierre Prud'homme, managed to get lost in the woods. Since there were signs of Indians about, La Salle worried that his man might have been killed. Never one to let these matters slide – it always made a bad impression on Indians – La Salle ordered the building of a stockade and sent out search parties. On the sixth day of their search, his men found two Chickasaw Indians. One was sent back to his village with presents and messages of goodwill – the other remained as a hostage. A few days later, Prud'homme, half-starved and delirious, was finally found, after what was no doubt the loneliest and worst week of his life. La Salle, with that touch of caustic irony we have seen before, named the stockade Fort Prud'homme and left the armorer with a few other men in charge of it. On March 3, he resumed the voyage down the river.

⚜

La Salle can't be blamed for what later happened with the Chickasaws, in the way that Champlain is sometimes blamed for inaugurating French-Iroquois relations with a blast of his harquebus. As was his wont, La Salle approached these Indians with cautious friendliness. It wasn't the way Hernando De Soto passed through here 130 years previously, killing Indians wherever he went. That's the difference between these two explorers who made their reputations beating everybody else to the Mississippi River. La Salle did not leave a trail of blood behind him.

The Chickasaws, when they ran into La Salle, were not interested in killing Frenchmen either, although they were famous for their martial spirit. In later years, the English settlers in Georgia and the Carolinas came to feel something like a warm regard for these Chickasaws, noting that they were taller and more robust than their neighbors, "a comely, pleasant looking people." The Chickasaws also compelled admiration from the English because they punished adulterers, although in other respects they lived in the kind of Iroquoian, sexually easygoing, matriarchal clan system, complete with primitive communism, which would so entrance Engels.

Unlike other Indians in the Southeast, the Chickasaws were more hunters than farmers. What farming they did they left to their slaves, and to their womenfolk – Chickasaw men displayed in full what Lord Macaulay termed "that dislike of steady industry, and that disposition to throw on the weaker sex the heaviest part of manual labour, which are characteristic of savages." They had more important things to do than to hoe corn. Fighting was religion. Fasting, sexual abstinence, and prayer preceded war parties, and if members of those parties encountered bad omens while setting out, they returned forthwith, with no suspicion of cowardice. It wasn't that often they returned without scalps, plunder, and captives, however. Their hereditary enemies were the neighboring Choctaw nation. As was the case of the Iroquois and the Hurons, these two mortal foes, Choctaws and Chickasaws, were very similar in language and culture. They both lived in fortified villages, with the great stronghold of the Chickasaw nation, the town of Akia, located in what is now northern Mississippi, not far from Tupelo.

Almost as soon as they established a permanent settlement near the mouth of the Mississippi River, the French realized they would have to come to terms with the Chickasaw. In 1702 the governor of the newly established colony of Louisiana, Pierre LeMoyne D'Iberville, convened a conference at his headquarters in Mobile, Alabama, at which both Choctaw and Chickasaw representatives appeared. D'Iberville called for peace, showered the Indians with gifts, and sent a fourteen-year-old boy named St. Michel among the Chickasaws to learn the language – and coincidentally to keep D'Iberville informed of Chickasaw movements.

It was a good start, but almost immediately the understanding fell apart. The year after the conference, a group of Chickasaws returned to Mobile to ask for French help in keeping the Choctaws in line. A French Canadian named Pierre Dugue de Boisbriant was dispatched to the nearest Choctaw settlement to help negotiate peace, but evidently the Choctaws were chafing at the idea of not harassing their old antagonists and were looking for pretexts to fight. They told Boisbriant that the Chickasaws had put young St. Michel to death in their typically gruesome fashion – an accusation denied by the Chickasaws accompanying Boisbriant, who offered to send messengers to bring St. Michel back, and to stay in the Choctaw village for a month as hostages. The messengers were duly dispatched. A month later, they had not returned. Boisbriant suspected that the messengers had been ambushed by the Choctaws, but he was alone in their village, surrounded by impatient warriors, and he gave in to their demand to kill the Chickasaw hostages. Later, it was learned that St. Michel was alive and well.

French-Chickasaw relations might have survived this disheartening episode if the French had been able to keep up their end of the understanding, which was to provide the Chickasaws with plentiful trade goods. They could not compete with the English, however. From the Carolinas a steady stream of pack trains loaded with blankets, tobacco, brass kettles, rum, needles and thread, hatchets, knives, and above all British muskets, came climbing over the Appalachian trails into the country of the Chickasaws. In return the British traders came back, not with furs, but with deer hides and Indian slaves bound for the West Indies. As the eighteenth century wore on, the Chickasaws became dreaded slave-hunters in the region, armed with their British muskets, ranging not only in the Southeast but across the Mississippi into Arkansas and Missouri and north into Illinois. This trade of the Chickasaws would be the tiger they dared not dismount. Once introduced to trade goods, they became increasingly dependent on them, particularly firearms, to maintain the military supremacy necessary to obtain more trade goods. It is a dynamic we have seen before, but it was particularly potent in the case of the Chickasaws, whose survival in the eighteenth century came to depend less and less on the traditional pursuits of hunting and farming and more and more on supplying deer hides and slaves to the English. Occasions when they turned back from raids because of bad omens became fewer and fewer. They could no longer afford old religious scruples.

The French were never able to supplant the trade with the English, largely because the English, with their more dynamic commercial and proto-industrial economy, always came up with cheaper and more plentiful goods than the French. What trade goods the French managed to transport from France were largely diverted to their reliable allies, the Choctaws. The Choctaws, indeed, formed the first line of defense for Louisiana for decades – in some cases, they literally fed the soldiers and colonists, as well as fending off the British and Chickasaws. But they could not stop the Chickasaws from ravaging French commerce on the Mississippi. Rowing a boat up the river between the French settlements in Louisiana and those in Upper Louisiana (Missouri and Illinois) remained a harrowing adventure for years, thanks to Chickasaw raiders.

Lacking economic inducements – and lacking the Jesuit missionaries who might at least have established a foothold in the Chickasaw nation and divided loyalties there the way they had divided Iroquois loyalties in the north – the French failed to woo the Chickasaws from the English. In frustration, they determined to destroy the Chickasaws by force of arms. In April 1736 the governor of Louisiana, Jean-Baptiste Le Moyne de Bienville (brother of Pierre Le Moyne d'Iberville), launched a pincer attack on the Chickasaws. From Mobile he proceeded north along the Tombigbee River with an army of six hundred men, including forty-five Blacks. The plan was to join forces with an army of over three hundred French and Indians, led by Major Pierre d'Artaguiette, marching south from Illinois.

It was always impossible to coordinate the movements of separate armies in wilderness warfare. Communications were too difficult and logistics too uncertain. Bienville's army was delayed in Louisiana, for example, because it had to wait for supplies and arms from France; the ships on which these provisions were carried ran into bad weather on the high seas. The plan had been for the two armies to meet at the end of March, but by the time Bienville reached the rendezvous point with d'Artaguiette he was two months late. By then, d'Artaguiette was nowhere to be seen. He had spent the month of March looking for Bienville and, having consumed nearly all of his provisions, was retreating back to his headquarters – at a hastily built post on the Chickasaw Bluffs, near La Salle's old Fort Prud'homme – when his scouts reported the presence of a nearby Chickasaw town. D'Artaguiette decided that capturing the town would not only replenish his provisions but make the whole exercise seem worthwhile.

Unfortunately, there were more Chickasaws present than he bargained for, and they were well armed and well positioned, behind their palisades, to pour a withering fire on the French. When d'Artaguiette attacked, his men were cut to pieces. Meanwhile, another Chickasaw force struck the rear of his army. Only twenty in his force managed to escape; the rest were killed or captured. Several of the French captives, including d'Artaguiette and a Jesuit priest, Father Antoine Senat, who had insisted on staying with the wounded instead of making good his escape, were burned alive. According to witnesses they endured their torments with remarkable fortitude. The victors then joined their fellow Chickasaws farther south and were present when Bienville finally showed up in front of Akia in late May. Bienville's men were also repulsed when they attacked this fortified town, and the governor was forced to retreat. The campaign had proved a disaster.

A second campaign, intended to remove the stain from French honor and deal with the Chickasaws once and for all, was planned for 1739. This time the rendezvous for troops coming north from Louisiana and south from Illinois and Michigan and Canada was set for November 1 at the Chickasaw Bluffs. Instead of going up the Tombigbee River, which was too shallow for boats in the fall, the northbound forces would proceed up the Mississippi River. The combined armies would then march to Akia directly from the staging area on the Mississippi.

In preparation for this campaign French engineers built a fort at the staging area, at the spot where the city of Memphis now stands. They cut a shelf at the base of the bluffs, formed an upward slope above it, a little taller than the height of a man, then cut another shelf, and so on, until the wall of the bluff had been carved into seven shelves and seven slopes. On top of the bluff they built bastions. All this was completed on August 15, the feast of the Assumption of Mary, and therefore the new post was named Fort Assumption. (The Assumption of Mary, for the curious reader, is an ancient belief of the Church that Mary, on her death, was "assumed body and soul into heavenly glory." This means that her body did not suffer corruption in the grave, did not turn into dust, and has been spared waiting until the end of time for its glorification.)

By the middle of November, Bienville had managed to assemble at Fort Assumption the largest army ever seen in that part of the world, thirty six hundred men, including Iroquois from Canada, Indians from many other nations (this was the expedition on which the ten-year-old Charles Langlade was introduced to the great game of wilderness warfare) *voyageurs*, French regulars from Europe, Blacks, colonial militiamen. The fort was loaded with cannons, mortars, grenades, bombs, gunpowder, and musket balls. An outside observer would have thought that the doom of the Chickasaws was sealed. The Chickasaws themselves, who had been watching the landing of men and supplies at the fort, came to the same conclusion. Late in November the Chickasaws left reeds stuck in the ground near the fort, attached to pouches of tobacco, ears of corn, and bearskins. These were old symbols of peace, signifying the desire to sit on a bearskin and share a meal and a good smoke. The French ignored the offerings.

Indeed, they had the upper hand, except for one problem. They did not know how to get to Akia with all their men and supplies and armaments. For months prior to this invasion, their scouts had been busy searching out routes to the heart of the Chickasaw nation, and different options were clearly available – the army could go by the Yazoo River, for example. For ordinary war parties there would have been no problem. But Bienville was not looking for a trail, he was looking for a military road through this land of swamps and streams to transport his baggage and artillery trains. With increasingly wet weather, and winter approaching, the problem was aggravated. Weeks and months went by without a solution.

The Indians amused themselves by skirmishing with the Chickasaws. When successful, they returned with scalps and prisoners and horses. The priests in the expedition tried to prevent the torture of these captives, but some men and women were burned to death with red-hot irons regardless. Drunkenness and desertion also began to take their toll on the Indian allies, who could not understand why the French were taking so much time. The French themselves were dying by the score from malaria, dysentery, and other ailments endemic to the insalubrious Memphis climate – it is no wonder that Indians never settled on this spot, and that only the insane white man saw fit to construct a city in this mosquito-ridden, torrid swampland. Before the winter was over, five hundred French soldiers had perished from disease.

At the beginning of February, Bienville finally ordered a party of 180 French and 400 Indians to set out for Akia on a road that scouts assured him was good enough for the purpose. Minus artillery, this band arrived at Akia on February 22. The commander, Pierre Céleron, had learned the lesson of Bienville and d'Artaguiette and refrained from a direct assault on the town. For the next two days the opposed forces exchanged fire, without much result. The Chickasaws were afraid, however, that more French might be on their way with cannon and mortar, and sought a truce. This time the offer was accepted. After preliminary talks, and some delay, a band of Chickasaw chiefs showed up at Fort Assumption on April 1 to make a deal with the French, just in time to see the

French burning their own fort in preparation to leave. This was colossally bad timing on the part of the French, who had made the decision to give up the expedition and the fort in the middle of February, while Celeron's force was still on its way to Akia: the sight was hardly an inducement for the Chickasaws to concede much in the way of a treaty. Nevertheless, Bienville proposed a few terms – banning English traders from Chickasaw settlements, surrendering any white or black prisoners held by the Chickasaw – to which the chiefs agreed. The last of the French then departed, happy to have gotten at least those concessions from their enemies.

The Chickasaws remained such a problem that a third expedition was mounted in 1752 by another governor of Louisiana, along the route of the Tombigbee River followed by Bienville in his first expedition. By this time, however, the Chickasaws had further improved their defenses, and the French contented themselves with burning a few cabins and destroying some crops. Their great opportunity had passed, in any case, with the failure of Fort Assumption and Bienville's army. With better planning, that army might actually have succeeded in destroying the Chickasaws. At least the French might have retained their fort and solidified their grip on the entire Mississippi Valley, with incalculable consequences for the future history of North America.

But the opportunity was lost. The Chickasaws, a Neolithic people who could never muster much more than five hundred warriors, had successfully defied a modern nation with a modern army. But as the experience of the United States in Vietnam and Iraq has shown, there are many ways that the advantages of overwhelming technological superiority in war can be nullified.

⚜

On my visit to Memphis I had arranged to meet an old friend named Bobby Landry. I picked him up at the airport and then we went to the Peabody Hotel to see the famous ducks. Twice a day, marching music is broadcast in the lobby of this grand hotel, the doors to the elevator open, and a line of ducks walks in single file down a red carpet to a fountain in the middle of the lobby. The ducks swim around the fountain a bit, and then, to the cue of music, walk back along the red carpet to the elevator, whereupon they are whisked up to their penthouse lodgings until their next appearance. Actually, Bobby and I barely glimpsed this famous ritual because it was in the middle of the tourist season and the crowd of spectators around the fountain and red carpet was impenetrable. But we did catch sight of one or two ducks, so we could truthfully tell our friends we had witnessed the event, surpassed on the list of Memphis tourist attractions only by Graceland and the Sun Recording Studios tour.

Bobby was from a small town in Ontario, and since his ancestry was half French — a cousin had traced the family tree back to seventeenth-century France — his presence at this point in my journey was fitting. A Landry ancestor, like one of mine, had probably worked a farm in the Canadian wilderness, swatting mosquitos and worrying when the next Iroquois was going to pop up and brain him with a war club. But he himself had grown up with minimal awareness of his French ethnicity. "There was nothing," he said to me. "No cooking, no music, no language. No nothing." But of course that was not so. He had been raised in the religion of his Landry ancestors, in the Church of Rome. He even joined the Knights of Columbus when he was eighteen years old.

Bobby, who now lived in Florida, where he was a senior manager in a nationwide corporation, had married a woman of Italian descent. His son, a preteen whose main interests were rap music, the Tampa Bay Buccaneers, and playing in-line hockey, seemed even less connected to his French heritage. Yet who knew? Perhaps when this boy retired forty or fifty years from now, he too might be bitten by the genealogy bug and pore over parish records on the Internet and visit old graveyards in Quebec. The bug bit some unlikely people.

We went to a five p.m. Saturday mass at St. Patrick's, a downtown church. I assured Bobby he didn't have to accompany me – he had moved farther away from the Church since we first met, thirty years earlier, while I had moved closer – but he said he wanted to. "I find churches comforting," he said to me. "Maybe it's just a throwback to when I was a child."

The next day we visited Graceland, a house soaked through with religiosity. It was evident in the living room with its stained glass blue peacocks – symbol of immortality in Christian art – in the dining room with its ceramic Taoist sages, and everywhere in the house with images of the tiger – symbol of strength and valor in the service of righteousness in Chinese art. It was kitsch, but kitsch is not without its depths. Even the "jungle room," with its Polynesian restaurant decor and green shag carpet on the ceiling, said something about Elvis's soul.

Confirmation of his spiritual yearnings came from a display of his office. Tourists could hear a recording of his daughter as they viewed this display. "He had stacks of books next to his bed," the voice of Lisa Marie informed them through their earphones. "He read all the time. Always of a spiritual nature. Always looking. Always searching for something. He would always underline." Sure enough, on his desk there were books "of a spiritual nature" – a Bantam paperback edition of Herman Hesse's *Siddhartha*, a paperback of *Gods From Outer Space*, the Holy Bible of course. On a wooden stand a book was open to a chapter entitled "The Coming Aquarian Age and the Emancipation of Women," which was indeed heavily underlined. Beside a sentence that read, "Great changes have already taken place in the mental outlook of humanity at large, and more particularly in the position of women," Elvis had written in ink, IN KARATE. Presley, of course, was a practitioner of that particular spiritual discipline.

The tour led to an annex of the main building, a split-level lounge area full of chocolate-colored leather armchairs and footstools and a sofa where a huge teddy bear sat. (The teddy bear has become a contemporary symbol of something – grief for an individual whose death was pathetic.) "Here, on the last morning of his life, Elvis played and sang with friends," a voice informed tourists through their recorders. "Two of the songs were 'Blue Eyes Cryin' in the Rain' and 'Unchained Melody.'" Not long after the last bar of the last song was sung, the spirit of the singer in its visible envelope of flesh was taken from us. Priscilla's voice was then heard. She recalled the moment when the news of her ex-husband's death hit home. "I had gone to a movie by myself and – I'd seen all these people, it was – I forget the name of the movie, in fact, because my attention wasn't even on it," the voice said. "I remember looking around and going, how is this world going to survive without Elvis Presley?"

The last stop on the tour was a "meditation area" with a fountain and the graves of Elvis and his parents. Here was a statue of Jesus Christ with his Sacred Heart, stained glass windows, an eternal flame, golden figurines of cherubs, and little teddy bears – all the symbols and charms forbidding the idea that the destiny of Elvis Presley was to lie in cold obstruction and to rot, as Shakespeare would say. Here was the last resting place of, what? A saint? No saint was so powerful the world conceivably would not survive without him. A martyr? The grounds of his martyrdom were unclear. A deity? That was closer. Still, even the weepiest, most obsessed Elvis fan would hesitate to go that far. The old pagans used such a term freely of the illustrious dead, but two millennia of Christianity have made us shy of it.

Presley was worshipped here, that was beyond dispute. Of course we didn't need Graceland to confirm this fact. All those pictures of Elvis in roadside restaurants, in rural Ontario and Connecticut and South Dakota – they were clearly more than a salute to a heartthrob, they were icons and they portrayed a sacred person.

Elvis also had a totemic animal represent him, which was still an audacious act even in this non-natural and sophisticated world of ours. The image of the tiger adorned his famous jumpsuits and appeared as a logo on much Presley paraphernalia. This animal, besides having symbolic resonance in Chinese art, was associated with the god Dionysus in Western mythology. As someone who was always reading books "of a spiritual nature," Presley might have been aware of this. He conjured up the Dionysiac spirit of the ancient world, in music similar to that described by Nietzsche in *The Birth of Tragedy*. The music, with its visceral nature, its incitement to sexual license, swept its listeners into an ecstasy of self-forgetfulness, Nietzsche wrote. "The entire symbolism of the body was called into play – not the mere symbolism of the lips, face and speech, but the whole pantomime of dancing, forcing every member of the body into rhythmic movement."

The other sides of Presley's nature – the sentimental, sweet-natured, shrewd, vulnerable sides – merely deepened the sense Presley worshippers had of his being an avatar of the god. Was Presley half insane? Dionysus was often stark, raving mad. Did Elvis have a benign grandmother, Minnie May, who was buried in Graceland? Dionysus had a grandmother named Rhea who saved his life. Did Elvis Presley become a global phenomenon? Dionysus also traveled the world, attracting worshippers wherever he went.

What had this to do with the French? Presley married a girl named Priscilla Beaulieu. Beaulieu means "beautiful place" in French – an echo, you might say, of "Graceland." Anyone who respects the occult power of names will not regard this as trivial. (A man's name, Marshall McLuhan observed, is a numbing blow from which he never recovers.) Beaulieu divorced Presley on October 9, 1973 – on the feast day, coincidentally, of the martyred bishop of Paris and patron saint of France, Saint Denys, otherwise known as St. Dionysius. While the divorce is said to have hastened the demise of Presley, who died less than four years later – a martyr, if you will, to prescription pills and a broken heart – it proved a feast day for Priscilla, whose career subsequently blossomed and whose later management of the Presley estate turned it into an even greater bonanza than it was in Presley's lifetime. Blessed St. Dionysius. He was beheaded, by the way, and various towns in France claim the holy relic of his head – a form of veneration compared by mythographers to the veneration of the head of the god Osiris in the ancient city known as Memphis.

❧

After visiting Graceland, I said goodbye to Bobby and went in search of the site of the vanished Fort Assumption, finished on the holy day that falls on August 15, the day that celebrates the assumption of the Virgin into heaven, which is the day in the calendar before Presley's own departure from this earth, on August 16. (Presley's ancestors were Scottish, but these ghostly tendrils of the French, these little coincidences, brushed ever so lightly against him.) Finding the place was not as easy as I had thought. In the Memphis public library I examined the file on Fort Assumption, which contained two or three clippings. One was a newspaper item from 1954 showing Dr. Marshall Wingfield, president of the West Tennessee Historical Society, in a suit and tie, and Mrs. Laurence B. Gardiner, regent of the Fort Assumption Chapter of the Daughters of the American Revolution, wearing a very becoming hat. They were dedicating a new bronze tablet. According to the newspaper, the inscription on the tablet read,

> Near this point, at the highest point of the bluff, on Assumption Day, August 15, 1739, this fort was erected by Bienville, French governor of Louisiana. This was the first structure built by white men in Shelby County, and the third such in Tennessee.

The item said that the bronze tablet was near the Hanrahan Bridge.

Shortly after noon on that day I drove down E.H. Crump Boulevard, named after Boss Crump, who ruled Memphis in the first half of the twentieth century, and turned into Crump Park. The park was near the Hanrahan Bridge and a good place, I figured, to look for that tablet. I left my car in a parking area near a battered yellow Lincoln Continental, the only other vehicle in sight. In the front seat of this car, a middle-aged white man and a black woman were eating Burger King french fries and laughing. I assumed they were having an affair. I walked around the park, but there was no tablet in sight. At the edge of the park, which overlooked the bluffs and the Mississippi, the view was blocked by a wall of kudzu vine. There wasn't much else to see – just a few magnolia and hackberry trees on the greensward.

I walked back through the parking area – the couple in the Lincoln were still talking and laughing – and came to a Super 8 Motel, which had a cryptic message on its marquee: NO MORE S W. I went inside to ask the desk clerk, a young man from south Asia, what the message meant, but he was as baffled as I was when I showed it to him. Beyond the motel was another park, the Chickasaw Heritage Park, which used to be known as De Soto Park, in the days when it was still acceptable to name civic spaces after Indian-killing Europeans. Like many parks in urban America, it was forlorn, and I doubted Chickasaw heritage gained much from taking back the naming rights from poor old De Soto. In fact, I had been warned to avoid it after dark.

I walked toward the bluffs, past an Indian mound that had been turned into a battery during the Civil War, and across a street. On the other side of the street there was a narrow space overlooking the bluffs. In a little grassy area on this space, somebody had put a park bench. That person must have thought it was an excellent place to put a park bench – weary passersby could sit and enjoy the view over the Mississippi. Since then, however, vegetation above the bluffs had spread, and when I sat down my view was of a dense tangle of shrubbery two feet from my face. The branch of a young tulip poplar tree reached out and practically touched my nose. I stood up and tried to see through the greenery – the bluffs at this point, I noted, fell very steeply to the edge of the river. Meanwhile, drivers slowed down as they passed and gave me suspicious looks.

I walked back to my car and drove down a dirt road to the bank of the Mississippi, a road between the Super 8 Motel and the park. I thought I'd finally get a clear, first-hand look at the mighty river and its bluffs, but at the end of the road a sign identified the spot as the American Commercial Liquid Terminal. The gate in the chain-link fence was open, but unfriendly signs were all over the place.

Warning!
This Area Is Under Camera Surveillance.
ABSOLUTELY NO FISHING ALLOWED!
Restricted Area.
Failure to consent to screening or inspection will result in denial
or revocation of authorization to enter.
ALL CARS: Unauthorized presence within the facility
constitutes a breach of security.

While I was taking this in, someone watching through a surveillance camera must have correctly deduced that anyone who would actually read these signs did not belong here. The gate quietly but firmly slid shut in front of me. I still had not seen any sign of the tablet.

The next day I joined Dr. Charles W. Crawford, director of the oral history research office in the department of history of the University of Memphis, and a colleague, Douglas W. Cupples, at a Kiwanis luncheon. It was a buffet lunch of cold cuts in the Venetian Room of the Peabody Hotel, a high-ceilinged room with chandeliers, mirrors, and parquet floor. A minister read a verse or two from the Bible, and then we all sang *My Country 'Tis of Thee* and recited the Pledge of Allegiance. The speaker was Tommy West, coach of the Memphis Tigers of the University of Memphis, who wore a black blazer with a white chrysanthemum on the lapel and a black polo shirt. I had no idea how good a coach he was, but he certainly was a terrific speaker. He grabbed the mike. "I promise I won't tell the same jokes I told a year ago." (pause) "Who said amen?"

(laughter) He eyeballed somebody in the room. "Tell me one joke I told last year." (pause) "I thought so." (laughter)

After lunch, a woman came up to Professor Crawford and he introduced us. "Are you writing about Doctor Crawford?" she asked me brightly. "No. I'm drawing on his expertise." "Oh, they all do that. He knows *everything*." Clearly Crawford was a respected, almost venerable, authority in these parts, a short, solidly built man who smoked a pipe, wore a blazer on this summer day, with a blue-striped shirt and gray pants, spoke in lucid, grammatical sentences, and looked like a cross between a courtly, homespun lawyer and Arthur Schlesinger, Jr. After lunch, he, Professor Cupples, and I went for a drive to Crump Park. En route they explained to me that the tablet had probably disappeared long ago, the casualty of highway construction or theft or vandalism. I was mildly shocked. For some reason I thought historical markers were as permanent as lighthouses. Not so. The fine efforts of Dr. Wingfield and Mrs. Gardiner fifty years earlier had gone for nothing.

We drove by Crump Park and the Super 8 Motel. This time the sign on the marquee read: NOW MORE. Professor Cupples, an expert on the Civil War, pointed to the Indian-constructed mound. "The Union army used it as a gun platform," he said. "If you look at this north-facing slope, you will see the entrance to the powder magazine." I saw what appeared to be a little door on the slope. "They could command the entire river from this mound." Professor Crawford turned down the dirt road to the American Commercial Liquid Terminal and drove through the gate without a second thought for all that nonsense about breaches of security and threats to the homeland and what not.

We passed the main building of the terminal and stopped a few yards farther on. "This is probably the original face of the bluff, wouldn't you say?" Cupples asked Crawford as we looked up at the slope of the bluffs now covered by the ubiquitous kudzu. "I would say it has changed little, if any," Crawford replied.

"I believe the bluff face is probably very much like the one the French climbed from their boats on the river behind us here," Cupples said. So this was where all those French soldiers and Iroquois Indians and *coureurs de bois* swarmed over two hundred and fifty years ago, to seize the heart of North America for the King of France. Now there wasn't even a sign to mark the spot. Professor Crawford turned around and looked at the gray-brown waters of the Mississippi. "Look at the powerful current," he said, with genuine awe, surprising for a man who had lived here a long time. "A great deal of power here," he said. "Fantastic." It reminded me of T.S. Eliot in his fifties, writing in wartime London, summoning his boyhood memories of St. Louis and the Mississippi River. "I think that the river/ Is a strong brown god – sullen, untamed and intractable." The Illinois Indians who had tried to warn off La Salle with tales of monsters and bottomless chasms were probably drawing on their own impressions of this river. Eliot's god who watched and waited before destroying – that was a river these Indians would have recognized.

"From here to the Gulf of Mexico, it's rare that you get high places like this one," Crawford said. "When you do, it's a great place to build a town or a fort." Professor Cupples pointed to the kudzu, a lush green curtain draped over the bluff. "There was a criminal who escaped from prison," he said. "They didn't find him for quite a while. It turned out he had been living under a thick cover of kudzu – lived there for a year. He built a little hut there and he'd come out at night, foraging for food."

As we drove back to the university, I said I thought Chickasaw Heritage Park was woebegone. "This is kind of an out-of-the-way park," Crawford said. "It's isolated by the expressway, and it's in a declining area of town. High crime rate. Lots of people avoid it. Really a shame, too. It's got a lot of potential. It has a past and it will have a future."

"I agree with you," Cupples said. "Someone will develop it in the next ten, fifteen years."

"Too good to miss." Crawford then pointed out to his right, as we crossed an Interstate. "At one time there was a place called Jungle Gardens. It was one of the first drive-in restaurants, where you could drive up and be served in your car. There was also a lot of greenery that could provide a certain kind of privacy where you and your girlfriend could get to know one another. Not too many history books are going to tell you that. Doug knows things about Memphis history beyond what you can find in the books, because he's lived through this. Doug, you went to Jungle Gardens, didn't you?"

"A time or two."

"And you were accompanied by a young person of the opposite sex?"

"Always."

I asked Professor Cupples if he knew Elvis Presley. "I met him a few times," he said. "I delivered newspapers to his girlfriend in the mid-town area. I was twelve years old at the time. On Fridays we would collect the bill – it was something like seventy-five cents a week. One day I noticed a Cadillac in the driveway of this girl's house, and when I rang the bell he opened the door. He asked me, 'How much is it?' and I said, 'Eighty-five cents.' He gave me a five-dollar bill and said, 'Keep the change.' Well, that five-dollar bill made my day. The next time I came around, he wasn't there, and she answered the door and gave me eighty-five cents. So I started looking there for his car or his motorcycle when I went collecting. One day I got from him twenty dollars. He was a very nice fellow. He really was."

FOURTEEN

Arkansas Post

La Salle makes some new acquaintances • A brief account of the French Canadians of Pittsfield, Massachusetts, including an attempt on the life of their priest • I am shown ghostly orbs and butt prints • A brief account of the French of Arkansas and their singular views on news media • A lonely cemetery in Jefferson County, Arkansas

La Salle and his men had pleasant journeying once more. "With every stage of their adventurous progress," Parkman writes, "the mystery of this vast New World was more and more unveiled. More and more they entered upon the realms of spring. The hazy sunlight, the warm and drowsy air, the tender foliage, the opening flowers, betokened the reviving life of Nature." The French discovered Spanish moss and made their first acquaintance with the alligator and the catfish, a creature of protruding eyes and exaggerated whiskers and mouth. It was hard to say which aquatic animal was more grotesque. The catfish, while not big enough to swallow a truck, were nonetheless large enough – six feet long sometimes – to capsize a canoe with a slap of the tail. Lurking in the waters as well were snapping turtles that could remove an unwary man's finger, and scaly gar, with teeth that could rend flesh.

One day, just about where Jolliet and Marquette had turned back nine years earlier, the river was covered in a dense fog. From the west bank came the sound of drumming and war songs. La Salle and his men hurried to the opposite side, where they landed and constructed a makeshift fort in less than an hour. By that time the fog had lifted, and the Indians across the river got a good look at the white men working so hard with their axes. A canoe came across the water and halted in midstream; La Salle held out the calumet. Soon enough La Salle and his men were in a village of the Quapaw Indians, near the junction of the Arkansas River and the Mississippi, where they were treated very well, according to Father Membré, one of the friars. "I cannot tell you the courtesy and fine treatment we received from these barbarians," he wrote in a letter to his superior. "They let us lodge where we wanted, swept the place clean for us, brought us poles to make our lodges, gave us firewood for the three days we spent with them, and treated us to one feast after another. . . . But my Reverend Father, this gives no idea of the good-hearted qualities of these savages, who are extremely cheerful, upright and generous [*joyeux, honnêtes et libéraux*]." As Membré's letter indicates, the French from the beginning fell in love with the Quapaws. They were to remain staunch allies for as long as the French laid claim to Arkansas. "They are so well formed [*si bien faits et proportionné*] that we were in admiration at their beauty and their modesty," Father Membré declared. A later priest, a Jesuit, Father Pierre de Charlevoix, said the members of this nation "are reckoned the tallest and most handsome of men of all the Indians of this continent." Granted that the "swarthy, stunted Frenchmen" of the seventeenth century were almost always bowled over by the robust physical qualities of the Indians they met – as witness Father Sagard's response to the Hurons – it is clear that the Quapaws were particularly healthy specimens in French eyes. What was also nice about the Quapaws, Father Membré added, is that they didn't try to steal anything.

On the third day of the party, the Europeans planted a cross with French arms in the middle of the village, thus formally claiming this people and this land as King Louis XIV's own. It is impossible to know how much the Quapaws understood of this ceremonial act. If it meant French help in killing their enemies, that was fine. Perhaps the cross itself was full of power and the sign under which they would conquer.

❧

My first stop in Arkansas, just south of Memphis, was the town of Helena – *A Main Street City*, according to the sign welcoming motorists. I parked my car and walked down that main street. It was deserted. Although it was the middle of a weekday, such stores as still existed were mostly closed. I passed Ed's TV Repair, with dusty television sets in the window and a handwritten sign on the door that read: "This store has an automatic alarm. IF you enter this store anywhere it will go off at the Police station, and you will be caught. Ed." It was hard to figure what other stores were actually selling, judging from the contents of their display windows – an old tennis racket and a swimsuit in one place that had an Open For Business sign, contradicted by another sign on the door, a green piece of cardboard. "Hi!" the handwritten green cardboard sign proclaimed. "Yes we're open. But ... only Friday's 10: Am - 5: pm and Saturday's 10: Am - 2: pm Come see me!! Bertha."

One store that really was open was Gist Music, with its pine floor and high ceiling, from which hung fluorescent lighting fixtures and rotating fans. The proprietor, Morse Gist, invited me to look around. Normally a store like this, selling mostly guitars, would have at least two or three aspiring young musicians inspecting the merchandise, but according to Gist potential customers were in short supply in Helena. "Well, truly there are not many young folks around here any more," he said. "Things are bad. It's got so an industrious young person almost *has* to move away." Once, Helena was such an important port on the Mississippi that President William Howard Taft visited its opera house (since burned down). Now, like a lot of Mississippi Delta towns, Helena was dying. Chemical plants, a tire and rubber factory, had shut down in recent years. Only agriculture – corn, rice, cotton, soybeans – and tourism kept the town alive. The King Biscuit Blues Festival in October, plus a motorcycle festival in the spring, pumped a fair bit of oxygen into the town's bloodstream, but the patient still looked peaked. The worst of it was that the town no longer nurtured the young blues musicians that made the Delta famous. "You just have a few cafés left, basically," Gist said. "There used to be a lot of juke joints – the Blacks had a community in the south part of town. But they're all gone. There's no place where you can play music now." And what of his customers, I asked him. Who came to buy or sell or have his guitar repaired these days? Tourists? "Oh, they come in to see the museum quality of the store," he said.

Outside, two men were talking in front of a pickup truck parked by the curb, and that was it for street traffic. It reminded me of the last time I visited North Street, Pittsfield's main drag – a thriving downtown when my parents moved away in 1962, but in the twenty-first century a rehabilitation project. It shared with Helena the same combination of empty storefronts, social agencies, and the odd marginal store. The England Brothers department store, the heart of North Street, was an empty shell. Pedestrians were few.

I headed toward the Magnolia Hill Bed & Breakfast on Perry Street, where I was staying for the night, and thought about the strange twists of history. If La Salle had had his way, Ed and Bertha would have written their notes in French. The hills of western Massachusetts, on the other hand, interested him not at all. That was the territory of *les Bostonnais*, and they were welcome to it. But in the nineteenth century his countrymen did come to western Massachusetts – and the growing city of Pittsfield. (The city, coincidentally, was named after William Pitt, the British statesman who was almost single-handedly responsible for the defeat of the French in North America.) They came as a conquered people, a race that produced reliable employees in the textile mills of that town because the French Canadians, with their large families, approached mill work in the same way they approached farm work, in family units. If the foreman was French Canadian, he was often supervising his own sons and nephews and cousins.

Pittsfield, however, never produced a French-Canadian ghetto in the manner of larger New England cities, such as Manchester and Lowell and Woonsocket. The textile industry began to fade at the end of the century, and Pittsfield might have withered like other mill towns had not a local engineer named William Stanley invented something called "a polyphase alternating-current generator." His factory was purchased by General Electric in 1903, and for most of the twentieth century that corporation ran Pittsfield. The G.E. works employed French Canadians, but the dominant immigrant workforce, at the start of the twentieth century, were the Italians, who frightened the locals when they first appeared with their gypsy-like tendency to camp out wherever they found employment, and their Sicilian-style feuds, complete with lethal knife fights. At St. Joseph's High School in Pittsfield, I ran across students with names such as La Croix and Lapointe, but we were scattered among the Irish, Poles, and Italians.

It was General Electric that brought my father to Pittsfield, just before the war. He had been trained as an architect at the University of New Hampshire, but graduated in the midst of the Depression and survived by taking odd jobs until he finally found permanent employment with G.E. In Pittsfield we lived an upper-middle-class existence, in a split-level home with a big lawn and a station wagon in the garage. My parents, in the manner of second-generation immigrants to the United States, spoke the language of the old country only when they didn't want the children to understand what they were saying. It would have seemed vaguely un-American for them to have taught us French at home. Odd bits of French-Canadian culture survived in our 1950s American lifestyle – the phrase *Joyeux Noël* for Merry Christmas, the word *caca* for shit, the stuffing of our Thanksgiving turkey with "French-Canadian dressing," which consisted of mashed potatoes, hamburger, pork, and onions instead of what my father disparagingly referred to as "Yankee dressing," i.e., pieces of bread.

Even the church where we worshipped was run by Irish priests. The pastor of St. Teresa's was Henry P. Sullivan, a heavyset man who occasionally regaled the children in catechism class with stories of his work at a juvenile reformatory. There were no bars on the windows, he informed us, so a visitor might be fooled as to the nature of the institution, but if an inmate tried to open a window, an alarm went off. The point of this story is lost in memory, but I believe it had to do with there generally being No Escape. Father Sullivan's methods of teaching the catechism were unusual – he liked to ask the younger children to "name the three gods." If they were so unwary as to answer Father, Son, and Holy Spirit, they soon discovered their mistake. Once he invited children at a first communion to test their parents' knowledge of the catechism, and one seven-year-old stood up and said, "Name the three gods." The audience of parents thoroughly enjoyed Father Sullivan's embarrassment – he was widely disliked in that parish. He was heavy-handed and maladroit in his relations with parishioners. He drank his whiskey in a teacup.

None of which is to say he was not a true priest or true man of God. He did his best, I'm sure. He was also, for what it's worth, a progressive of sorts. St. Teresa's was built in 1954, and at the time it was unique among the fourteen thousand or so Catholic churches of America – a flat-roofed, brick structure, with minimal adornment and a plain altar, consisting of a slab of Italian marble, surrounded on three sides by pews. "Harking back to the mass sung by the early Christians, the altar is traditional in the deepest sense of the word," Father Sullivan told a reporter from the *Berkshire Eagle*. He was anticipating the liturgical reforms of the Vatican Council, a decade in the future. In the same vein, and much to the annoyance of the congregation, he tried to introduce a "dialogue mass," in which the faithful were asked to join in the responses to the celebrant, instead of silently following the mass in their missal, or, more likely, pondering what they were going to have for Sunday dinner. It was at St. Teresa's that I learned to say "Holy Spirit" instead of "Holy Ghost" when referring to the Third Person of the Blessed Trinity. (Or the third god, if you were misinformed.) Change was in the air, and Father Sullivan was no slouch in picking up the scent.

Unlike Father Chiniquy and some of his parishioners in Illinois, we Catholics of French-Canadian descent didn't chafe under the ecclesiastical rule of the Irish. By this time we were all Americans. If Father Sullivan was unpopular, it was not because of ethnic reasons. More persistent was a long and lingering suspicion between Protestants and Catholics. Pittsfield had been in existence for sixty-five years before a Catholic set foot in the town, in 1825. That was the Marquis de Lafayette – a French Catholic, but decidedly not of the Canadian variety – en route to lay the cornerstone of the Bunker Hill monument in Boston. Less distinguished Catholics came soon after. In an unpublished book entitled *Catholic Pittsfield*, written in 1897 by Katherine F. Mullaney, we read of an incident in 1835 when a visiting priest named Jeremiah O'Callahan was walking the streets of Pittsfield in company with an Irish settler, one Thomas Coleman. A member of the local gentry spotted the pair and said, in a voice loud enough for them to hear, "What's that? A Catholic priest! I would give ten dollars for his head!" It was not a wholly idle threat – this was in an era when Catholic churches were burned and priests tarred and feathered in the good old Commonwealth of Massachusetts. "Irish fire gleamed in the eyes, and Irish wrath doubled up the fists of honest Tom Coleman when he heard this truly Cromwellian remark," Mullaney writes. "Meeting the same haughty bigot on the way back, he marched up to him with true Celtic indignation and courage that is never a respecter of 'Gentry' when his priest or church is assailed, and said, 'Look ye here, Mister, if ye ever make a remark like that again, your own head won't be worth ten cents, ye small minded spalpeen.'"

Bravo Paddy! But why couldn't honest Tom Coleman have been honest Pierre Laframboise? (Peter Raspberry, in English.) Where was somebody to display that true Canuck indignation and courage? There's no answering these questions. The French who came to New England in the nineteenth century were not a very aggressive lot. In fact, they were deeply resigned, and it is not easy to discern exactly where their resignation came from. The bone-chilling Canadian winters, the vast, dark wilderness at their doorsteps which would never be settled, never be tamed, the profound historical sense of being hopelessly under siege by enemies, the unfathomable rigor of the God brought to these shores by Bishop Laval, who drank the pus of diseased men – all these might have been its ingredients. In his novel *The Country*, David Plante describes his response to some of his Franco-American relatives:

> For me, they brought with them a crude air as of a settlement
> in the woods . . . a settlement which was not really a success: the
> cabins were falling apart, the chimneys of the wood stoves were
> rusting, the cooking pots had holes, and soon, the settlement
> would be abandoned, but no one in it knew where to go. They
> had not really expected the settlement to be a success, but, now,
> they did not know what to do, and perhaps they would do
> nothing; or perhaps they would go to a city, where, somehow,
> they would continue to live in the woods.

In a way the French-Canadian mill workers of Manchester and Lowell and Woonsocket and Pittsfield continued to live in the woods, spiritually, in settlements they never expected to be a great success. In his *Visions of Gerard*, Jack Kerouac writes of meeting a childhood acquaintance from Lowell, a man with the surname Plourdes. Kerouac bursts out, "Plourdes – A Canadian name containing in it for me all the despair, raw hopelessness, cold and chapped sorrow of Lowell." The Franco-Americans, Kerouac included, viewed worldly ambition as intolerable vanity. It would be punished in some way or other. "That anyone should realize his will and be honored for realizing it filled me with enough jealousy of his vanity that I would have liked to see his world end," says the Franco-American narrator of Plante's novel *The Accident*.

The same narrator reflects, "But I love everyone," and that is also true, in an odd way. If Yeats is right when he tells his daughter that "an intellectual hatred is the worst," the Franco-Americans were spared the worst of history's vices. "After centuries in the Canadian forests, my family had not only lost all sense of an intellectual whole, of any system, they were hardly capable of conceiving ideas," the narrator of *The Accident* informs us. (The Church is not an intellectual system, by the way – the Church is the body of Christ.) For this reason, or for others, the Franco-Americans were never great haters.

Certainly the French Canadians who came to Pittsfield did not frighten the locals as much as the Sicilians who arrived later, and they were hardly as pugnacious as the Irish. They were tolerated, more or less. In 1867, Katherine Mullaney tells us, the first French parish was founded in Pittsfield, to service the approximately one hundred French-Canadian families in that town. The following year someone fired several bullets through a window into the confessional at a time of day when the pastor, Father Derbuil, customarily heard confessions. Fortunately, Father Derbuil was away, and so his life was spared. The shooter was never apprehended, of course.

It must be said that by the time I arrived on the scene, Catholic priests could walk the streets of Pittsfield and go about their pastoral business without fear for their lives. Shortly after my family left Pittsfield in 1962, the Second Vatican Council began and relations between Catholics and Protestants became even warmer – it would soon be possible for Catholics to walk into a Protestant church and not anticipate a blast of lightning. Meanwhile I did not miss St. Teresa's. And I rarely returned for a visit to the city, and so was not around to witness the blight that fell on Pittsfield when General

Electric scaled back its operations in the 1980s. So devastated was the city that it became a case study for researchers. In 1998 an anthropologist named Max H. Kirsch published his study about Pittsfield, *In the Wake of the Giant: Multinational Restructuring and Uneven Development in a New England Community*. In 2004, a writer named Joanna Lipper published a rather more popular account of teenage mothers in Pittsfield, *Growing Up Fast*, setting the sad lives of these abused and disheartened women against the background of a depressed and disintegrating community.

"Tourism is still regarded as a savior for the Pittsfield region," Kirsch notes in his book. But are there enough tourists in the world to save Pittsfield, as well as places such as Hallettsville, Texas, and Helena, Arkansas? Will half of the United States, littered with abandoned factories, be turned into a theme park for new waves of visitors from more bustling places on the earth?

⚜

After I checked into Magnolia Hill, I went back to the only bar/restaurant I could see open in the downtown area for a night-cap. At the bar a local asked me where I was staying, and when I mentioned Magnolia Hill he said, "That's the old Tardy place. It's crawling with ghosts." The bartender gave him a look, which I interpreted as, stop pulling the Yankee's leg. Back at Magnolia Hill – where I had chosen the Ruby and Blue Room, which had nice oak furniture and a door that opened on to a porch – I crawled into bed and experienced an uneventful night, except for a visit to the bathroom at three in the morning. When I rose for breakfast, my hostess, Jane Insco, joined me. I forgot how we got on to the subject, but she told me the house did have a number of supernatural inhabitants.

"The first thing I started hearing when I moved in, it would sound like five or six footsteps in the house," Insco said. "I'd run to the door and there was nobody there and the doors were all locked.

But it really hit me one day when my daughter and I were working on the house, doing restoration, and my little grandson, he would stand and point like this," Insco pointed her finger at a patch of air in front of her, "and say, 'What's that?' We would say, 'Nobody's there. Who's there?' And he would just point. He did that a number of different times. It used to terrify my daughter. Since then there's been times I've heard a baby crying inside the house. You couldn't hear it outside, but I would come in and hear it. I've heard someone call my name on a couple different occasions. Once it was a female voice, a very soft voice, you know, and the other time it was like they were shouting at me. They would call my name, and nobody was at the house but me."

Jane Insco was a trim, dark-haired woman, who was friendly but also business-like, in the manner of a hard-working real estate agent. She was not obviously a devotee of the paranormal, like those men and women who wear rings on every finger and a half-dozen silver ornaments around their necks. Her guests – solid citizens, no-nonsense ordinary Americans – had also encountered a spirit or two. "In the Emerald Room there's a picture on a wall," Insco said, "and I had a couple staying there, they told me they were lying on the bed and the picture turned sideways. I said, really. That was a new one. I didn't know about that. Well, one day, while I was cleaning the room, I saw it, the picture turned sideways. I thought, oh my God, they told me the truth.

"It's usually mischievous teasing things. It's not like people are trying to harm you."

Still, some guests do not like being teased by beings from another dimension, no matter how harmless. "It's typically men who it scares more than women," Insco said, and related the story of some computer technicians who were staying at Magnolia Hill while working on the slot machines at the local casino. One of the men, who was sleeping in the Ruby and Blue Room, reported a dream he had of a woman standing at the foot of his bed – a dream often experienced by guests at Magnolia Hill. The woman appeared to have long, light brown hair and wore a long dress. "He came down in the morning," Insco recalled, "and he said, 'Last night I looked up and there was a woman standing at the foot of my bed.' He said, 'It really scared me. She went away, but I couldn't get back to sleep. Then I heard someone stomping up the stairs, and I thought, I shouldn't be hearing anybody on the stairs at this hour, and then I felt someone sit on the bed beside me. I felt the weight on the bed. The strange thing was, I felt very calm and comforted and I went right back to sleep.' Then the guy in the Peridot Room came down, and he said, 'I was sleeping last night, and I woke up and a woman was standing at the foot of my bed.' Same night, same time. I said, 'What happened?' 'I don't know, I covered my head,' he said. 'But then I felt someone sit on the side of my bed, I could feel the weight.' He told me the very same thing the guy who had come down earlier had told me. He said, 'I felt very calm and comforted.' 'Was she gone then?' He said, 'No, I never uncovered my head.' And the fellow who was in your room said, 'I don't know if I can stay here any more.' Most people don't get that freaked out about it. It's more men, like I say. But when he came back later that day, he said, 'I told everybody at work and they thought it was fun. They were all excited. I called my wife and she's keen to get down here. She's coming down on the weekend.'

"One weekend I had a couple from Mississippi that stayed in the Emerald Room, where more things like this happen. They stayed three nights and the last morning her and her husband came down, and she said, 'You know, we've had some horrific things happen in our room.' I said, 'Like what?' She said, 'I'm very, very sensitive to things. Everywhere I go, usually if they're around, I see them.' And she said, 'Last night a woman came in the room.' Described the same scene as everybody else. And she said, 'We talked for hours.' She said, 'Not out loud. And she was telling me about her life.' She said, 'When the woman left, I just started sobbing and crying.' And her husband said, 'She did. She woke me up sobbing and carrying on. We've been through this before when she sees things.' She said, 'We went outside in the yard, and she had some children out there and she was showing me all of her children.' This all happened in her room, by the way. It was a mental thing, being out in the yard. She said in her mind they were out in the yard and she saw all of her children. And she said, 'When she left, I was inconsolable.' I don't know. As far as I know, nothing tragic has happened in this house. I'm not aware that anyone has died in the house. She said she was just picking up on the woman's sadness, is all it was, nothing tragic going on. It appeared she was just telling her about her life. She said the conversation was not audible, it was telepathic."

Insco showed me a photograph, hanging on the wall, of the man who built the house in 1895, a cotton merchant named Charles Lawson Moore. Beside his portrait was that of his wife, Mary Horner Moore, her hair swept up in a pompadour, her chin set firmly above a high collar. She must have been the woman whose sad tale made the woman from Mississippi cry. It was hard to judge from the photograph what this woman's life had been like. She was unsmiling, but nobody smiled in nineteenth-century photographs. Her gaze was solemn, and a little wistful perhaps. Insco also showed me some snapshots taken of the inside of her house by some visiting "ghost stalkers." The photographs showed these little round white balls floating in the air. The color was the same as that of the substance Suzanne Tetrault had captured on film in the powder magazine of Fort Niagara, but unlike the latter phenomenon, the shapes on Insco's photographs were perfectly round. "The ghost hunters tell me they're called orbs," Insco said. "They think it's spirits that are still here on earth, and it's their energy." She showed me another photograph of a quilt on a bed, and what appeared to be a slight depression on the surface of the quilt. Actually, you had to look really hard to see it. One of the ghost stalkers had been sitting on the bed when a ghostly something sat down beside her. The depression on the quilt marked the spot. The ghost hunter called it the invisible entity's butt print.

I felt disappointed that Mrs. Moore had not appeared at the foot of my bed during the night. I felt like somebody who pays full fare for a show and then the star doesn't show up. I had to remind myself that the existence of ghosts is considered laughable by every rational person and that my disappointment indicated weakness of intellect. Then again, as Samuel Johnson said on the question of the existence of ghosts, "All argument is against it; but all belief is for it." Most of us can never completely rid ourselves of that belief. Moreover, it was appropriate that ghosts would be prevalent in a town, like Helena, that was disintegrating. In literature, as critic Northrop Frye has observed, the ghost is often presented as "a fragment of a disintegrating personality." Mrs. Moore might not be a fragment, but she would be more at home in an earthly environment heavy with a sense of loss.

If she was indeed lurking in the Ruby and Blue Room during the night I spent there, I think I know the reason she didn't appear to me. Before I went to bed I said my prayers, like all good Christians should do, especially when traveling. That might have repelled her, or any of her fellow ghosts – not because they are evil, but because they are as yet unreconciled to God.

✤

After breakfast I drove south from Helena to the Arkansas Post National Memorial, about eighteen miles upriver from the mouth of the Arkansas. The post was first established in 1686 by Henri Tonty, who had been granted the land four years earlier by La Salle as they proceeded upriver on their return journey from the mouth of the Mississippi to Illinois. Tonty was too occupied by affairs in Illinois to take immediate advantage of the grant, but when word reached him in 1686 that La Salle was somewhere on the Gulf, he set out with a search party to find him. Once again Tonty and his men voyaged down the Mississippi, but they never found La Salle.

Before returning a second time to Illinois, Tonty did, however, leave six men to establish a trading post on his concession, and for a while it enjoyed the distinction of being the only white settlement west of the Mississippi. But it was ill-starred. The problem was that these six men had very little to trade with. Four of them lost heart and returned to Illinois. A year later, Henri Joutel and a few other survivors of La Salle's Texas expedition who had escaped from the grip of their leader's assassins and spent six months in the wilderness trying to find their way to the Mississippi caught sight of their house and the great wooden cross they had erected. It was a moment of inexpressible joy both for the two lonely traders left at the post and for Joutel's party.

For another dozen years the post struggled to maintain itself, until a depressed European market for furs led to its closing. Whether the wooden cross remained standing as the house the Frenchmen had built fell to ruins and the site was reclaimed by deer and fox and the odd black bear – whether the Quapaws occasionally consulted this strange *manitou* before going off to war – is unknown to us. In 1717, meanwhile, the financier John Law launched his campaign to make Louisiana a paying proposition. He soon realized that the site of Tonty's defunct establishment, equidistant between New Orleans and the Fort de Chartres in Illinois, was too strategically valuable to leave unclaimed. In 1721 fifty or so Frenchmen took possession of a tract of land not far from the old trading post, and the settlement known as Arkansas Post was reborn. It would move a few miles up and down the river, according to the exigencies of war and flooding, but it would remain French until Louisiana was given to the Spanish at the end of the Seven Years' War. When Spain joined the cause of the American revolutionaries and declared war against Great Britain in 1779, the outpost immediately became a British target. In April 1783 a Scot named James Colbert, a former British officer who married into the Chickasaw nation and became one of its great men (he owned 150 black slaves), led an assault on Arkansas Post in what was probably the last engagement in the Revolutionary War and one of only two battles in that war fought west of the Mississippi River. He was repulsed.

With the Louisiana Purchase, Arkansas Post became an American town, and for a very brief period the capital of the new Arkansas Territory. Confederate troops built a fort there during the Civil War but failed to prevent its capture in January 1863 by Union forces. This was the third, and final, siege of Arkansas Post, following a Chickasaw attack in 1749 and the Colbert raid. Where the first two had failed, northern General John A. McClernand succeeded. It has been said that the town never fully recovered from the destruction wrought by that campaign. But what really destroyed Arkansas Post as a community was a force more powerful than armed combatants. The near annual flooding of the Arkansas River and its unpredictability were to Arkansas Post what hurricanes were to Indianola, a death warrant. In the early years of the twentieth century, the river changed course permanently, and Arkansas Post found itself no longer a river port. In 1929 the site became a state park, and in 1960 it was incorporated into the national park system as the Arkansas Post National Memorial.

It was five in the afternoon when I arrived at the park. Nobody else was in sight, but by this time I was used to the loneliness of these places. I followed a walkway to a bench that overlooked a thirty-foot wooden cross – a replica of the original erected by Tonty's men – and a channel of the river. It was only about a quarter of a mile across to the other side and what looked like an impenetrable wall of trees. I sat down on the bench and enjoyed the view, with the light of a declining sun imparting a mellow tone to the light green scum and a field of lotus plants on the water. There was no breeze, and no motion on the river, and the quiet was restful, interrupted by the whistling of some birds and the percussive calls of others. Occasionally I would hear a plop in the water, or thrashing in the woods, but what creatures were responsible for these disturbances remained out of sight.

Arkansas Post, in the days of the French, was never much of a place, even though it was the only European settlement worthy of the name in what is now the state of Arkansas. (It is true that French-speaking hunters formed a more or less permanent encampment at a place called Petit Rocher, later called by the Americans Little Rock.) "Even as late as 1790, the Arkansas Post commandant reported a population at his village that barely exceeded one hundred," writes Morris S. Arnold in his book *Colonial Arkansas 1686–1804: A Social and Cultural History*. Arnold, who is described in the book jacket as a "United States Circuit Judge for the Eighth District," is one of those diligent and savvy amateur historians, or independent scholars, we have met before. Much of what follows is pillaged from *Colonial Arkansas* and also his book on the Quapaws, *The Rumble of a Distant Drum*. In the former work, Morris sums up one important question: "It is safe to conclude that there were never more than eight or ten real farmers at any one time at the Post in the colonial period." The periodic flooding of the Arkansas River discouraged agriculture, but that was incidental. Arkansas Post was not meant for *habitants*. It was meant for soldiers, merchants, and the hunters these merchants outfitted.

Hunting was the economic mainstay of French Arkansas because of the amazing plenitude of game in that region – buffalo, deer, and bears, chiefly. Arnold quotes a traveler to Arkansas in the late eighteenth century: "Without exaggeration, it can be said the world does not have a country where more excellent and abundant meats can be taken out or with greater ease." Another Arkansas Post observer quoted by Arnold noted that "people subsist mostly by hunting, and every season send to New Orleans great quantities of bear's oil, tallow, salted buffalo meat, and a few skins." Bear's oil was melted bear fat. The French used it instead of olive oil in cooking stews or frying food or even as salad dressing. It was tasty. Tim Kent and his wife used to take bear oil with them on their own wilderness expeditions.

French hunters, in the manner of French fur traders, freely added to the gene pool of the Quapaws, as well as to that of the

Osage, Kansas, Loup, and Paduca nations, so that by the time the Americans arrived at the beginning of the nineteenth century, they found virtually the entire population of Arkansas Post to be of mixed blood. Generally the Arkansas hunters made fur traders look like models of bourgeois respectability – they were even more lawless and uprooted and had almost no ties to the Church, since priests were scarce at Arkansas Post. Many of these hunters had come up from New Orleans, Arnold notes, as men already on the run from the law, hardened criminals or deserters from the army or navy. A Spanish official declared that the Arkansas River, on the banks of which the hunters roamed, was "the asylum of the most wicked persons, without doubt, in all the Indies."

Of course, many of the hunters were simply men who enjoyed freedom and the outdoor life. When they hit town and had settled their accounts with the local merchants, they enjoyed drinking and gambling and dancing, which gave Arkansas Post the same frolicsome air as Kaskaskia or Ste. Genevieve. Everybody at Arkansas Post, it seems, enjoyed attending a ball, or playing cards or billiards. Once again, visiting Americans disapproved. A Presbyterian preacher aptly named Timothy Flint, who arrived around the time Arkansas was organized as a territory in 1819, recalled, "The French people generally came to the place of worship arrayed in their ball-dresses, and went directly from worship to the ball. A billiard-room was near, and parts of my audience sometimes came in for a moment, and after listening to a few sentences, returned to their billiards."

Highly literate Americans were also struck by the indifference of the locals to printed matter – like French Canada, Louisiana under the Bourbons had no printing press. Washington Irving, who had recorded the colorful but not very intelligent antics of the *voyageurs* in Michigan, found himself among the French in Arkansas and was struck by their antipathy to newspapers. According to Irving, the French thought that newspaper-reading Americans "trouble themselves with cares beyond their horizon and import sorrow through the newspapers from every point of the compass."

In the decades after the Americans arrived, the French drifted away from Arkansas Post. The market for bear oil, evidently, was no longer lively. The place had never been particularly enticing, anyway – the climate and the mosquitos were deadly. "The greatest torture, compared to which everything else is positively amusing, and which passes all belief – certainly nobody in France could imagine it – is the cruel persecution of the mosquitos [*les maringouins*]," wrote the Jesuit Father Poisson, who visited Arkansas in 1727. "This little creature has caused more swearing among the French of the Mississippi than has been uttered since the beginning of the world." During the evening meal, he reported, "we are eaten, devoured; they enter our mouths, our nostrils, our ears; our faces, hands, and bodies are covered with them." The *petit animal* made sleep at night impossible.

No wonder a Spanish commandant called Arkansas Post "the most disagreeable hole in the universe."

⚜

In 1998 archeologists found a buried settlement in the lower reaches of the Arkansas River that clearly belonged to the time of the French. It was named the Wallace Bottom site. As they continued to dig up hand-forged nails and glass beads and tinkling cones – a common ornament among the Indians of eastern North America – and musket balls and fragments of iron tools and shards of green-glazed earthenware similar to that produced in Quebec at the time, the archeologists concluded that Wallace Bottom was the place where Tonty established his trading post. As in Texas, the precise geographical outlines of the empire – an empire in embryonic stage – were being filled in. The wandering footsteps of La Salle and Tonty were being charted. You could almost be sure, if you followed those charts, that you were standing in the same soil as had these men. Except in Arkansas the soil kept shifting. The river shifted it. I found this a mildly unsettling notion, coming from New England, where the mountains and lakes had been nailed in place since the end of the last Ice Age. They had stayed put. In eastern Arkansas, the surface of the earth was still being molded. It was like a taste of the Pleistocene Epoch.

"We haven't found evidence of agriculture – either maize or anything like that," John House told me. Professor House was the station archeologist at the University of Arkansas, Pine Bluff. I talked to him in his office at Pine Bluff, in what looked like a small warehouse filled with boxes and drawers. Inside the boxes and drawers were piles of Ziploc bags, and inside the Ziploc bags were objects about the size of fingernails, in shades of gray and brown. They were things that had been dug up. With god-like patience, the archeologists and their volunteer assistants had separated these valuable little objects from the very similar-looking but worthless pebbles and clods of dirt they were embedded in, and they had brushed the dirt off them and saved them. The objects in the bags would tell a story, and give it a date, except for the little glass beads, which drove archeologists nuts because they had been the same for hundreds of years.

The story these objects told about Wallace Bottom was very similar to the story Morris Arnold told about Arkansas Post. "They did a little bit of farming and raising of livestock, but the real main-stay of the colony was either trading with the Indians or hunting," House said. The story, however, was far from finished. "We think that maybe ten years from now, when we've done a lot of work, there will be some big surprises – when we've dug more in the site and have more material," House said. "We're in such a very early stage of investigating the site."

What did the story, in the meantime, have to tell us today? The motto of the Arkansas Archeology Survey, of which Dr. House was a part, was "The Past Should Be Forever." But Tonty and the French traders and hunters had blown through the plains of eastern Arkansas like dust in the wind. What was their piece of forever? For a start, they gave names to places in the state, such as its capital, which was something. The two thousand residents of the southern Arkansas town that gloried in the name of Smackover, for example, could thank the French, who called the place *Chemin Couvert*, the "covered way." In the fullness of time, English speakers converted the French syllables into Smackover. Why did the French call it the Covered Way? House shrugged. No one knew.

Some family names in the state also testified to the presence of the French. A hunter in the eighteenth century might have been French enough to have a first name like André, but Indian enough to be called *le Sauvage* by a trader or post commandant. *André le Sauvage.* André the Indian. As time went by, some of his descendants might have left with the last of the Quapaws to live in the northeast corner of Oklahoma. Other descendants might have become European enough to identify with the whites and end up in the Little Rock telephone directory under the name of Savage. The descendant living in Oklahoma with his fellow Quapaws might have blue eyes, like George Gilbert in Kahnawake, and the descendant in Little Rock might have brown eyes and high cheekbones and still be regarded as much of a white man as William Jefferson Clinton. I imagined Mr. Savage of Little Rock residing in a neat bungalow with a backyard, but being still kin in spirit to the Franco-American family in New England mentioned by David Plante, living like them in a metaphorical settlement in the woods, with the cabin falling apart and the chimney rusting. Spiritually, the past should not be forever, but often it feels like that.

The social structure of Arkansas Post, Arnold writes, was quite similar to the "more familiar Latin republics to the south of us, with the very interesting difference that in Arkansas the mestizo peasant component of the society were hunters rather than subsistence farmers." John House agreed. "I have spent some time in Latin America, so I know what it looks like down there," he told me. "When I came back I started seeing hints of that here." He mentioned the place names and the family names, and the Virgin of Guadaloupe, symbol of the *nova raza*, the new race, because the minds of her devotees had been prepared for her coming by a centuries-old worship of the goddess Tonantzin. There was no equivalent of the Virgin of Guadaloupe among the hunters of Arkansas, but the same mix of European and native Indian religious sensibilities could be seen in other ways. "At Wallace Bottom we came across some graves showing hints of European or Christian burial customs," House told me. "Their heads were to the east and the graves were more rectangular than we were used to seeing. But there were also grave goods – these tinkling cones and hundreds of beads."

As the United States becomes generally more Hispanic, this old echo of a French-speaking *nova raza* will be overlaid by the real thing, in the way that Mexican Americans now fill the pews of St. Anne's in Detroit, once the parish of Johnny Couteau. What does remain of *André le Sauvage* in Arkansas is hard to pin down, but it survives most visibly in the countryside, where families live in real – not metaphorical – cabins in the woods, or mobile homes, or weather-beaten old farmhouses, where the chimneys rust and the cooking pots have holes in them, and everybody has a gun and everybody hunts. These are tougher and more eccentric country people than their counterparts in Tennessee or North Carolina. They are not southerners and they are not westerners. They are marginal in every sense of the word, and it is likely that one of the sources of their stubborn unwillingness to come out of the woods is the mixed blood of the Quapaws and the French that flows in their veins. They may have inherited only a few drops of such blood, but it tells.

⚜

Before I left Arkansas I visited a spot that John House told me about, a place called St. Peter's Cemetery. It was located in a town called New Gascony that doesn't exist any more. Once I had found it I parked my car and climbed over the rusty chain-link fence surrounding the cemetery. It was not large – four rows of graves, with nine or ten graves in each one. A granite monument told the story. One Antoine Barraque, a veteran of Napoleon's army, came to the United States in 1817. "After living briefly in Arkansas Post," the monument read, "he moved up river and established a landing named for his home land. Floods forced the settlement inland." For a century, the little town hung on. Immigrants from Italy, twenty-nine families, came to farm the land in 1905 – a few of their number were buried in the western-most row of graves. "Following the flood of 1927 and a period of depressed farm prices most of these hard working families living around St. Peter's Cemetery moved away," the monument said. New Gascony joined Arkansas Post and innumerable other American towns in oblivion.

Thunder sounded from a bank of clouds to the south, but overhead the sun was shining. It was a beautiful day. To the west was a line of trees, to the north rows of corn about the height of a man, brown in the late July sun. To the east grew dark green cotton plants with their tufts of white, to the south a field of grass that ended in another line of trees. That was all I could see on the horizon. Inside the cemetery, pecan trees shaded the mown grass. Near them was a group of six tombstones belonging to the Bogy – or, as they were originally known, the Baugis – family. According to the information on these tombstones, they came from the province of Poitou, France, to Quebec, Canada, in 1641. A scion of this family, who spelled his name Joseph Beaugi, settled in Kaskaskia, Illinois, in 1768 and then removed to Arkansas Post twenty years later. He was not a fur trader or a hunter. He was a good bourgeois who served as an appraiser when the Americans arrived. His descendants eventually became known as the Bogy family, and they were prominent in this part of the country.

While I was examining the final resting place of the Bogys I heard a low hum. It came from a swarm of bees in a hollow of a dead juniper tree. Something about the hum stirred a literary memory of bees in a graveyard, and later it came to me – Emily

Dickinson's poem that begins "Safe in their alabaster chambers,/ Untouched by morning and untouched by noon,/ Sleep the meek members of the resurrection . . ." The Bogys and the Dumonds and the Dardennes and the Gracies and the Palazzis and the Mangonis were not housed in "alabaster chambers," they lay in humble graves, but they, too, were untouched by morning and untouched by noon, and they, too, were awaiting the resurrection. "Light laughs the breeze in her castle of sunshine;/ Babbles the bee in a stolid ear . . ." Dickinson could have been writing about St. Peter's Cemetery on this summer day. "Ah, what sagacity perished here!" Typical of Emily. You didn't know if she was expressing hope or despair. Despair always seemed more likely, given the facts of the matter — we knew for a fact that the sagacity of Joseph Beaugi, which must have been considerable, had perished from this earth, and that his ear could no longer take in the happy buzz of the hive in the rotting juniper. That ear was dust.

"Diadems drop and Doges surrender," Dickinson wrote. The kingdoms of this world would pass away, Christ assured us while he was living on this earth, and with those kingdoms the shrewdness of their rulers, the worldly sagacity used for good or ill by kings and by village appraisers in Arkansas. Only soul would survive. But a visitor still had to possess a great deal of faith to believe that the ear of Joseph Beaugi, lying in this graveyard, would hear the trumpet of the last day.

FIFTEEN

La Pointe Noire

*La Salle meets some Aztec wannabes • Why Henry Wadsworth
Longfellow put Francis Parkman in a grumpy mood • Awful Cajun
food products • The persistence of blood and the curse of White Mule*

La Salle and his men drifted past the great pine forests of northern Louisiana and Mississippi. In what is now the parish of Tensas,
they came across a rudimentary city in the wilderness, the capital
of the Taensas nation. For the French, this was something new in
America – square buildings of sun-baked mud and domed roofs,
surrounding an open rectangular area. The two main buildings
were the lodge of the chief and a temple to the sun. Inside the
lodge they met the chief, surrounded by three of his wives and sixty
old men dressed in white cloaks, his senators. Like members of
Congress applauding the entrance of the president to deliver his
state of the union address, they howled like wolves in homage to
their headman. "After the chief had spoken to them they all sat
down," Tonty wrote. Later the French visited the temple, which
had an altar and three wooden sculptures of eagles turned toward
the east. (Perhaps the Taensas shared the ancient belief in Western
culture that eagles could look directly at the sun.) On top of the
walls were spikes where the heads of the Taensases' enemies were

impaled. Here was a human society – influenced clearly by the civilizations of Meso-America – groping toward a future of social classes, bureaucracies, literature, priests learned in geometry, and armies commanded by generals.

After giving gifts to the chief, the party continued their progress on the river. At one point, they were met with a shower of arrows from some Indians on land; a short while afterwards they came across a village that had just recently been attacked and burned. Corpses lay stacked on the ground. The French took in the sight, got back in their canoes, and kept paddling. Now they were in the country of marshes and lakes and streams that the local Indians called *bayuks*, a term that the French would alter to bayou. It was a country of cypress trees with their trunks in the water, and water lilies and palm trees and gorgeous flowers and herons and flamingos and hummingbirds. The French fought off mosquitos and killed alligators for their food, dangling a fish in the water for bait; when the reptile swam up, somebody whacked his skull with an ax. They relished neither the hunting nor the eating of that animal, but it was the easiest thing for them to kill. In this fashion they made their way to a destination that promised only more of the same, beauty and horror mixed equally, until the salt water put an end to their wandering.

⚜

When I was in the eighth grade I sat in the auditorium of South Junior High School, in Pittsfield, with the rest of the student body and watched a pageant based on Henry Wadsworth Longfellow's poem *Evangeline: A Tale of Acadie*. Only the beginning and end of this performance remain in my memory. The beginning was the opening line of the poem, chanted in sing-song by my fellow eighth graders: *This is the forest primeval, the murmuring pines and the hemlocks.* This string of words will stay with me until my brain begins its final deterioration, this *TUM ta ta TUM ta ta TUM ta ta*

TUM ta ta TUM ta ta TUM TUM. Technically, it's a hexameter – five dactyls and a spondee or trochee – the classic meter of Virgil. It's a form almost never used in English verse, which doesn't like to go beyond ten syllables a line. Somehow this lumbering, slow-paced line fit the mood of Longfellow's poem perfectly. It's a mood I associate with my memory of the pageant's ending, when the heroine Evangeline, after a life spent searching North America for her lost lover, Gabriel, finally discovers him on his deathbed, in a hospital in Philadelphia, where she has come to nurse the victims of a plague. I must have been moved enough by this scene to retain a memory of it – and re-reading the poem now, after more than forty years, I have no trouble believing it's the finest expression of sheer pathos in American literature.

Longfellow, who wrote *Evangeline* in 1847, was in the nineteenth century considered the greatest of American poets, and *Evangeline* his masterpiece. His reputation took a beating in the twentieth century, however – he was a little too sweet, a little too sentimental, a little too addicted to moonlit scenes (he was, by the way, universally considered to be an extremely nice man, unlike his grand-nephew, Ezra Pound). For every person who reads Longfellow now, a thousand read Whitman or Emily Dickinson, those two eccentrics and borderline nutcases. It is true that as late as 1960 you could expect your average eighth grader in Massachusetts to recognize the opening line of *Evangeline*, but then Longfellow was a New England poet who spent most of his career in Massachusetts. Now even in Massachusetts you would spend a very long time asking thirteen-year-olds about the forest primeval before finding one who knew what you were talking about.

Still, the poem has called a myth into being, and the myth will never die. How did *Evangeline* manage this feat? It is a narrative poem with a pair of lovers and other notable characters, but Longfellow did not employ vivid or realistic characterization to achieve his effects – even Evangeline is barely sketched. Although long, it is not a true epic, either – there are no real adventures, no enemies overcome, no lively escapes, no rising action. The closest analogy to the poem is a story ballad written with a lot of minor chords. Everything is sad, dream-like, nostalgic.

And what is the occasion of all this emotion? It was an incident that took place in 1755 in Nova Scotia, a land that had been settled by French-speaking farmers since 1604, three years before the first English settlement at Jamestown. It was known as *Acadie*, or Acadia. The name derives from the sixteenth-century navigator employed by the French king, Giovanni da Verrazzano, who termed the beautiful coastline occupied by the present state of Delaware *Arcadie*, after Arcadia, the region in ancient Greece legendary for its pastoral innocence, for its hills and groves and streams where nymphs and dryads sported. Subsequent map-makers, confused by Verrazzano's geography, dropped the "r" and applied the name to present-day Nova Scotia. There is, I should add, an alternative derivation from the language of the native Mi'kmaqs. According to this theory, the name derives from a Mi'kmaq suffix *-akadie*, meaning "place of abundance." I like the first theory, however, with its suggestion of misplaced identity, suited to land that would always be more a country of the mind than a well-defined geopolitical entity. And Acadia was Arcadian. Its farmlands were rich and beautiful, carved out of the Annapolis Valley and bounded by salt marshes and forests and a bay full of cod and mackerel and lobster. As for pastoral innocence, Longfellow plays that note for all it's worth. His Grand Pré, where Evangeline and Gabriel are promised in marriage, is a village where "the richest was poor and the poor lived in abundance." It is distinguished by "the homes of peace and contentment," inhabited by "the blithe Acadian peasants . . . simple people, who lived like brothers together." It is a village where the priest is kindly, the blacksmith robust and open-hearted, the notary humble despite his learning.

Over this paradise fell the shadow of imperial rivalry. The Treaty of Utrecht in 1713 transferred Acadia from France to

England. The new British rulers pressured the French inhabitants to take an oath of allegiance to the British Crown. The Acadians, fearful of being forced to bear arms against their fellow French, and of losing the privilege of practicing their religion, insisted on taking only an oath of neutrality. The question became acute when war broke out in 1755. British authorities, notably William Shirley, the royal governor of Massachusetts, resolved on settling the question of Acadian loyalty once and for all by removing the Acadians from their land and shipping them somewhere else. When British and New England troops captured, with ridiculous ease, a French outpost that bordered Acadia called Fort Beauséjour, their hands were freed to implement this policy. New England troops did most of the dirty work. In Grand Pré, for example, a Massachusetts colonel named John Winslow summoned all the men of the village, read out the order of their deportation, and marched them aboard waiting British ships. Winslow, in his diary, acknowledged the "scene of woe and distress" this order caused. In a satisfying historical irony, that same diary provided Longfellow with much of the material of his poem.

Francis Parkman was very annoyed by the success of *Evangeline*. Creating great historical myths about the French in North America was his department, not Longfellow's. Moreover, in his eyes, the Longfellow version was a needless insult to the shades of their Massachusetts ancestors. "New England humanitarianism, melting into sentimentality at a tale of woe, has been unjust to its own," Parkman wrote in *Montcalm and Wolfe*. In that same book, he set out to undermine the Longfellow version of the expulsion of the Acadians by evoking a people not so much simple and living like brothers, as just plain simple. The Acadians, according to Parkman, were illiterate and "very ignorant," as well as "enfeebled by hereditary mental subjection." More to the point, the real villains of the story were French authorities and clerics who kept stirring up the Acadians against their British rulers, insisting they not take the oath of allegiance and encouraging them to give whatever covert help they could to French and Indian raiders. According to Parkman, Shirley was right to view the Acadians as an intolerable security risk.

Today nobody bothers to defend the removal of the Acadians, or *le grand dérangement*, as it is known in Acadian history. It was a terrible thing to do. There was something both very ancient and quite modern about this drastic measure. The action of clearing out the possessors of land so that others closer to God – Protestant New England farmers – could settle it and enjoy it has a definite biblical ring. At the same time the Acadian removal evokes concepts such as ethnic cleansing and homeland security. From the British point of view, at any rate, it was a very successful military operation. Nearly six thousand Acadians were put on board ship and scattered to various locales in the thirteen colonies, while the New Englanders methodically went about burning the homes and barns and killing the livestock the Acadians left behind them.

"Their lot was a hard one," Parkman admits of the Acadian exiles scattered in the thirteen colonies. The British tactic of herding the men on board ships first – knowing this would force their women and children to follow them as best they could – meant that families were often separated, a hardship that gave Longfellow his plot line, the story of Evangeline's lifelong search for her fiancé, Gabriel Lajeunesse. Intact or not, the Acadian families received an extremely frosty reception from the English colonists with whom they were supposed to assimilate. With no land or livelihood to sustain them, they were forced to rely on the assistance of people who feared their compatriots, hated their religion, and didn't understand their language. Many Acadians tried, sometimes successfully, to make their way back to their homeland. Others looked for alternative ports of call where their language and religion and nationality would not count against them. The most likely such refuge was the territory that Cavelier de La Salle had claimed for France nearly a hundred years previously. After 1763, when peace was declared, Acadians who had spent the war scattered in the thirteen colonies, or on the French islands of the Caribbean, or even in Great Britain or France, made their way to Louisiana. King Louis XV had just ceded this territory to Spain, but it was still French-speaking, Catholic, and unoccupied except for *les sauvages*. About three thousand Acadians ended up in southern Louisiana, where in the course of time they intermarried with other ethnic groups, including Indians and Africans, and evolved into the people now known as Cajuns. At present they number over half a million souls.

Their symbol remains Evangeline. It is perhaps not the symbol contemporary Cajuns would have chosen. Intellectual Cajuns sneer at her as the idealized creation of a sentimental old nineteenth-century Harvard professor, and ordinary Cajuns give little thought to her. But in the end Evangeline – this fictional creation who is often treated as a real, historical personage (the town of St. Martinville, Louisiana, has "Evangeline's tomb" and a bronze statue of Longfellow's heroine, cast in the likeness of the Mexican actress Dolores Del Rio, who starred in the 1929 movie *Evangeline*) – has no real rival for the honor. Such symbols are the fortuitous creations of poets or storytellers, and once embedded in the collective imagination they are not easily removed. Longfellow did his work too well. *Patience and abnegation of self, and devotion to others, / This was the lesson a life of trial and sorrow had taught her,* he wrote of his heroine Evangeline, the woman who eventually gave up hope of personal happiness and became a Sister of Mercy. It is not a popular theme today; we now want women who are strong and take control of their lives and live by their own rules and do things on their own terms and can, if they're beautiful young actresses on screen, break a man's jaw with a roundhouse punch. There's something extremely brittle about this new ideal woman, however. Instinctively we prefer the old-fashioned saint. The old-fashioned saint, even though she may be a stranger to us, is kind and attentive to our needs. That's who we want by our bedside in our lonely moment of death, not a woman who's proved to herself that she's strong.

Patience and abnegation of self is the explicit theme of *Evangeline*. The poem has another theme, however, which is implicit: the transformation of Evangeline and Gabriel into Americans. In his exile Gabriel wanders the territory of the future United States, hunting and trapping in the Ohio Valley and the bayous of southern Louisiana and the great western plains and the woods of northern Michigan, finally dying in the city where Americans declared their independence. By the end he is far from the blithe, simple Acadian peasant he was at the beginning of the poem. He belongs to this new country as much as Daniel Boone or Kit Carson. The same is true of Evangeline. She changes from a woman needing, like other exiles, assistance and charity from the English-speaking people around her, to a woman who dispenses assistance and charity. The end of the poem suggests that the people of Philadelphia no longer care if Evangeline is French or Catholic; they simply revere her. She, too, is an American.

That's why Longfellow wrote the poem, and why public school teachers in Massachusetts in 1959 had their students dramatize the poem on stage. *Evangeline* demonstrated that victims of oppression and injustice anywhere could come to this land and acquire a new identity as Americans. Unfortunately, while that was true of Evangeline, it took a long, long time before it became true of the Cajuns as a whole. Louisiana historian Shane K. Bernard, in his book *The Cajuns: Americanization of a People*, quotes an observer's remark, in the middle of the nineteenth century: "These people [the Cajuns] seem to be living in the year 1500, such are their limited ideas, singular habits and unparalleled ignorance." The situation worsened during the Civil War, when Cajun farms and homes were often targeted by Yankee raiders. The poverty and isolation of this people deepened. Even local Blacks were considered more progressive and intelligent than this race of swamp-dwelling,

French-speaking, alligator-wrestling hunters and trappers and subsistence farmers. They made few appearances in American literature, one of the most notable occurring in William Faulkner's 1939 novella, *Old Man*. That work concerns a convict in a Mississippi state penitentiary who is sent in a boat to rescue some people stranded by the great flood of 1927. The rescue attempt turns out to be an epic voyage lasting weeks. In the course of this voyage, hopelessly lost in swampland, the convict floats by a cabin on stilts inhabited by a "little wiry man with rotting teeth and soft wild bright eyes like a rat or a chipmunk." This half-human creature doesn't speak English; he utters, in a "fierce hissing gobble," a language unknown to the convict, which of course is French. As the two commence a partnership in hunting alligators, they are joined by other "pint-sized dark men" – close cousins to Kenneth Roberts's "swarthy, stunted Frenchmen." The convict, who is tall and has pale greenish-blue eyes, stands out physically from these Cajuns, but the cultural contrast is even greater. Faulkner's tale highlights the stereotypical contrast between the stoic, silent Anglo-Saxon and the Frenchman who gesticulates wildly and acts hysterically in tense moments.

That's where things stood on the eve of World War II. With the coming of that war, everything changed – the great Americanization of the Cajuns, foretold in *Evangeline*, finally took place, as Cajuns, for the first time in their history, ventured outside their traditional domain in huge numbers as servicemen and defense workers. "The war exerted a profound influence on Cajun GIs, giving them a new sense of national identity and beginning the process of rapid, widespread Americanization," Shane Bernard writes. "Proud of their wartime contributions, they came home staunch patriots, defenders of the American way of life. They had at long last become part of the national melting pot." As part of the deal, they claimed their full share of post-war prosperity. Subsistence farmers who had barely fed their families became plumbers, carpenters, electricians, making good wages. They used the G.I. Bill, Bernard writes, "to complete their schooling, buy homes, and start businesses." They made happy acquaintance, in short, with the American style of getting and spending. "The Cajuns had always frowned on consumerism, especially conspicuous consumption," Bernard told me in conversation. "But along with greater educational attainments came more income, and with more income they bought into the same American consumer values as everyone else had. Now they wanted that car with the big tail fins and the chrome."

They also stopped speaking French. Today only about 30 per cent of Cajuns still speak French as their first language, and they are almost all middle-aged or elderly. "Unless a linguistic revolution occurs," Bernard writes, "Cajun French will cease to exist as a means of everyday communication in south Louisiana."

⚜

The town of Richard lies on the flat plain of southern Louisiana. This is not the Cajun country of swamps and bayous but the Cajun country of the prairie, and if you drove there in the spring, as I did, you would pass rectangular fields of water that could be either rice fields or crawfish ponds. Not far from the main crossroads of the town stood St. Edward Church, with its cemetery next door. It was a church built in the 1960s, with walls of brick, an airy, well-lighted interior, and clean lines inside. The statuary, however, was Victorian. Two white angels flanked the front entrance. They were mortuary angels – androgynous, with long, flowing locks and feminine features, except no breasts. They had no pupils, either, but they were facing upwards and one of them pointed with a torch to the heavens.

A few yards away, the bodies lay under the earth. It was a beautiful Sunday when I strayed alone among the graves in that cemetery. You could hear a bird singing from the oak trees in the distance, and across the street a cow in a pasture lowed, and once in a while a car passed by, but otherwise it was quiet. I paused at the grave of a young woman named Charlene Richard, who had once been part of this parish, who had been baptized here and made her first communion and was confirmed here. It was an ordinary grave except for a few exceptional touches: a wooden prie-dieu by the side of the grave, a foot-high statue of the Blessed Virgin at the head of the gravestone, a glass case on top. Inside the glass case were pieces of paper, folded sheets of lined paper ripped from the spiral bindings of memo books, filled with handwriting. I thought momentarily of opening the case and reading some of the messages, but couldn't bring myself to do it.

The quiet was shattered by five motorcycles roaring up the highway. They halted by the entrance of the cemetery and three women got off the bikes and joined me by Charlene's grave. We stood there in silence for a while. Occasionally we heard a burst of laughter from the five men who sat by the bikes – they wore beards and wraparound sunglasses and those black T-shirts that have the skull of a longhorn or a snarling wolf on the back. I asked one of the women if they knew about Charlene Richard. "Oh, I heard about her a long time," one of them answered. "But I didn't know where she was or nothing. Then last week I read an article in the paper and they said this is where her grave is, so we thought we'd come up." I left them alone and strolled past other graves and then eventually the women walked back to the entrance and climbed on the bikes and they all roared off.

Shortly after, I left as well and drove back to the house of Dean and Sylvia McGee, a retired farmer and his wife, about half a mile away. "McGee" hardly sounded Cajun, but like the Ryans and Johnsons of Quebec, who started out Irish but over the course of time became deep-dyed French Canadians, some Louisiana McGees were pure Cajun. "McGee, that's a French name," the famous Cajun musician Dennis McGee once said. "I don't know anyone named McGee who doesn't speak French." Dean McGee grew up in Richard speaking French, with the sons of tenant farmers who planted cotton and plowed their fields with mules. It was the Great Depression, but these farmers hardly noticed – they were already dirt poor. Dean's father, though he also farmed with mules, was more prosperous than most; he owned the town's only flatbed truck, and he took his kids and their friends on the back of that truck to the Liberty Theater in nearby Eunice, where they watched Buck Jones and Hoot Gibson westerns. Sylvia's father was a policeman in the town of Church Point, where she grew up, eight miles from Richard. She showed me a black and white snapshot taken in 1955 of her father and a man named Wilbur Landry, chief of police of Church Point. The chief wore glasses and looked more like a high school principal nearing retirement than a cop. He looked like a thoughtful man who didn't throw his weight around but quietly exercised his authority for many a weary year because somebody had to do it. Most of his policing involved decent fellows who'd had a little bit too much to drink. Then one day, in a blaze of madness, a man turned on him with a gun and shot him. "It was a terrible killing," Sylvia told me. "A man tried to take his wife back and she didn't want to go back and so he killed her and his daughters and two police, all in about thirty minutes. He ran into a corn field to hide but then he shot himself." Sylvia's father survived the incident.

When the war came, Dean served in the air force at a base in the Azores. "It was a nice place to be in time of war," he recalled. "It's a pretty country." When he returned after the war he married Sylvia. In 1955 they built the ranch-style bungalow they still live in. Dean continued to farm rice on the land his family owned, but the tenant farmers departed and the mules were taken from the cotton fields to haul carriages of tourists around the streets of the French Quarter in New Orleans. It was the familiar story of the heart of a small town fading, the population diminishing, the young moving away, a Wynn Dixie and a Wal-Mart down the highway monopolizing all the business that was left. Now, some city folk had moved to Richard – commuters who worked in Lafayette, a small city about a forty-five-minute drive to the south and west. "People don't visit a hell of a lot," Dean said of his long-time neighbors. "Most of them do like us, watch that boob tube all day."

Sylvia and I left the house in my rented car and she directed me down some country roads past fields of rice and soybean and fallow earth to a corner of Richard where a cluster of bungalows stood, inhabited by members of the Richard family. "They all live together around here," Sylvia told me. "It's like a *commune*." She pointed to a man and a woman standing in the yard of one of the bungalows. "These are her people here. Ask them where their mama's house is." The couple directed us to a mobile home with a deck and awning around it, and a washing machine and a four-by-eight recreational vehicle and other items scattered in front. A couple of pickup trucks were also parked in the yard, and a few feet away stood a little yellow house. We walked up to the front porch and knocked on the door. Mary Alice Richard, the mother of Charlene, was inside cooking chicken. "You can tell you're in Cajun country when you smell something good like that in the kitchen," Sylvia said.

Mary Alice Richard, the mother of ten children, was a seventy-eight-year-old widow wearing a short-sleeved shirt loose over a pair of slacks. She moved about her kitchen with the deliberation of a stout woman troubled by arthritis, hypertension, and congestive heart failure. Perhaps because her ankles were swollen, she was barefoot. "I'm a real Cajun," she joked. "I don't have any shoes on." There was no embarrassment behind the joke. She had the dignity of an old woman who had worked hard all her life at indisputably useful tasks and had never fretted much about herself, and didn't talk just to fill the silence. "Look at Charlene's picture there," Sylvia said. "She was a pretty girl." On one wall hung an oil painting of Charlene Richard, based on a photograph, which showed her sweetly smiling, her chin up. The artist had created the impression of an aureole of light around her head. Mrs. Richard pointed to another framed portrait on the wall. "That's my young son who got killed." This second portrait was a photograph of a young man in an open-necked shirt, with reddish hair, a grin, and a handsome face, fresh as the morning. The surprise that overcame him one day in his twentieth year was an accident on the highway.

In a bedroom with a wooden Mexican crucifix on the wall and other religious artifacts on display, I saw a workbook for a "Health Improvement Class" from Charlene Richard's last year in school. It was filled with her careful handwriting, a mysterious code her father had failed to crack, because in his childhood he had been sent to pick cotton under the hot sun instead of sitting in a classroom. As a truck driver he had to memorize the traffic signs he could not read. But Charlene had mastered the code thoroughly. Any teacher could tell at a glance that this girl was going to make life in the classroom easier. "I have taken Health Improvement for two years," she wrote. "It has been a great help. It has taught me to eat beans and corn. By eating the right kinds of food it will make me healthier. I have learned not to bite my nails. . . . To keep up with the growing and improving world a person must be healthy to do his part."

Charlene was ready to do her part. She had always done her part. "She was a big help to me," her mother said. "She would cook dinner and serve it and then she'd tell me she was going to clean the kitchen. 'You can lie on the couch and sleep,' she'd say to me, and then, when she was through with that, she was going to make some coffee and wake me up." She loved her father, too, though there were evenings in the Richard home when tension was high as the family waited for Elvin, a smart man who had never had a break, to come home from his cards and his beer.

In January 1959 she celebrated her twelfth birthday. During the following months, she began to experience pains in her hips and legs. Her animal spirits began to fail. That spring a woman in black appeared to her. She had no face. When Charlene tried to question the apparition, it vanished. In July that year, diagnosed with advanced leukemia, she entered Our Lady of Lourdes Hospital in Lafayette.

The hospital chaplain was a young priest from Pennsylvania, a curate at the nearby Our Lady of Fatima parish named Joseph Brennan. Father Brennan had been ordained just two months earlier. "It was a life-turning experience for me," he told me, when I visited his home in Lafayette. "I remember the night she died, I went back to the rectory I was living in, and I sat down and said to myself, nobody is going to believe in this story. But as you know, ten thousand people a year now visit her grave." The story he had told many times, but he was not tired of it, despite the decades and despite the infirmities that now visited his age. Like Mary Alice Richard, he had grown stout and suffered from arthritis and heart problems. After he greeted me at the doorway, he used a walker to maneuver himself into an armchair, while a piebald dachshund named Danny Boy went into paroxysms of yelping. Father Brennan was stern with the dog, but it was a while before the animal calmed down. "One of the nuns who staffed the hospital called me and asked me to come and be with Dr. Voorhies when he had to confront the parents after he examined Charlene," Father Brennan said. "The news was that she had about two weeks to live – it had developed that quickly. They asked me if I would tell her. You know, if they had asked me right now, a priest of forty years' experience, that would be a hard thing to do. And I was just two months into my ministry. But I went into her room and I said, 'Charlene, you're a very sick little girl.' She said, 'Yes, I know.' 'A very beautiful lady is going to come soon to take you.' She looked at me and said, 'When she comes I'll tell her, Blessed Mother, Father Brennan said hello.'"

Danny Boy was now curled up in a basket by Father Brennan's feet, satisfied that his responsibilities regarding the intruder were over. Father Brennan leaned slightly toward me as he spoke. What he said was the same thing, almost word for word, that he had said to many others over the years, but he still seemed moved by it. "I saw her every day for two weeks," he said. Every day he talked to her about offering her sufferings for others. It is an old Catholic concept. "When you are sick, offer up all your grief and pain and weakness as a service to our Lord, and beseech Him to unite them with the torments He suffered for you," St. Francis De Sales wrote in his classic 1608 treatise *Introduction to the Devout Life*. The concept can be traced ultimately to the letter of St. Paul to the Colossians. "Even now I find my joy in the suffering I endure for you," the apostle wrote his flock. "In my own flesh I fill up what is lacking in the sufferings of Christ for the sake of his body, the church." Biblical scholars are not entirely clear as to what St. Paul means by this – possibly he is saying that the suffering and persecution he has endured while spreading the gospel is helping to extend Christ's church. The church needs this extra suffering, as it were, so that Christ's own sufferings can attain their full fruition in the growth of the church.

That is not exactly what St. Francis De Sales meant, or what Father Brennan meant when he urged Charlene to offer her sufferings to God for others, but it's close enough. In this variation of St. Paul's idea, the suffering person asks that her offering of pain be instrumental in helping somebody. Charlene Richard, apparently, took to the concept immediately. "Okay, Father, who am I to suffer for today?" she would ask Father Brennan as he entered her room. And she did suffer. In 1959, the only painkiller available was Demerol. "Her pain was excruciating," Father Brennan recalled. "But despite all her pain, she could always smile. I guess the thing I will always remember were those big brown eyes smiling at you."

At their last meeting, Father Brennan remembered, "She said, 'I want you to lean over. I want to kiss you goodbye. I'll be praying for you in heaven.' Then I left and the next day I was busy over at the church, and when I returned from church there was a note from Charlene's room, Room 411. I rushed over there, and when I got there Dr. Voorhies was just closing her eyes. I sat in that room quite a long time until the funeral people came. It was one of those occasions you just want to stay and be part of something, and I knew I was. I just felt I was in a holy place. You know, she was an ordinary kid, but she had an insight into redemptive suffering which was so unique. She knew the power of offering her pains for other people."

In 1989, five thousand people showed up at an outdoor mass near St. Edward Church, celebrating the thirtieth anniversary of Charlene Richard's death. They were calling her the Cajun saint. In a way, she had reaffirmed the continuing relevance of that old symbol of her people, Evangeline. Like Evangeline she had been an otherwise ordinary girl who purified her heart in sorrow and silence. It was not surprising that a television crew arrived to record the occasion. "When I saw that CNN truck I thought, 'Charlene, honey, they believe you now,'" Father Brennan said. Her story has since been featured twice on television, and her grave is listed in such Web sites as the "Haunted Places Directory" and "Haunted Sites of Louisiana." "According to visitors to the church, there is a grave of a twelve year old girl in the cemetery behind the church that has the power to cure," the *Haunted Sites of Louisiana* informs the prospective visitor to St. Edward church. "There is a box on top of the headstone where visitors can drop in their requests." No one seriously maintains that Charlene's grave has occult powers, of course, and it is worth remembering that during her lifetime Charlene herself did nothing more paranormal than face her painful death with hope rather than despair or bitterness. Call that an unsolved mystery, if you will. "She is a symbol of what a person can be in a time of crisis," Father Brennan told me. "We never know who we are until the crisis comes. I remember one time somebody who grew up with her said to me, 'I remember Charlene. She wasn't all that great.' I said none of us are great until the crisis bell rings and we have to answer."

⚜

That week Sylvia McGee and I went to the regular Saturday morning jam session at the Savoy Music Center, just outside Eunice. The center is a music store owned and operated by Marc Savoy, who was born in 1940, grew up in Eunice, obtained a B.S. in chemical engineering, but then decided to pursue his great passion for building and selling Cajun accordions. About fifty people sat or stood in the front room of the store listening to six fiddlers, six guitar players, a singer, an accordion player, and a triangle player. Admission was free, and so was the boudin passed around at break time. Like a stupid *Américain* I tried to eat the skin casing of the pork and rice mixture, which can be done if your teeth and stomach are up to it, but it was awkward and made me spill pork grease on a couple of books I had just bought from the store, *Cajun Sketches* and *Cajun Healing*.

Marc Savoy was a tall, robust-looking man who kept an eye on the proceedings and introduced one of his guests, a nonagenarian named Rodney Fontenot, who wore a cowboy hat, a dark gray suit, and a big brown and white polka-dot bow tie. Fontenot was a noted fiddler who played the way he heard Dennis McGee play eighty years ago. "Looks like they dug him up from the *grave*," Sylvia said to me. Mr. Fontenot did look as if they had just drained the blood from his body. But he represented Authentic Tradition, which is something Marc Savoy will go to great lengths to support and uphold. On one wall of his store hung a hand-lettered sign that read:

So you tell me that you can't speak French even though you have lived in a French speaking area all your life.

You say you have never learned how because no one ever showed you. Yet somehow you managed to become a normal, stereotype, clone of "Anywhere, U.S.A," even though no one ever showed you that either. BULLSHIT! I'll tell you why you can't speak French. It's because, as you were growing up, you were so busy pursuing mundane American trivia and making fun of those who did speak French that you could never find time to recognize the beauty of your heritage. You turned your back on a hot bowl of gumbo in favor of a cold, tasteless hot-dog. Now that Cajun

Culture attracts worldwide attention you have decided to be Cajun also. That's fine but don't make a second mistake and try to take credit away from the people who kept the torch lit when Cajun was a dirty word. I pledge myself not to let that happen.

Marc Savoy
December 1987

You could tell Marc Savoy had strong feelings about a number of issues. Underlying his irritation seemed to be a fear that Cajun culture, now fashionable, was turning into a fad, a commodity, a tourist spectacle, like Indians doing a dance at a powwow. In the space of a few decades, the Cajun had evolved from swamp scum and greaser, to an earthy, sexy, devil-may-care fellow who really knew how to have a good time – the only white man with rhythm. No wonder some fallen-away Cajuns wanted to rejoin the church. Most Cajuns, however, took all this new-found Cajun chic with a grain of salt. Outside the store, Sylvia and I met a short, compact gentleman named Hilliard, with slicked-back gray hair and a soft-spoken, almost melancholic tone of voice, who hailed from the nearby town of Rayne, Frog Capital of the World (so-called because one of its prominent citizens, the late Felix Perres, had been a fanatical devotee of the Louisiana Jumbo Bullfrog, *Rana catesbeiana*, and its tasty legs). "He's from Canada," Sylvia told Hilliard, after we introduced ourselves. "I lived here all my life – I don't know what a Canadian looks like," Hilliard answered.

"You're a real Cajun," said Sylvia. "Everybody wants to see a real Cajun."

"Don't know why. Don't know what we're good for."

"We *eat* good."

"Eat too much," declared Hilliard sadly.

Sylvia's remark about real Cajuns reminded me of something Carl Brasseaux, a University of Louisiana history professor, had said, that the biggest complaint the Lafayette Tourist Information Center received from visitors was that they hadn't seen any Cajuns during their stay there. Half the people walking the streets of Lafayette were Cajuns. What did these visitors expect to see? Pint-sized dark men with rotting teeth and eyes like rats and chipmunks, talking French in a fierce, hissing gobble? I suppose the information center could have given people Hilliard's address. Of course, if you put Hilliard in downtown Toronto, he could be easily mistaken for a Canadian, and then nobody would want to see him unless he was dressed in a red Mountie uniform and riding a horse.

Later I watched Hilliard play the guitar in the store, contributing to the jaunty rhythms of the music whose soul was expressed by the high tenor wail of the singer. It was a wail that could easily have turned into a funeral dirge. Behind me a middle-aged man wearing shorts and a T-shirt sat with his wife. "We're from central Iowa," he told me. "We don't hear much of that Cajun music." He had a very pleasant smile. Is there a more amiable race of people on earth than retired, affluent Americans on the road? "We're on our way back to Iowa – we winter in Texas, and they don't have any crawfish deals like they do here. Back in Iowa we have corn and soybean and pork products. We have a lot of chicken leg farms there, too." But no Cajun bands and boudin and crawfish. This was well worth stopping for an hour or two on the trip back to Iowa. You couldn't beat the price, either. The free admission was one way of saying this was not a tourist attraction. This was real.

When I asked Hilliard if anything had changed since the tourists had started coming to watch them play on Saturday mornings, he said, no, nothing had changed. He was surely right. Yet the presence of spectators who had no ties to the community or to individual musicians did alter the nature of the event, however subtly. It made the gathering more aware of itself, more vulnerable to irony, and that was the first step in the transition from folk happening to part of an entertainment package. That damned self-consciousness is the curse of our times.

How can a local culture like the Cajun culture remain distinctive and connected to the past while admitting change and development? On one crucial front, language, people like Marc Savoy have been clearly fighting a losing battle. That was the front that the French of Quebec staked everything on, by the way. And they won. The French language is alive and well in that province. In other respects, however, their cultural distinctiveness is nothing to brag about – it's *Sex in the City* with an *accent aigu*. Cajuns get tired of seeing Québécois visitors shake their heads over the loss of French in Louisiana. "They point with pride to the viability of their language," Carl Brasseaux said to me. "We wonder what has happened to their French culinary traditions." Ouch.

To be sure, it's a pity about the loss of the French language. If someone like Marc Savoy sounds a little cross it may be because he remembers the 1950s, when there was zero pride in Cajun tradition, especially in a place like La Pointe Noire, the most isolated and backward region of all Acadiana. Teachers there and elsewhere punished children for speaking French in the classroom or the schoolyard. Like the punishment of Indian children who spoke their native language in residential schools during this same period, the act was not necessarily malicious or perverse – Native American parents, and Cajun parents, really were anxious that their children learn English. English, then and now, was a passport to a life of opportunity. The shame was that both Cajun French and Native languages were considered a badge of low mental ability by the teachers who suppressed them. In the case of the Cajuns, it was as if Francis Parkman's sneer that the Acadians were "enfeebled by hereditary mental subjection" just would not go away. Even today, partly as a pre-emptive measure, Cajuns like to tell Boudreau and Thibodeaux jokes, celebrating the dim-wittedness of two Cajun good old boys. It is okay of course to laugh at these jokes if told by a Cajun, but perhaps unwise to tell one yourself, in a bar in Eunice or Lafayette.

When the late sixties arrived, everything changed. The Council for the Development of French in Louisiana (CODOFIL) was founded in 1968 with the aim of restoring French by teaching it in school at all grade levels. At the same time, traditional Cajun music was revitalized, particularly after the appearance of Cajun musicians at the 1964 Newport Folk Festival, and then after a landmark concert in Lafayette ten years later called the Tribute to Cajun Music. This concert popularized not only music but Cajun culture and folklore generally. It only remained for crawfish and gumbo to seize their day, and that happened in the early eighties with a nationwide craze for Cajun cuisine. As Shane Bernard points out in his book *The Cajuns*, this craze had some decidedly odd manifestations: supermarket shelves across the country offered such dubious treats as Ass Kickin' Cajun Hot Sauce and California Cajun Pistachios, fast-food chains put Cajun Popcorn Shrimp on their menus, and a cookbook entitled *Kosher Cajun Cookbook* was published, "the cover of which showed an Ultra-orthodox Jew enjoying south Louisiana's spicy cuisine." The irony, as Bernard points out, is that this burst of Cajun pride represented the final Americanization of the Cajuns, since it was part of a nationwide trend of celebrating ethnic heritage. Once, the Cajuns – described by Marc Savoy as possessing "the most powerful ethnic culture in America" – had been impervious to national trends, but no longer.

Cajun food and music were certainly worth celebrating, and it is not surprising that both were marketed successfully across the country. But corporations could not market the inner principle that gave life to both food and music – the principle of community and family.

It was family and community, with their traditional feasts and celebrations, that kept bringing back the children who had left. It was also what made La Pointe Noire the nursery of a long line of great Cajun musicians, including the accordion player Iry LeJeune. "In Iry's music is all the cruel loneliness of our Cajun history," writes historian Pierre Daigle.

Not only the loneliness at the time of our exile, but the later years of poverty, the poor little tenants' shacks in cotton fields and along forests, with their mud chimneys or the big sad old houses with a stairway to the attic and their mournful shutter in the gables. It's all there in Iry's music. A young man hurrying to pick a bale of cotton in the fall so he could marry his bride, the struggle of small farmers trying to survive, the threats of so many diseases that doctors could do nothing against, the lone horseback rider singing his love or his sorrow on a dark country road at night; the clop, clop, clop of a horse hitched to a buggy. It's all there in the music of this almost blind man.

The Franco-Americans are different from the Cajuns in many respects, but "the big sad old houses" certainly would strike a chord of memory among New England French-Canadian families. Their forebears did not work in the cotton fields, they worked in the textile mills, but they too lived in the kind of settlements that David Plante conjured in his writing – settlements in the woods with cabins falling apart and chimneys rusting, the habitations of failure and resignation, the homes of hewers of wood and drawers of water.

Franco-Americans, however, did not develop the music that would give voice to their condition. In La Pointe Noire, by contrast, music is still played in practically every home. In part because of this love of homemade music, the French knack of combining deep religious piety with roaring good times reached its maximum intensity in La Pointe Noire, in the years before World War II. The great social institution was the Saturday night *bal de maison*, when people would gather to dance at somebody's house – much like the parents of Art Papin in Ste. Genevieve. The musicians would bring their accordions and triangles and fiddles, the furniture would be removed, extra chamber pots put in spare bedrooms, and then the guests would arrive in their good clothes and pay ten or fifteen cents at the door. Now that was a Saturday night.

❖

One evening Sylvia McGee and I visited an elderly couple who lived down the road, Frozine and Hilton Thibodeaux. Like the McGees, they inhabited a ranch-style bungalow. The unpainted wood siding was a weather-beaten gray, and the front lawn was devoted not so much to grass as to a collection of interesting objects: there was a statue of the Blessed Virgin Mary in a grotto ("Our Lady of the Bathtub"), a birdbath, a miniature windmill. When we arrived Hilton and Frozine were sitting in a pair of La-Z-Boy armchairs – one in green leatherette and the other in brown corduroy – watching their wide-screen television. Hilton turned it off as we walked in, while his dog, a black and white chihuahua named Tiny Tim, did his pro forma duty as guardian of the household. Hilton told him to quiet down. "Let me tell you," Frozine said to us, "he loves his master." Frozine remained in her chair while she spoke – blotches on her calves showed where the blood no longer flowed freely. Hilton was more mobile. You couldn't tie him down, not even at the age of eighty-seven. He no longer sang, and he couldn't play the accordion for long without his arms hurting – age had taken that much from him – but a pool of nervous energy within had not evaporated. Both he and his wife had the lean alertness of birds of prey.

Like many homes in La Pointe Noire, their house was full of ornaments and art objects, many of a religious nature. On top of their television set, for example, were two statues of the Blessed Virgin Mary, a statue of Christ holding a lamb in his arms, a Mexican crucifix, a couple of ceramic angels, two ceramic Boston terriers, photographs of family members, and little pots of artificial flowers. The family photographs had an obvious place in this collection; so did the Boston terriers when you knew more about the Thibodeaux.

They loved dogs. On one wall of their dining room was a framed group of photographs of Tiny Tim with the caption "It's a Dog's Life." There were also photographs of a black and white Boston terrier. "He was twelve years old when he died," Frozine said. "I cried like a baby." Outside, under a slab of concrete by the miniature windmill, whose blades were spinning in the night breeze, lay the body of the Boston terrier. The birth and death dates of the dog's twelve-year life were inscribed on the concrete, by a conch shell.

Yet it was the religious artifacts that were dearest to Frozine and Hilton. Hilton showed me a picture on the wall. When you flicked a switch it revealed a crucified Christ, with a series of crucified Christs mirrored behind him, receding into an infinite distance. It was a gift from one of their grandchildren. "They always give me a cross or a statue. They know I like that," Frozine said. This was one thing, the Catholic faith, constant in their lives – lives that had begun by breathing the lingering air of the nineteenth century and were now experiencing the dawn of the twenty-first century. The couple still prayed the rosary every night before going to bed. "*Les affaires changent,*" Hilton said. "*Oui,*" Sylvia replied. "*Pas pour le meilleur.*" Hilton cradled Tiny Tim in his lap. "*Les femmes se marient ensemble, et les hommes se marient ensemble,*" he said. Sylvia shook her head. "*C'est peut-être la fin du monde.*" Frozine laughed. "Hilton said a man would have to be pretty good looking before he would kiss him."

We all laughed at that. Then the conversation turned to the past, and Hilton showed me his wedding photograph, taken sixty-eight years earlier. "They were hemming my dress because it was too long for me," Sylvia recalled, "and Father LaFleur – I don't know why he came up there, where they were doing the hemming, but he saw me standing with my wedding dress on and he said, 'What are you doing?' I said, 'I'm getting married.' 'You're too young.' 'I know, Father. But I want to get married.' He said, 'Okay,' and he gave me a ten-dollar bill to put on my dress. Then he gave a big box of chocolate kisses for my wedding. A *big* box. It lasted a long time." Frozine laughed. "But he was nice to us."

"He was a good priest," Sylvia agreed. Smart priests, then and now, know better than to argue with young women, even seventeen-year-olds, who say they want to get married. Perhaps Father LaFleur had an intuition this marriage would go the distance, and then some, when he parted with that sawbuck.

Not all change since those days has been for the worse, of course. "Everybody's friendly now," Frozine said. Now, youths from this part of the country do not wear black shirts and put red handkerchiefs in their back pockets as a challenge to the Marais Bouleurs. Now men do not "fight with handkerchiefs" – engage in a form of duel in which the two participants hold on to a handkerchief with one hand and slash at each other with knives in the other. "That was bad, yes," Hilton said. "People were so crazy. You saw them drink – they drank that whiskey they made themselves, they called it what? White Mule? I drank White Mule."

"It didn't kill you?" Sylvia said.

"It came close."

"He's paying for it now," Frozine said. Hilton grinned. Actually at his age he was a pretty good advertisement for White Mule.

"My brother was so dumb," Frozine said. "He was going out with a girl and that girl had another man. My brother, he loved her and he wanted her bad. You know Fred Blanchard from Church Point?"

"Oh, yes," Sylvia said.

"One Easter Sunday my brother, he was drunk, and he went over to the house where the girl was and he got there and his enemy was there. But when he got ready for that man, that man Fred was ready for him. Oh, he cut my brother."

"The Blanchards weren't afraid of nobody," Hilton said. "If you wanted to fight with them, they were ready to do that. He was crazy, your brother."

"Not crazy, *dumb*. Crazy is when you don't know what you're doing. Dumb is when you know what you're doing and you do it anyway. That Blanchard would have killed him, but his knife was not pointed, it was round at the end so it didn't go to his heart.

They picked him up and brought him home. I was young, about fifteen I guess, and I remember the doctor sewed him right there on the table. I'll never forget that day. And you know, those two, they died enemy. They didn't talk to each other. And my brother, he didn't marry the girl. He got married with another lady, and Fred Blanchard also got married with another lady."

❧

The last day I was in La Pointe Noire I visited the Thibodeaux again to talk about Frozine's history as a *traiteuse*, or healer. The *traiteur* (male) and *traiteuse* (female) have long played an important role in Cajun culture. Folklorists love them; articles about these healers are constantly appearing in one folklore journal or another. We dote on things that are passing away – the new, by contrast, always appears to be corrupt. And there is no denying that *traiteurs* are dying off. "There are not too many *traiteurs* left," Dean McGee told me. "When Frozine and her generation are gone, there won't be any."

Frozine's "treatments," she said when I asked, were mostly prayers – chiefly the prayer Christ taught in the New Testament, known to Catholics as the Our Father and to Protestants as The Lord's Prayer. Her repertoire was also limited. She didn't treat for cancer or rheumatoid arthritis. She treated for sunstroke, and twisted ankles, and burns, and shingles, and worms in the intestines, and to stop the flow of blood from somebody's wound. They were very simple treatments. For cases of sunstroke, for example, she told me, "You put water, a little thing of water, and you dip your hand into that water and while you dip your hand in the water you say a prayer. First of all, you pray to God. You say, 'God, please take away the sunstroke. You came into the world to save us, so make this sunstroke go away.' And then you say Our Father, and you say it three times. That's for the sunstroke." For a burn, she said, "You blow on it, say Our Father, and then you make your cross on top of it." Hilton, who was standing in the kitchen listening, with Tiny Tim in his arms, nodded. "I burned myself on my hand, I came right in here, and she treated me for the fire," he said. "Man, it just go away. Oh yeah, that's a good treatment. If you burn yourself and she treat you, it's going to heal right there."

"For the shingle, you make a lot of crosses," Frozine continued. "Everywhere it is, you want to circle it. While you circle it you say Our Father. It's the same prayers. When you pray Our Father, you ask God that that go away. My treatment is all prayer." I asked her if she used prayers other than the Our Father. "There's one treatment with Hail Mary," she answered. "Sometimes little kids have some worms in their bellies. When you circle his little belly, you make a cross and you say Our Father and Hail Mary. That's the prayer for that."

The treatment to stop somebody from bleeding was more complicated – the healer had to have something with the person's blood on it. "For the blood you take a piece of white material or white paper or rag – anything with the blood on it," she said. "You put it between your hands like that –" She made a gesture like a person praying. "You say, 'Oh blood, I judge you in the faith of Jesus.' You say that nine times. And then you throw the rag away. Make sure it disappears." Recently a man she knew hit his head and opened a wound in his scalp that was bleeding profusely. Someone from his house came rushing over to Frozine's with a rag covered in the man's blood. "I met her at the door," Frozine recalled. "She said, 'This is the rag. Go treat him.' I treated him right away. I just put the rag between my hands and prayed to Jesus for Him to treat him. That's what you do. You say that prayer nine times, and then you take the rag and disappear it so nobody knows where it is. You wrap it up and put it somewhere, and nobody knows where it is. You can burn it or throw it away. Just make it disappear. Put it in the bottom of the trash can and put the trash on top of it. Nobody knows what's on the bottom of the trash can."

This emphasis on hiding or eliminating the rag with the person's blood on it made me wonder if there were people in La

Pointe Noire who were not above witchcraft. Traditionally, of course, such people hankered after the blood or nail parings of the person they wanted to curse. This was not the case, however, according to Hilton and Frozine. But a blood taboo does not depend on fear of witchcraft – it is a very old and powerful taboo in the history of the race, which is why God forbade the children of Israel from partaking of blood in their animal sacrifices. Blood is intimate. Blood is sacred. If you have a cloth or a rag with a person's blood on it, you must not leave it hanging around. You must do as Frozine says: Make it disappear.

SIXTEEN

The Devil's Empire

The usefulness of a notary in a wilderness expedition • The importance of helping the king put on his pants • The significance of writing XXX on a tomb • What to do with a corpse that's taking up too much space • The final resting place of the Emperor of the Universe • Hoodwinking a priest in the confessional • How you can be a star at the Mother-In-Law Lounge • The eerie and magical properties of a certain wig

On April 6, 1682, a few miles south of the present town of Venice, Louisiana, La Salle discovered that the river he had been following since the beginning of the year split into three channels. He sent a party of men down each channel. His was the one on the right. Before long, he could smell the salt air of the ocean, and then he saw the breakers. "The broad bosom of the great Gulf opened on his sight," Parkman writes, "tossing its restless billows, limitless, voiceless, lonely as when born of chaos, without a sail, without a sign of life."

La Salle rounded up the other two parties and then paddled back up the river looking for ground solid enough to set foot on. Near Venice they beached their canoes, cut down a tree, planted its trunk in the earth, and from it hung the flag of France. Hymns were sung, muskets fired in the air, and then La Salle, in the good scarlet coat that he used for important occasions, proclaimed:

In the name of the most high, powerful, invincible, and victorious Prince, Louis the Great, by the grace of God King of France and Navarre, fourteenth of that name, I, this ninth day of April one thousand six hundred and eighty-two, in virtue of the commission of His Majesty, which I hold in my hand, and which may be seen by all whom it may concern, have taken and do now take, in the name of His Majesty and of his successors to the crown, possession of this country of Louisiana, its seas, harbors, ports, bays, adjacent straits, and all the nations, peoples, provinces, cities, towns, villages, mines, minerals, fisheries, streams, and rivers within the extent of the said Louisiana . . . hereby protesting against all who may hereafter undertake to invade any or all of these countries, peoples, or lands, to the prejudice of the rights of His Majesty, acquired by the consent of the nations dwelling herein.

At that a notary, brought expressly from Canada for the purpose, stepped forward and signed the document from which La Salle had just read. It was official. The Mississippi River and all the rivers that flowed into it and all the lands that were watered by all these rivers belonged to France. Parkman's comment on this pathetic and brave gesture has often been quoted. It is worth quoting again:

On that day, the realm of France received on parchment a stupendous accession. The fertile plains of Texas; the vast basin of the Mississippi, from its frozen northern springs to the sultry borders of the Gulf; from the woody ridges of the Alleghenies to the bare peaks of the Rocky Mountains — a region of savannahs and forests, sun-cracked deserts, and grassy prairies, watered by a thousand rivers, ranged by a thousand warlike tribes, passed beneath the sceptre of the Sultan of Versailles; and all by virtue of a feeble human voice, inaudible at half a mile.

When he heard the news, was Louis XIV impressed by his "stupendous accession"? No. Other things claimed his attention. A month after La Salle read his proclamation, while he and his men were still making their way through the wilderness back to New France, the king officially moved his court to his new palace of Versailles. Louis XIV, a serious student of architecture and gardens, loved his palace and the routine that developed around him. Each morning at eight his valet would draw the curtains of his bed and gently wake him – "Sire, it is time" – and the favored few would enter the bedroom to see him sit on the john and be rubbed down with rosewater and spirits of wine, be shaved and dressed, with the great duke so-and-so wrapping the dressing gown around him, and another great duke pulling on his breeches. It wasn't the luxury and the servility that the king loved, it was the order. Order was all important. Everyone in his place and a place for everyone. The king's own place was deep in the remoteness of the palace, in the epicenter of the nation where he could decide and regulate and say yes or no to requests and ultimately shape the destiny of his subjects, from the peasants in the fields of France to the fur trappers and missionaries in the forests of America. Again, it wasn't the power the king loved, but the order. Order meant the nation could be united and prosperous and powerful and civilized.

Order in this world has her outworks and fortifications. Versailles was a fortress of art, a public expression of inner majesty, a helmet and breastplate for the king's sacred aura, but the body of the nation also needed a bulwark to protect and define it. The Alps and Pyrenees provided a natural bulwark for most of the nation. The plain of Belgium, however, was a highway for invaders. Louis XIV spent most of his energy trying to block it. At the time La Salle claimed Louisiana, in the early 1680s, it seemed that Louis XIV had finally succeeded. In 1679, after several years of war, the king concluded a favorable peace with Spain and other enemies of France. It left France in possession of a belt of fortified cities in the area known as Franche-Comté, once a part of the Spanish Netherlands (Belgium) and now part of France.

This period of triumph for the French monarchy was brief. France's enemies, goaded by further French aggression, formed a coalition against her and war was resumed near the end of the decade. For the rest of his reign, Louis XIV would be in a nearly constant state of armed conflict with other nations, fighting over this small piece of Europe. In the process, he drained the wealth of his country to raise and equip armies.

From our vantage point, all this seems like lost opportunity. What was this strip of European real estate worth weighed in the balance with the North American continent? For a portion of the expense that he lavished on his armies, and on the conquest of middling-sized towns in Franche-Comté, Louis XIV could have fortified his navy, garrisoned the Mississippi, made good on the claim that his loyal servant, La Salle, had made for him. Did not the great king have eyes and imagination? His minister, Colbert, seemed to possess an awareness of the stakes involved in La Salle's explorations – it was Colbert who prodded the king into building a respectable navy in the first place.

Part of the explanation for Louis XIV's indifference to La Salle's exploration was no doubt the king's temperament. He rarely visited his ships, but he loved his armies, loved the spectacle of their orderly maneuvering, their marches and counter-marches. He enjoyed watching sieges, which were also orderly pageants, with an orchestra ready to burst into music when the mines were set off and the enemy's walls blasted. Siege warfare was relatively predictable – it was something that Louis XIV could control. By contrast, the struggle in the wilderness of America, with little wooden forts strung out among the forests and the swamps, seemed shadowy, inglorious, fraught with uncertainty. "You must hold to the maxim that it is far more worthwhile to occupy a smaller area, and have it well populated, than to spread out and have several feeble colonies which could easily be destroyed by all manner of accidents," Louis XIV wrote to Governor Frontenac, six years before La Salle's trip down the Mississippi. Trying to control the sea lanes to the colonies was even more risky and less predictable – a bad storm on the ocean could wipe out an investment of many thousands of *livres*. If there was a model for Louis XIV's empire, it was the empire of King Solomon, land-based and centered on his magnificent temple, with its orderly religious cult, rather than the bold, secular seafaring empires of Phoenicia and Athens. (The Israelites never did like the sea – the Bible rarely mentions it without a hint of dread.) Near the end of his reign Louis XIV used the navy Colbert had given him almost entirely to protect the coast of France from sea-borne raids – the navy became another one of order's necessary bulwarks.

The truth was that a single fortified town on the northeast border of France was of more interest to Louis XIV than all of North America. That might not have been so perverse. It is possible the king knew what he was doing. The stretch of real estate in northeastern France, over which so much blood was spilled, has remained French ever since the reign of Louis XIV and is now part of the very definition of the country. Louis XIV's annexation of Franche-Comté has proven necessary to France, in a way that naval bases in the Pacific are necessary to the United States. There may also have been an even deeper instinct at work in Louis XIV. His rival, Great Britain, did indeed end up possessing most of this vast North American continent – and what good did that do Britain? Britain's conquests in North America merely spawned an English-speaking child that grew up to dominate the parent. Those who surveyed the globe from Versailles, by contrast, may have felt deep down that there was room only for one great French-speaking nation on this planet, and God clearly intended that nation to be France. Finally – and this is a point that goes back to France's interest in trade monopolies as opposed to agricultural settlement – France did not really have a good idea of how to exploit that potential in any case. When the French ceded all their possessions in North America to the British in 1763 and went back home, they were happy enough to go. They had lost a huge empire – but so what? It left barely a scar on the national psyche. They still possessed Martinique and Guadaloupe and St. Lucia in the Caribbean, as well as the fishing islands of St. Pierre and Miquelon off the coast of Newfoundland. These little islands were real money-spinners, as opposed to Canada and the Mississippi. Years would go by and the Bourbon monarchy would fall and blood would run in the streets of Paris and Napoleon would create and lose his own empire, and the monarchy would return, and then the republic, and in all that time nobody in France seemed even to remember what had once been their vast possessions in North America. It was as if La Salle had never existed.

If there was a real loser in France's failure to make good on La Salle's claim, it was the Indian nations, who were thereby deprived of a counterweight in their diplomatic and military struggles to retain their independence. It might also have been better for the world if the United States, early in its history, had to share the middle of the continent with a racially and religiously and linguistically alien power. The United States might not have been such a colossus, in that case, but it might have retained the vigorous democracy it lost in the late nineteenth century, it might have kept faith with the Jeffersonian dream of smaller-scale economic and political institutions, it might have had a greater tolerance for difference.

Of course none of this was Louis XIV's problem.

❧

The French were not completely indifferent to what La Salle had wrought. In 1699 Pierre Le Moyne d'Iberville, a French-Canadian military hero, returned to the area and built Fort Maurepas, near the present-day site of Biloxi, Mississippi. In 1718 his brother, Jean-Baptiste Le Moyne, sieur de Bienville, founded the city of New Orleans. The growth of these settlements was slow – there wasn't much in the way of resources to lure settlers or merchants. The region, moreover, had a well-deserved reputation for disease and famine. High officials and military commanders did build impressive homes and plantations, but it was hard to find labor to keep them going. For the first few years of the colony's life, in fact, the government used Louisiana in the same way Great Britain later used Australia, as a dumping ground for convicts and social misfits. When that didn't work out, slaves were imported. Priests and nuns came in their wake. The France they left was very different from the France that had produced the heroic missionaries and Jesuit martyrs of Canada one hundred years earlier. The saint and the ascetic no longer set the tone. The intellectuals of the Enlightenment set the tone, and it was not friendly to the Church Militant.

Such a tone undercut any extraordinary evangelical fervor among the clergy sent to Louisiana. But even if members of this clergy had all been of the stamp of that indomitable old Bishop of Quebec François de Laval, they would have had a hard time regulating the morals of their flock, which consisted of converted Indians, African slaves, and desperate whites. These whites were more like the *coureurs de bois* in the northern wilderness – living lives half-European and half-native, intermarrying with Indian women – than the farmers along the St. Lawrence River. "Religion for the fireside, freedom for the woods" was the credo of the fur traders; Frenchmen held the same credo in Louisiana, where it was almost all woods – cypress swamps – and virtually no fireside. "Religion is little known and practiced even less," an Ursuline nun named Mother Tranchepain said of New Orleans in 1728. That same year, another Ursuline, Marie Madeleine Hachard, put it even more strongly: "The devil here has a very large empire, but this does not discourage us from the hope of destroying him."

We may be sure the nuns gave the devil a severe pummeling, but it is doubtful that bad spirit entirely quit the field. Piety never took root here like it did in French Canada, which was like a machine for producing religious vocations up until the middle of the twentieth century. By contrast, Louisiana didn't even have a seminary to train local priests until 1858. It wasn't until the twentieth century that New Orleans had an American-born archbishop.

The most assiduous churchgoers, in early Louisiana, were Blacks. That was not the most unusual aspect of race relations in the colony. As in Ste. Genevieve, slavery in New Orleans was a more relaxed affair than it was in British and American jurisdictions. This was partly because of the influence of the *Code Noir*, but also because in New Orleans the white population remained relatively low, and its control over the slaves tenuous. These slaves, consequently, had bargaining power. They possessed skills, in construction, cabinet making, ironwork, even medicine, the white settlers could not do without. They formed part of the militia and the armed forces that defended the territory. They had a trump card, finally, in the cypress swamps that sheltered many a runaway and were never far away. "New Orleans under French rule was a permeable frontier village with a small, often dwindling white population whose survival depended on maintaining good relations with France's Indian allies, mainly the Choctaws, and the labor and military skills of its African slaves," writes New Orleans historian Gwendolyn Midlo Hall. The slaves suffered bitterly from bondage of course, as all slaves must suffer, but they were not without resources, a strong culture of their own, and some protection from the tyranny of their owners.

In time, many of these African slaves became part of an important class of New Orleans society known as "free people of color." These were the freed slaves, and the descendants of freed slaves, who formed a cohesive community with close ties to the white settlers and to the slaves and Indians. They were go-betweens and intermediaries, insiders and outsiders simultaneously. (They could do everything white people could do except vote and marry whites.) Some of them became wealthy slaveholders themselves. They were probably the most alert and best mannered people in New Orleans.

New Orleans during the French period, in short, was an interesting multiracial society. Segregation was minimal – Indians, whites, African slaves, free people of color did business with each other in the markets of the city, drank together in taverns, worshipped together in churches, jostled each other in the streets, danced with each other in dance halls, even had dinner together in their homes. The greatest strength of the French and Canadian settlers, Hall writes, "was their openness to people of other races and cultures. This attitude was surely the main reason for their survival in such a dangerous and inhospitable land."

⚜

In the city of the dead, Robert Florence spotted an empty bottle of Alize Red Passion near one of the tombs and picked it up. "I want to get rid of this because people will see it and think, 'Oh, this must be a voodoo grave,' and they'll put all sorts of junk on it," he explained. If anyone doubted that possibility they had only to look at the nearby tomb of the famous Voodoo Queen, Marie Laveau. The tomb, the most notorious in the state of Louisiana, was covered in XXXs and was draped in trinkets, such as those multicolored strings of Mardi Gras beads that are made, like everything else these days, in China. Laveau was a free woman of color, born in 1794, who presided over many a voodoo ritual while remaining an adherent of the Church of Rome. Her devotees believed that their requests would be granted if they performed rituals at her tomb and scratched or chalked those XXXs on its surface. This annoyed Robert Florence, who was co-founder of the Friends of New Orleans Cemeteries, an organization devoted to the upkeep and preservation of these sites.

Florence loved the cemeteries. "They reflect the city in a more vivid, accurate, and poetic way than any other historical site," he said. "They really reveal aspects of every type of history there is – geological history, social history, economic history, the history of immigration, the history of slavery and race, legal history, artistic history." A native New Yorker who wandered the country in his youth and, like many, was captivated by New Orleans, Florence was an actor, playwright – his play entitled *Bones*, about a pet cemetery, was produced by the city's Contemporary Arts Center in 2003 – and founder of his own company, Historic New Orleans Tours. He was showing me around the most historic of all New Orleans cemeteries, St. Louis Cemetery No. 1.

What made St. Louis Cemetery No. 1, and the city's other burial places, so distinctive were two things, Florence said. The first was that the graves were above-ground. This was partly cultural – above-ground cemeteries are common in Spain and France – and partly for geological reasons. When the first settlers buried their dead in normal fashion, in the earth, they had the unpleasant experience of seeing the coffins and corpses of their near and dear float past their front doors in the spring, when the water table rose and the river flooded. The other distinctive feature of the city's cemeteries was that, because of land shortage, the tombs were re-usable. By law, the recently interred individual was entitled to rest inside his or her coffin for a year and a day. After that, the tomb owner could open the tomb, haul out the coffin, put the remains inside in a bag and shove it to the back or the side and put a new coffin, with a new body, in its place. The old coffin was often dispensed with unceremoniously; Florence told me about a man who was shocked by the sight of a coffin sticking out of a Dumpster.

The year and a day was supposed to allow enough time for a corpse completely to decompose – which was reasonable given the city's heat and humidity. Cemetery workers opening a tomb would usually be greeted by the sight of hundreds of cockroaches scurrying around. These insects were doing the job that earthworms did in the earth. If the departed was not completely decomposed, cemetery workers would have to improvise. "This guy told me he opened one coffin and the woman inside was still pretty intact," Florence told me. "He thought about it and then he just bent her into an 'L' shape, so she would fit around the new coffin. Another time, the corpse hadn't broken down at all. Clothes and everything still there. He just picked up the corpse and put it on top of the new coffin." "It must take a particular kind of temperament to be a cemetery worker," I suggested. Florence shrugged. "You got to kinda make a joke of it after a while."

We left St. Louis Cemetery No. 1 and drove to St. Louis Cemetery No. 2, where Florence, whose business includes the restoration of tombs, had recently whipped a tomb into shape with Portland cement and a fresh coat of yellow latex paint. He showed me the tomb, a flat, rectangular structure, like a little house for a dead person. Near the door of this house was a bronze plaque. It read,

> Emperor of the Universe and Friend of New Orleans Cemeteries, Grand Marshall Ernie K-Doe was buried in this tomb on July 13, 2001. Along with the Star Spangled Banner, his signature R & B Classic 'Mother-in-Law' will be one of only two songs to ultimately be remembered. His wake and funeral comprised the most spectacular send off New Orleans has ever experienced. Tomb owner Heather Twichell of the Duval family graciously donated the burial space.

"After we put on *Bones*," Florence recalled, "the producer said to me, 'Robert, now you need to write the greatest story ever told.' And I said, 'What do you mean, the Bible?' 'No,' he said. 'Ernie K-Doe.' This isn't going to mean anything to you, but if you knew Ernie K-Doe, man, he's a major, major story. You could call him a has-been or a one-hit wonder, but that's missing the point. It was his eccentricity in his radio broadcasts, the way he talked. Nobody ever used language like that man. No one could."

I was wondering about Heather Twichell, however. Who was she and why did she donate her tomb as a final resting place for the Emperor of the Universe? Florence gave me the phone number of Twichell's mother, a woman named Anna Ross Mauldin-Twichell, who lived in the French Quarter. I called on her the next day. We sat in a courtyard in the rear of her house, which is a standard feature of houses in the French Quarter, while she held her golden Pomeranian in her lap. Anna Ross was a high-spirited, middle-aged woman who wore red sneakers and was a member of that much discussed class of Louisiana citizens, the Creoles. It is much discussed because the definition of "Creole" has always been uncertain. It is also much discussed because of the myth of the Creole as the descendant of French aristocrats, attuned to the finer things of life, such as thoroughbred horses, fine wines, and silver-plated dueling pistols. It's a pretty myth, which still has some life to it.

The best definition of "Creole" is somebody whose family roots go back to the colonial period of Louisiana. (This included the descendants of slaves and free people of color – but not Cajuns.) By this definition, Anna Ross was a Creole. Being a descendant of the Princesse de Noailles, she was also a Creole by the narrower definition of the word, meaning somebody in whose veins the blood of Bourbons flows. Her family had been in Louisiana since 1703, even before New Orleans was founded. This was as Creole as you could get. I noted the same pride of lineage in other people in the city, however. "We're not a melting pot," Ross said to me. "Ain't nothing melting about this mix. America might be a melting pot but down here we know who we are and where we're from. *And don't be rude.*" She smiled. "Manners are everything."

She grew up on a dairy farm in New Iberia, in the southeast part of the state, near Lafayette. Her family did its part to maintain the image of the Creole culture as an elegant survival of a better era. "It was linen on the dinner table at noon and damask in the evening," she recalled. "We always ate off china and used sterling silverware. It's just because that's what we did. We could go to the dinner table without our shoes on, but we had to eat properly." While we talked, water spilled gently from a fountain surrounded by ferns, hibiscus, little tangerine trees, ginger plants. Towering banana trees rose in front of us alongside empty terra cotta jars that looked like they dated from the Minoan era. "Everybody knew who we were," she said. "Everybody called me 'miss.' Everybody. When I was nineteen years of age I misplaced my driver's license, and I remember I walked into the courthouse on a Friday evening, and there were these farmers standing around in their good suits that were thirty years old because they only had one suit, and I walked in there and the clerk said, 'Oh, Miss Anna Ross, what can we do for you?' I said I had lost my license. Of course, the license bureau was closed for the weekend, but he said, 'There's no problem with that. Just a minute.' And they got somebody from the sheriff's office to get on the Teletype and type out a message to the whole state – my name, my social security number, and instructions that if I got stopped by a policeman on the highway, anywhere within the state, not to arrest me for not having a license." She scratched the ears of her golden Pomeranian. "I grew up in a world of privilege," she said.

So privileged were they that the local bishop personally gave her grandfather the sacrament of extreme unction, although her granddaddy hardly ever darkened the door of a church. Anna Ross was educated in a convent school and considered herself a Catholic in good standing – "It's part of who I am, like having red blood cells" – but knew by experience that Creole Catholicism can be a somewhat lax affair. "When I was a girl going to confession my mother would sometimes make me rehearse." She mimicked her mother, listening to her daughter's litany of offenses. "Anna Ross, you were rude to me more times than that!" Don't try to minimize those sins against the fourth commandment! Anna Ross smiled at the memory and sat back in the wrought iron chair that had once belonged on her mother's porch, back in New Iberia. "But my grandmother would say things like 'When you go to see the priest, remember he's just a man, and you sweep that under the rug. It's none of his business.' This is a woman who *lived* in the church. 'You sweep all that under the rug.' And she meant it, too."

We talked about the tomb. "When I got married, my husband and I were given a very historic tomb from his parents," Anna Ross said. She paused for a second, as if a thought had just struck her. "I never did write that thank you note – and I'm a very proper

Southern girl. But I just don't know how to write a thank you note for a tomb. Do you?" I shook my head. "Then my husband and I got a divorce. I left him in '95, I think. It was hard because I thought I had to be in it until the day I died, because that's what marriage meant. I couldn't leave him until I went to see a nun I knew from college, who was on the marriage tribunal for the church. I went to see her and I said, 'Sister, this is what's been going on.' She knew I wasn't telling everything, either. What I told her was bad enough. Then she said I could have an annulment, and once she said that, I thought to myself, that's it, I'm leaving him." Anna Ross narrowed her eyes, like a teacher who's been dying to give some bratty kid a good, swift kick in the pants and now feels she can get away with it. "I got permission to go. And I *took* it."

In the divorce settlement, the title for the tomb went to the couple's daughter, Heather. "I think she's the ninth title holder of the tomb," Anna Ross said. When Anna Ross heard that legendary rhythm and blues artist Ernie K-Doe had expressed a desire to be buried in St. Louis Cemetery No. 2, which is where the tomb happened to be, she told Heather, and Heather told Ernie's wife, Miss Antoinette, that she had a perfectly good tomb that she wasn't using, and probably wouldn't be using for another fifty or sixty years, and she would consider it an honor if her husband wanted to be laid to rest there. Miss Antoinette accepted the offer, with pleasure. This generosity in sharing burial places is not unlike people in Minneapolis, say, offering friends the use of their cottage on Lake Superior. "I have thirteen invitations for places to be buried around town," Anna Ross said. "It's a really serious deal. When you're at a dinner party with friends and they say, 'Why don't you come and be buried with us?' – that's a real compliment."

Miss Antoinette was having a Friday evening fish fry at the Legendary Ernie K-Doe Mother-In-Law Lounge. It was easy to spot the place, even for someone who had never been there – on the front of the building an artist had painted larger-than-life-sized faces of some black men wearing feathered war bonnets. One was

Tootie Montana, Big Chief of the Yellow Pocahontas New Orleans Traditional Mardi Gras Indians. Another was Chief Alfred Doucette of the Flaming Arrows tribe of Mardi Gras Indians. Inside, where you were served some lightly breaded fried catfish, seasoned by Miss Antoinette herself, potato salad, green beans, triangular slices of white bread inside a clear plastic bag, and dessert, for six dollars, there was also much to greet the eye. A banner hanging from the ceiling over the bar read, Emperor of the World Legendary Ernie K-Doe. From the ceiling hung hundreds of paper stars with names on them. "That was Ernie," Miss Antoinette explained to me. "When he was here, he said he wasn't the only star in the house. He started that. If you wanted to be a star you made one of them and signed it and he put it up on the ceiling." You, too, could be a star on the ceiling of the Mother-In-Law Lounge, along with such names as Ella Fitzgerald, Curtis Mayfield, and Professor Longhair.

The really eye-catching feature of the lounge, however, was a mannequin sitting in a corner. The mannequin wore a black curly wig, a yellow suit with a white shirt and matching yellow collar, a white carnation on his lapel, and white Stacy Adams High Tops. His head was turned to the left and there was a faint smile on his face. This was Ernie K-Doe, or the closest that Miss Antoinette could come to an earthly representation of him.

Miss Antoinette wore a black baseball cap, a short, white pleated skirt, and white running shoes and was finishing a cigarette when I met her. I commended her on the fried catfish. She told me she came from a long line of people, a mixture of African-American and native Indian, who loved to cook. "I have some recipes from my grandmother that a lot of people are trying to get from me, my grandmother's okra gumbo, with a very, very special seasoning," she said. "My grandmother and I taught it to Ernie K-Doe. I told Heather, that I'm sharing the tomb with, I'm going to leave it in my will for her. Everybody's been trying to get the recipe, but I won't give it out."

She opened the lounge in 1994, and two years later married Ernie K-Doe, after they had been going out with each other for fifteen years. "He wanted to get married sooner, but I told him he had to give me one special wedding gift and that was to get back into his music, full bloom. He realized we wouldn't get married until he got back on the stage. Four years ago, he gave up drink, so he was clean and sober when he went home to God." After his death, Miss Antoinette turned the lounge into a shrine for her husband.

As we spoke, a young woman sprawled on a sofa with a beer in one hand laughed at something on a wide-screen television. She was a friend of Miss Antoinette's, as were most of the people at the fish fry. The lounge, in essence a living room with a bar at one end, was really for her and the other "fans" of Ernie K-Doe, Miss Antoinette explained. It belonged to them. "Sometimes they might come at nine or ten in the morning, and I might still be in my PJ's, but I'll let them in because this is home," she said. "They all loved Ernie and this is his place. I tell a lot of my fans, when I'm out there paying bills or doing errands, I can't wait to get home because I feel a lot safer at home with the statue of him. He looks after me." Sitting in his chair in the corner, the mannequin did seem to have a talismanic power. I asked Miss Antoinette if she ever felt the presence of her late husband. "A lot of times I get a warning from him," she replied. "If I'm talking to somebody, if it's the wrong person I'm talking to, or if something's not right, I can smell his odor, his body odor. It's like a warning that this is the wrong person I'm talking to."

From his vantage point in the beyond, Ernie K-Doe had to be pleased with his widow's care of the mannequin that was his visible presence in the world he no longer inhabited. She changed his suit regularly – and of course his socks and underwear. The hands of the mannequin could be removed as well, so occasionally Miss Antoinette took them across the street to TNT Nails to get a good buffing. In life, Ernie K-Doe had enjoyed going over to TNT Nails for a manicure. I noticed that the current state of the fingernails on this mannequin was excellent – they were a deep, shiny pink.

Occasionally, the mannequin got to perform for the public. "He has two sets of legs," Miss Antoinette explained. "He can sit down or stand up. We feel he's more comfortable sitting down, but when he performs we stand him up. What we do, we get the band that was his last band. And we work with the sound man and the band actually be playing his music and the CD playing at the same time and the statue is standing up with a mike in his hand and it's as if he's performing."

Later that night I returned to the Mother-In-Law Lounge for a nightcap. The main room was empty except for Miss Antoinette and another woman, but in the back room three musicians were playing some terrific blues. They shared the room with a painting of Ernie K-Doe. In this portrait, he wore a red suit and red slippers and seemed to be hovering in the clouds. The painting evidently represented the apotheosis of Ernie K-Doe. It reminded me of the city's statue of Robert E. Lee, which is mounted on top of a soaring column, a column so high the message is unmistakable: this mortal has become a god. (Elvis Presley would understand. At Graceland there was a similar painting of him floating in the clouds, only he was dressed in white.)

As the evening wore on, and I drank and chatted with Miss Antoinette, I kept looking at the mannequin. It made it hard to concentrate sometimes on what Miss Antoinette was saying. She told me how Ernie K-Doe had gotten along extremely well with her mother, as opposed to the mother-in-law who inspired his famous musical lament back in 1961. (The song hit No. 1 on the pop charts.) "It sounds like a fairy story, but it actually be true," she said. "I like to call her his good mama." His good mama died shortly after Ernie K-Doe died, and is also buried in Heather Twichell's tomb. I glanced again at the mannequin, with its faint smile and piercing eyes. This Ernie K-Doe looked pleased with what he saw in the room – everybody having a good time – but he also had a distant air, as if he were viewing everything through another level of awareness, which is the knowledge that dead people have. I asked for another beer and looked at the mannequin from a slightly different angle. This time the eyes seemed more piercing, as if he were definitely seeing something in the room the rest of us weren't. I began to think I was making too much of an inanimate object and had better stop.

The next morning I dropped by the lounge and picked up Miss Antoinette – she was wearing the same pleated skirt and running shoes she had on the day before – and drove to the cemetery. The Interstate 10 overpass was close by, and as we stood at the tomb the traffic was constant, but nobody else was in the cemetery and birds were singing and the sun was shining and it felt quiet and peaceful. I asked her if she came here often. "Oh, very often," she said. "I come out sometimes with a folding chair and sit here and read, and bring a portable radio and play his music." She picked up a withered wreath at the foot of the tomb. "The caretaker won't take this away from the grave, because they know I like to do that. I'll come out here on Monday, usually, and sweep in front of the tomb and the whole aisle here. They know that's one of my peaceful times that I like to do."

On All Saints' Day, Miss Antoinette and her friends come out to the cemetery to party, as is the custom in New Orleans and other Latin, Catholic cities. "We bring tables with umbrellas and an ice chest and we bring some flowers and say hello to our loved ones," she said. "People bring lots of food, all kinds of food. You never know what they're going to bring. They know I'm going to bring my Ernie K-Doe gumbo and the Ernie K-Doe red beans. They do know that." In Anne Rice's *Interview with the Vampire*, the vampire Louis remarks that All Saints' Day might seem like a celebration of death to people who don't understand the festival. It isn't, Louis insists. It is "a celebration of the life after." And this is true. Read what the plaque welcoming visitors to the St. Louis Cemetery No. 1 has to say: "The Catholic cemetery is the last resting place of the bodies of the faithful departed, awaiting re-union with their souls at the resurrection on the last day. Blessed by the Church and dedicated to God, the Catholic cemetery testifies to a faith in the immortality of the soul and the promise of resurrection with Christ the Lord." So these bones will dance on the day of resurrection, and the dust of the long dead will shine brighter than the sun. Knowing this, people can have a fine old time eating gumbo and red beans in the graveyard.

⚜

I wish I could tell you something about other descendants of French Creoles I met in New Orleans, like the man who owned and operated Mid-City Lanes, a very popular bowling establishment with hot live bands playing every night and a portrait of Our Lady of Medjugorje over the stairs. The night I was there I saw the actress Kate Hudson bowling with her husband and some friends, and I was very impressed to see her do the scoring with a pencil and a sheet of paper. Mid-City Lanes does not have computerized scoring devices. "It would kind of destroy the whole feel of the place," the owner, John Blancher, told me. Blancher, it seemed to me, had perfected the synthesis between Catholicism and having a good time that eluded this child of New England Franco-Americans.

And I wish I could tell you more about black French Creoles, like Jelly Roll Morton, the man who invented jazz. Morton was born Ferdinand Lamothe and liked to boast, "All my folks came directly from the shores of France." It would be pleasant and instructive to mention St. Augustine Parish, built in 1842, still the heart of black French Catholic life in New Orleans, and to say something about its pastor, Father Jerome G. LeDoux, a black French Catholic priest in his mid-seventies, who was a vegan and liked to stay up all hours of the night. One evening near midnight we visited a friend of his, Vernon Jude Dobard, called "a vampire artist" by Father LeDoux because Dobard also liked to work late into the night. In his studio we saw a striking portrait of the Blessed Virgin Mary, based on a model from the Victoria Secrets catalogue. We also saw a very sexy portrait of Marie Jeanne Aliquot, a Frenchwoman who came to New Orleans in 1832 and dedicated her life to teaching catechism to slaves. Father LeDoux was writing a romantic historical novel about her.

Later that week, on Palm Sunday, Father LeDoux, wearing a cinnamon-colored dashiki, began the service in his traditional fashion, by riding a mule up to the front of the church. The mule's name was Susie, her owner said to me. "She's a wonderful animal," he said. "She's very affectionable, she loves children. You don't get many mules like that." With her large, liquid brown eyes, Susie did look infinitely patient, without putting on that subtly self-dramatizing air of patience, as some mules do, who want you to know that it's killing them to pull this carriage of tourists, but they're doing it anyway because you asked them. Susie's owner also volunteered that he was a descendant of the Naquin Indians. "My ancestors from the old Indians, they talk about them in the Bible," he said. I could find no reference to Naquin Indians in the Bible, but I did come across a reference to the tribe in a book entitled *Cajuns in the Bayous*, published in 1957 by a journalist named Carolyn Ramsey. Ramsey discovered this lonely, isolated band of Indians living on an island called the Isle of Paradise, near the town of Houma. They were led by a man named Chief Victor Naquin, a "tall, broad-shouldered, copper-skinned man of great calmness and solemnity," according to Ramsey. He also served the best meal of boiled crab she ever had in her life.

I wish I could say more about these people, because they were very interesting individuals and carried in their bones the history of this region, but my narrative is already too long. In New Orleans I could feel the spirit of La Salle tugging at me. He and his men had not gone down the Mississippi to have a good time and enjoy a break from fort building and fur trading, their shades whispered to me. They had traveled with a purpose. They had traveled to find something. And so had I, difficult though my purpose was to define, and elusive the object I was looking for. But if I were ever to get a handle on it, now was the time.

So one day I decided to drive southwest from New Orleans down Route 23 to Venice, where La Salle planted his cross. I thought it might be a nice outing – I had a vision of a beach and some sort of monument to La Salle where I could commune with the spirit of the dead explorer while the broad bosom of the gulf tossed its restless billows, as Francis Parkman would say. The highway to Venice passed through flat, featureless country, and towns with names like Port Sulphur. At Venice, I found a strip mall, which seemed to be the equivalent of downtown, and clusters of mobile homes. Where was the beach? Where was the La Salle monument? Where was the Mississippi River?

A channel of the river was visible if you turned off the highway and drove into any one of various docks and marinas. I did that a couple of times but quickly returned to the highway and continued to drive south, to where land's end must be. But I never saw land's end. Instead I saw industrial monuments like the Venice Gas Plant, and shipyards and depots and warehouses and more docks and marinas sprawled across the landscape. That landscape seemed like one continuous construction site, except that nothing was being built. You would be driving along the highway and every once in a while, if you wanted, you could take a left on a gravel road and drive by parking lots where the pickup trucks far outnumbered the cars. You would proceed past chain-link fences behind which were storage areas full of huge tanks containing frightening liquids, and sheds and derricks and cranes and forklifts and flatbed trucks and Dumpsters and endless barrels and square metal containers and construction equipment and unfriendly signs. Private Property. Unauthorized Persons Keep Out. No Trespassing. Violators will be prosecuted. All visitors must report to office. The sale, purchase, transfer, use or possession of illegal drugs, narcotics and other unlawful substances and materials on the premises of this facility or while conducting business for this facility are prohibited by law. Concerned Citizens for the Community: There is no YOU in unions. Pedestrians and vehicles are subject to search while on this installation by authority of AR 190-22.

What was really strange was that every site seemed to be deserted. Once in a while a truck appeared and then drove off, but no workers were visible. It was as if the area had recently been evacuated. The only living things in motion were the seagulls flying above, through air that was hazy with dust.

Then there was a green stretch along the highway. I passed a settlement of mobile homes set back in the trees. On the other side of the road, which bordered a channel of water, there was a four-foot-high slab of wood sticking up from a mailbox. Somebody had painted on it the name Jesus. It seemed less like a witness to Christ than a cry for help. In the settlement, some of the residents had fired up their barbecues, while children ran underfoot. The scene reminded me of some post-apocalypse village of survivors, huddled in a clearing in the forest, with their children and their cooking fires, amid the debris of an industrial civilization that had suddenly collapsed: an old school bus painted blue, defunct cars, houses collapsed into piles of rotting plywood and shingles. Their only hope was a few boats with outboard motors that still seemed in trim shape – but in this country of oil and gas deposits, was there still, after the apocalypse, fuel for these boats? And where could they go with them, except to catch dubious seafood?

Shortly afterwards, the highway came to an end at the Chevron Texaco Dome Dock. I got out of the car and walked to the edge of a channel of water. From somewhere came the relentless, rhythmic pulsing of a motor. At my feet were cans of pop and a heap of alligator snouts, with their rows of delicate teeth still in place. Out on the water, the setting sun was burning an image of white light on the water, a very narrow channel of water bordered by a wall of reeds on the other side. Black and white birds with stork-like legs waded through it with immense dignity. The water was the color of the fluid that comes out of your oil pan when the oil in your car is being changed.

While I was standing there a pickup truck pulled up by my car, and a man in his fifties, wearing rubber boots, got out. He came over and asked me if I wanted to buy any fish. He had just caught some this afternoon. I said no. We looked at the channel for a moment and then I asked him what was the name of that green plant that was spreading across the channel like water lilies. "That kind of beats me," he said. He thought for a moment. "I don't know if that's what they are, but I seen something like that they call elephant ears. Once you plant 'em, you can hardly stop 'em from spreading. I got some on my property, I tried to poison them with Roundup, and they're still growing. That stuff costs seventeen, eighteen dollars a quart. It's supposed to *work*."

I commiserated with him, and then he went back to his pickup truck and drove off. I remained there for a few more minutes, wondering if this was the place where La Salle had planted his tree trunk and claimed most of the continent for his sovereign. If it was, were his men impressed by their country's new acquisition? Or did it make them long all the more for the pleasant fields of Normandy?

⚜

On the last Monday I spent in New Orleans, I was aimlessly wandering the French Quarter when I came across an unusual sight, even for the French Quarter. A small brass band was standing in the middle of the street, in front of a pink Cadillac convertible about the length of a telephone pole. The driver wore the headdress of feathers and beads of a voodoo priest. In the back seat, a man was wearing evening dress – a maroon, three-piece suit, complete with tails – and white and brown shiny patent leather shoes. On top of a back seat draped with leopard skin, he sat flanked by two beauty queens. He was a princely figure. But that wasn't what struck me. What struck me was that this individual was none other than Ernie K-Doe.

It had to be him. No one else could wear a black curly wig like that. I asked somebody on the sidewalk what was going on, and he said they were shooting a television pilot about two lady detectives in New Orleans. All the extras and actors were standing around waiting for something to happen, the usual procedure in these cases. I noticed Ernie K-Doe stepping out of the car for a moment, so I went over to ask him what he was doing here. This avatar of the god was also known as Harold X. Evans, an actor of note in the city. "It's not part of this thing here, but I've recently been doing impersonations of Ernie K-Doe with the assistance of his wife, Miss Antoinette," he explained. "Most people say I look like Ernie K-Doe. Miss Antoinette says I look like Ernie K-Doe, and she's his wife. I don't see it myself. It's got to be the wig. I don't even copy his mannerisms – except one thing he used to do, I started doing recently, pulling his pants up. Mostly I don't have to do or say anything. I just walk out in this outfit and people see Ernie K-Doe. Although a few people say, 'Little Richard?' I say no. 'How about Ricky James?' No. It's definitely the Ernie K-Doe spirit. Some people think – for those who believe in that sort of thing – that the spirit of Ernie K-Doe comes up through this wig." He pointed to his wig. "This is the wig that used to belong to him."

The phenomenon of Ernie K-Doe was obviously bigger than I thought. "Miss Antoinette's doing a great job of marketing him," Evans said. "She actually takes the mannequin out on gigs. I think she has something planned where Ernie K-Doe comes out of a coffin. Which is consistent with the culture of New Orleans. Death is a big thing here. Always has been. I don't know of too many other cities that market their cemeteries for tourists. We certainly do in New Orleans. It's all part of the mystique of death in New Orleans. We put fences around our cemeteries not to keep people out, but to keep the dead in. That's from the days of the floods, when the waters would wash up the coffins. Oh yes. Keep them dead people where they belong."

Somebody called to Evans, and he got back on top of the rear seat of the convertible with the two beauty queens. I gathered the scene they were shooting involved a chase. One of the lady detectives was running after a bad guy dressed as a policeman down the streets of the French Quarter. Because the streets were crowded with a parade led by the brass band, the bad guy was supposed to scramble over the Cadillac convertible in his headlong flight, thus incidentally contributing to the color and drama of the scene. The director was ready to start shooting. His assistants tried to herd the spectators on the sidewalks – real tourists, like myself – to the rear of the Cadillac so the street would look crowded. "Everybody down to the Cadillac," one of them shouted. "Slide on down, folks."

"Who's the guy in the Caddie?" one tourist, a burly young man, asked. "Ricky James?"

"Slide on down here," the assistants kept shouting to us. "No flash photography!"

"Don't look at our cameras!"

"Ignore our cameras!"

"Enjoy the parade! Slide on down!"

I saw the director, a man wearing Hush Puppies, khaki pants, a loose Hawaiian short-sleeved shirt, wraparound sun glasses, and a black wire sticking out of his ear, conferring with a woman who was supposed to be chasing the cop. She was a stunt double and not the real actress, obviously, although she was trim and sexy, but she was not cute enough to be the star. She wore jeans and a caramel-colored leather jacket, and a cop's badge on her belt and a pistol. "You guys set?" the director shouted. "Let's do it!"

"No flash photography!"

"Slide on down, folks!"

"Let's see some energy in the band!" the director shouted. The brass band started to play. "Okay! Cameras up? Slide on down, people. I want to see crowds here. I want to see she can't get through the crowd. Fill it up there, folks. Here we go, folks. Cameras up? Ready?"

"Ready."

"No flash photography!"

"Don't look at the cameras!"

"Roll cameras!"

The Spirit of Ernie K-Doe, flanked by his smiling beauty queens, looked up at the second-floor balconies on the street, smiled benignly, and waved to his invisible fans. Suddenly the bad cop came racing down the street and jumped into the back seat. Shock and consternation registered on the face of the Spirit of Ernie K-Doe. The bad cop climbed over them, and the Spirit of Ernie K-Doe grabbed the beauty queen on his right as a protective gesture. The bad cop leaped out of the other side of the car and kept going. Then the young woman in the jeans and leather jacket appeared in front of the Cadillac. In a single, graceful movement, she sprang onto the hood of the Cadillac and slid its entire length on her left buttock. Still in that fluid motion, she got to her feet and continued running down the street.

The Communion of Saints

After reaching the mouth of the Mississippi and returning to Canada to tell the tale, La Salle's work in history was done. Ahead lay the futility of Texas, and the sighs of historians over La Salle's willful mismanagement of affairs, and the handing down to us of a story in which death triumphed. But like most gripping narratives the story has a subplot — it is, in fact, the mysterious dynamic between main plot and subplot that gives such narratives their depth and vibrancy. The narrative of La Salle in Texas is no exception.

In this case the sub-plot has to do with the Talon family. The reader may remember this family, introduced in the first two chapters of this book. It was headed by a man named Lucien Talon, who left his native Picardy in France to move to Canada in 1666. Lucien Talon was then twenty-two, a member of what we would now call the working class — he was a soldier and a servant before he obtained a small tract of land along the St. Lawrence, and evidently a man willing to take risks. In Canada, he married a woman named Isabelle Marchand, another native of France, and sired five children in ten years while working his modest farm. When La Salle's party returned from its expedition down the Mississippi, one of its members, who knew Talon, told him about La Salle's plan to return to the warm and fertile lands that bordered the river near the Gulf of Mexico. He must have painted a pretty picture, because Talon was eager to sign on. Perhaps Talon had had enough of Canadian winters and the difficulty of feeding five children on a small plot of land.

In the spring of 1684 the family returned to France, just in time to board ship for the Gulf of Mexico. While still on the high seas, Isabelle Talon gave birth to her sixth child, a boy. He was named Robert, in honor of the leader of the expedition, who also agreed to be the boy's godfather. That the infant survived his first few weeks on a disease-ridden ship was perhaps the first great stroke of good fortune in Robert Talon's amazing life. Landing in Matagorda Bay in January 1685, with nearly two hundred other French settlers, he would need good fortune – his tiny body would potentially be exposed to all the microbes, blistering sunshine, venom of snakes and insects, insufficiencies of food and water, and enemy arrows that felled nearly everyone else in the company. His oldest sister, Marie-Elisabeth, died in the first year of the settlement – we do not know how – and so did his father, Lucien. The latter apparently accompanied La Salle in one of his first exploratory expeditions and got lost in the woods, where he died alone, presumably of starvation. Of all the hard ways to die in this new country, that surely was one of the hardest.

Then came the day, in January 1687, two years after the founding of the settlement, when La Salle told the dwindling band of settlers that he was going to walk to Illinois for help, with sixteen selected men. The pathetic remnant left behind watched La Salle and his men march off through the grasslands. When the departing company disappeared from sight, the men, women, and children living in huts above Garcitas Creek must have felt like the last humans on earth, except for the hostile Karankawa. Perhaps they told themselves that if they could just hang on for a few months they would be rescued. But the months passed and no sail was spotted on the ocean and no men arrived from the north with a message from La Salle. Robert Talon learned to walk under the watchful eye of Madame Talon, and to speak a few words of his mother tongue, and to survive the threat of fever and diarrhea. The bones of the man who had pledged to protect and educate him in case of his father's death, but who had forgotten or ignored that obligation, now lay scattered on the Texas earth. The first anniversary of the departure of Robert Talon's godfather came and went. More months passed.

Not long before the approach of the second anniversary, the Karankawa appeared before the settlers making gestures to signify that they had come in peace. Although La Salle had warned them not to do this, the settlers welcomed them. In an instant, the Karankawa produced their weapons and fell upon them. The four-year-old Robert Talon must have heard everything, including the cries of his mother as she was hacked to death — cries that meant the stubborn dream of Lucien Talon for a prosperous life had finally came to its end. Robert Talon knew nothing of this. He and his siblings and another child, the only survivors of the massacre, were adopted by the Indians. Apparently they were treated with every kindness. Robert Talon's older brother Jean-Baptiste later recalled that, in cases of conflict, the Karankawa elders took their side "even against their own children." As part of their new identity they were tattooed in Karankawa fashion, by having charcoal mixed with water injected beneath their skin with sharp thorns. Later their Spanish rescuers tried every method they could think of to get rid of the tattoos, but without success. The tattoos proved permanent. The boys also learned to shoot arrows and run great distances, and to bathe in the river every morning. Jean-Baptiste maintained that he never followed one Karankawa custom — eating the flesh of their enemies. In all other respects, the boys seemed perfectly integrated into their new culture. In the process, Robert Talon forgot his French vocabulary and learned to speak a language known by only a few hundred other mortals on this planet.

At that point it seemed that Robert Talon was destined to disappear from history, living in the wilderness with a people themselves destined eventually to disappear. But then another extraordinary thing happened. In 1690 General De León revisited the site of the settlement at Garcitas Creek, having heard of these French children living among the Indians. At a Karankawa settlement on Matagorda Bay, not far from the fatal settlement, he found them. Robert Talon and his siblings were taken to Mexico City, where they were brought up, Robert Weddle tells us, as servants in the household of the viceroy. When the viceroy was recalled to Spain, Robert Talon went with him. In 1714, when he was nearly thirty, Robert Talon, as if to vindicate his father's dream, made his way to the new French settlement at Mobile, Alabama, married a Frenchwoman, had children, and practiced the peaceful and useful trade of carpenter. Whether he grew tired of explaining to people how he got the black marks on his face and hands and arms, or enjoyed the attention and curiosity aroused by them, or experienced both feelings, is something we will never know. We do know, according to a Mobile census of 1721, that he prospered sufficiently to acquire six slaves – five Africans and one Indian – and one cow.

Two hundred and ninety years after Robert Talon returned to the New World, I drove to the New Orleans suburb of Metairie, on a warm spring night, to meet a native and long-time resident of New Orleans named Paul C. Newfield III. Newfield, then sixty-two, was a "Certified Professional Landman," a person who investigates the title of properties sought for oil and gas exploration, and who negotiates leases for these properties on behalf of oil companies. Evidently Newfield had a bent for gleaning facts from documents, a useful skill in his avocation as a genealogist. Drawing upon this skill, he had traced his line of descent directly to Robert Talon. In his veins, and in the veins of his two grown daughters, flowed the blood of that family.

This pedigree meant something to Newfield. "Five years ago I walked the Camino de Santiago across northern Spain and part of France," he said to me. "Five hundred miles. At first I had my doubts. Can I do this thing? Then I started to look back on people like the Talons and thought, hell, they were able to walk all over the place, and surely I can too." I understood his doubts. He was just under average height, a little chunky, perhaps ten pounds heavier than he should have been. Add to that his age, the late fifties, at the time of his pilgrimage, and a man in such circumstances might well wonder about his powers of endurance and the reliability of his heart. Then there were the blisters and aching leg muscles Newfield suffered on the pilgrim's trail. "It was when my feet were hurting that I would focus on the Talons."

Newfield certainly would have had no difficulty explaining to Robert Talon just what he was doing. There were pilgrims on this particular trail to Santiago de Compostela in northwestern Spain during his ancestor's time, and for centuries before that, ever since the remains of St. James the Greater – one of the twelve apostles of Christ – were discovered there in the ninth century.

"It's a beautiful experience," Newfield said to me. "There's a religious, spiritual aspect to it, and a physical aspect – it's a multifaceted thing. You meet wonderful people. I was walking with a guy from Brazil who was living in New York City, a fellow from France, a woman from Australia, two French Canadians from Canada. I remember we stopped for lunch at one point and the guy from France – he had also been to the Himalayas – he said he was trying to decide what he wanted to become. He didn't know whether he wanted to become a Catholic priest or a Buddhist monk."

There will always be a time, as Chaucer says, when folk long to go on pilgrimages, like his men and women bound for the shrine of the martyr, St. Thomas Becket, in Canterbury. Part of the soul responds to the challenge of a journey to a holy place in a strange country, a journey that strips us of certain comforts and complications and material things. But it is important to remember that pilgrimages in our tradition have a specific religious meaning, as well as a broad spiritual appeal. They are not journeys to mystic sites radiating awesome vibes. (Some New Agers apparently believe that the five-hundred-mile trail to Compostela directly reflects the energy of our star system – the term "El Camino de Santiago," or "St. James's Way," is the Spanish term for the Milky Way.) These pilgrimages are Catholic in their origins, and Catholic in their essence, that is to say, open to everybody, and not just a spiritual elite. (Chaucer's pilgrims are a case in point.) The pilgrimages are devoted to the historical reality of Christ and His saints. They say, this holy man existed once, and he did this or that on this spot under the heavens. They say, these individuals are not myths, or figments of our imagination, but human beings who existed once and still exist. Pilgrimages will never go out of fashion. Hundreds of years from now people will still be traveling to the shrines of saints, for the sheer joy of arriving at a cherished destination after arduous travel, or to heal some ill of body or soul with the assistance of the saint, among other reasons. If they have no Robert Talons in their genetic makeup to inspire them when the going gets rough, they will still remember the example of other heroic men and women who have gone before them.

Unfortunately, there was very little spirit of pilgrimage in La Salle's final walk – encumbered with buffalo hides, shadowed by personal enmities, infected with hopelessness – an act irresponsible in its abandonment of the weak. Newfield shakes his head at the thought. "La Salle says, 'We have to do something about this, we're in a real jam – let's take half of these folk and walk to Canada and get help.' That's just – it boggles my mind that someone would just say, 'Let's walk to Canada and get help.' I mean, these people had been watching their numbers being decimated, when all of a sudden seventeen guys take off and head up north, and who was left – two or three priests and incapacitated soldiers and Isabelle Talon and her kids." More than most, Newfield had grounds for being upset with La Salle – his actions, in placing his godson in grave danger, almost doomed Newfield to nonexistence. "It's an amazing story, and it's fun to tell people about it," Newfield said, as we sat at his kitchen table. "Man, they hear about it and they can hardly believe it because it's such a strange story, with so many unique characteristics – it's an adventure story and it's touched me personally, of course, and I don't know . . ." He paused for a moment, keeping guard on his emotions. "I'll back off on that," he said finally. "I don't want to use the wrong words."

We were approaching the sacred, is what he was saying. Our feelings of what our fathers and mothers did in the long ago should not be spoken of except in fitting language. "It makes me appreciate America, it makes me aware of the richness of the heritage we have. We don't have a lot going for us in terms of antiquities. I mean, people in Europe go back hundreds and hundreds of years. We here only go back three or four hundred years, but the people came from all over and everybody has their own story, and that, to me, is interesting." Newfield then sounded a theme I had heard a few times in my journey. "I think the voyage of the *Mayflower* has its primary importance because of the general northeastern bias of American history. I think there were people in the southwest and Spanish territory who were doing things every bit as important, but we look to the people on the *Mayflower* as the founders of this country. My ancestors who were here earlier, they did things that were important too, but they were not directly involved in the evolution of the government of the United States." He gave a faint smile. "I don't think the Pilgrims sound like fun people at all. I think I would rather have been a Frenchman than a staunch Pilgrim."

Me too. I think of Mrs. Drennan, God rest her soul, in our fourth grade class in Pittsfield, Massachusetts, telling us that the United States of America was such a great country, the greatest in the world, because it was founded for religious reasons, and she was thinking, of course, of those staunch Pilgrims who landed on the shore of my native state, carrying Bibles and muskets. She was not thinking of Father Marquette in the woods of Michigan and Illinois, or Robert La Salle promising his king that he would spread the gospel in the swamps of Louisiana. For Mrs. Drennan, as for most Americans who think about history, there was a direct line between these Pilgrim fathers and the embattled farmers who defied the British at Lexington and Concord and the statesmen who wrote the American Constitution and the brave soldiers in blue who preserved the Union, culminating in this great republic from sea to shining sea. That was the story. French fur traders and Jesuits and farmers in Illinois were no more important to that narrative line than the Gibeonites and the Edomites and the Ammonites were to the great narrative of Israel. On the highway of history, these people were dead ends. Of course the North American Indians were dead ends too – the Last of the Mohicans, the Vanishing American. Yet as dead ends they are not all that dead. They bequeathed their curious psychic legacy to America, even as they were commemorated in romanticized paintings and statues, as part of a sublime landscape that never existed. Their psychic legacy persists, and we are still trying to deal with it. The French are another matter. Their alternative vision of America has been more or less effaced from our history. It's just not part of the picture.

Those who do think about it, like Newfield or Timothy Kent, harbor no resentment against the veneration of *Mayflower* passengers. They do, however, give thanks to their own forebears, who did not end up in Massachusetts. "I have a great deal of admiration for these people who boarded a ship in Europe and said goodbye to their families, knowing that they would never see them again, sailing off into the endless ocean and getting ready for whatever life gave to them," Newfield said. "A lot of them didn't survive, but I happen to be a product of those who did survive, and that makes me special. That gives me a feeling of my own uniqueness. It makes me realize how fortunate I am, to be where I am, and who I am." Thank you, Robert Talon, an ordinary man placed in an extraordinary situation. His story infused meaning into the story of La Salle. "I'm not a Shinto," Newfield said, lest he leave a wrong impression. "I reflect to some measure my ancestry, but I don't believe in ancestor worship, though sometimes my wife accuses me of it. I don't define myself in terms of my ancestry or anything like that."

I saw no shrines in his living room with bowls of tasty rice and fish, set out so that the souls of his ancestors could inhale the flavor. I believed him when he said he was no Shinto. Yet the spirit of

Shinto was not completely alien to this household – or to my own journey for that matter. A Japanese practitioner of that religion has written, "In Shinto, we are merged with our fellow men about us and with the unseen host of ancestors that have gone before us and, as a great spiritual body, united with the divine." That reminded me of the phrase "the communion of saints" in the Apostle's Creed, which Catholics recite at mass. The phrase refers, among other things, to the interchange of supernatural gifts and graces among the living and the departed. We are forging a unity of love and prayer, those of us on earth, the souls being purified in purgatory, and the souls in full communion with God in heaven. Only the damned are excluded.

The Camino de Santiago, the pilgrimage to the shrine of St. James, was a potent expression of this idea – a pilgrim, almost by definition, was somebody acutely aware of all the other pilgrims, over the centuries, who had done the same thing and sought the same goal. It was predicated on the blessings of a particular saint, which in turn was predicated on the boundless love of Christ for His brothers and sisters. Was Robert Talon in that company of the blessed dead? If so, then he was waiting for Newfield. "A great number of loved ones await us in heaven," wrote the third-century bishop St. Cyprian. "An enormous host is filled with longing for us. Their concern is only for us." That was a thought to cheer the weary, the footsore, the discouraged. But even if one did not believe in this supernatural dimension, it was natural to feel a kind of awestruck gratitude for the Robert Talons in all of our lives. In her family memoir, *Cousins*, the poet and novelist Paulette Jiles writes, "If you come from people who were neither wealthy nor lucky, you are here because of the cardinal human virtues. Courage, persistence, fortitude, hope. You are here because they took it on the chin."

Just before I left, Newfield gave me a message for a colleague at the newspaper where I work who had also walked the Camino de Santiago. "Tell him you met a fellow pilgrim and give him a warm *abrazo*," he said.

Of course we are all fellow pilgrims on this earth, and as such all owe each other a warm *abrazo*. That goes for you, too, René-Robert Cavalier, Sieur de la Salle, who could be such a bastard, and who, for your sins, met a violent end and lay unburied on the earth. By now, we trust, your faults have been purged in the fires of purgatory and your soul has found rest. Send a blessing on this book. Help us to realize that nothing in the universe is lost and that our existence is richer than we know.

Conclusion

In February of 2006, on assignment with the *Toronto Star*, I went to New Orleans, along with a small army of reporters – estimates I heard ranged from eight hundred to twelve hundred visiting journalists – to report on the stricken city's first Mardi Gras after Katrina. I took the opportunity to look up Miss Antoinette and others I had spoken to on my previous visit. With the exception of Anna Ross Mauldin-Twichell, who had moved to Atlanta for reasons other than the hurricane, and the artist Vernon J. Dobard, whose house had been flooded and remained uninhabitable, all were still in town.

Miss Antoinette was undaunted, although the Mother-in-Law Lounge had been destroyed. Fortunately, she managed to save Ernie K-Doe from the flood waters, and at the time I spoke to her was considering running him for mayor in the forthcoming civic election. (The election was subsequently won by the much-maligned incumbent, Ray Nagin.) To transport her husband to various functions, and to haul building supplies to the Mother-in-Law Lounge, she had purchased a magnificent, maroon Cadillac hearse. "We celebrate down here," she said on Mardi Gras day. "We're not sad people down here. We celebrate if your dog dies. To other people, that might be crazy, but that's the way it is in the Bible. It says you're supposed to rejoice."

Robert Florence was also doing fine, as was his business, Historic New Orleans Tours. Since historic New Orleans, including the French Quarter, had been built on relatively high ground, it escaped hurricane damage. "The cemeteries are fine, they're great," he told me. Those corpses who had ridden the floodwaters of Katrina were the newly dead.

John Blancher, owner of Mid-City Lanes, was not quite as fortunate as Florence. The neighborhood of his bowling alley was devastated. "Everything was brown," he recalled. "Trees, grass – it was one colour of brown. No birds, no animals, no squirrels, not even insects. It was just barren desolation. Everything living had moved." His bowling alley was intact – it was on the second floor of a shopping centre – but for weeks suffered the horrific stench of rotting food from a grocery store and restaurant on the first floor. When these establishments were finally gutted, Blancher hired a man with a Bobcat to bulldoze five feet of trash from the parking lot in front of his bowling alley into the street.

Father Jerome G. LeDoux was still pastor of St. Augustine, still a vegan – "Nine years, ten months and counting, no meats of any kind, no sea foods, no dairy products, no sugar" – and his historical romance about Marie Jeanne Aliquot was a work still in progress. Many of his parishioners, however, had been hard hit. The church itself had been damaged – copper blown off the steeple, asbestos shingles off the roof. Roof damage alone came to about $400,000, Father LeDoux said. His church, often described as "the oldest African-American Catholic parish in the United States," was slated to be closed by the archdiocese, along with numerous other Catholic parish churches. The hurricane had been a crushing financial blow to the Catholic Church in New Orleans.

Paul Newfield, whose own neighborhood of Metairie had been largely spared, drove me to the hurricane-ravaged neighborhood of Araby, where his uncle, a Catholic priest, had lived before the flood. Newfield came here after the flood to retrieve an old chalice – Newfield suspected it dated back to the seventeenth century – that his uncle had used throughout his entire life as a priest. Newfield showed me where the glass door of the bungalow had been smashed by National Guardsmen looking for bodies floating in the house. Through a window I could see the interior, covered almost to the ceiling with heaps of fiberglass insulation, once pink, now beige. On one of these heaps, a television set rested upside down. Newfield then showed me the window of his uncle's bedroom and through that window the closet where the chalice had been stored. Clothes still hung in the closet. You could see the lines of rust on a light green polo shirt, where it rested on a metal clothes hanger. No one would ever wear that shirt again. But the chalice – inestimable for what it was and for what it represented – had been saved, ready for renewed use in celebration of the sacred mysteries.

Select Bibliography

Anderson, Fred. *Crucible of War: The Seven Years' War and the Fate of Empire in British North America, 1754–1766*. New York: Alfred A. Knopf, 2000.

Arnold, Morris S. *Colonial Arkansas 1686–1804: A Social and Cultural History*. Fayetteville: University of Arkansas Press, 1991.

———. *The Rumble of a Distant Drum: The Quapaws and Old World Newcomers*. Fayetteville: University of Arkansas Press, 2000.

Axtell, James. *Natives and Newcomers: The Cultural Origins of North America*. New York: Oxford University Press, 2001.

Balesi, Charles J. *The Time of the French in the Heart of North America 1673–1818*. Chicago: Alliance Française, 2000.

Belting, Natalia Maree. *Kaskaskia Under the French Regime*. Carbondale: Southern Illinois University Press, 2003.

Beneteau, Marcel, ed. *Passages: Three Centuries of Francophone Presence at Le Detroit*. Windor, ON: University of Windsor, 2003.

Bernard, Shane K. *The Cajuns: Americanization of a People*. Jackson: University Press of Mississippi, 2003.

Blaise, Clark. *I Had a Father: A Post-Modern Autobiography*. Toronto: HarperCollins Publishers Ltd., 1993.

Chatellier, Louis. *The Europe of the Devout: The Catholic Reformation and the Formation of a New Society*. Cambridge: Cambridge University Press, 1989.

Cox, Isaac Joslin, ed. *The Journeys of René-Robert Cavelier, sieur de La Salle*. New York: Allerton Book Company, 1922.

Delanglez, Jean, S.J. *Some La Salle Journeys.* Chicago: Institute of Jesuit History, 1938.

———, trans. *The Journal of Jean Cavelier: The account of a Survivor of La Salle's Texas Expedition 1684–1688.* Chicago: Institute of Jesuit History, 1938.

Doughty, Howard. *Francis Parkman.* New York: Greenwood Press, 1962.

Eccles, W. J. *Canada Under Louis XIV 1663–1701.* Toronto: McClelland & Stewart Ltd., 1964.

———. *The French in North America, 1500–1783.* Toronto: Fitzhenry & Whiteside, 1998.

Ekberg, Carl J. *Colonial Ste. Genevieve: An Adventure on the Mississippi Frontier.* Tucson: The Patrice Press, 1996.

Faragher, John Mack. *A Great and Noble Scheme: The Tragic Story of the Expulsion of the French Acadians From Their American Homeland.* New York and London: Norton, 2005.

Flenley, Ralph, ed. and trans. *A History of Montreal 1640–1672.* London and Toronto: Dollier de Casson, 1928.

Foster, William C., ed, and Johanna S. Warren, trans. *The La Salle Expedition to Texas: The Journal of Henri Joutel, 1684–687.* Austin: Texas State Historical Association, 1998.

———. *The La Salle Expedition on the Mississippi River: A Lost Manuscript of Nicolas de La Salle, 1682.* Austin: Texas State Historical Association, 2003.

Gaither, Frances. *The Fatal River: The Life and Death of La Salle.* New York: Henry Holt, 1931.

Gutierrez, Barbara Dever. *Charlene: The Little Cajun Saint.* Lafayette: Lynd Publishing, 2002.

Johnson, Donald S. *La Salle: A Perilous Odyssey from Canada to the Gulf.* New York: Cooper Square Press, 2002.

Kerouac, Jack. *Visions of Gerard.* New York: Penguin Books Ltd., 1991.

Margry, Pierre. *Lettres de Cavelier de La Salle et correspondance relative à ses entreprises, 1678–1685.* Brooklyn: AMS Press, 1974.

Muhlstein, Anka. *La Salle: Explorer of the North American Frontier.* New York: Arcade Publishing, 1994.

Osler, E. B. *La Salle.* Toronto: Longmans Canada Ltd., 1967.

Pare, George. *The Catholic Church in Detroit.* Detroit: The Gabriel Richard Press, 1951.

Parkman, Francis. *La Salle and the Discovery of the Great West.* Boston: Little, Brown, and Company, 1895.

Plante, David. *The Family.* New York: Farrar, Straus and Giroux, 1978.

———. *The Country.* New York: Atheneum, 1981.

———. *The Woods.* New York: Atheneum, 1982.

———. *The Accident.* New York: Houghton Mifflin Company, 1991.

———. *American Ghosts.* Boston: Beacon Press, 2005.

Power, Michael. *A History of the Roman Catholic Church in the Niagara Peninsula.* St. Catharines, ON: Roman Catholic Diocese of St. Catharines, Ontario, 1983.

Ramsay, Carolyn. *Cajuns on the Bayous.* New York: Hastings House, 1957.

Robinson, Percy J. *Toronto During the French Regime: A History of the Toronto Region from Brûlé to Simcoe, 1615–1793.* Toronto: University of Toronto Press, 1965.

Sagard, Gabriel. *Long Journey to the Country of the Hurons.* Translated by George M. Wrong and H.H. Langton. Westport, CT: Greenwood Press, 1968.

Terrell, John Upton. *La Salle: The Life and Times of an Explorer.* Toronto: Clarke Irwin, 1968.

Thwaites, Reuben Gold, ed. *The Jesuit Relations and Allied Documents.* New York: Albert & Charles Boni, 1925.

Utley, Henry Munson, and Byron M. Cutcheon. *Michigan as a Province, Territory and State, the Twenty-sixth Member of the Federal Union.* New York: The Publishing Society of Michigan, 1906.

Wade, Mason. *The French Canadians 1760–1945.* London: Macmillan, 1955.

Weddle, Robert S. *The Wreck of the Belle, the Ruin of La Salle.* College Station: Texas A & M University Press, 2001.

Williams, William Carlos. *In the American Grain.* Norfolk: New Directions, 1925.

Index

About the Author

PHILIP MARCHAND is the books columnist for the largest circulation newspaper in Canada, the *Toronto Star*.